AF328434

To Marlene

Peter Ahrends

Stream of Sketches

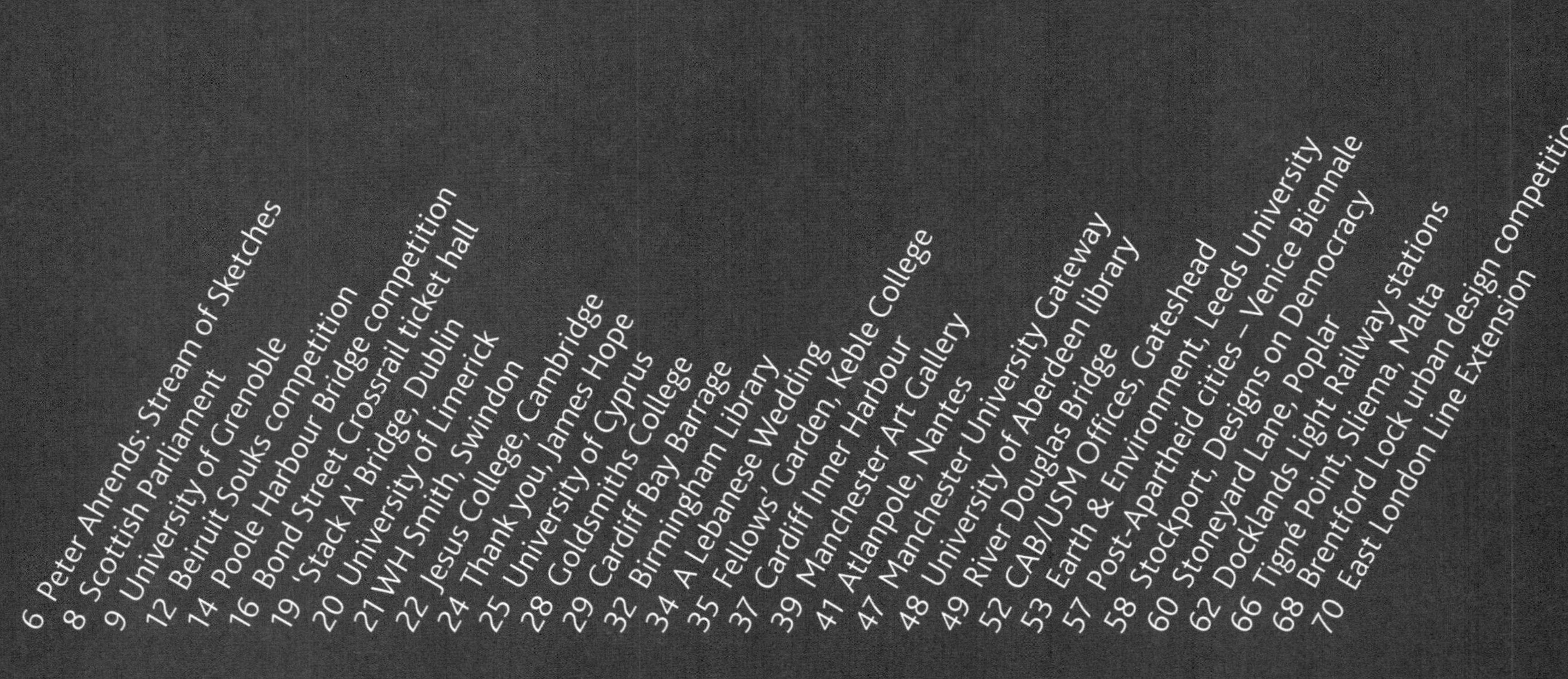

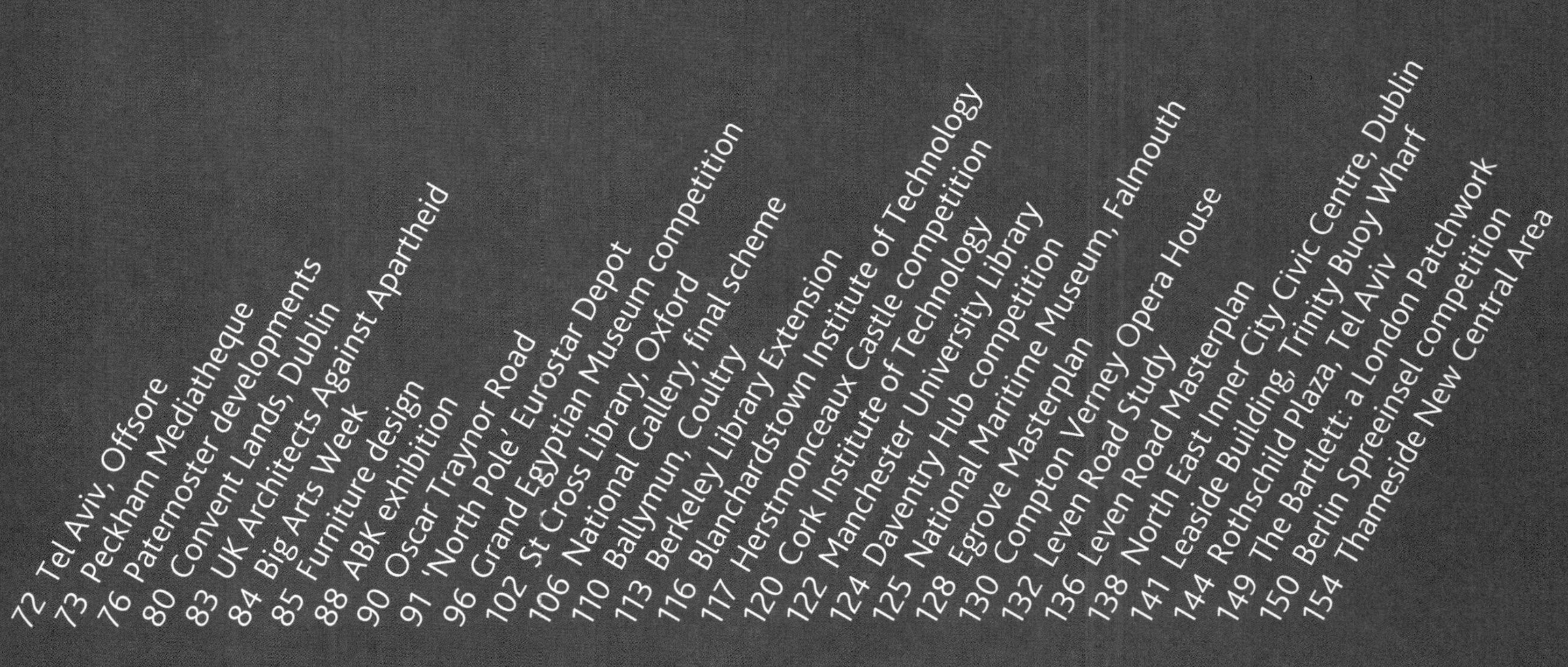

Like the meander of a river, the process of architectural design seldom follows a straight line.

During the early stages of design, working with others in a spirit of collaboration, minds explore, absorb and consider the multiplicity of a brief; not only the client's stated requirements but, just as important, those that develop as you work on possible interpretations with a flow of sketched design ideas. By the analysis of a series of barely recognisable layers of meaning you reach ways of seeing the project with a set of underlying views that encourage design flows.

In these early meanders across unknown fields, much will be thought, felt and said of a guiding design sense; during this stage of design nothing should be fixed; all avenues should be kept open until a preferred direction becomes evident. A process of oscillation takes place, forming an interplay of seemingly restless conscious and unconscious mindflows in which the process of 'easy' sketching seems, as though by itself, to encourage new connections. For it is the making of marks on paper that stir and awaken interpretations as design iterations encourage clarity.

Within this somewhat restless search for ideas the satisfying magic of sketching plays a fundamental part in the birth and growth of design concepts. The hand, activated by the feel of pen or pencil, is seemingly unconcerned by the mind's possible uncertainties in the face of ambiguities; carelessly confident, the action of drawing gives shape to images with a fluent authority, making marks that speak about the concrete meanings of the emerging forms. This is not to suggest that analysis, rationality and the demands of functionality play no part in this process but rather that, by themselves, written descriptions have a different and complementary value in the design process.

The first glimmerings of ideas for this book crossed my mind during the closing stages of the production of my last book, 'A3, Threads and Connections'. In that period Richard Burton, Paul Koralek and I had contributed individually to interviews of our lives and work for the British Library's oral archive. Plans were also being made for a joint interview: three of us in an interactive conversation covering the longstanding dynamic of our work at ABK, in practice. Jeremy Melvin had successfully managed this format for an evening's showing and discussion of ABK's work at the Royal Academy, confirming my thought that it would be interesting to so do for the oral archive. Arrangements were being made for this but it never quite came to anything… funny how things can disappear; or less mysteriously, how sometimes they remain no more than an idea, never to be realised.

Instead, I thought: consider assembling a book of our sketches, we three, illustrating our differing ways of making marks on paper as we each reach out to find and express the freshness of conceptual ideas. But this idea, then no more than a swirl of good intentions, didn't materialise.

With this selection, collection, of my own sketches I thought to show a wide variety of ideas and meanings that were latent in areas of ABK's work over a period of several decades in the late-twentieth century. Later, when thinking about possible graphic arrangements I came to the notion of a river of ideas, a stream of sketches, a scroll and a stroll through time and place, whose energy would carry and convey meanings; not from beginning to end, but from cover to cover.

Later, I came upon Geoff Dyer's introduction to his book 'Anglo-English Attitudes' where he recounts the suggestion that he'd made to his editor of publishing a preferred type of book, 'a collection of my bits and pieces'. These, his bits and pieces, each being an essay, form a very different type of collection from this set of my early-stage sketches which, in their way, 'speak' about the marks of architectural beginnings. And although in their making such drawings are solitary actions, they more often than not serve to open ideas to a collective field, first to a small design group working on the project but also, later, to a wider collaborative field.

While most of the projects in this book weren't built, ABK did complete buildings, in abundance, over a period of about five decades. The sketches shown and the ideas that they represent are of my making, but I'll generally use the pronoun 'we' when describing work which formed the stuff of our practice.

During the first twenty years of our professional life and, perhaps in common with other architects practising in that period, I did not sufficiently value the significance that such early freehand sketches have as a significant part of our design processes. Or, if I half-recognised this evident reality, it seems that I felt no need to keep and file such sometimes fuzzy manifestations of an unquestionable search for ideas; at least these were an essential part of the practice's theoretical output, if nothing else.

Many sketches about ideas were ditched at that time in favour of the more formal convention of hard-line presentation drawings. As I remember it, these early sketches seemed to have little or no significant archival place in our set of values at that time; perhaps a deliberately careless and almost cavalier oversight which may now be seen as an unconscious denial; one that may have been rooted in the more widespread architectural culture of graphic representations at that time? In the years that followed this seemingly censorial position eased as recognitions of the value of the process grew. I had thought to say more: the value of unbuilt work; the significance of plans, seeing each project as one that shapes bits of the city; sketches but not artworks, digital graphics now, and so on… but enough said!

First, some preparatory sketches made for our competition interview for the new Scottish Parliament building in Edinburgh. For the submission ABK had formed a one-off association with Behnisch & Behnisch, architect of the excellent parliament building in Bonn (1973-92), then capital of West Germany. The selection panel advised that no design work was expected for the interview so we presented only our aspirations alongside the work of our two offices.

I made a preparatory visit to Edinburgh to remind myself of the powerful character of the Royal Mile, the Old Town urban spine that extends from castle to palace in a steep uphill alignment. I sketched this simple plan to remind myself of the complexity and diversity of buildings along the route; it also served as a preface to an idea that went something like this:

Considering the nature of the context, formed by the relatively small, unitary scale of the Royal Mile buildings, I wanted to reflect the varied, quite ordinary character of this urban reality, together with the need to house Scottish democratic processes in the new building. Holding this in mind, and preceding any detailed brief, I sketched a plan in which small-scale parts at upper levels would relate to the spatially larger elements (such as the debating chamber) at lower levels. The forms were intended to be 'of the street', providing a contextual fit while expressing the dynamic structures of parliamentary democracy; a relatively modest set of parts, free of the traditional idioms of power, hierarchy and the grandeur of 'civic order'.

1998

Devolution led to the creation of a new Scottish Parliament in Edinburgh, the competition for which was won by Enric Miralles and Benedetta Tagliabue.

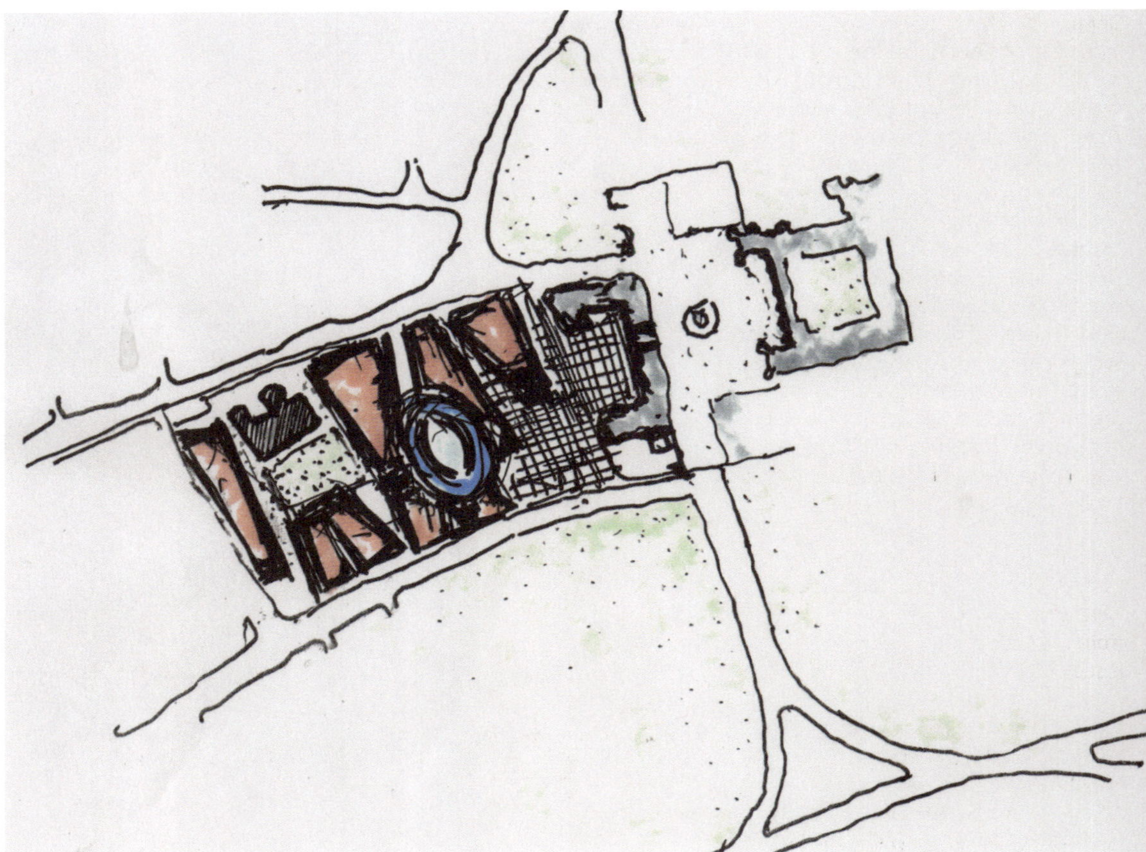

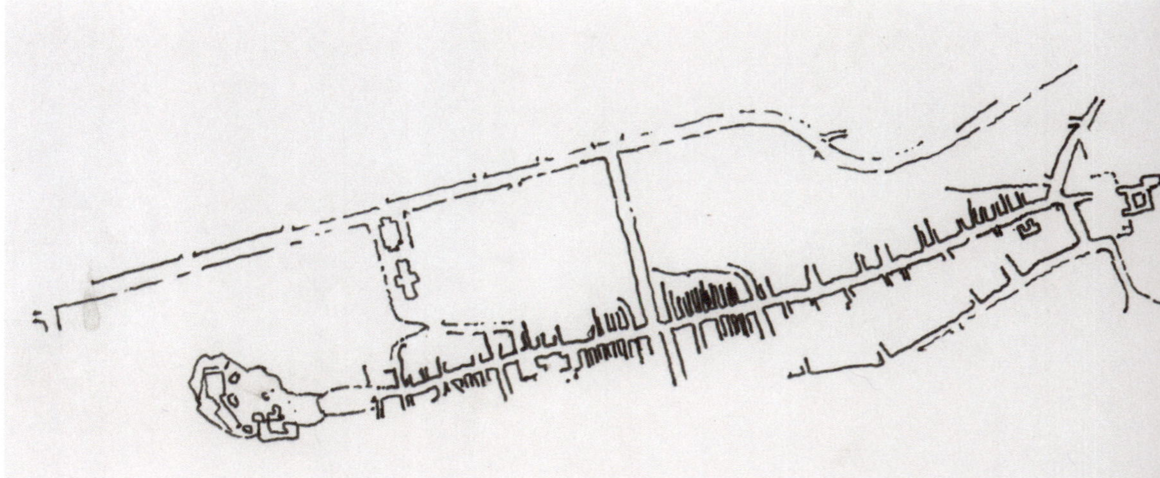

The Royal Mile links Holyrood Palace to Edinburgh Castle, embracing a multitude of different buildings and cross connections along the way. The initial idea for the Scottish Parliament sought to reflect this complexity, using built forms to achieve a fitting place in the street scene.

During a family holiday in the Languedoc in the early 1990s, the office contacted me about an international competition to re-plan the University of Grenoble campus. Might I like to pay a visit 'on my way back'?

My first impression was of the generous expanse of greenness at this out-of-town 1960s campus, with individual buildings spaciously scattered across swathes of well-landscaped open space. But I had no sense of a centre of gravity that would help one to read the the campus. Just a road-patterned layout serving a collection of generous, freestanding 'villas' that said little of 'university'. Modern? Yes. But legible and coherent? Not yet.

Walking through an outlying wooded area I came across the clear boundary of the Isère river, of which I'd been unaware from the built-up area of the campus. It seemed as if this remarkable riverside location with its magnificent Alpine views had been either overlooked or thought inappropriate for development when the original masterplan was devised. An alternative plan to exploit this key opportunity came to mind – but that, I realised, was not the issue.

We submitted a proposal for a dense alignment along a new spine to contrast with the loose layout of the existing campus. We were shortlisted for the competition and, in due course, found that we'd won.

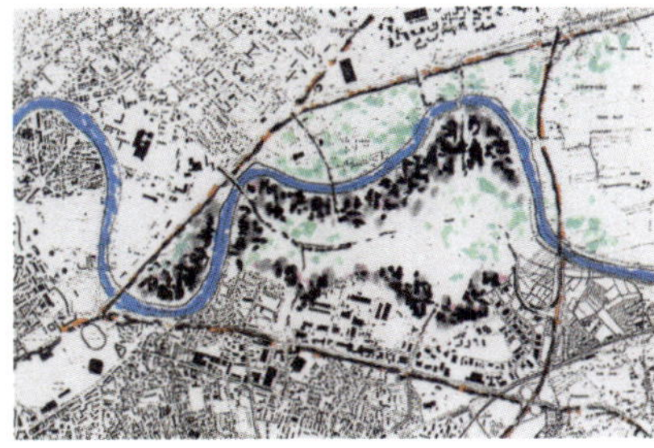

A wooded area, bordered to the north by the meandering loops of the river, came to mind as an area for the potential campus expansion.

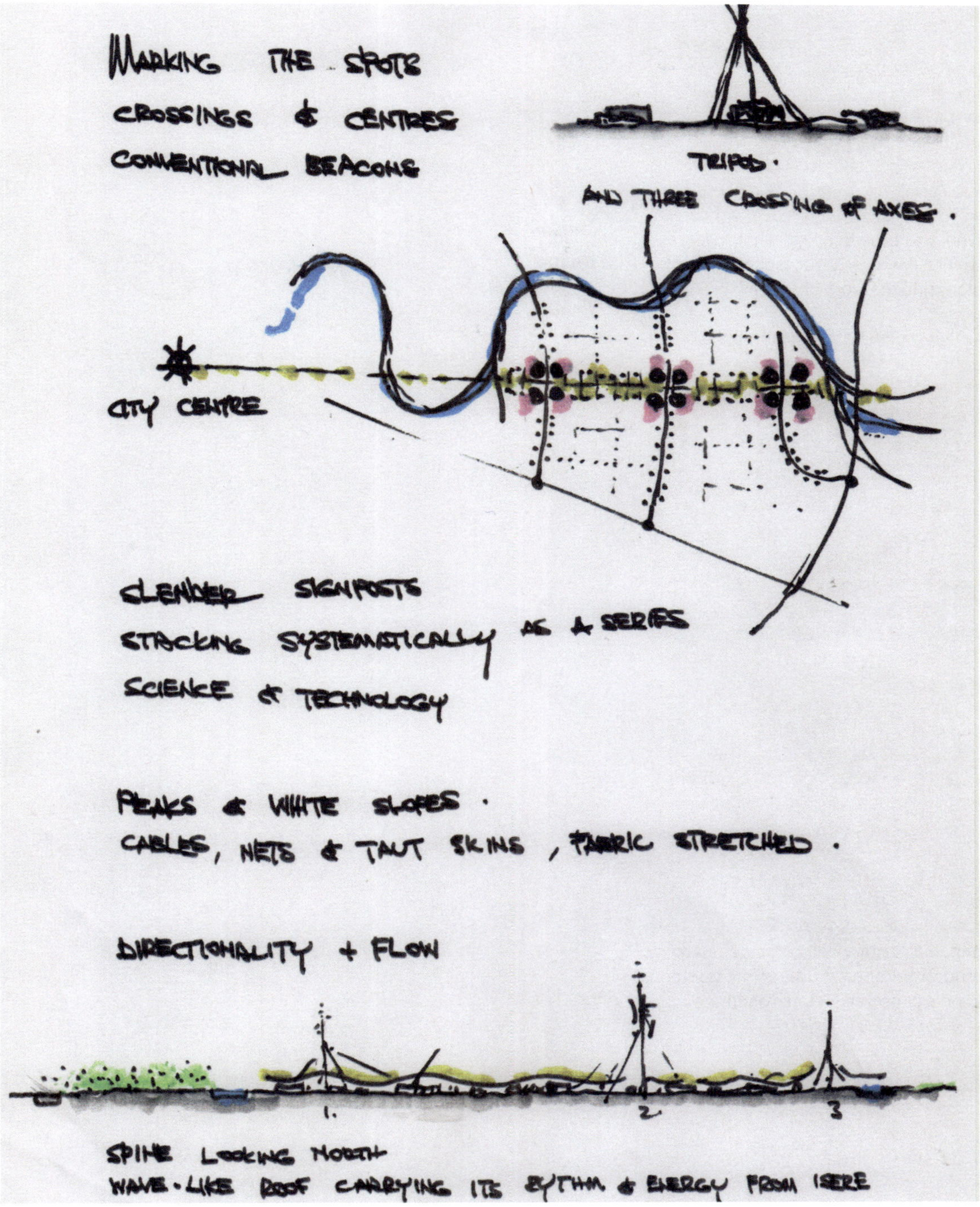

The proposed developmental axis, aligned towards the city centre, would provide a structuring spine for new university faculty buildings.

So what was the brief? In essence it called for a significant increase in the number of academic buildings, to be built over the following decade. Why then did we propose this different type of plan when the relaxed overall character of the campus had been so effective and well established?

We considered options to establish urban character by means of a centralising element. But what lay behind this ambition, and why would we not, for example, simply add more buildings in the same idiom that had prevailed since the inception of the original campus plan? Why this compulsion to effect a different plan type for this new phase of growth?

With hindsight, the answer lies in a number of thoughts. The first concerns the location of the campus in relation to the city; being just out-of-town, it seemed neither greenfield nor urban – 'on the edge' yet with no sense of 'edginess'. Given the university's academic status and its importance to the city, we thought it would better represent both campus and city to initiate a shift to a more urban character, a modest implant of a kind of 'City Strip' that would locate and intensify without disturbing the almost-parkland character of the whole.

Second, the existing 'salt and pepper' spread of buildings across the campus-green-tablecloth would, if continued in a like manner, lose the essence of its character, becoming no more than an extended, not-quite-suburban 'mat'.

Third, as though serendipitously awaiting our arrival, was the central part of the campus road layout, a formal axis of two one-way streets separated by a strip of nondescript open lawn-land that seemed destined to become the urban alignment we had in mind – an obvious gift.

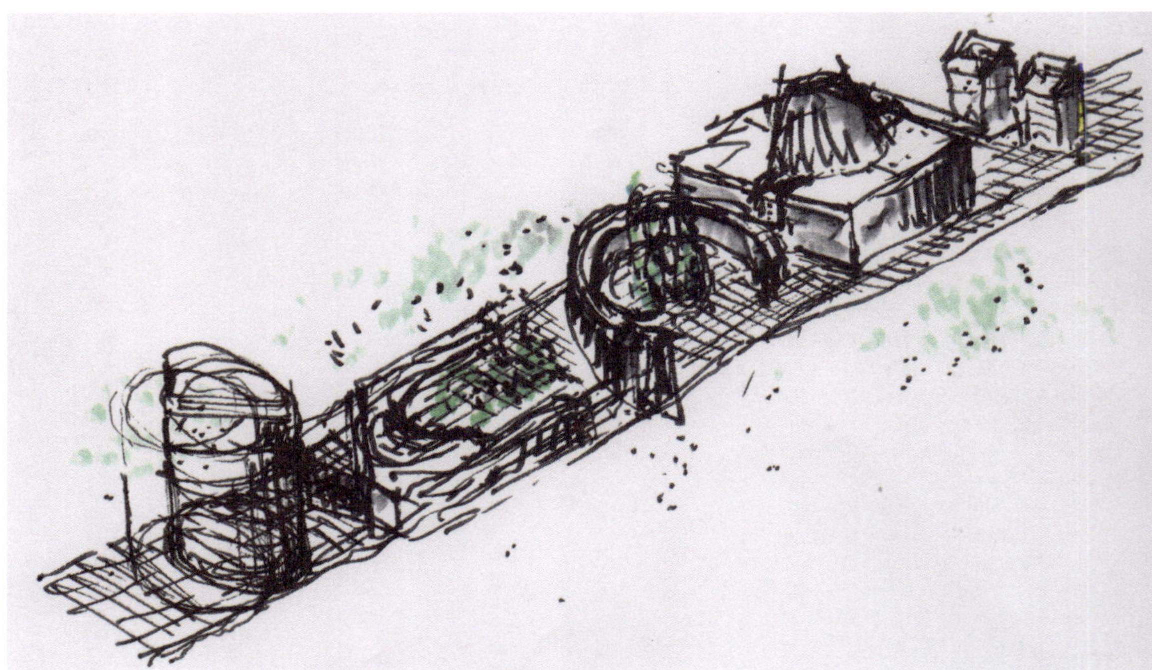

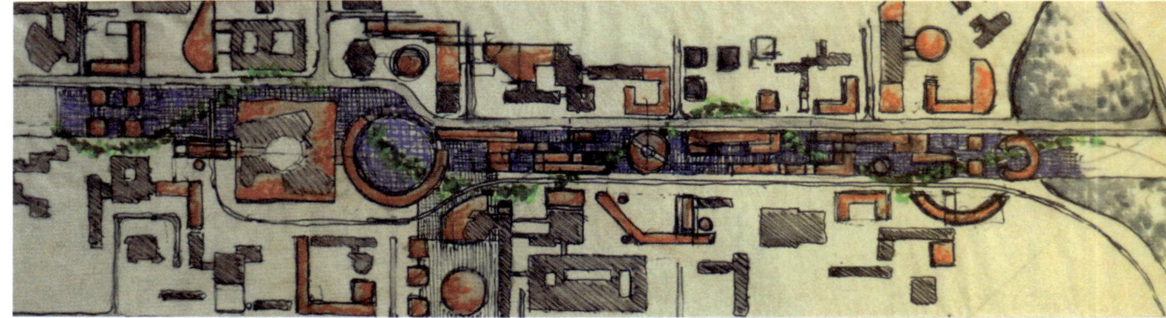

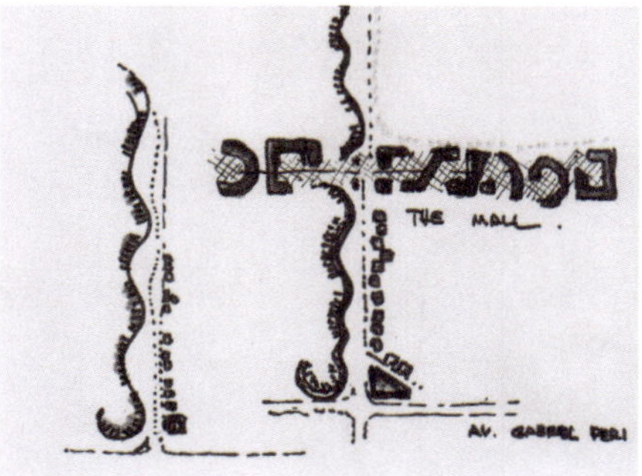

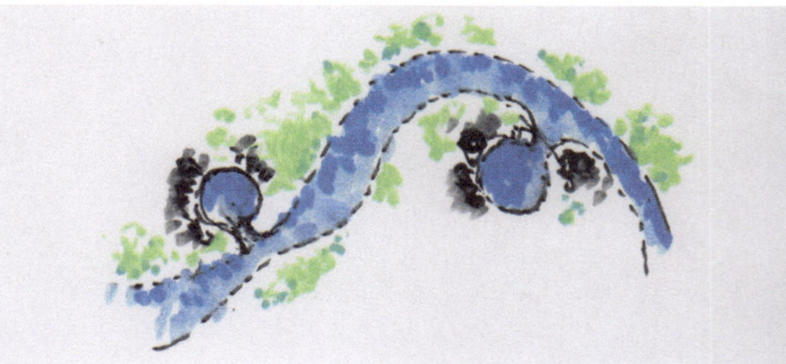

A sequence of built forms animates the development, lending an urban scale and adding a linear strip, allowing for permeability at street level.

Sheltered 'basins' are formed as inlets from the river to act as focal points for development.

thought to make a new city-link of a different kind. A wide inhabited bridge would establish an easy-flowing, safe link for pedestrians and cyclists. This, an ideas-gift that lay beyond the university brief, was not to be. No funds, no means.

Finally, we imagined a different set of built forms set along the uninhabited curvaceous road alignment that then formed the main entrance to the campus. Here, working with free-flowing curves, we formed a differentiated 'crossing' of the straight-lined geometry of the strip, introducing stretches of 'river-water' as elements of an alternative landscape language. This too was to be set aside; beyond the brief so, at best, a land-bank for the future stages of growth that are bound to occur.

1993

The addition of a linear organising 'spine' was intended to introduce an urban character to the University of Grenoble campus. ABK's competition entry was successful and adopted.

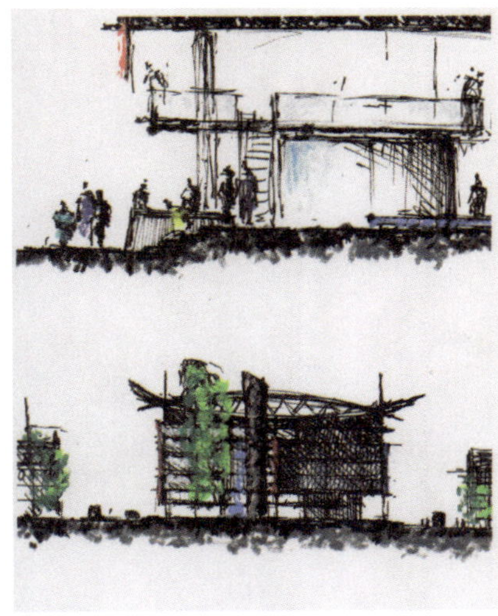

Faculty buildings would be designed so as to enhance social interaction and legibility at street level.

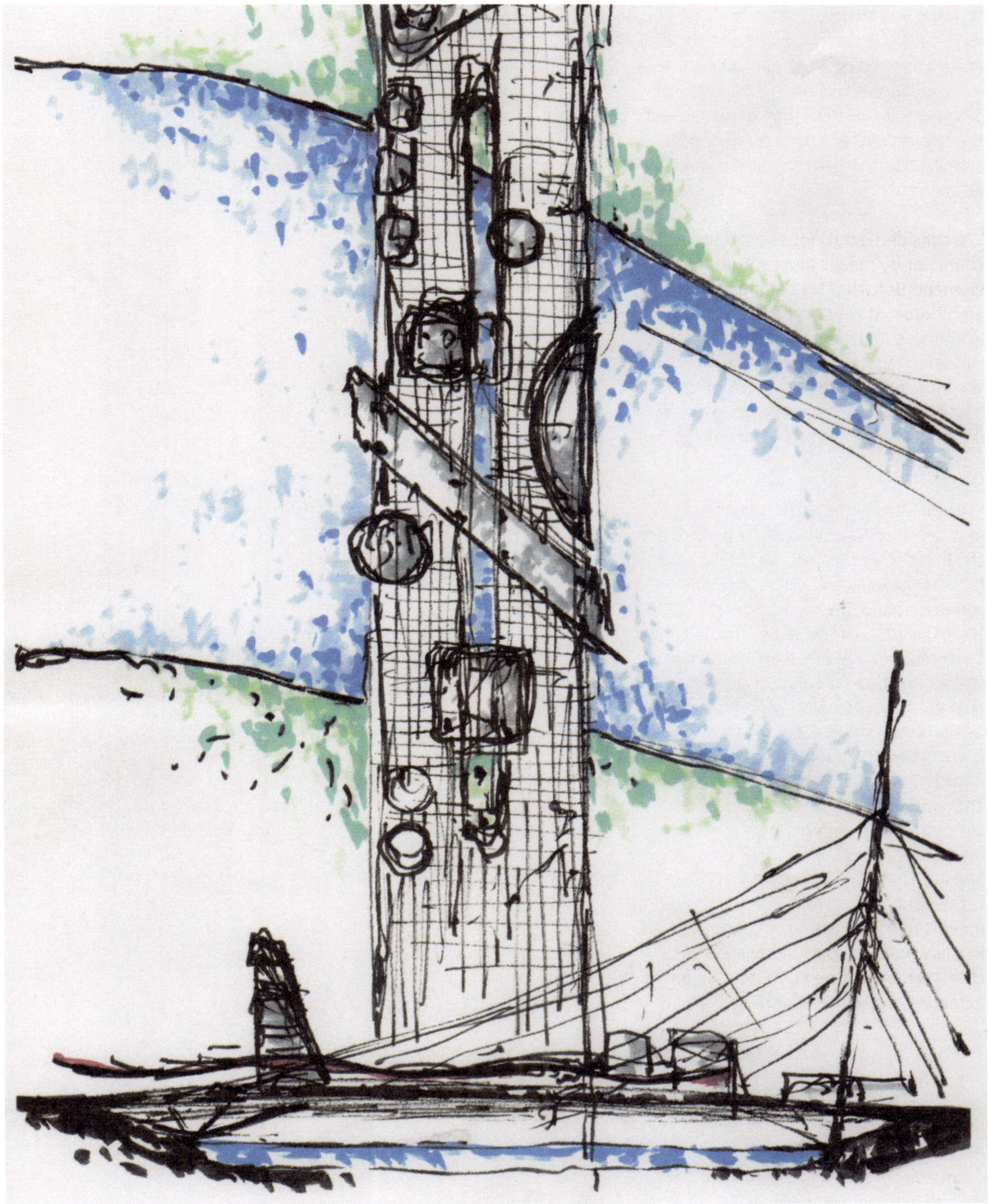

A broad, 'inhabited' suspension bridge would extend the linear development axis across the Isère river.

Beiruit Souks competition

With no such thoughts in mind we considered, designed and submitted an entry for an open competition for the souks of Beirut. Collaborating with Antoine Raffoul, a London-based Palestinian architect who had worked at ABK in earlier years, we paid a visit to Beirut to meet the authorities, see the site and, by chance before leaving, enjoyed the overnight celebrations of a Lebanese wedding in a village in the mountains to the east, towards Syria.

We walked through the mine-cleared streets of Beirut's war-torn souks, thinking how, by architectural design, we might help to bring positive notes and melodies to this bomb-raw sector of the city. Destruction and construction, a powerful coupling of contradictions that had yet to come alive for me as the idea of 'notes and melodies' grew in my mind.

Fresh, unmarked music sheets, a graphic structure of parallel-lined staves, offer notation opportunities for music-making. Perhaps with this image somewhere in mind, we designed a matrix of paralleled streets and tightly-spaced low-to-medium-rise souk buildings, a dense mews-like urban fabric, crossed and connected by two curvaceous streets

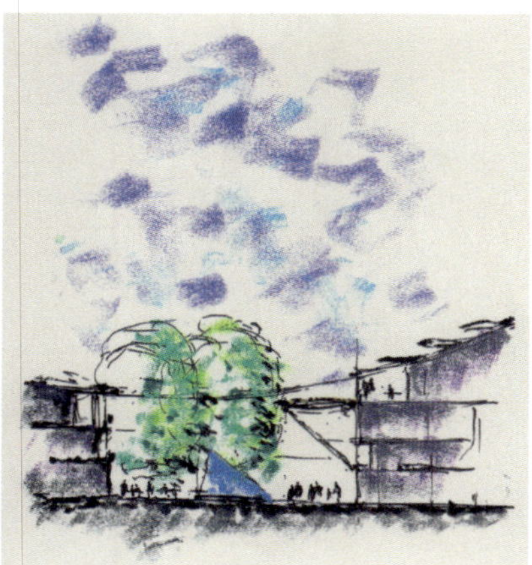

Trees, watercourses and canopies would provide respite from the summer heat.

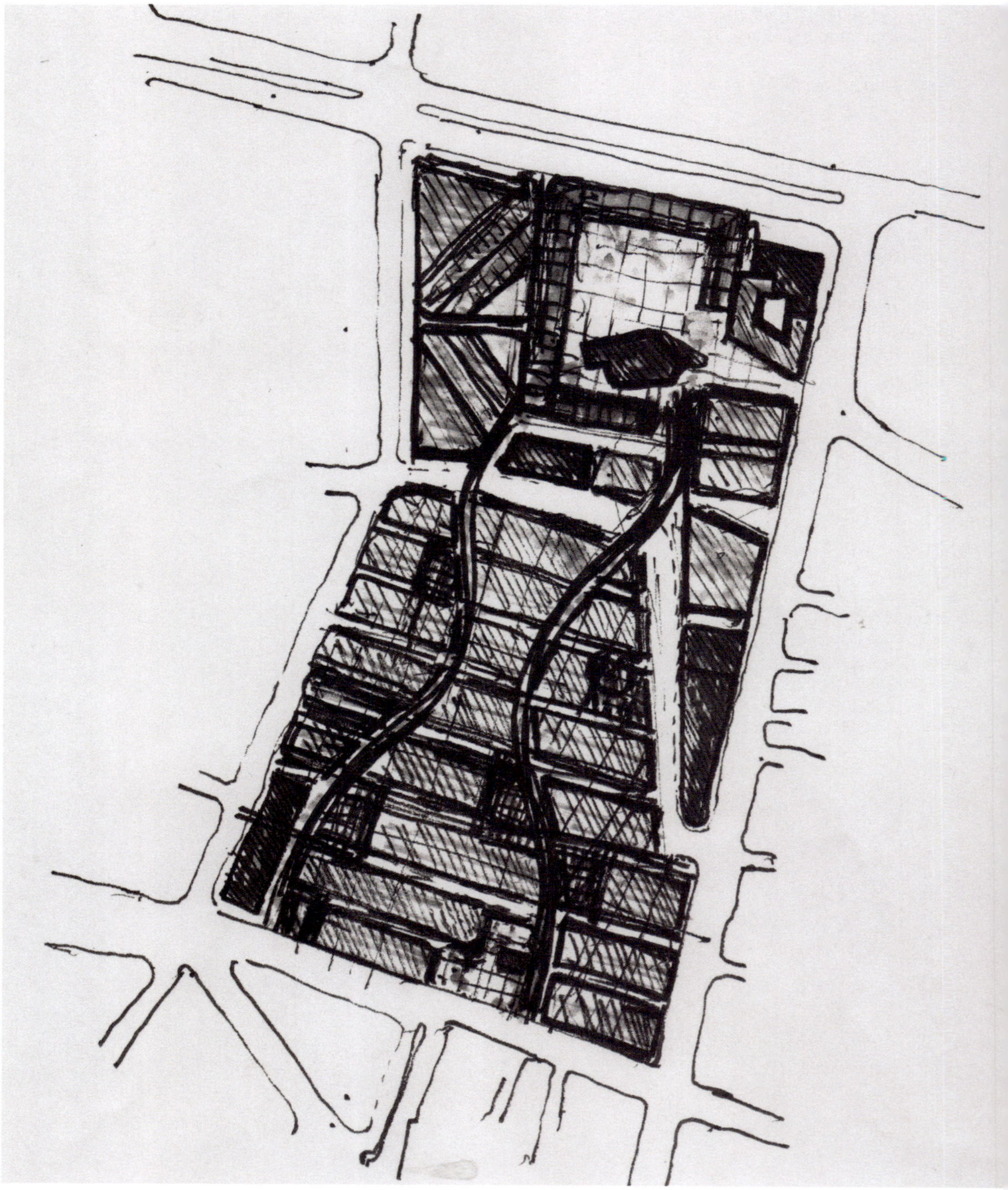

Two principal curving streets weave through a dense arrangement of parallel market buildings.

offering contrapuntal market-place melodies; references, perhaps, to DNA's interlocking helical structure and, more generally, the power of free-flowing binary couplings?

Looking through these sketches some years later, I felt that, had we been successful in the competition, I may have come to relax from the strict uniformity of parallel lines. A few straight-line deflections would also have favoured the formation of occasional public gathering places. But now, seeing the sketch plan afresh, I think the design is fine as it was.

But this scenario wasn't to be. After the competition winner had been announced, Antoine visited the exhibition of entries in Beiruit, but he couldn't find our drawings. Directed to a store, he located the panels that we'd safely dispatched by courier, crumpled on the floor. We never got to the bottom of what had happened.

1994

Largely destroyed in 1975 during the Lebanese Civil War, Beiruit's historic souks were rebuilt following an international competition and finally reopened in 2009.

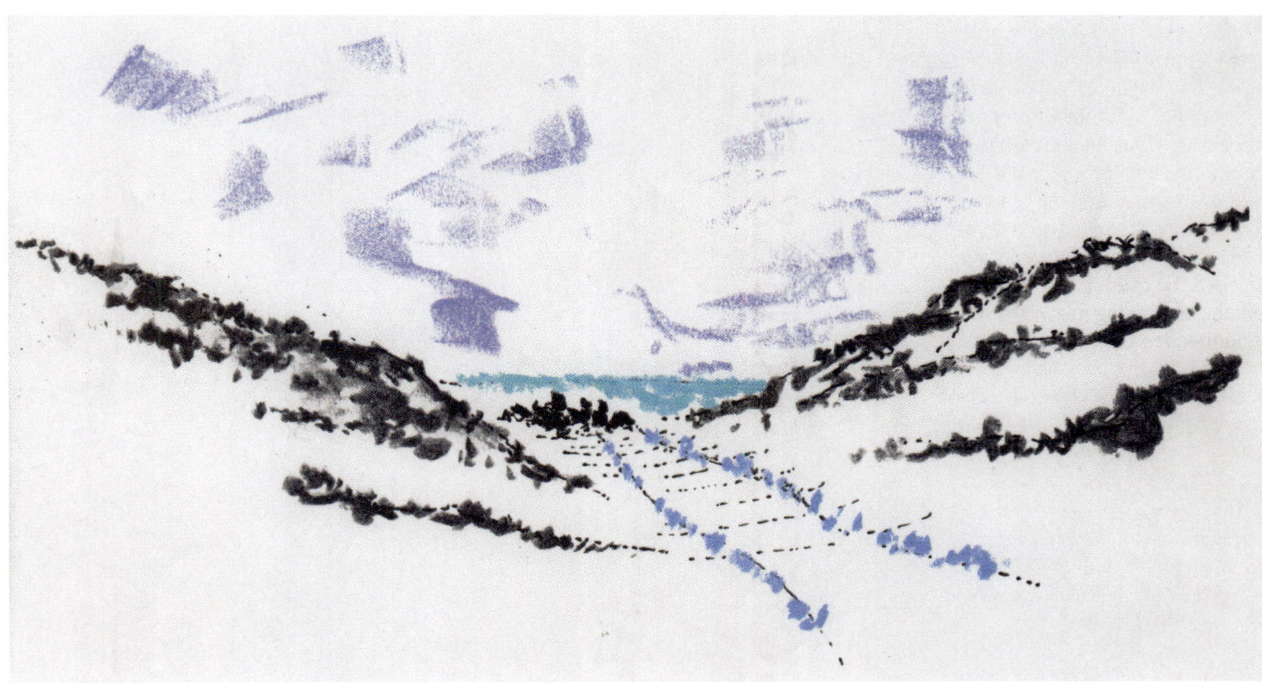

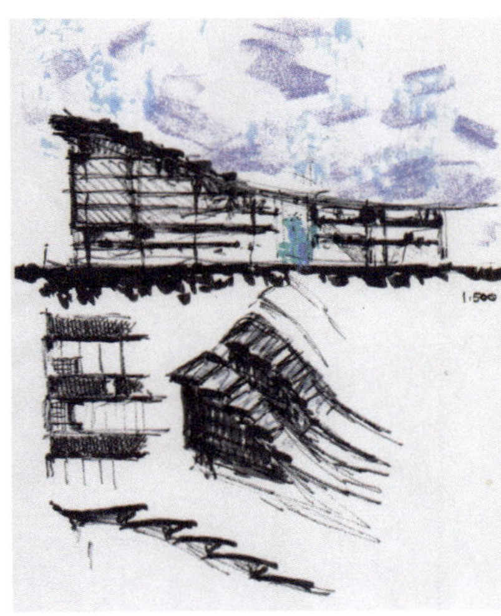

Stepped building forms with external louvres as shading devices.

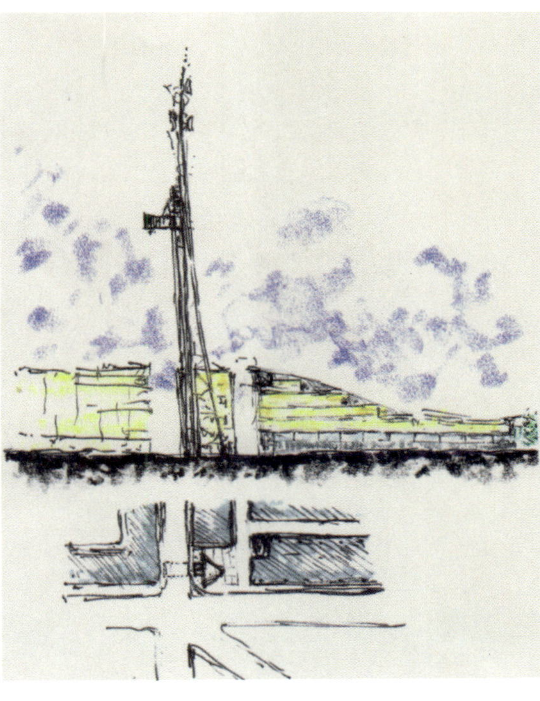

The plan draws on the landscape of hills and valleys at the edge of Beiruit, as well as the dense urban matrix of the medieval souks.

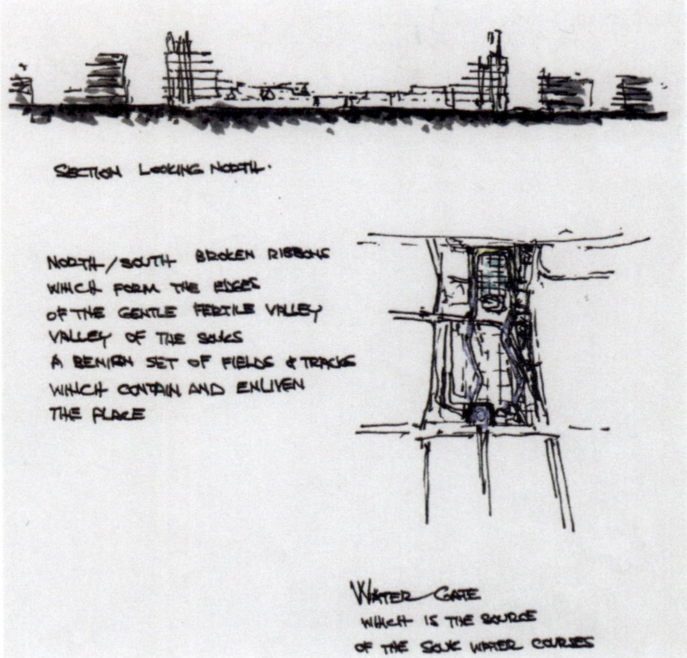

I include these sketches not so much to illustrate the character of the proposal, nor to suggest the importance of bridge design within the lexicon of ABK's work, but rather to show how on this occasion I found myself taken, for a while, by an unforeseen design idea that had a powerful appeal.

When I visited the site, while wandering along the water's edge, I was attracted by the beauty of a cluster of reeds. Their random, almost vertical alignments suggested an idea for the columnar structure of the bridge: an abundance of thin supports rather than the convention of having relatively few weightier columns. But ideas come and go, and I realised that the extent of foundation disturbance along an ecologically sensitive stretch of water would have been unacceptable; time to move on.

1995

The Highways Agency held a competition for a new bridge across Poole Harbour in Dorset, that was intended to set a benchmark for bridge design in sensitive areas. The £26m winning project, by Flint & Neill with Ramboll, was abandoned in 1998.

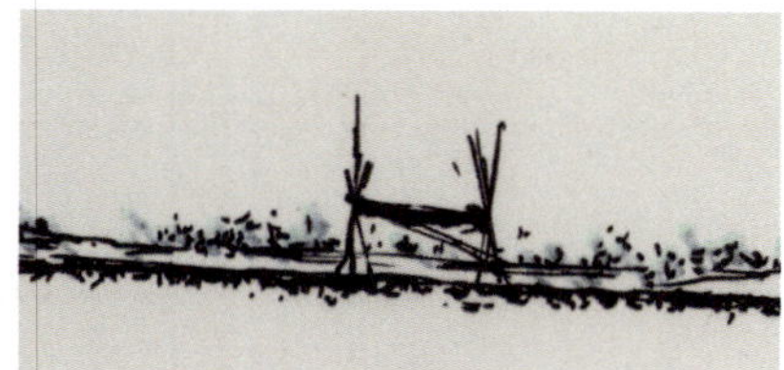

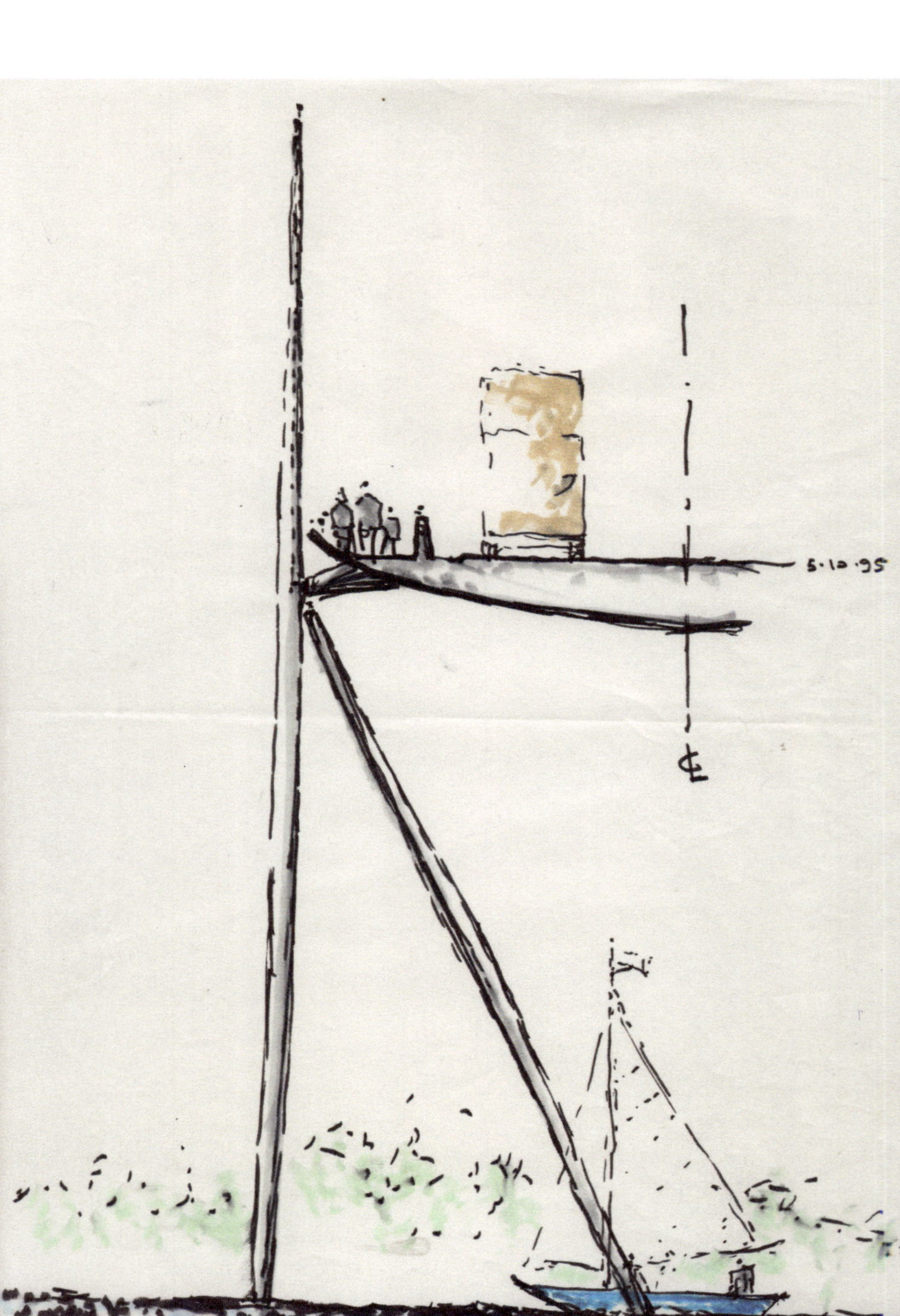

The bridge rises in a gentle curve, allowing boats to pass beneath at its highest point.

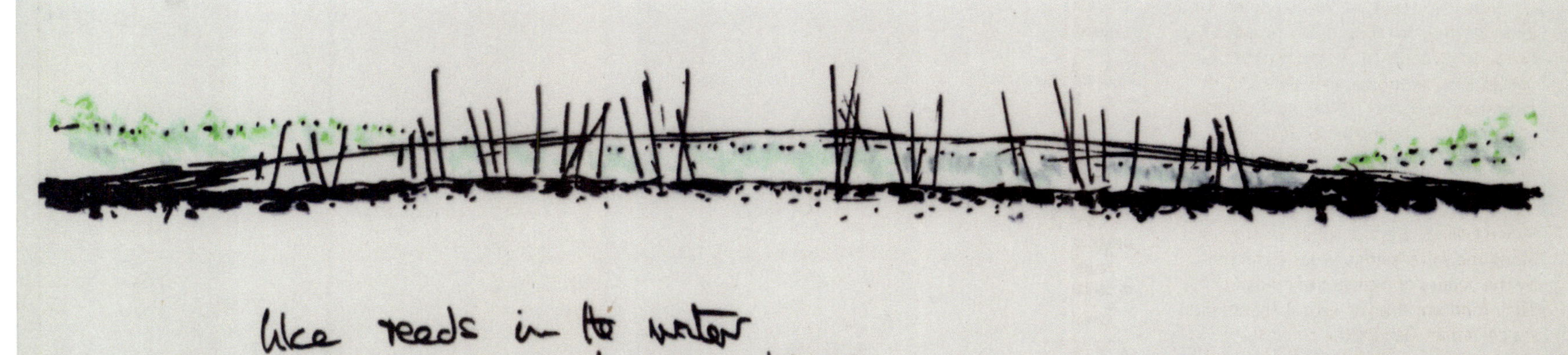

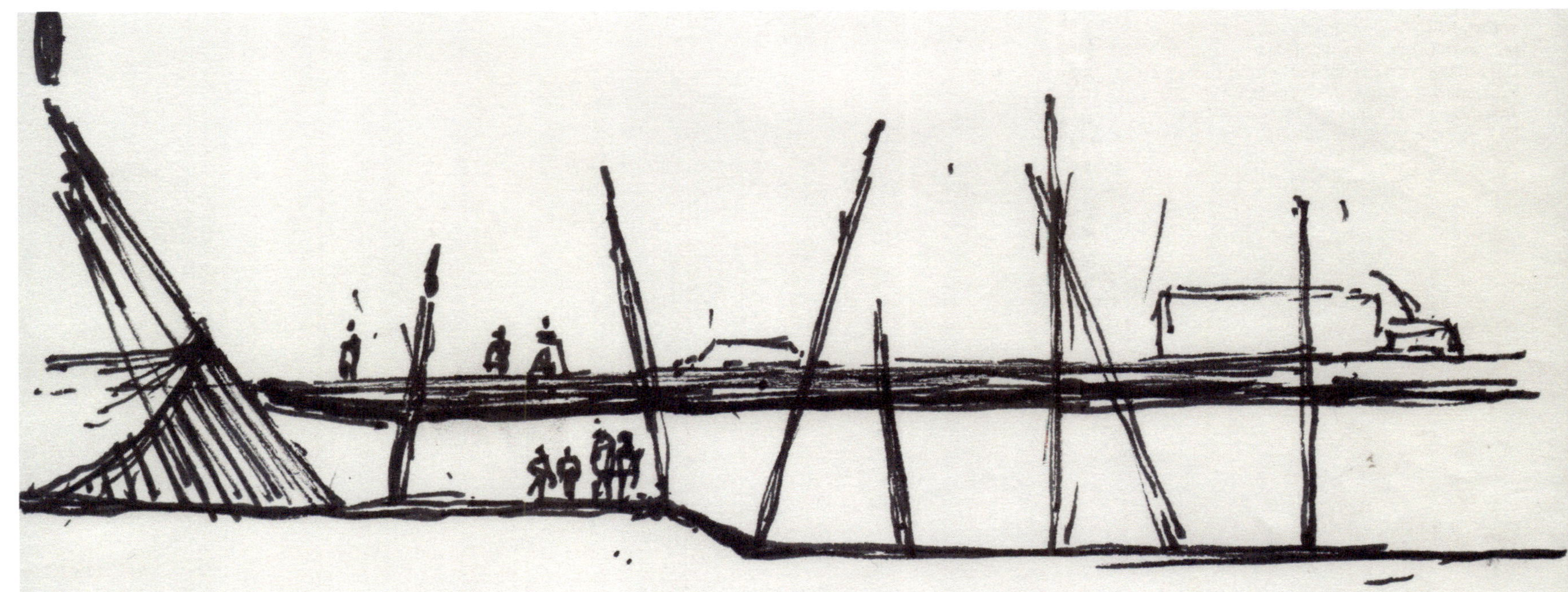

Slender struts, randomly spaced and angled, provide a structural system that at first seemed appropriately tuned to the ecologically sensitive context of Poole Harbour.

15

Coming upon these sketches for a below-surface ticket hall for one of the new Crossrail stations, I'm reminded of the circumstances that gave rise to the ideas. I was away on a springtime family holiday at our house in the Languedoc when I heard from our office about the impending deadline for this submission.

Perhaps the weather wasn't great on that day, but I had some time. Or was it that this particular Crossrail site triggered memories of our earlier roof-lit studio, tucked-away in a mews near Hanover Square? In any case, by then we'd done several rail schemes, so it may have been a natural opportunity.

But, as it later seemed, these snapshot holiday ideas of a 'luminescent ticket hall' with 'cracks in the earth above', were not thought by our Crossrail client to be of environmental interest.

1990-92

The 73-mile-long Crossrail project, linking east-west across Greater London, arose from a 1989 study of three options. The central section of the adopted scheme passes through Bond Street, for which ABK designed a proposal for a daylit ticket hall.

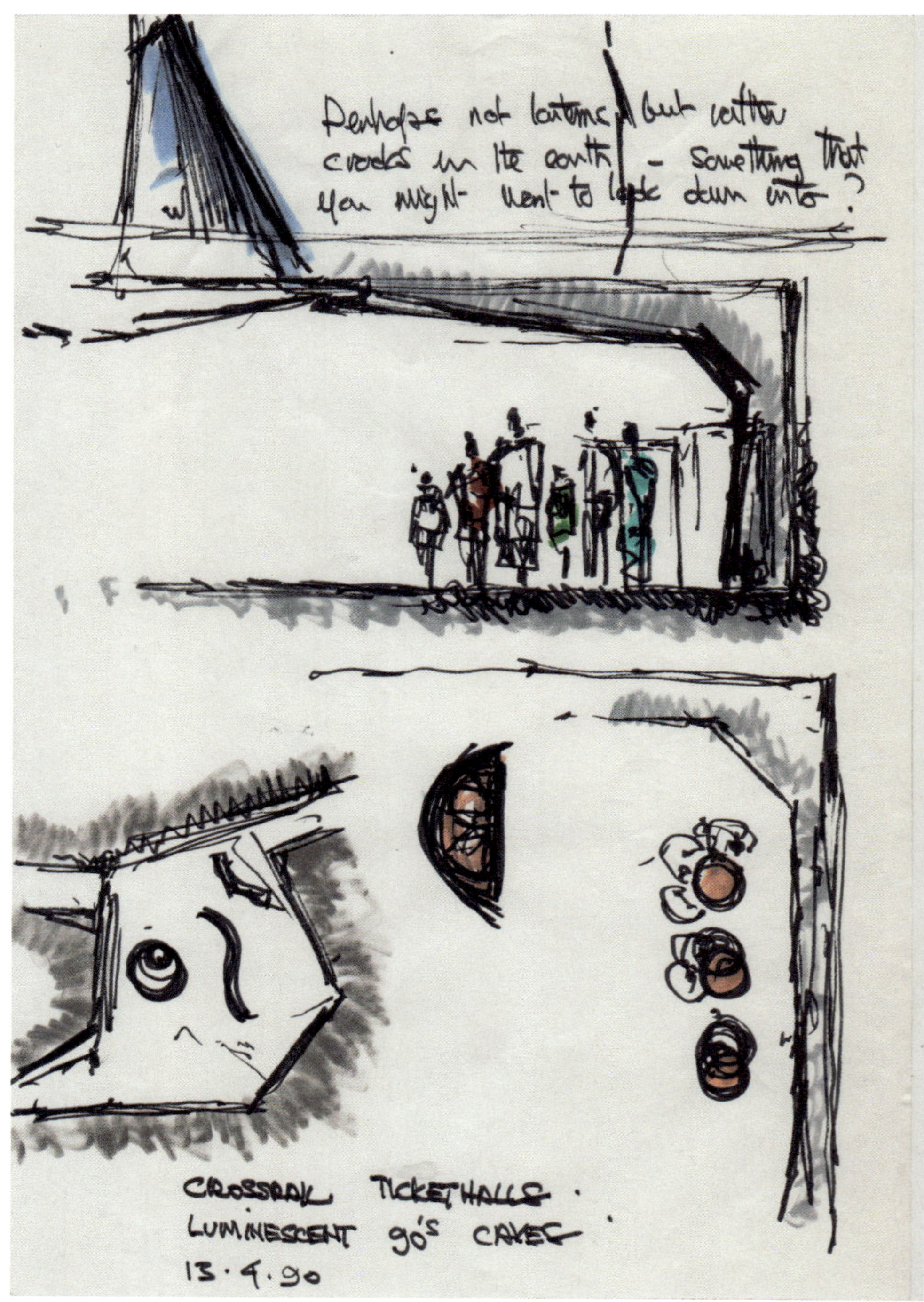

These preliminary sketches explore the idea of introducing natural light to the below-grade ticket hall while also allowing views in from the pavement level above.

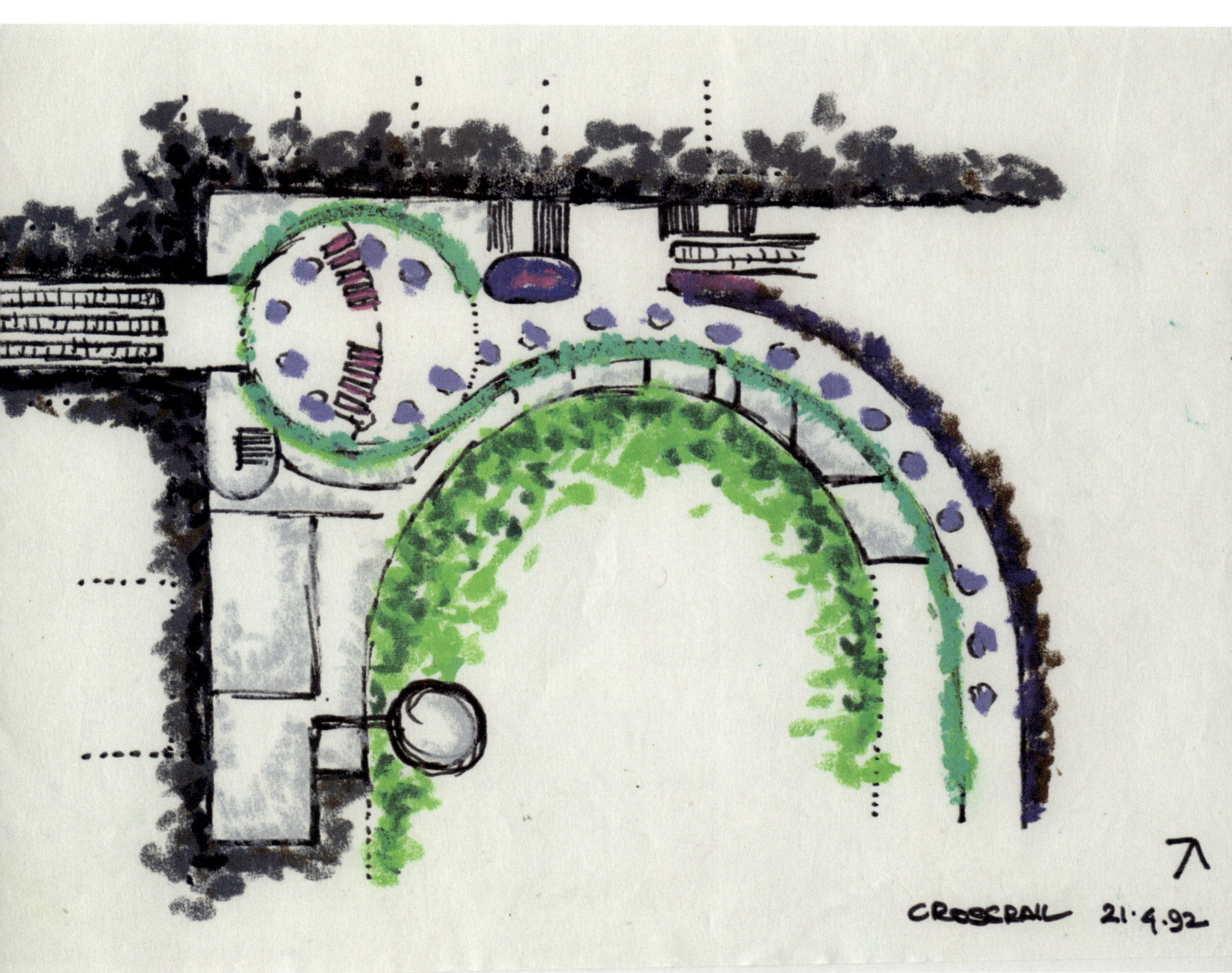

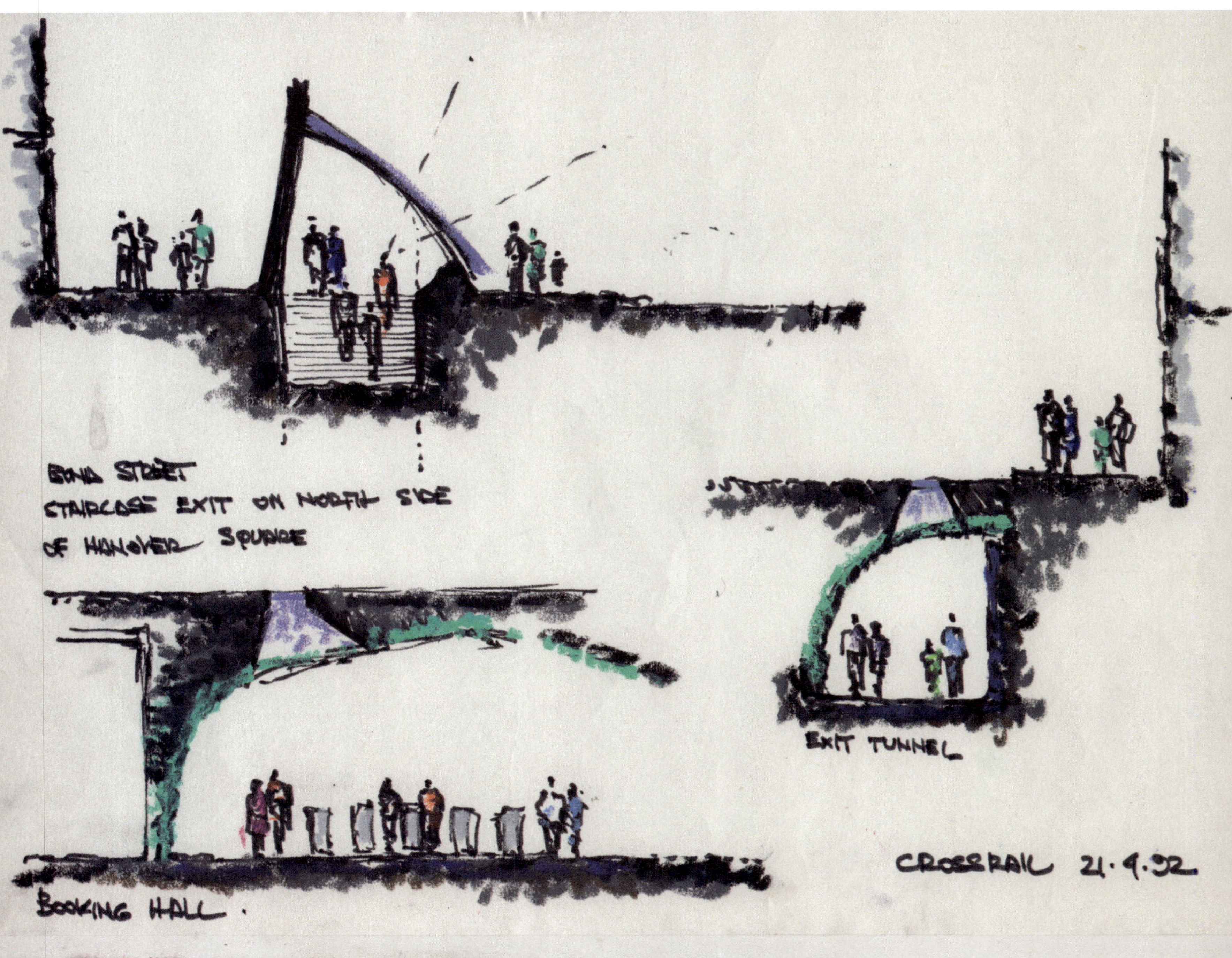

BOND STREET
STAIRCASE EXIT ON NORTH SIDE
OF HANOVER SQUARE
EXIT TUNNEL
BOOKING HALL.
CROSSRAIL 21·9·92

We worked on this proposal for an open competition for a new opening footbridge of the counterweighted, 'bascule' type to span across the lower, navigable reaches of the River Liffey in Dublin.

Like a huge boomerang, it was poised so as to rock elegantly, opening and closing on its elbow using a minimum amount of motor energy to effect its movements.

We received a special mention from the competition panel. Thanks, but together with our engineers we felt that our distinguished design should have won, and could have been built with style and confidence. The night and day computer images we submitted were, I thought, stunning. I had a bundle of design sketches that haven't come to light, so for now this can be no more than a rather thin showing.

2002

A competition entry for the 'Stack A' bridge, the first opening bridge on the downstream river journey in Dublin, forming a symbolic gateway to the docklands and the sea.

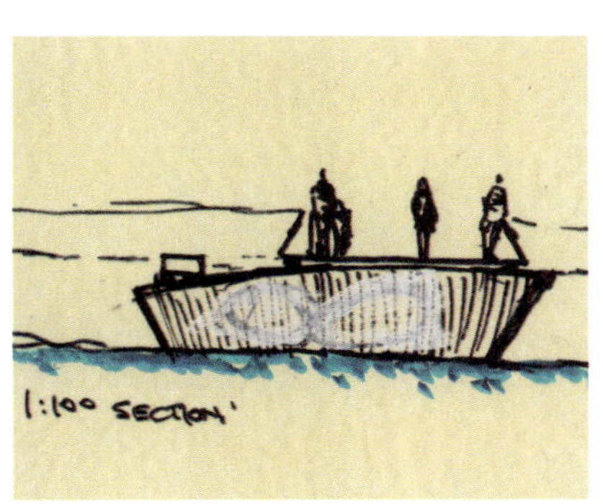

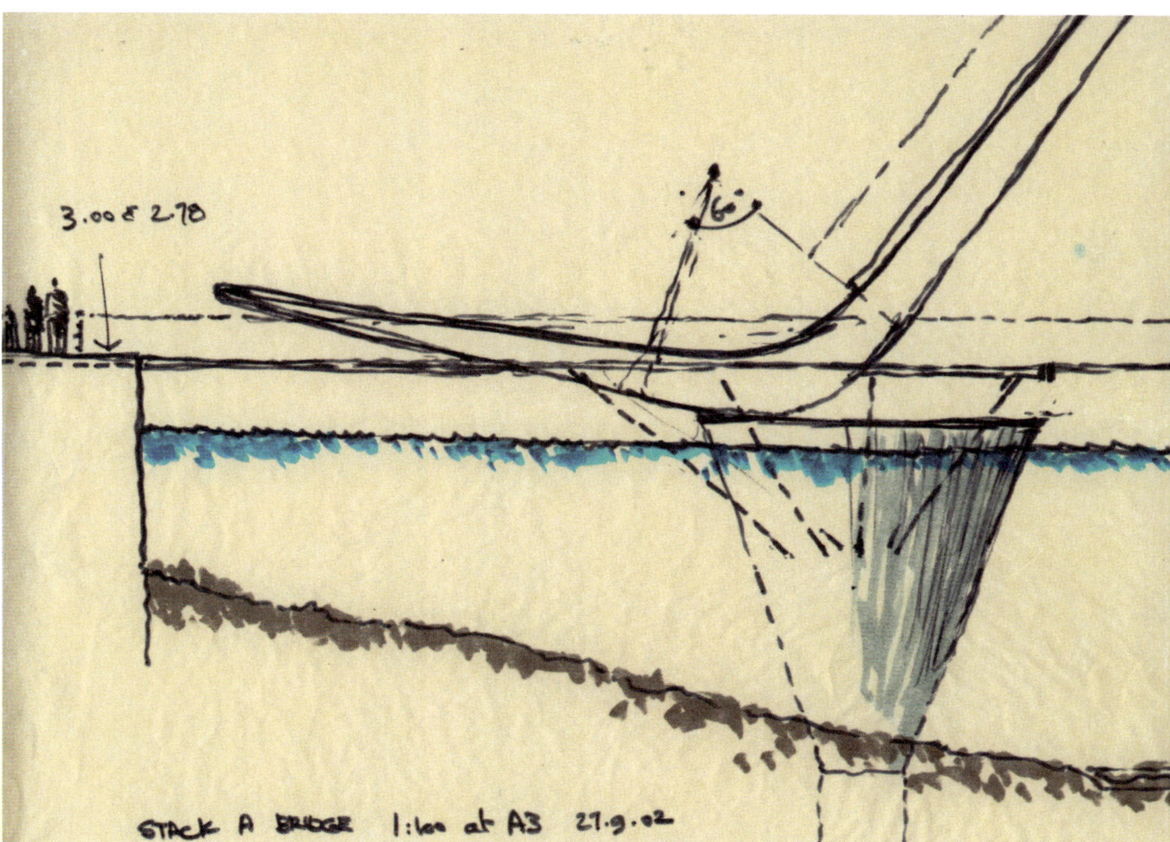

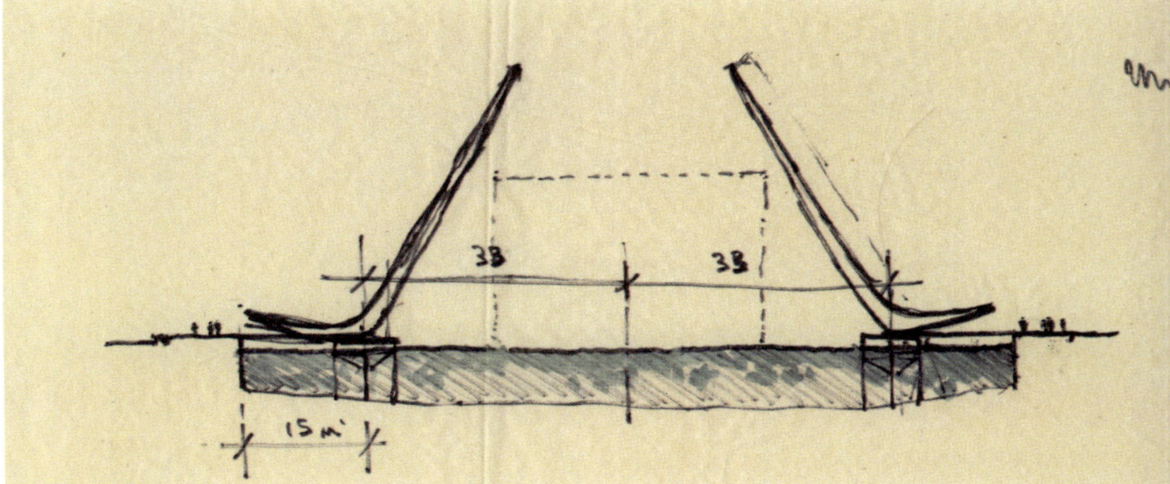

Counterbalanced 'wings', like two opposing drawbridges, open to allow river traffic to pass beneath while also forming a potent landmark.

I visited the University of Limerick campus to help prepare a quick study expressing our interest in the university's advertised development programme for new academic buildings on its greenfield site.

Here my interest in the riverside site gave rise to a number of design options. These sketched proposals show a possible new route towards a bridge across the River Shannon, by way of its mid-stream islands, to serve clusters of new buildings situated on both banks.

Physically and metaphorically, the idea related to the formation of an additional 'anchorage' on the campus, while reaching out towards a new territory.

2000

Established in 1972, the University of Limerick campus is bisected by the River Shannon, which posed a challenge for its future expansion plans.

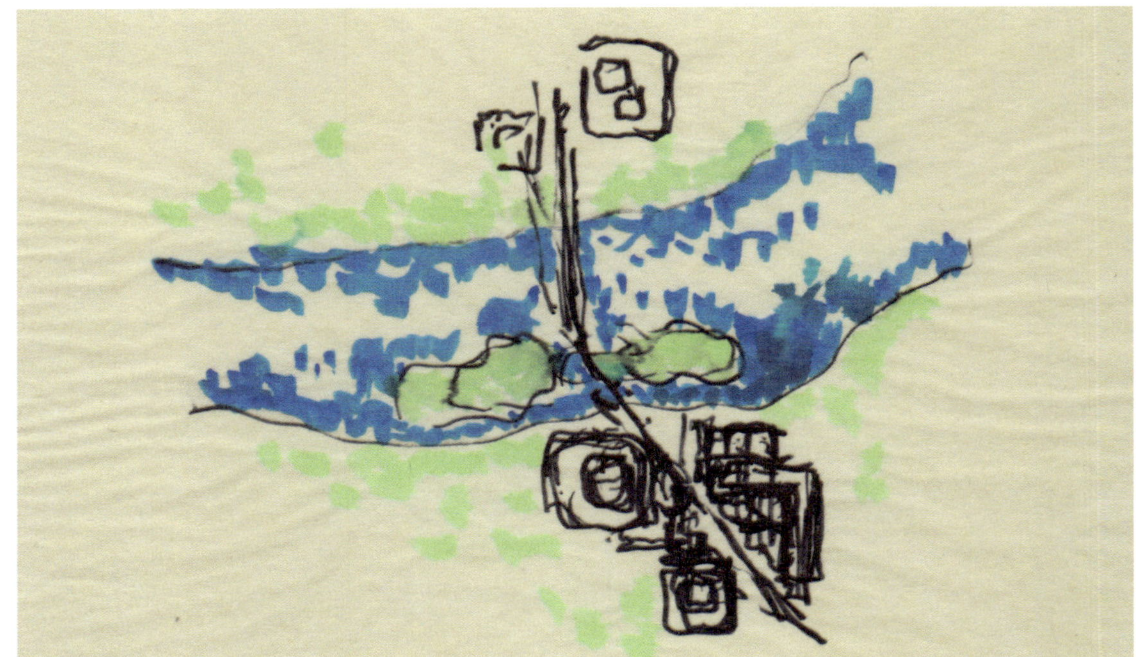

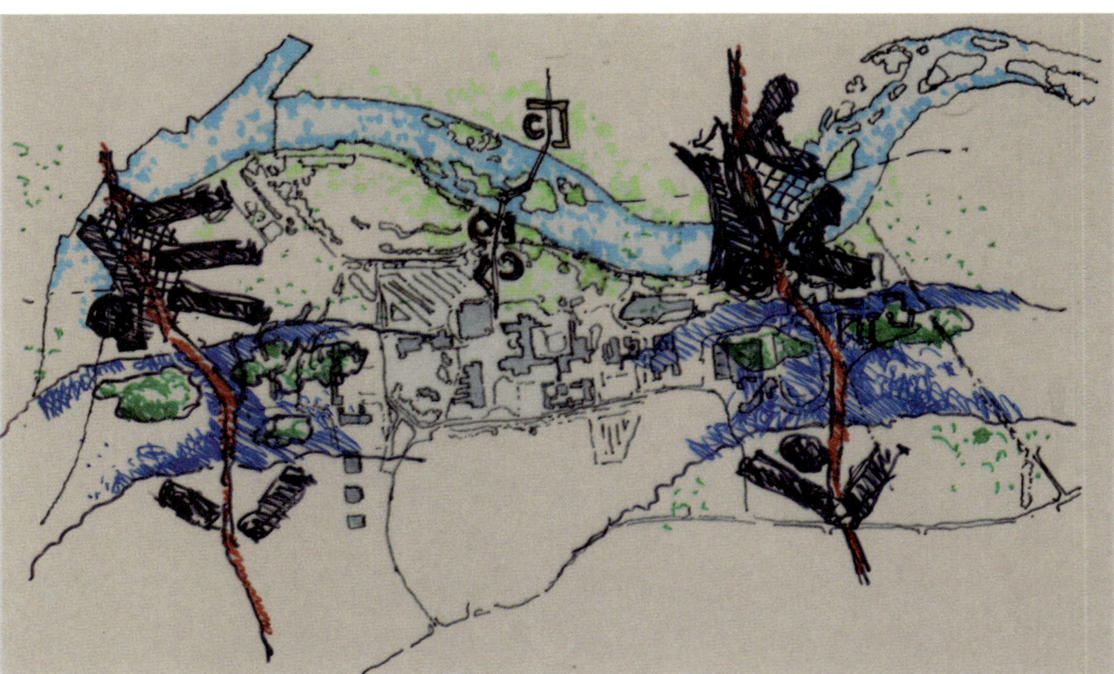

Initial sketch ideas seek to unite the campus across the river by means of bridges that provide armatures for potential future faculty buildings.

WH Smith, Swindon

Having built the first phase of a relatively dense, low-rise office building for WH Smith's regional headquarters in Swindon in 1985 (employing a gridded plan with a 'noughts-and-crosses' matrix), we were asked in 1994 to devise the development plan for a new conference suite.

We prepared a number of options, most of which formed groupings around the existing stair cores that were situated at intervals along a diagonal access route, so as to form a functionally active edge to the existing plan.

At first these clustered animations were appealing, but on analysis they seemed less flexible in use and management than the alternative of a single unit, a cylindrically-planned suite of rooms whose terminating form echoed the cylindrical hub that marked the existing entrance to the route. Whereas the original 'drum' form had comprised an assembly of opaque wall materials lit by rooflights, this new hub became fully glazed – a clear and deliberate contrast in architectural language.

1994

ABK was asked by WH Smith to revisit its earlier project for the company and plan a new conference suite.

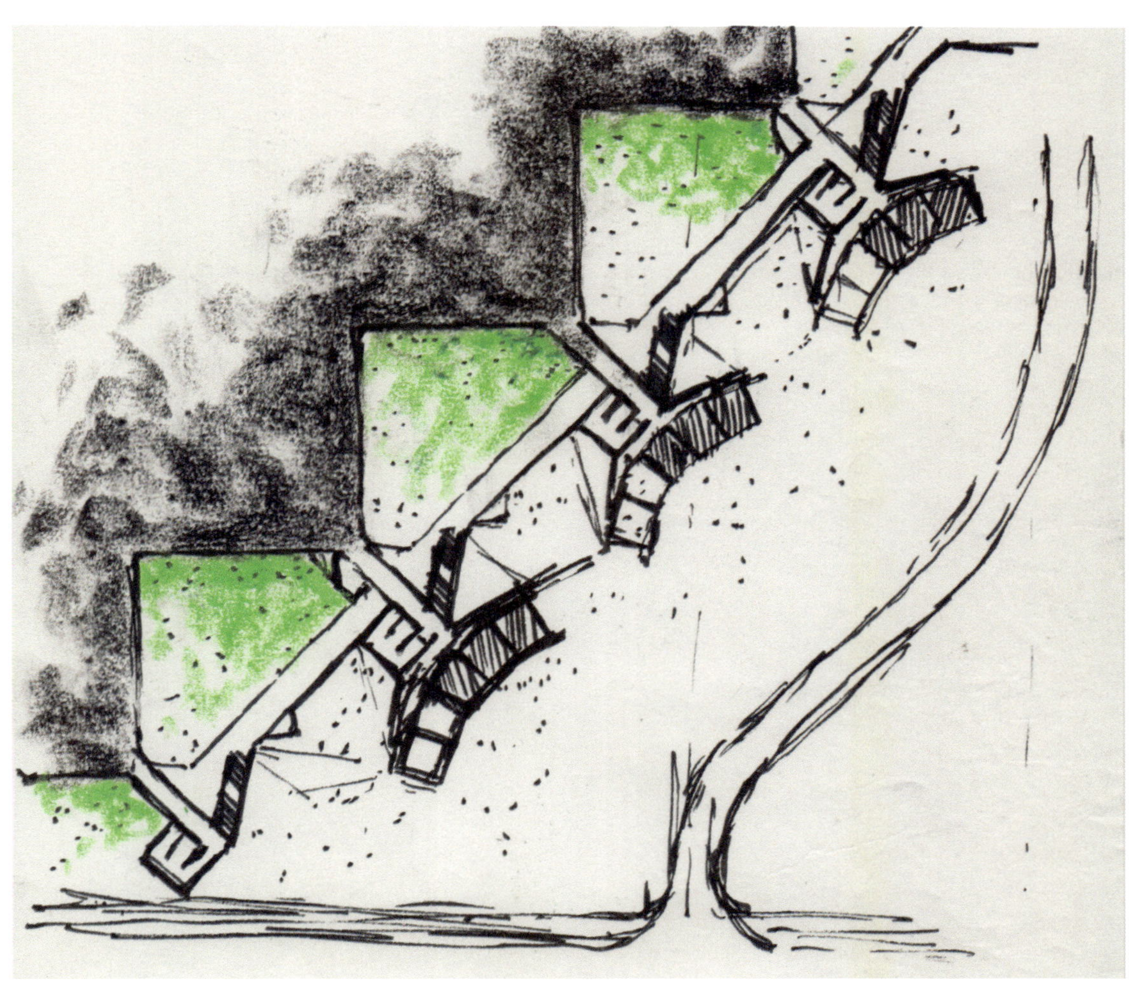

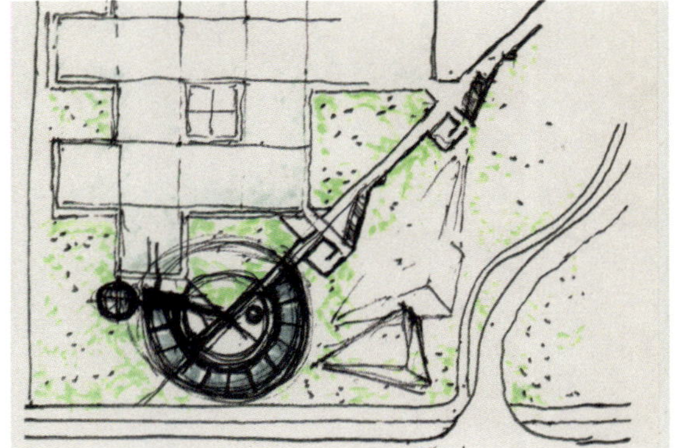

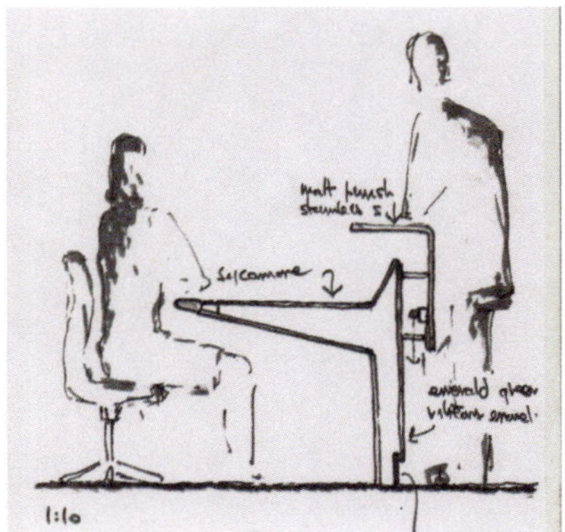

Clusters of conference suites were planned to link with the existing stair towers.

These sketches illustrate a first-ideas response to Jesus College's brief for a new library. Our proposal engaged with the character of the existing 'Chimney' (the walled passage to the college entrance) to establish a new low-rise entrance and library building. This was to extend, formally, to link with the quadrant-shaped plan of the auditorium and its loggia. The ensemble was designed so as to nestle modestly and comfortably at a low level in the corner of this newly formed quad.

1991

Jesus College at the University of Cambridge held an architectural competition for its Quincentenary Library. The winning scheme, designed by Evans & Shalev, was completed in 1995.

Jesus College, Cambridge

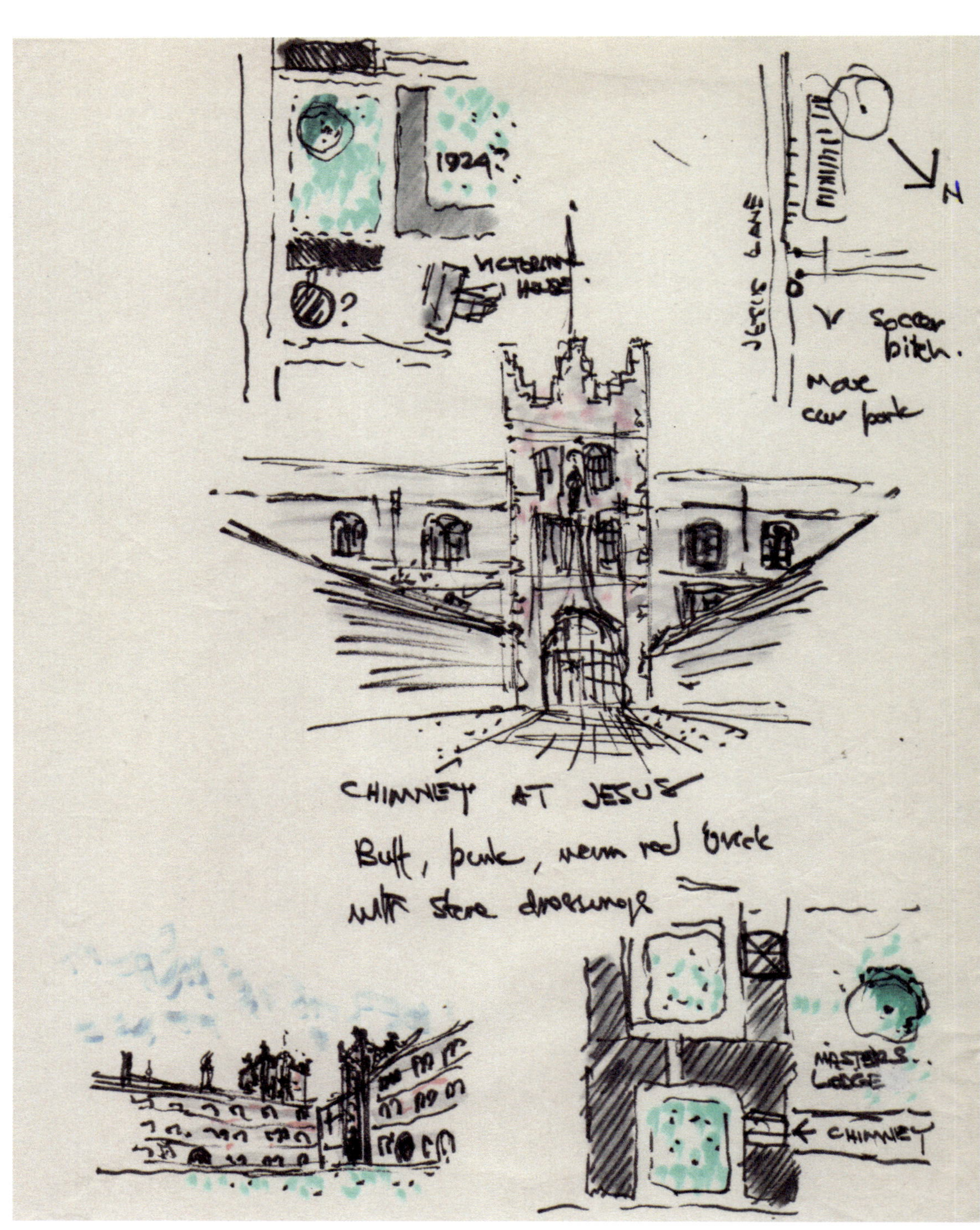

Analytical drawings of the existing college buildings informed the proposal for the library building.

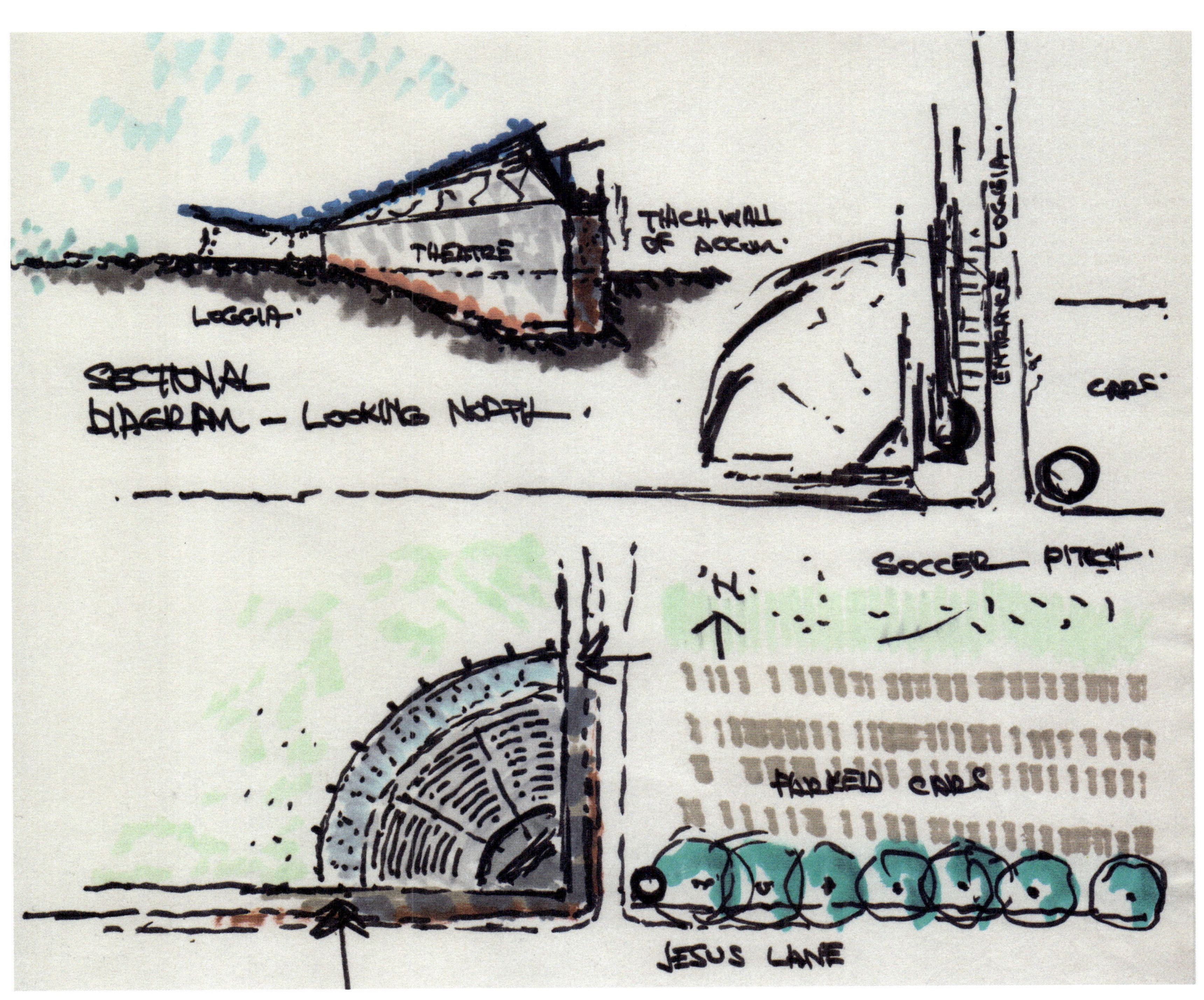

'Great quadrant with welcoming loggia facing the green new quad. But also presenting two entrances: one internal, facing the new car park to the east, and one external onto Jesus Lane. The bulk of the building is buried, with only the gentle roof as clear dominant form, whilst the loggia speaks for itself'.

Thank you, James Hope

In the late-1970s, during the early design stage of our scheme for the Cummins diesel factory at Shotts in the Scottish lowlands, I made a visit to Edinburgh to interview a number of prospective landscape architects.

The meetings took place amidst the hustle and bustle of the lobby at The Caledonian, the distinguished railway hotel in Edinburgh. For a number of reasons, James Hope stood out, not least because he asked challenging questions about one particular aspect of our design that related to his set of landscape interests. In the years that followed, we much enjoyed and valued working together on the high-paced Cummins project, and his contribution was memorable.

On one of my working visits, I stayed overnight with the Hopes at Birdsmill, just west of Edinburgh. Before breakfast, I made a visiting card, a composite sketch of some of the landscape elements that James had planned and built for his rural home. Looking at the sketch much later, I wondered whether De Chirico had been staying overnight in spirit.

1977

Landscape elements inspire a thank-you card.

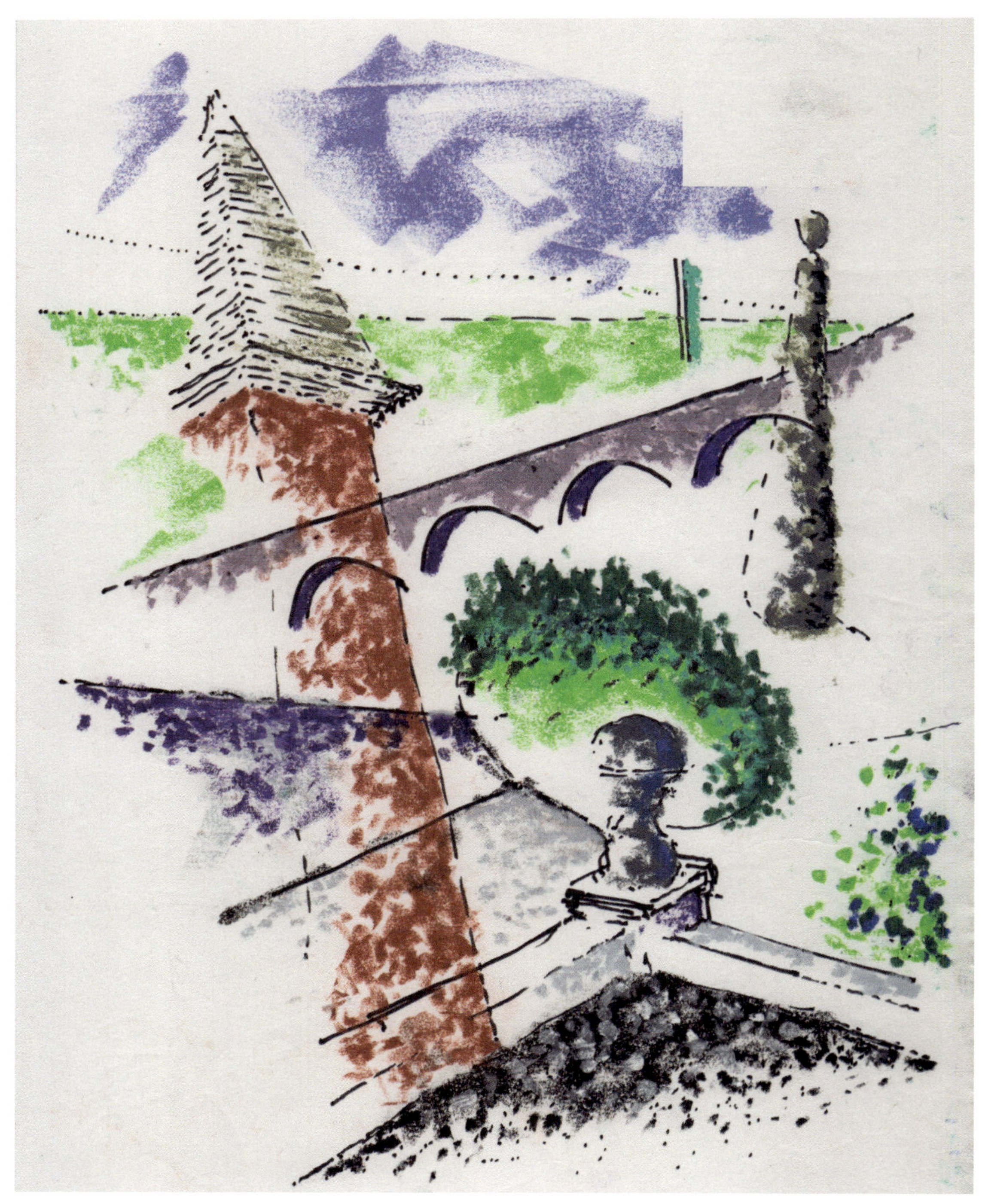

Familiar with Camden Town's many Greek Cypriot restaurants, where we ate so well in earlier times, I decided to have a go at the 1992 competition for a masterplan for the new campus of the University of Cyprus on a greenfield site near Nicosia.

I received the competition papers and, grabbing a weekend to make a quick site visit, arrived on the island without making any prior arrangements with the university. Next morning, with much interpretive map reading, the taxi driver took me to the remote site. Pointing towards the mountains a few kilometres away, he warned me in broken English about the proximity of the 'green line' border of the disputed Turkish territory.

Walking along the flanking dusty road beside the site, I crossed a barb-wire fence to get a close-up feel of the lie of the land, only half-registering the presence of a military settlement on the distant higher ground. Enjoying my relaxed walkabout I suddenly noticed the dust-path of jeep, speeding in my direction. Soon and quite seriously this became: "Passport, papers" – with little English, and in my case almost no Greek, sweet talk of baklava wasn't going to help. My best attempt at pleasant persuasion, with reference to the university papers, was followed by a Greek, but well-understood, instruction: "Get off the land".

Later, thinking about the new campus and its adjacency to the military zone, I sketched out two protective, cupped hands, wondering whether something positive might come of this gesture in relation to a new masterplan.

1992

The University of Cyprus held an 'International Design Ideas Competition' for its new campus at Athalassa, near Nicosia.

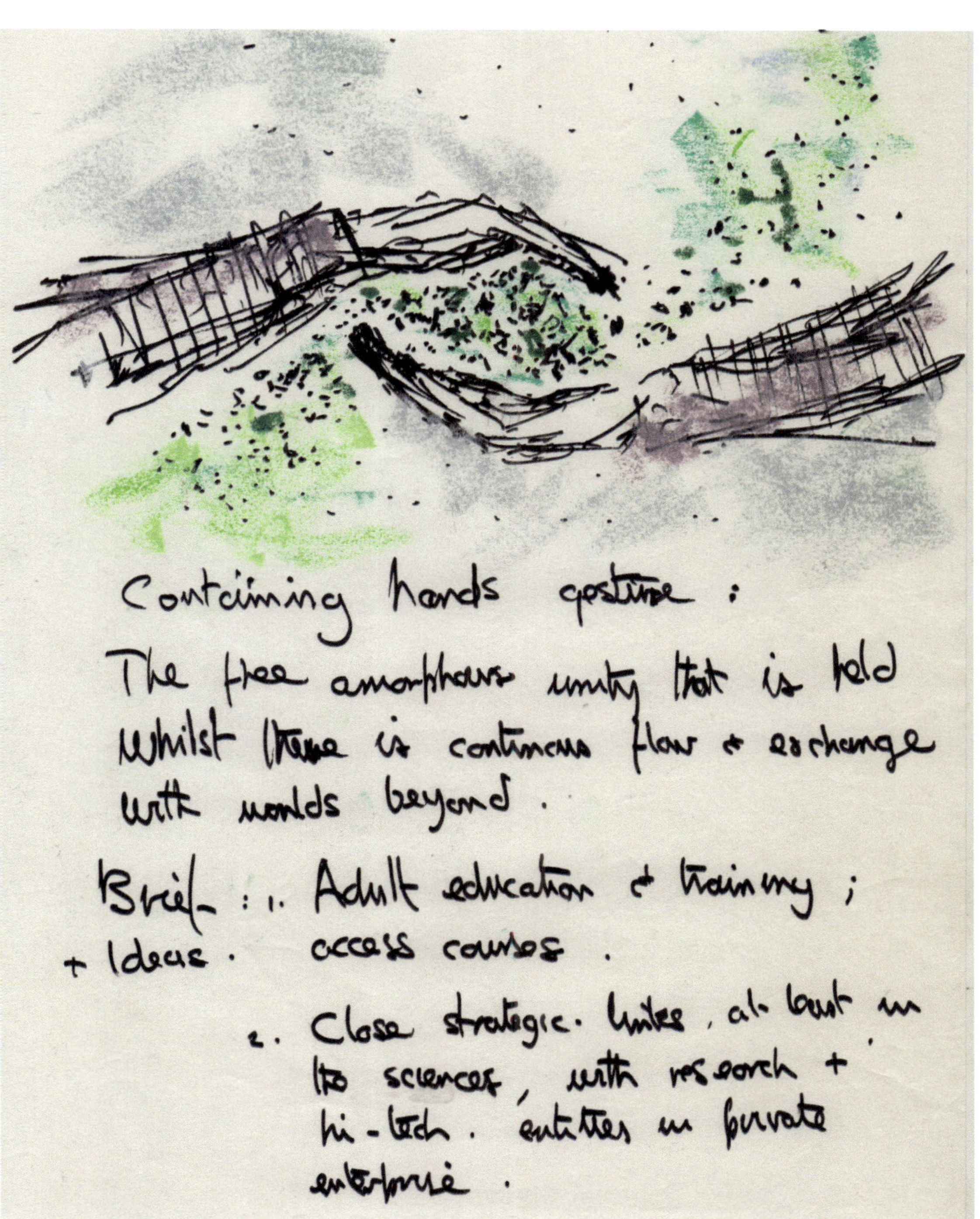

An implicit expression of unity and togetherness for the divided island.

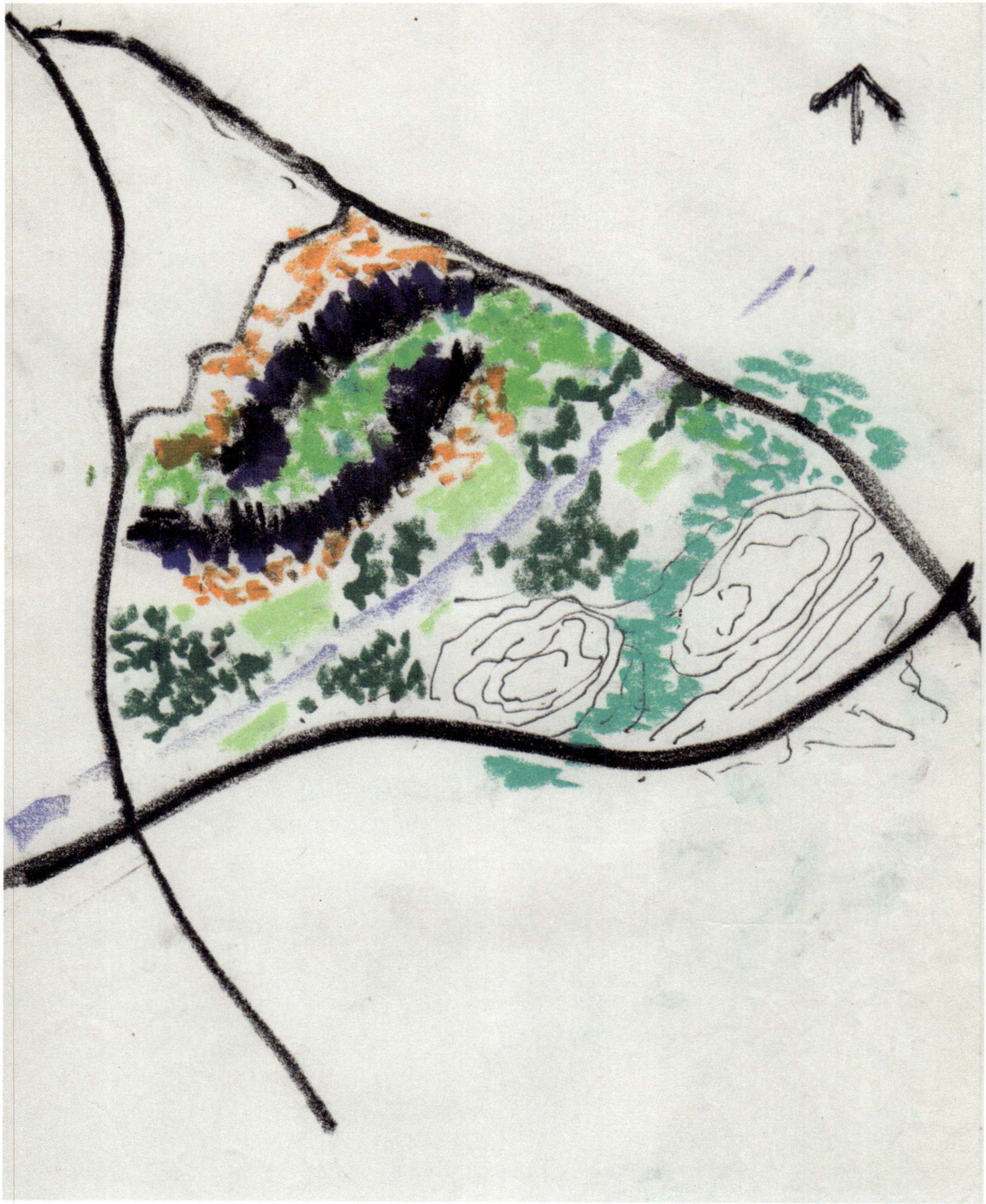

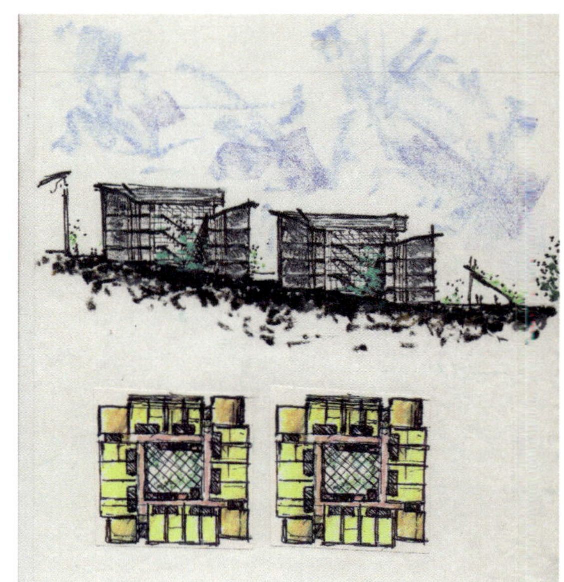

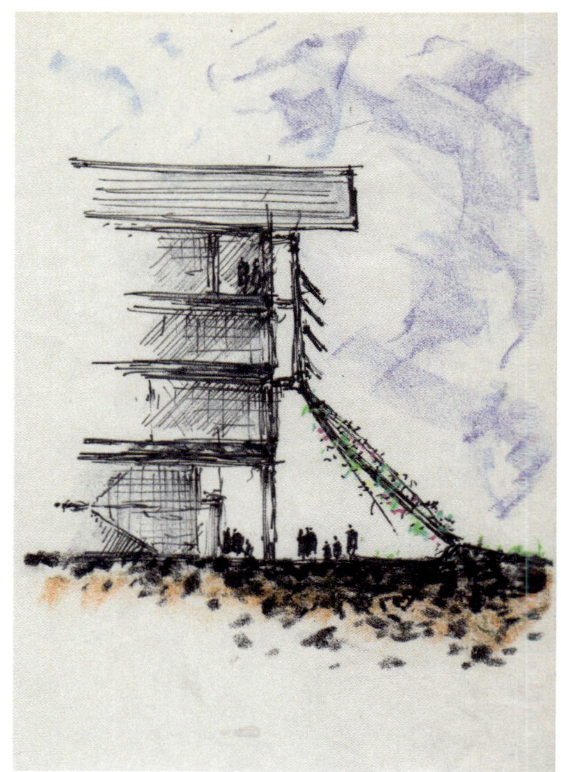

Study for a student residential building, with rooms accessed from galleries defining a central court. Faculty building section with a combination of louvred and planted shading devices. A covered walkway links to the car park.

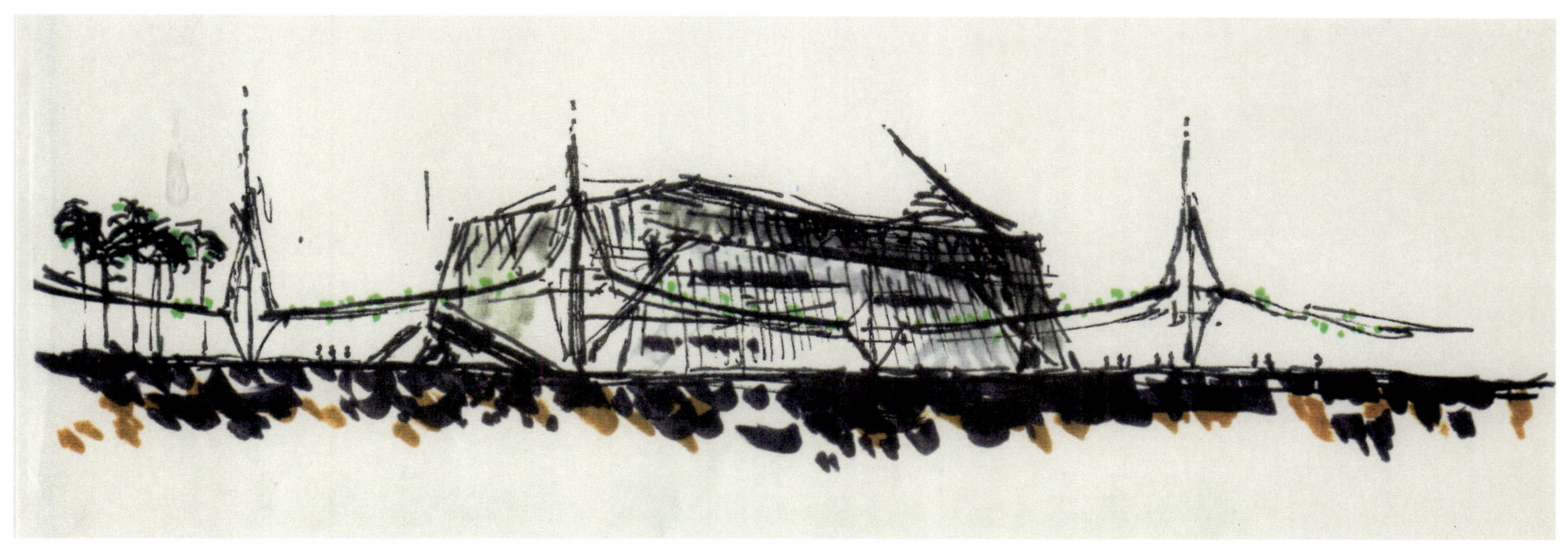

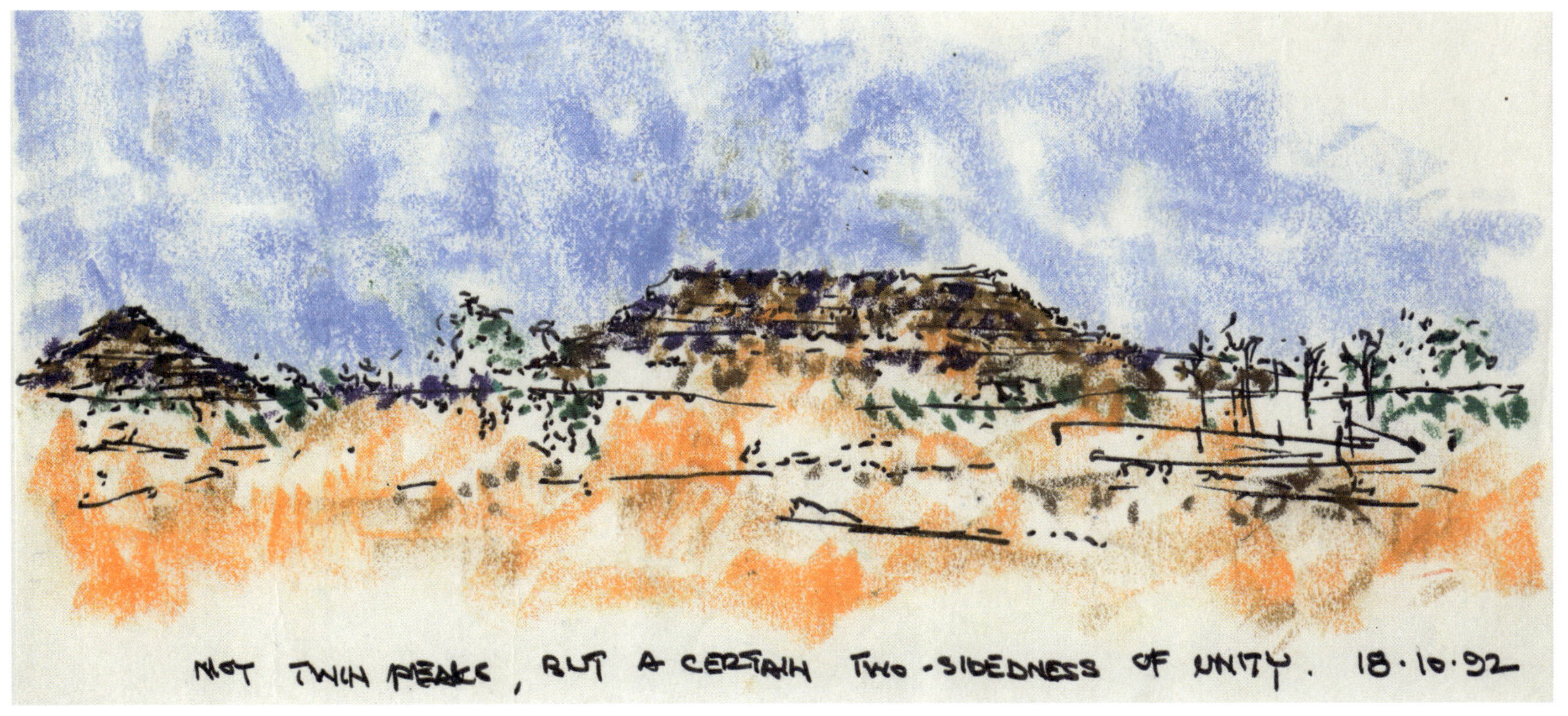

NOT TWIN PEAKS, BUT A CERTAIN TWO-SIDEDNESS OF UNITY. 18·10·92

We 'expressed interest' in the competition to design a new teaching building for Goldsmith's College. The site was on the college's loosely-assembled campus, which was characterised by a collection of smart, renovation-in-progress parcels of urban land in south London's fast-changing New Cross.

Twenty-five years later, I still have an image in mind of our submission. Most of the drawings are in the ABK archive, I assume, so I can show just a few sketches. These touch on various site-planning options and show a building form based on diagrams for a deep-plan solution.

2001

Goldsmith's College held a competition for a new teaching building on its south London campus. It was won, and built, by Will Alsop.

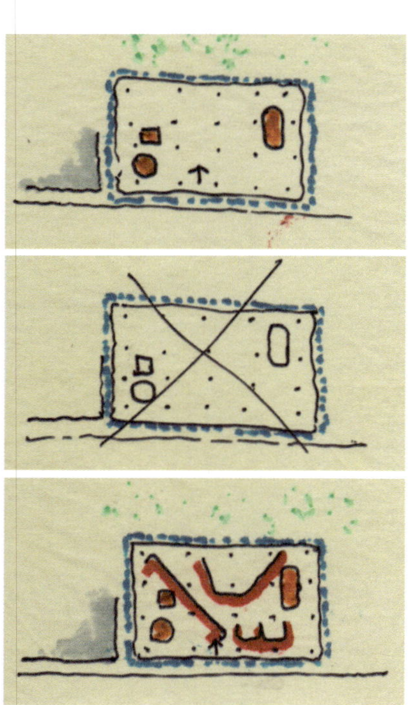

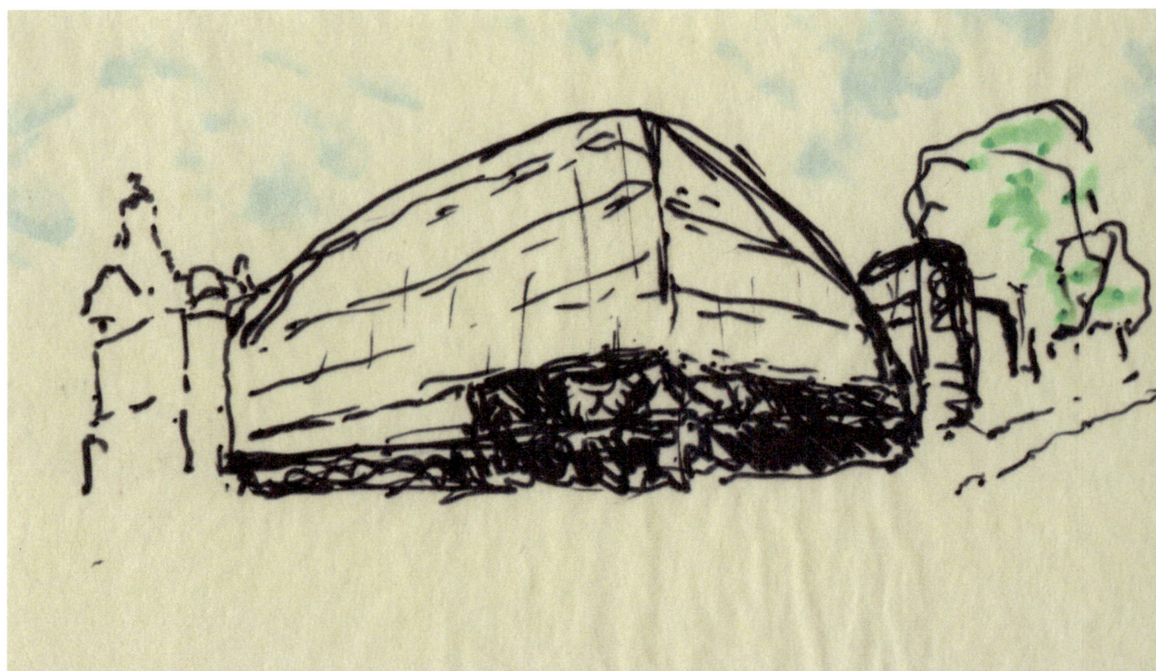

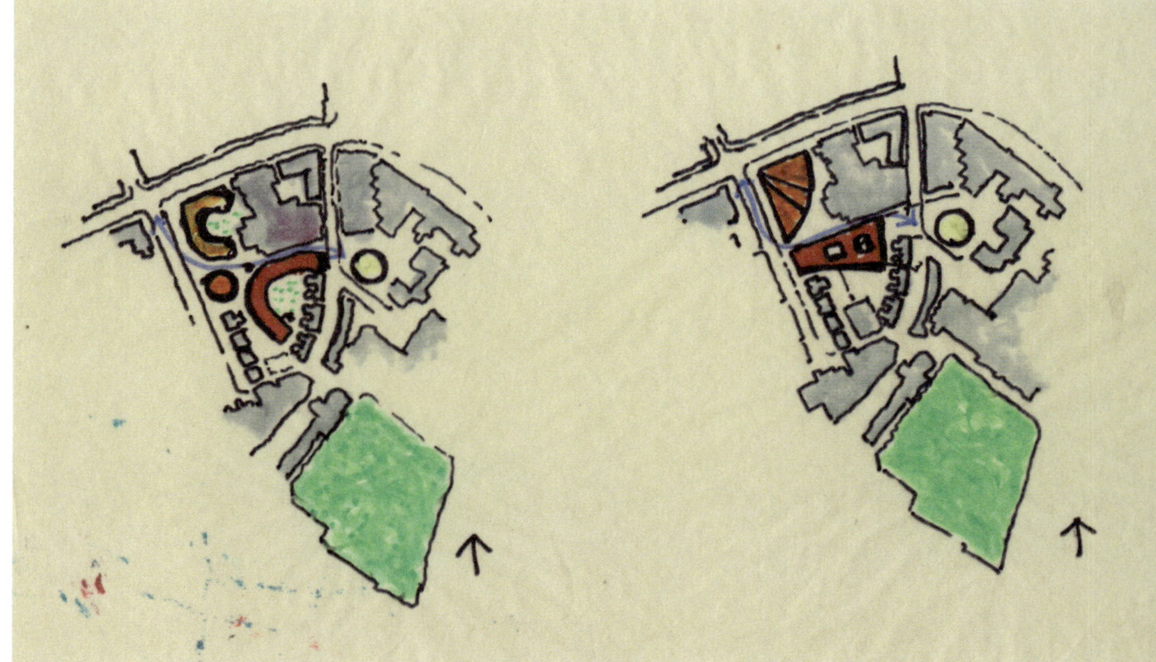

These initial ideas explore ways of making interventions so as to create coherent and pleasant places within the campus.

In the 1990s we completed a building for Techniquest's science-related visitor centre in Cardiff Bay's docklands. Soon afterwards we were asked to prepare a study for the Inner Harbour area in which, among other things, we made proposals for the Oval Dock and its adjacent land. Following these schemes I felt that I couldn't but respond to the open invitation to prepare a set of ideas for the treatment of the Cardiff Bay Barrage.

I took the interestingly open brief to mean that fresh ideas for the treatment of the upper part of the barrage (in effect its whole character) would be considered: a grand project. My notes on the drawings, little more than cryptic messages to myself, suggest something of the lines of thought:

'The arched forms at the base of each of the coupled "tetrons" symbolise a seaside gateway to Cardiff. The unequal heights of these structures represent the peaks of Cardiff as an Industrial Revolution port and [its] aspiration to become an internationally renowned city.'
'Water, wind, sky: make a ribbon that lies between calm and turbulence.'
'Wave, switchback, as an elevated walkway, a route taking its own course.'
'Wind music/wind machines as sculptures – refuges, gathering places for performances and outlying new jetties.'
'The dynamic of the twin spiral is good – cycles of resolution and irresolution, but think how to skew the image.'

I now see a kind of resonance in this type of structure, designed to serve Cardiff as a city-scale marker – in Anish Kapoor's 'Orbit' at Stratford's Olympic Park.

1999

An open competition sought ideas for the landscaping of the barrage that encloses Cardiff Bay, built from 1994-99.

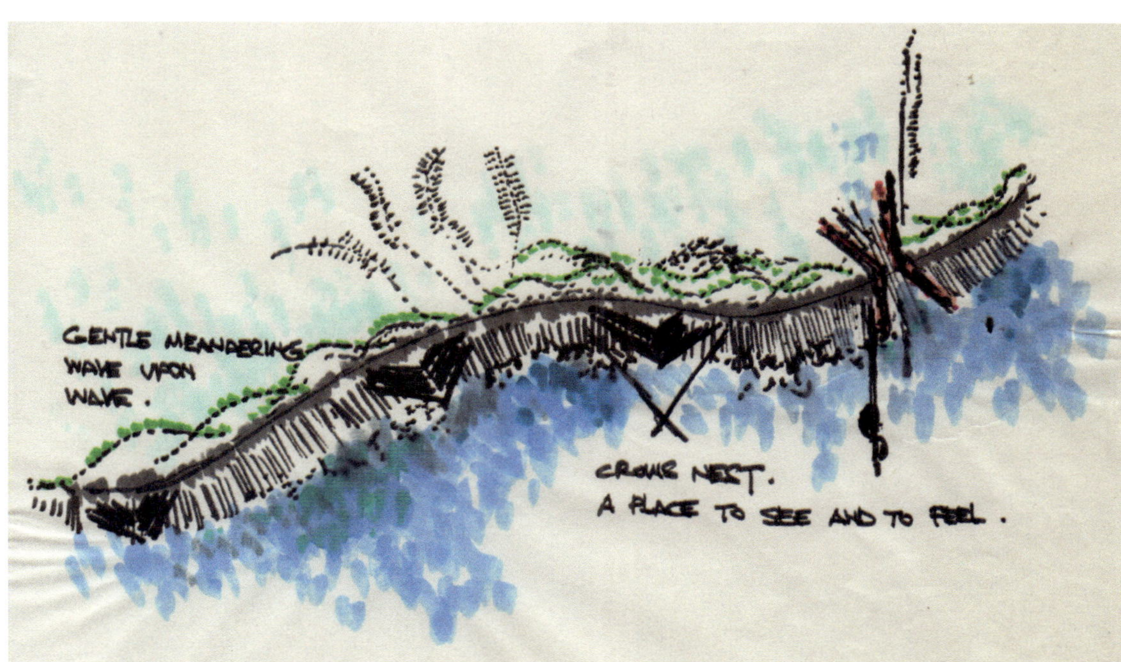

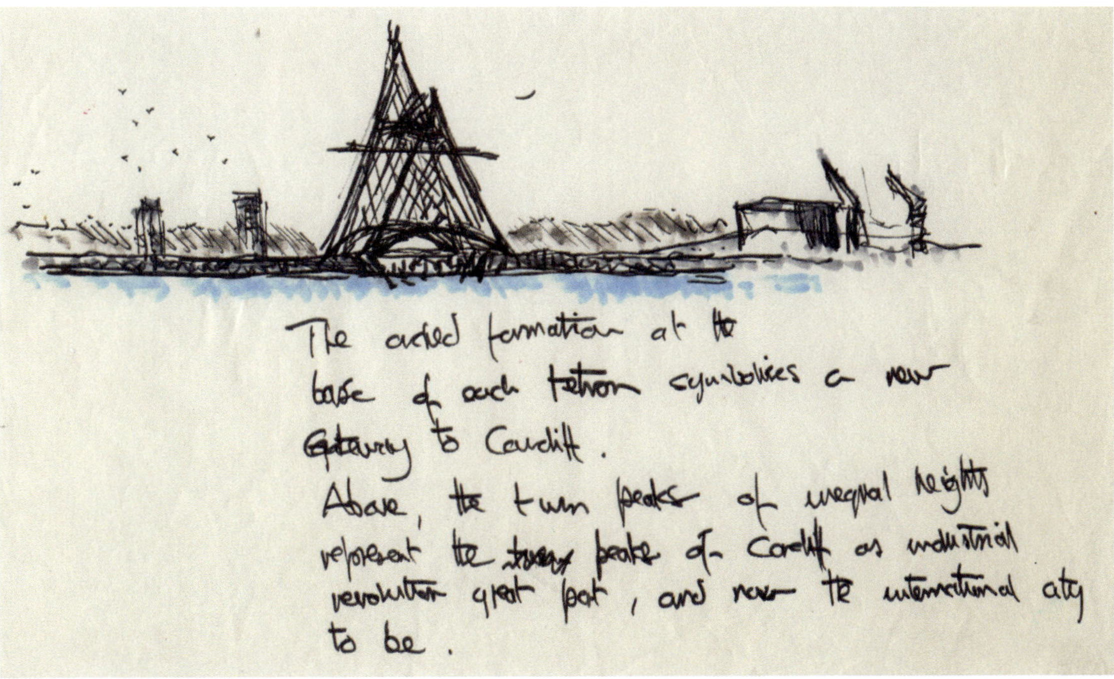

Sketches focus on enhancing the experience of visitors, as well as announcing the major engineering project from afar.

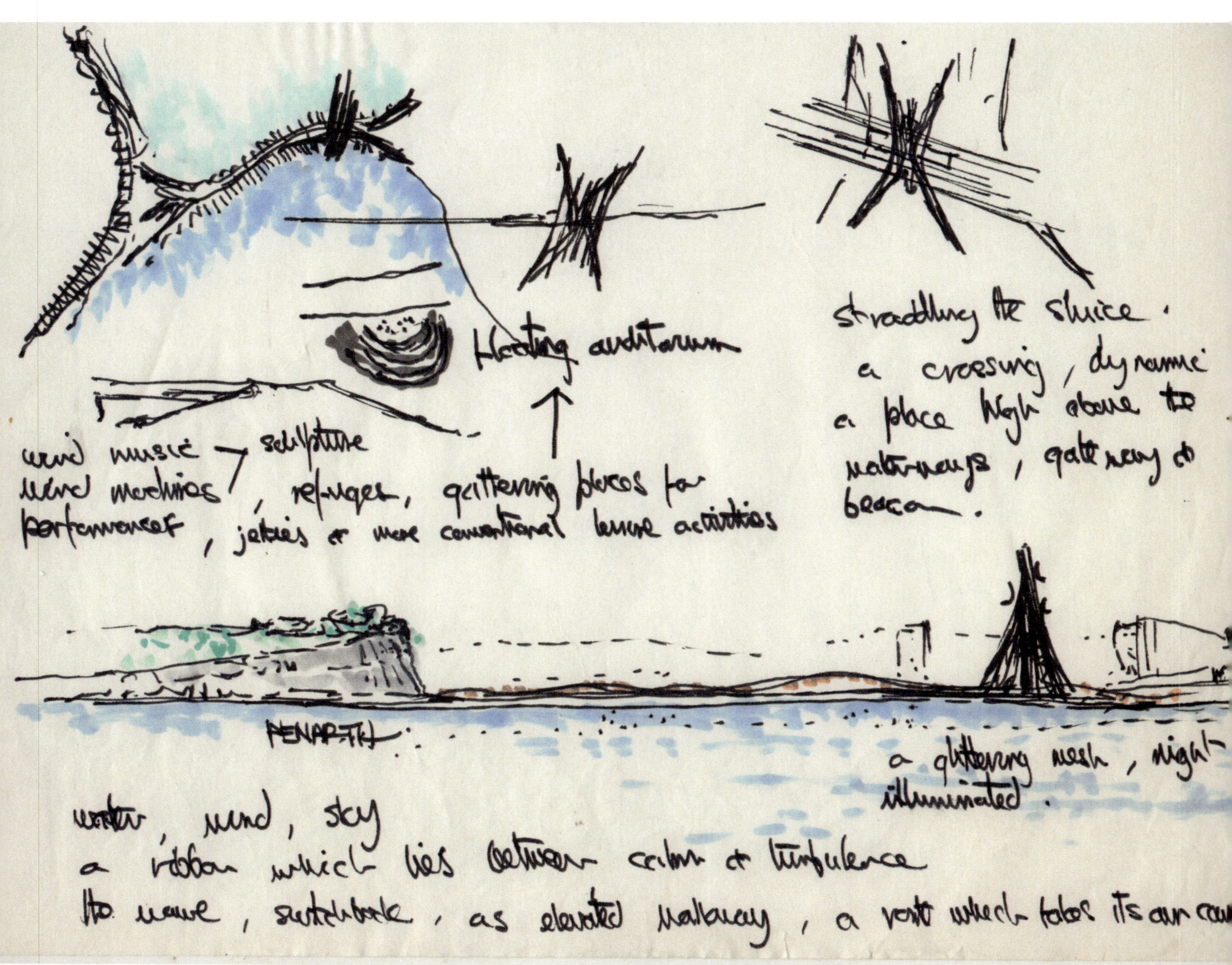

The range of ideas included marker bridges across the barage sluices and a helical tower based on the structure of DNA.

Make diaphanous duodone
self-supporting fabrics
which provide homes for
objects which seem to intercode
to suggest a prevailing condition
of order / chaos.

Consider peace parks.

DNA, twin towers (towers)
of our life. Beware the geometric
perfection of the figure as an
appropriate symbol!

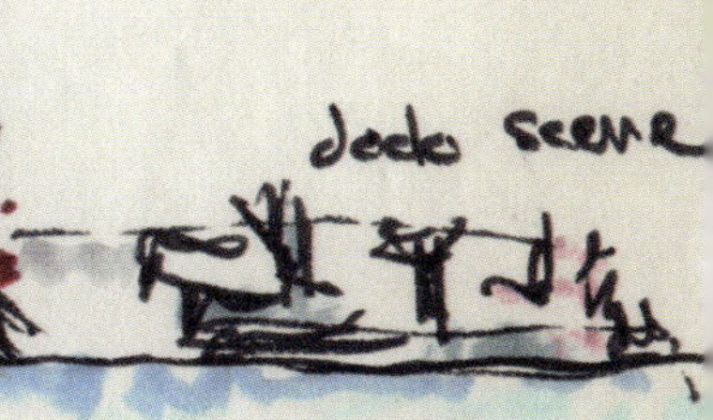

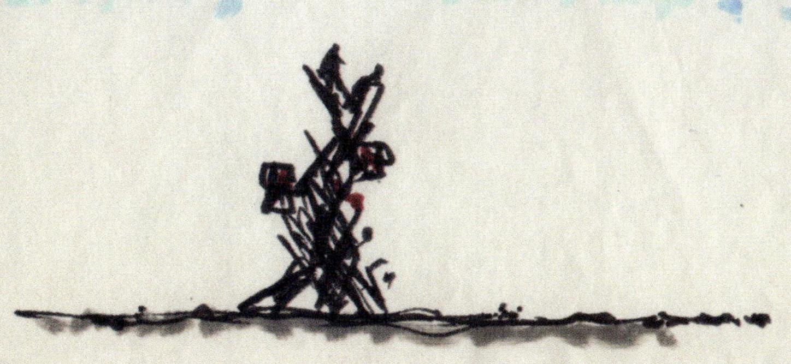

The dynamics of the twin spiral
is good; but think how to skew
the image. Represents cycles of
resolution AND irresolution!

The announcement calling for 'expressions of interest' in designing Birmingham's new central library suggested a commitment to addressing what might be the key aspects of a city library for the twenty-first century.

This selection of sketches, conveying some initial thoughts about the spatial characteristics of different areas of the library, formed part of the submission. They served as a kind of notebook summary of the building's constituent elements that we would want to explore further with the client.

Today (and perhaps even then) I think it likely that a selection committee would have expected clearly-stated design proposals rather than the more open qualities implicit in our questions and sketches – a hard lesson to learn when your inclinations favour early consultation in the design process.

2001

Birmingham City Council launched a competition to replace its unloved 1970s central library. Plans by the winner, Richard Rogers Partnership, foundered, and it was not until 2013 that a new library, designed by Dutch architect Mecanoo, was built.

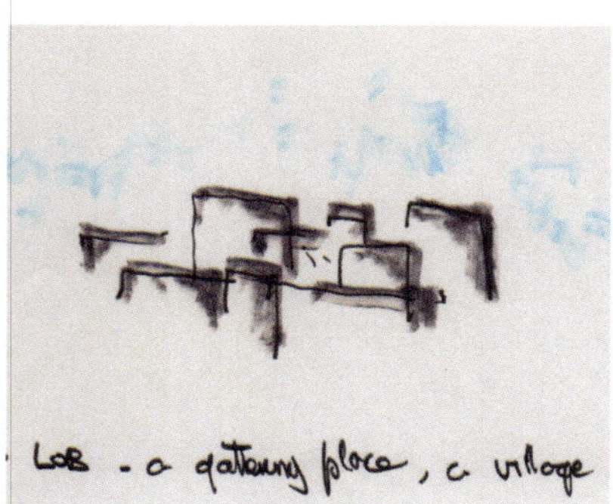

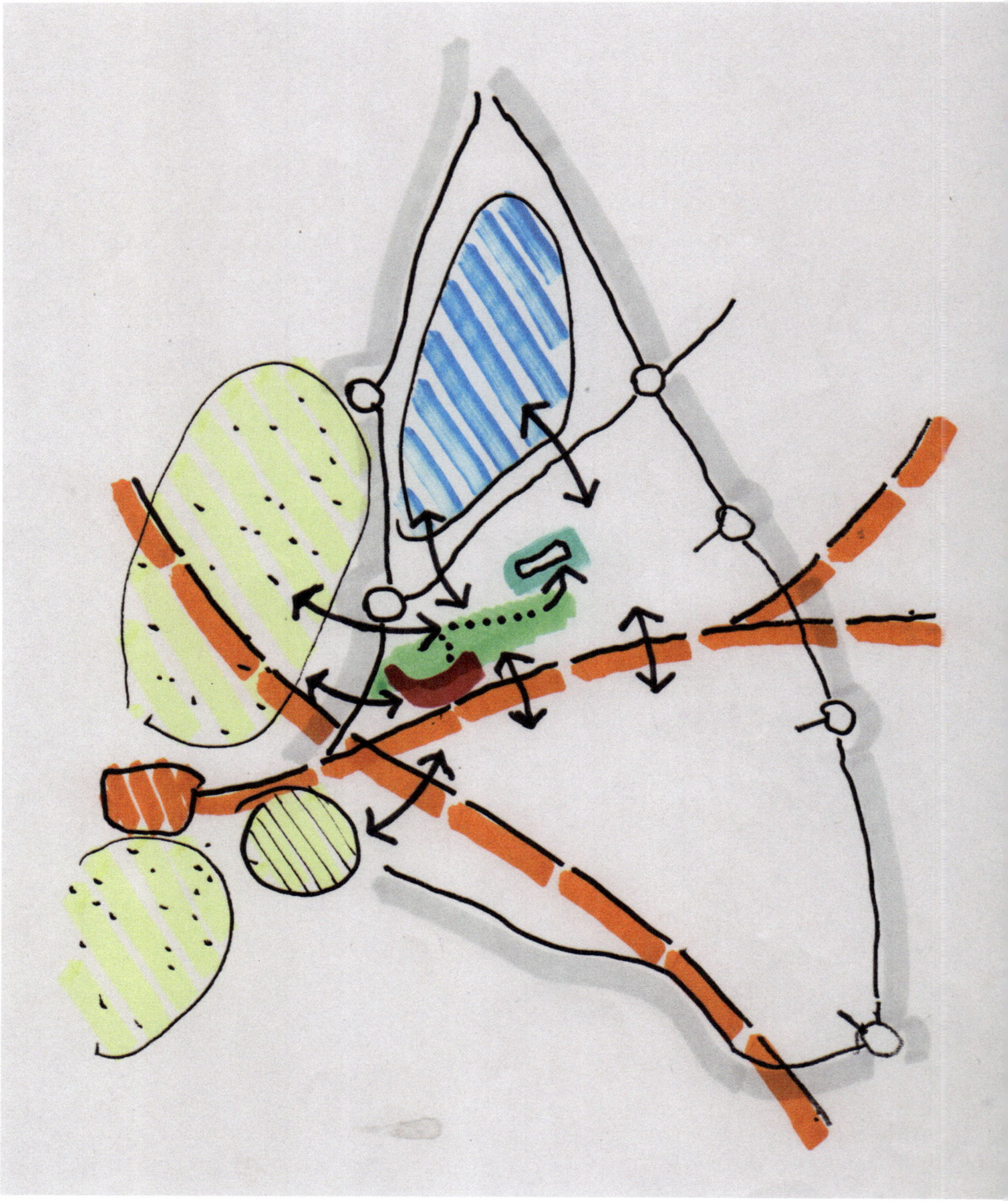

Initial conceptual ideas regarding
the massing and site planning.

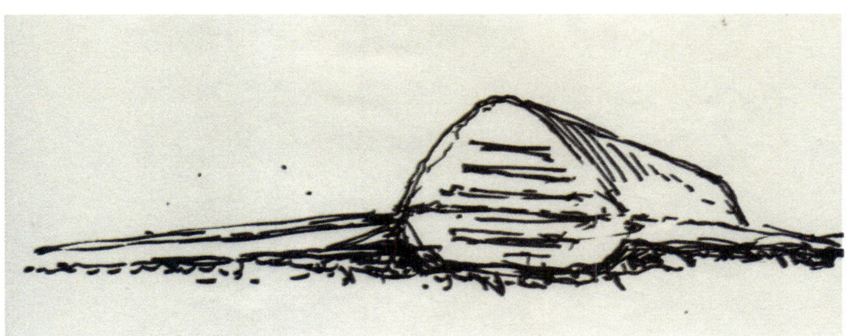

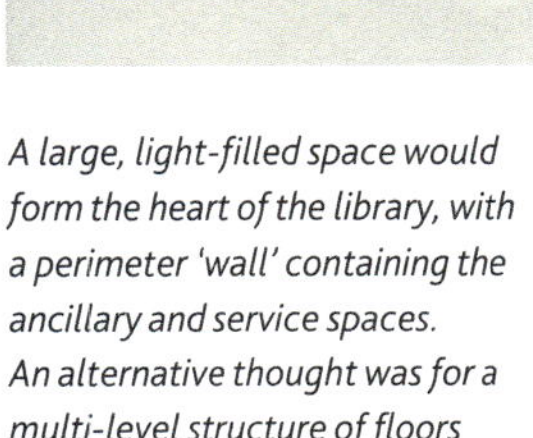

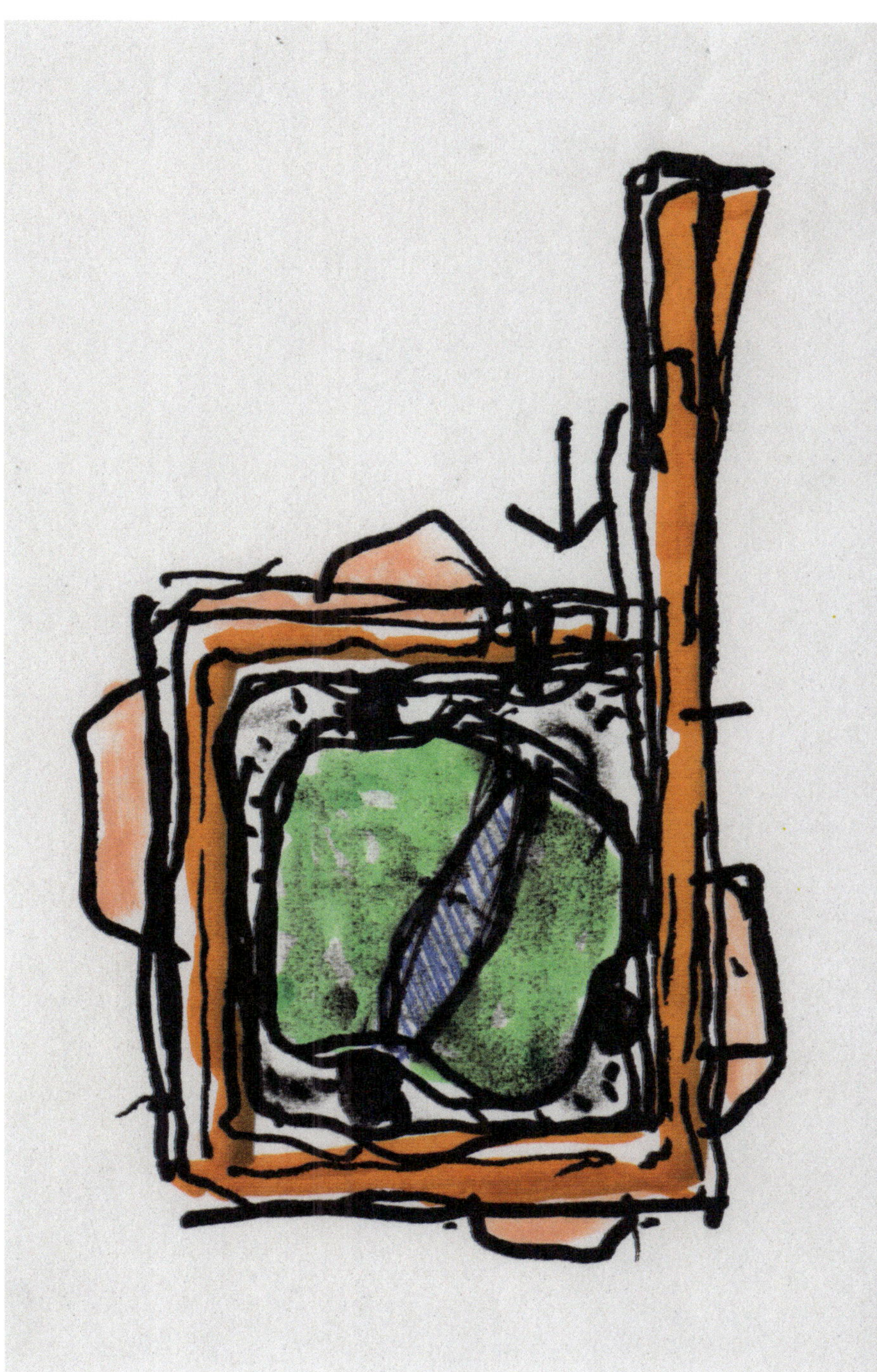

A large, light-filled space would form the heart of the library, with a perimeter 'wall' containing the ancillary and service spaces. An alternative thought was for a multi-level structure of floors within a curving, enveloping skin.

Unexpectedly, we were generously invited to what was to become a remarkable evening of delicious Lebanese food and joyful traditional dance, celebrating a wedding in a remote village in the mountains near Syria. It was a circuitous drive eastwards that evening, and then back to Beirut the following morning – perhaps somewhat hung over – as the beautiful landscape rolled by.

At the time that I drew these sketches I hadn't thought that they had any obvious connection to the ideas that had begun to stir in my mind for the architecture of the Beirut souks. Today, perhaps fancifully, I wonder whether our drive across some of the valleys eastward of the city may have given rise to later-imagined ideas of the twinned roads (as though they were rivers, perhaps) crossing the fabric of our competition scheme for the souks.

In the past few years my memory of this quick visit has become especially poignant as we receive daily news of the plight of Syrian refugees, camping out in makeshift homes in Lebanon and elsewhere.

1994

An unanticipated invitation to attend a village wedding in the hills beyond Beiruit.

A Lebanese Wedding

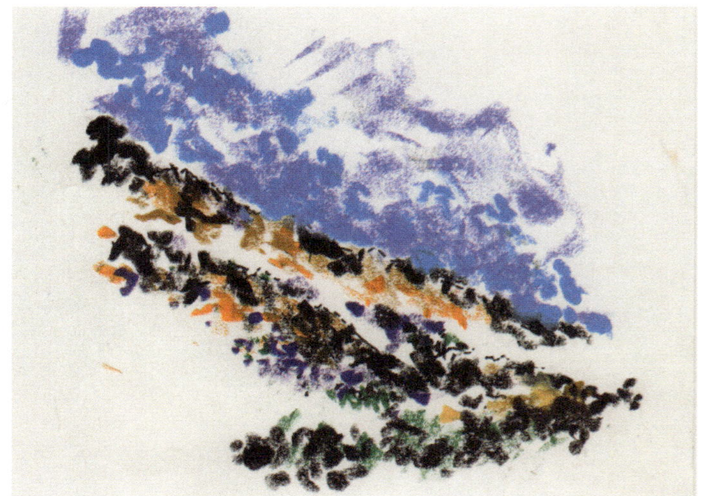

About 15 years after we'd completed our residential building for Keble College, Oxford, along the south-western edge of William Butterfield's late-Victorian perimeter boundary, the college decided to build another new building, this time at the north-western corner of the Fellows' Garden.

It had been a pleasure working with Keble's progressive group of Fellows on its building committee, and I had reason to think that they valued the architecture of our project, so I was looking forward to the shortlist interview for the new building. We presented our ideas but, on leaving, felt that on this occasion the selection panel's interest lay elsewhere.

We had welcomed the opportunity to explore the materiality of a different set of ideas in relation to the characteristics of this site, marked by its adjacency to Butterfield's well-established Gothic-Revival idiom along this stretch of Keble Road. Whereas in the first phase of our earlier scheme we'd formed an unusually tight open space (a 'mini-quad'), here it seemed opportune to contain the lecture theatre with a similar wrap-around plan.

The study bedrooms were to be a more spacious development of the room plans in our 1960s building for the Theological College in Chichester. I now wonder whether the 'redness' of the sketch elevations (referring loosely to the field of Butterfield's decorated red brickwork), may in time have developed, leading us on to… just what?

1990

An invited competition set up by Keble College, Oxford, offered ABK the chance to design a counterpoint to its 1970s residential building. The proposal by Rick Mather was chosen and built.

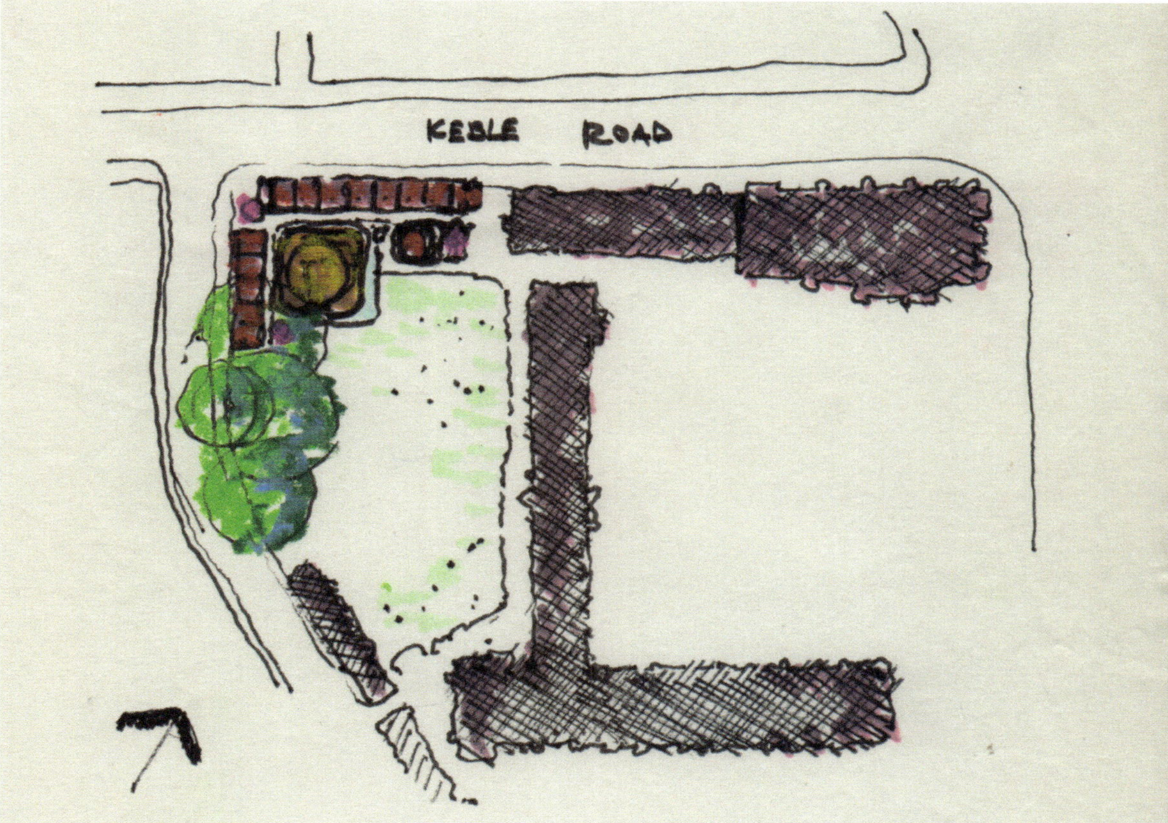

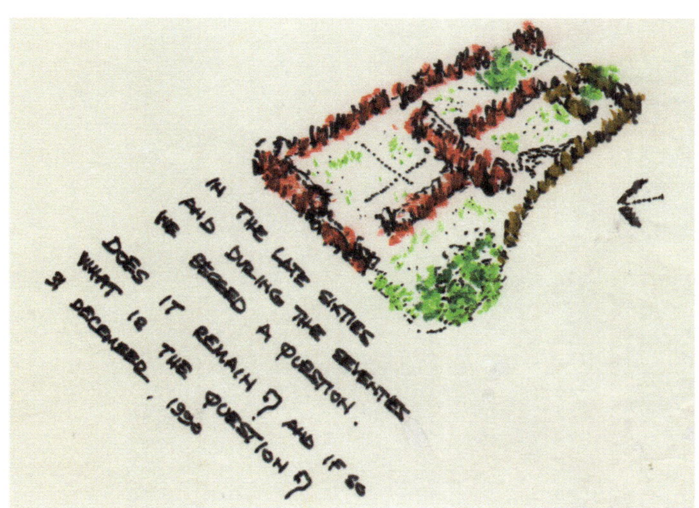

The site offered the opportunity to again propose a 'wall' building that anchored the corner of the college precinct.

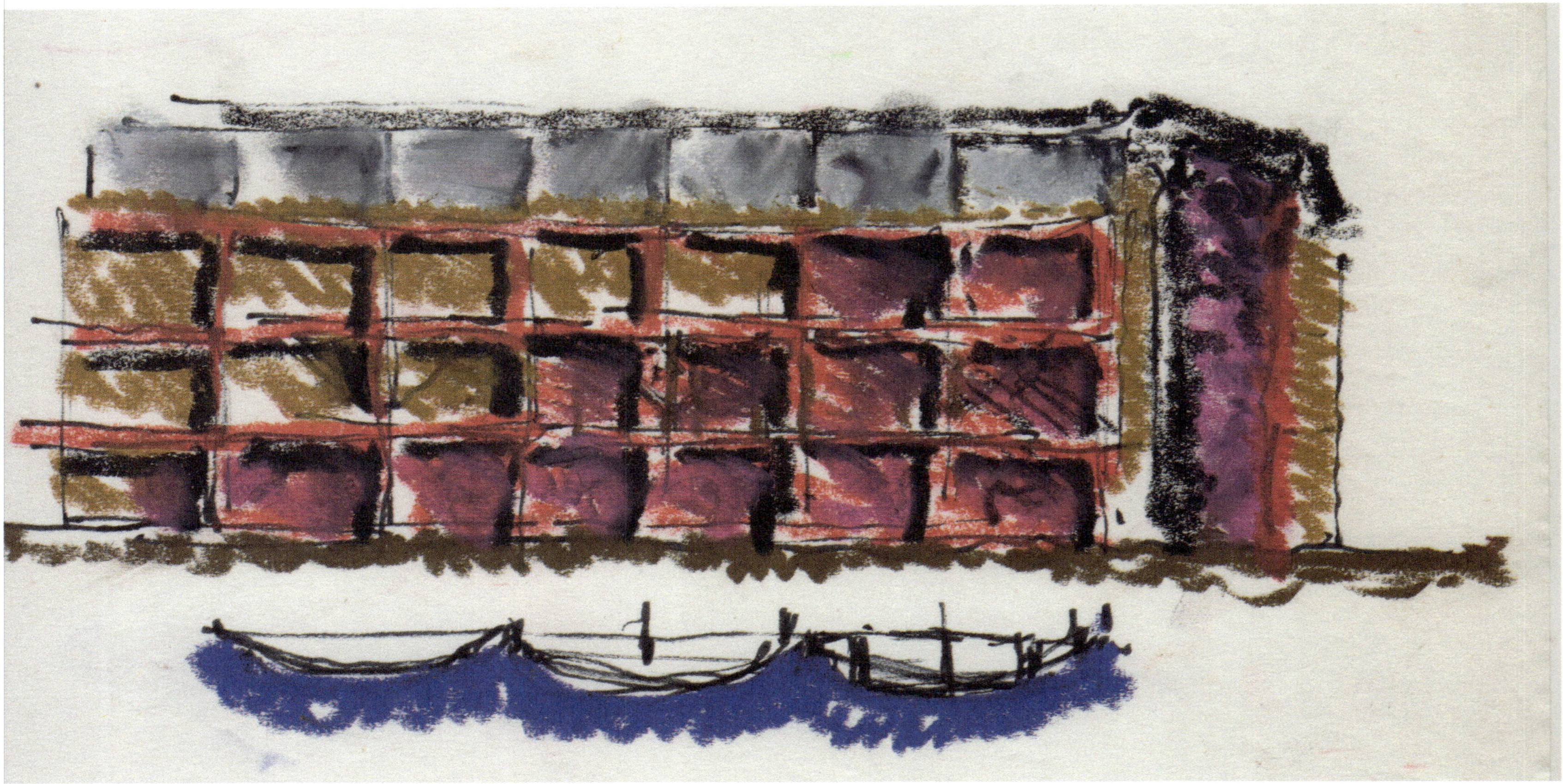

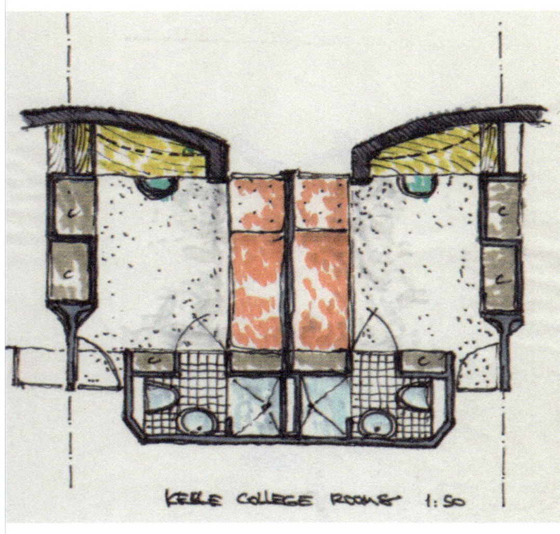

Paired study bedrooms provide
desks in projecting bays.

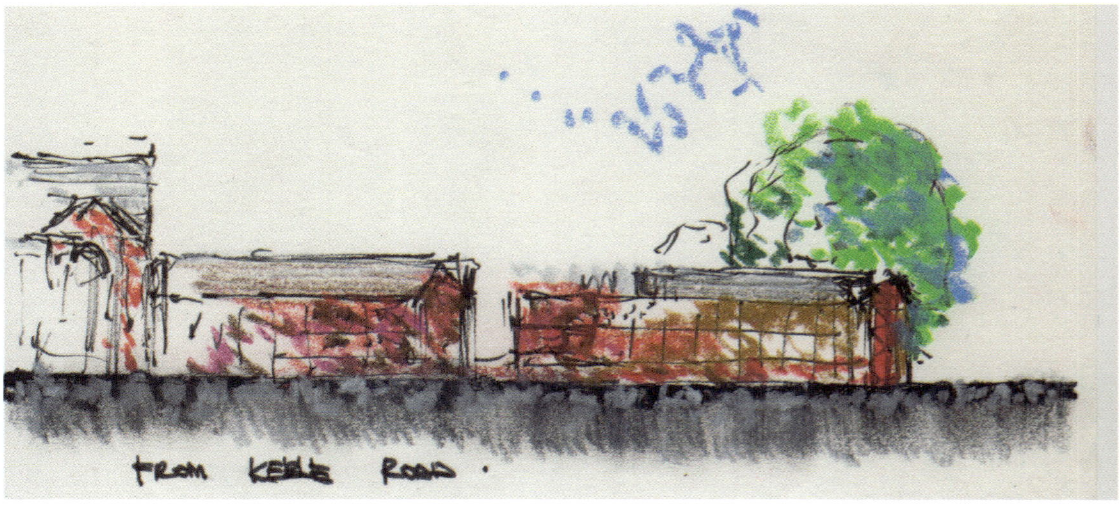

Elevational studies suggest a
colour palette that responds to
the red brickwork of William
Butterfield's Gothic Revival
college buildings.

These ideas for enhancing the listed structure of the Oval Basin formed part of our development plan for Cardiff's Inner Harbour Area, where we were completing the Techniquest visitor centre.

The ill-fated competition for Cardiff's new opera house, planned for the neighbouring site, was in progress at the time. Zaha Hadid won first prize but, disgracefully, and in spite of a robust and well-managed campaign, she was not appointed for the job.

Our proposal was to help bring new life to the area, suspending the planned tram terminus structure over a disused basin re-filled with water and encircled by a glazed canopy that would house a variety of retail outlets. In retrospect, the proposal seems to anticipate developments in retail design that would emerge more than a decade later.

1995

Preliminary ideas for developing the potential of Cardiff's historic Oval Basin, subsequently the subject of a competition.

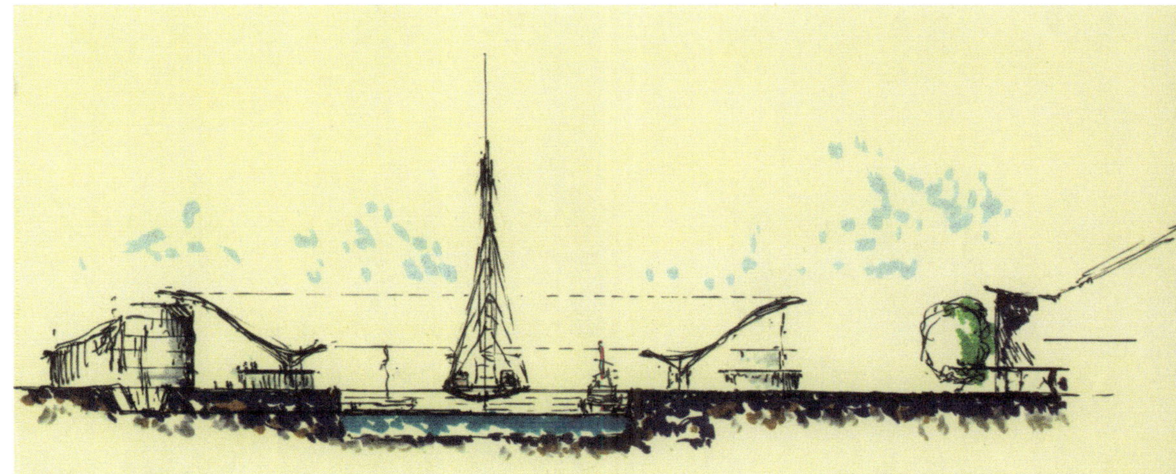

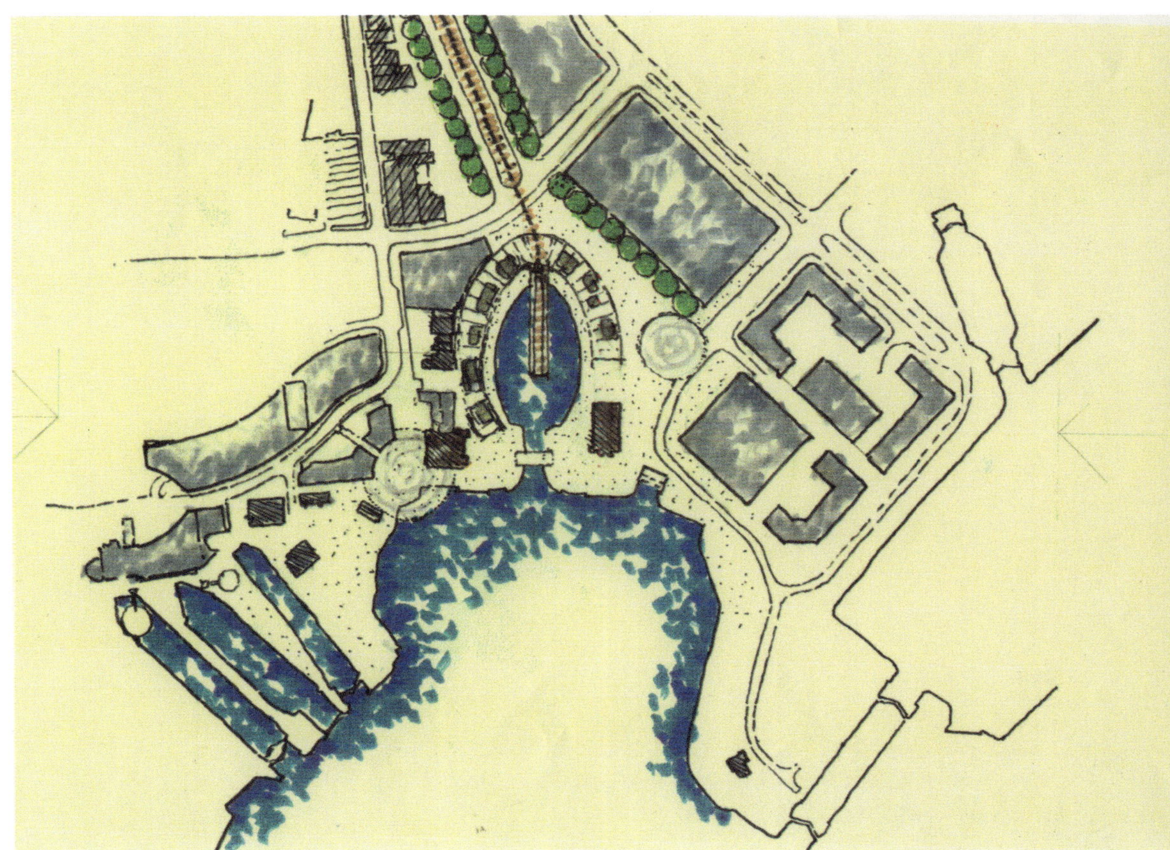

The proposed tram line terminates at the basin, suspended above the water. A surrounding glazed canopy echoes the oval plan, sheltering leisure and retail units.

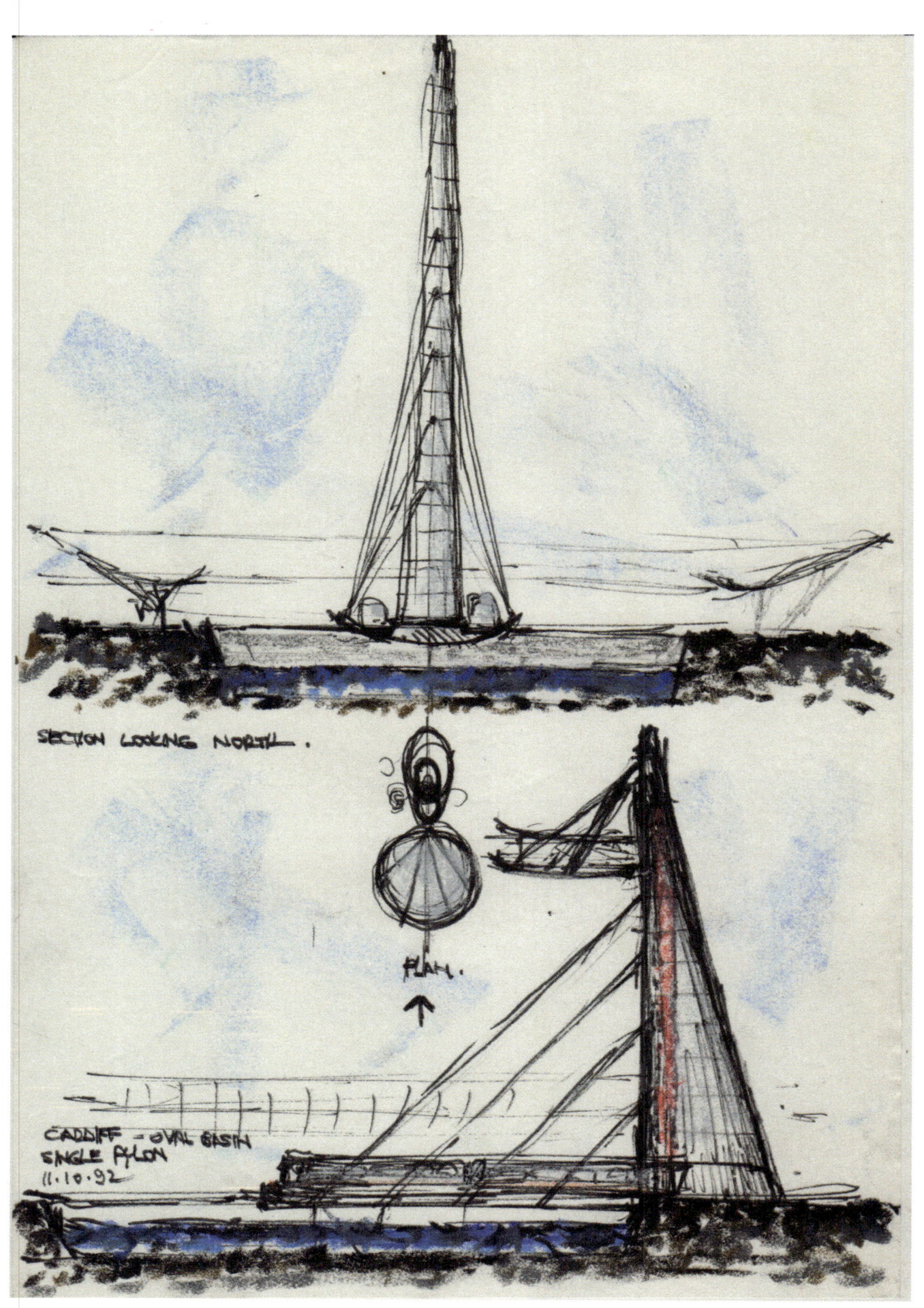

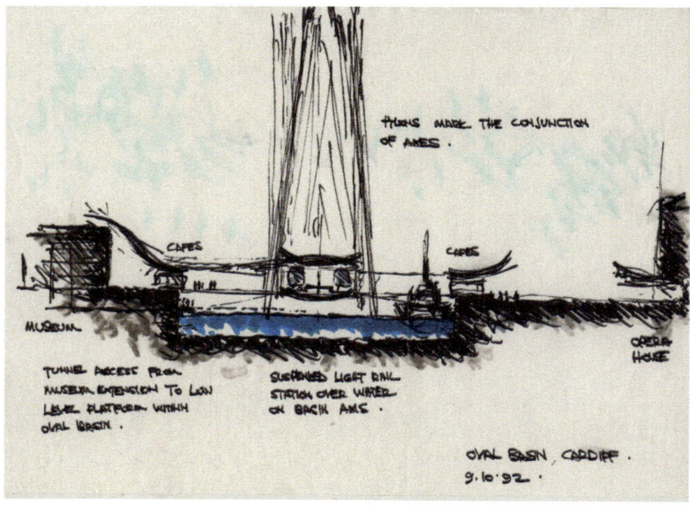

A landmark pylon structure
supports the tram station above
the water level of the Oval Basin.

Having completed a development plan and built a new gallery at Manchester University's Whitworth Art Gallery, we were pleased to be invited to participate in a limited competition to extend Manchester Art Gallery.

With the retention of the two existing buildings on the city block, we proposed a kind of swollen triangular plan whose gently sinuous hypotenuse formed the edge of a rooflit interstitial space between old and new buildings, an articulation of the closely-placed adjacencies of these now internally-oriented facades. We thought this lively assembly of new and old held much potential, but our submission became somewhat marked by two unforeseen events.

First, we received a phone call to say that the model that formed part our submission had fallen apart in transit. This was certainly concerning, but with just 24 hours to go before the presentation, our modelmaker set off to Manchester and reassembled the pieces in good time. Was this to be a sign of troubles to come? In earlier times it would have been thought that the gods weren't favouring us in the realisation of our art gallery projects. Shades of the royal behaviour in relation to the National Gallery extension in Trafalgar Square? Second, during our morning presentation, the chair of the selection committee kept nodding off to sleep as I explained our scheme (we later learned that he had flown in overnight from Asia). Others on the panel seemed knowingly wide awake but, of course, nothing was said…

1994

Entry for the competition to design an extension to Manchester Art Gallery, won by Michael Hopkins & Partners.

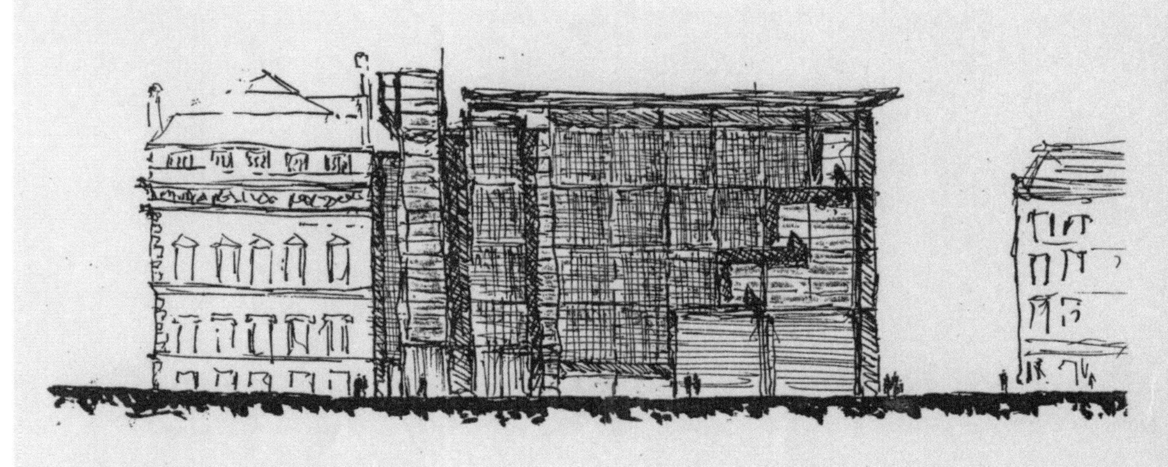

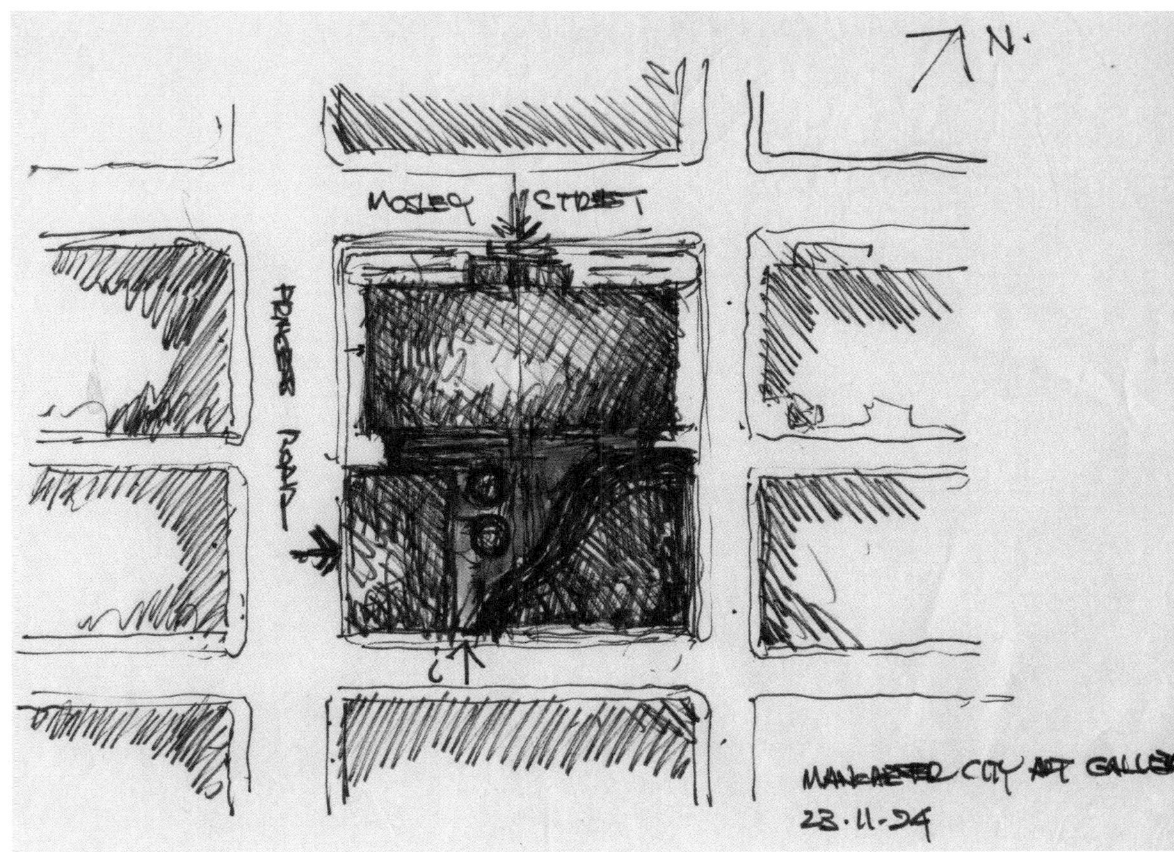

Elevation study showing the proportional relationship with the principal 1823 neoclassical gallery building, designed by Charles Barry. The plan suggests an internal court, linking new and old and articulated by full-height glazed shafts that face the surrounding streets.

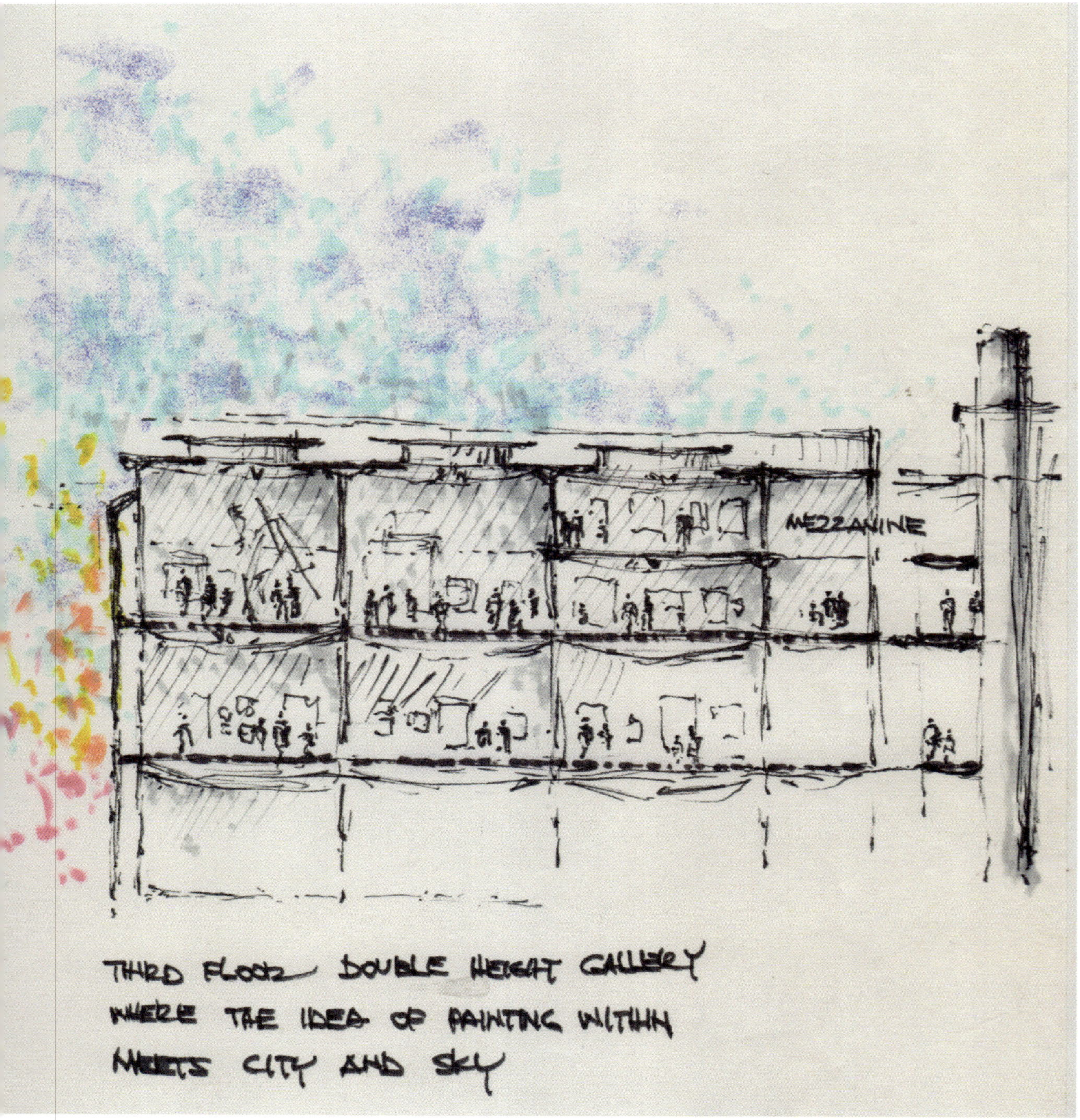

THIRD FLOOR DOUBLE HEIGHT GALLERY
WHERE THE IDEA OF PAINTING WITHIN
MEETS CITY AND SKY

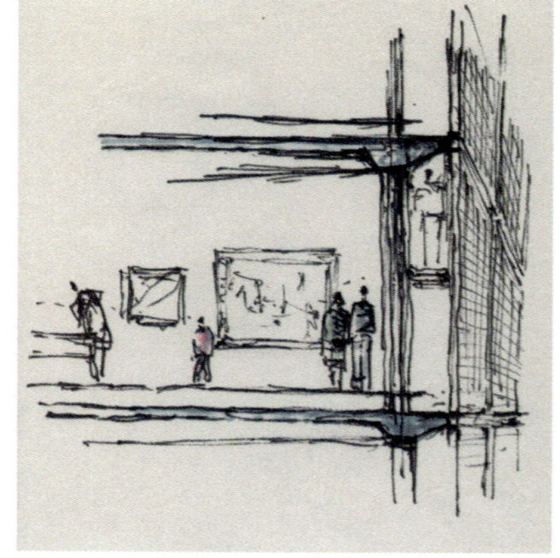

Section studies showing double-height gallery spaces at the top of the building. A double facade would allow separation of structure and enclosure, forming a buffer zone to mediate external conditions.

This interesting and unusual ideas competition was for a large, open stretch of land rising from the banks of the river Erdre at its confluence with the Loire on the outskirts of Nantes. The city authority had invited one architect from each of five western European countries, anticipating that each would respond differently to the open brief. This unusual strategy was vindicated, however, when a wide variety of approaches was presented publicly in succession, thanks to the university's well-managed IT resource; it was a remarkable morning of ideas, ideas, ideas.

In contrast to some of the other fully-developed schemes illustrating clear, hard-line buildings set within structured masterplans, we had focussed on the landscaping. This would underlie our exploration of the art of making a new 'science park', asking questions (with ideas in sketch form) about the making of science-related settlement-places, sculpture-lines, water-courses.

This could be a completely different kind of public place, we thought, designed for work and ideas in the fields of science, together with new elements of habitation. Not so much a masterplan as glimpses of a different world… above all, there was an implicit message about the importance of facilitating structured discussions about the character of the place that was to be made.

So the notes accompanying the drawings were but reminders of aspects of the content-character that I had in mind, rather than being outcome instructions.

1988

Competition project for a high-tech science research and technology park near Nantes.

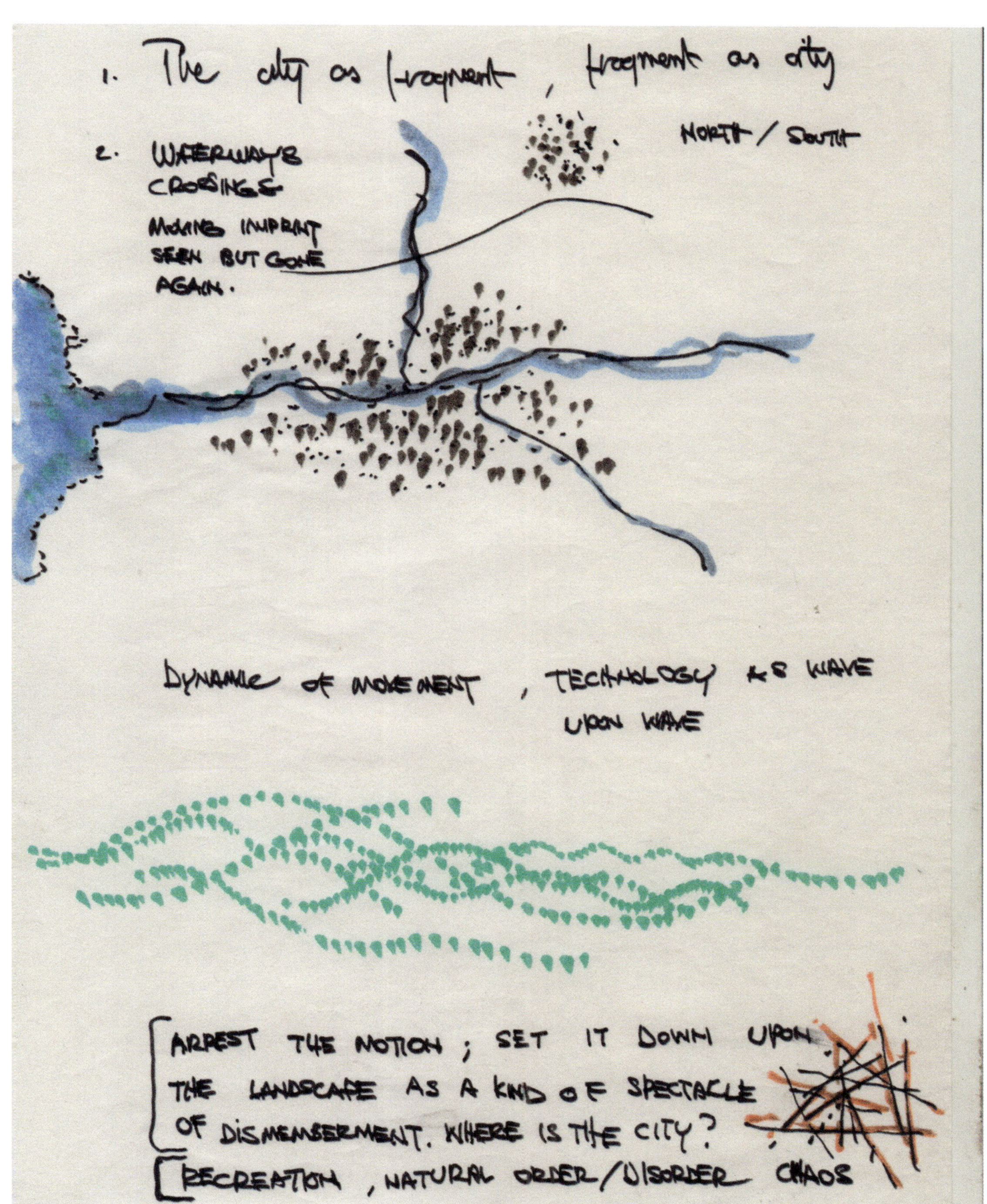

Initial thoughts draw on the natural ecology of the parkland site that borders the Erdre river, and an interplay with the rational world of science and technology.

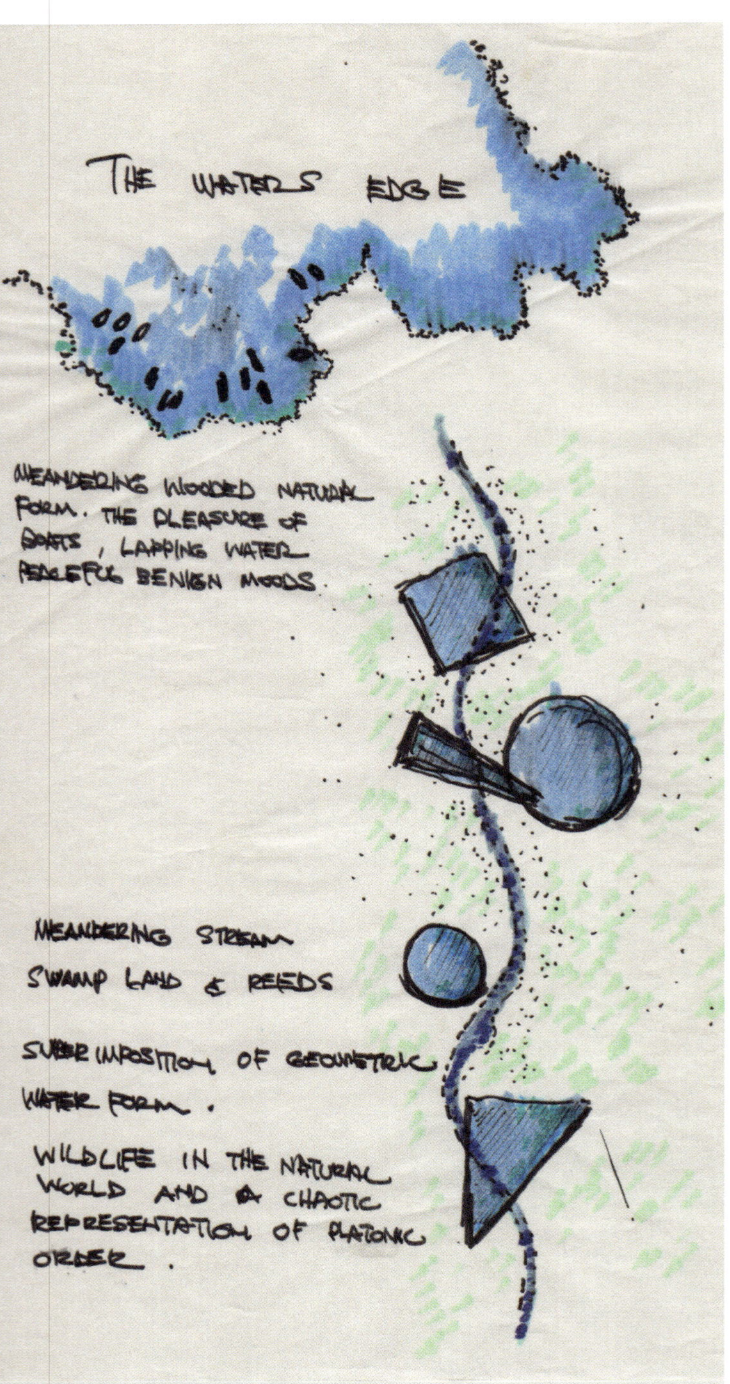

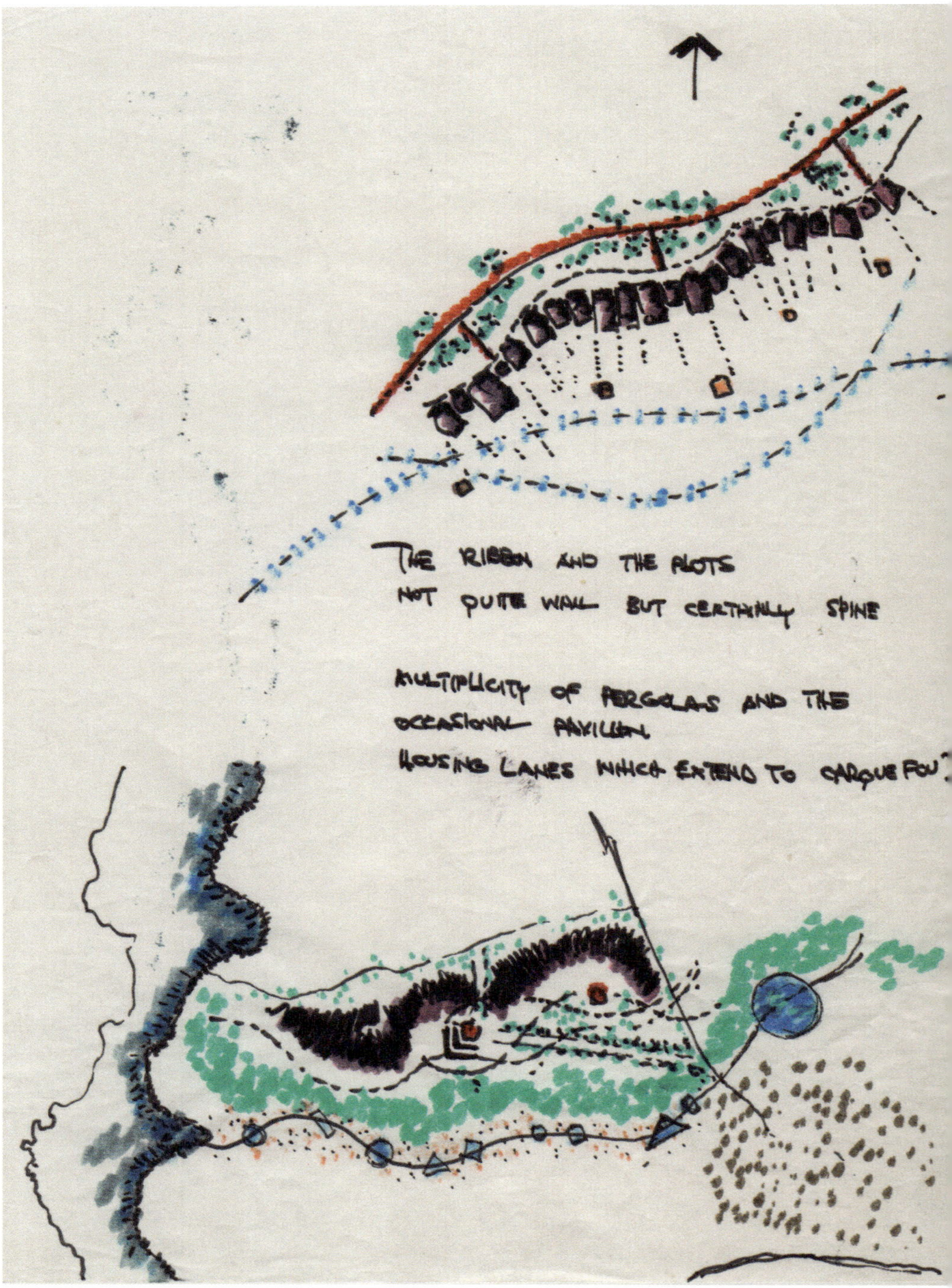

The underlying planning strategy comprises a landscape of features and forms.

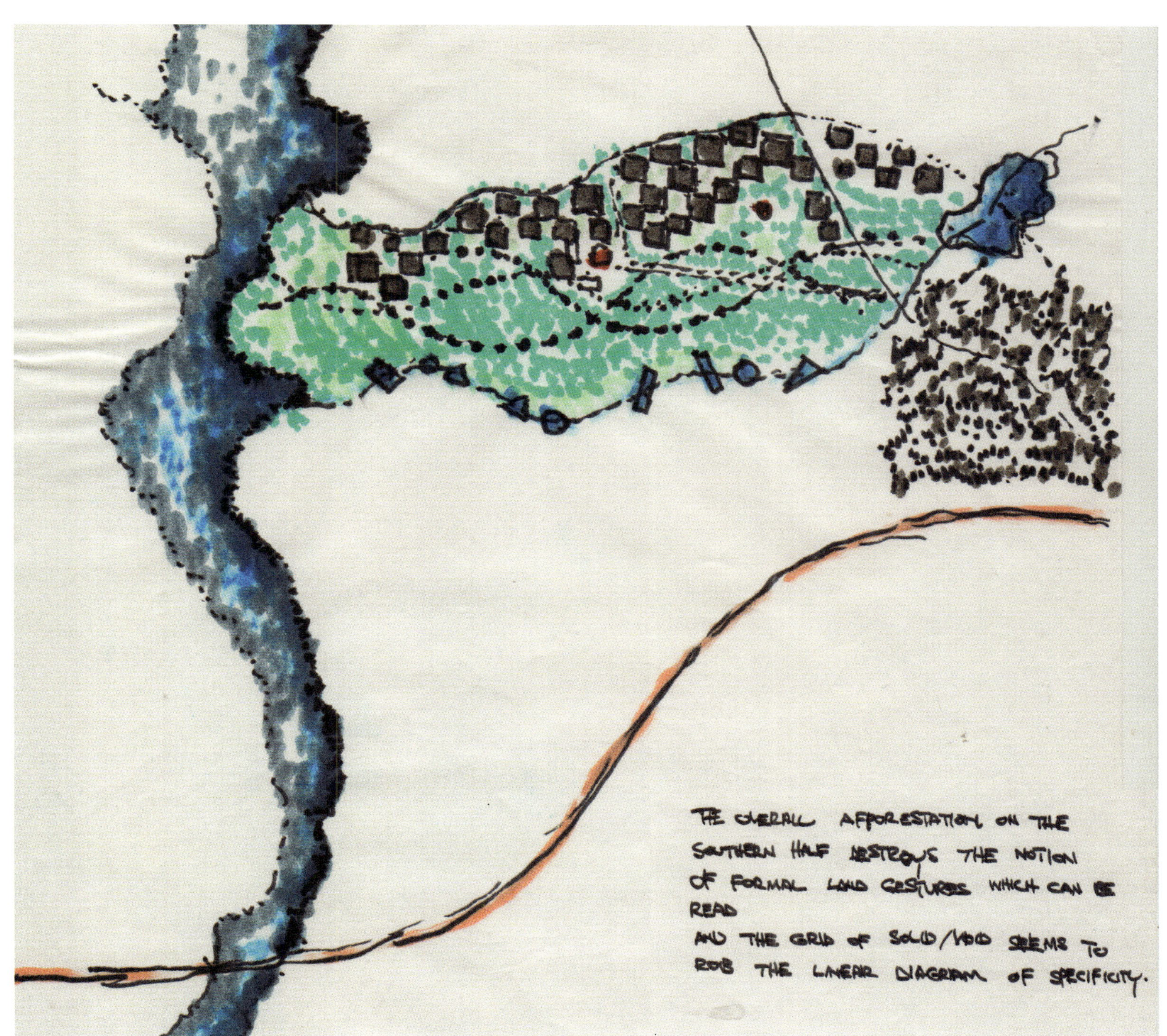

The variety of different building types and forms would be unified by the relationship with the flowing, meandering lines of the landscape plan.

THE COMMUNITIES AND WORKSHOPS

Cells aggregate to make the curvilinear spine

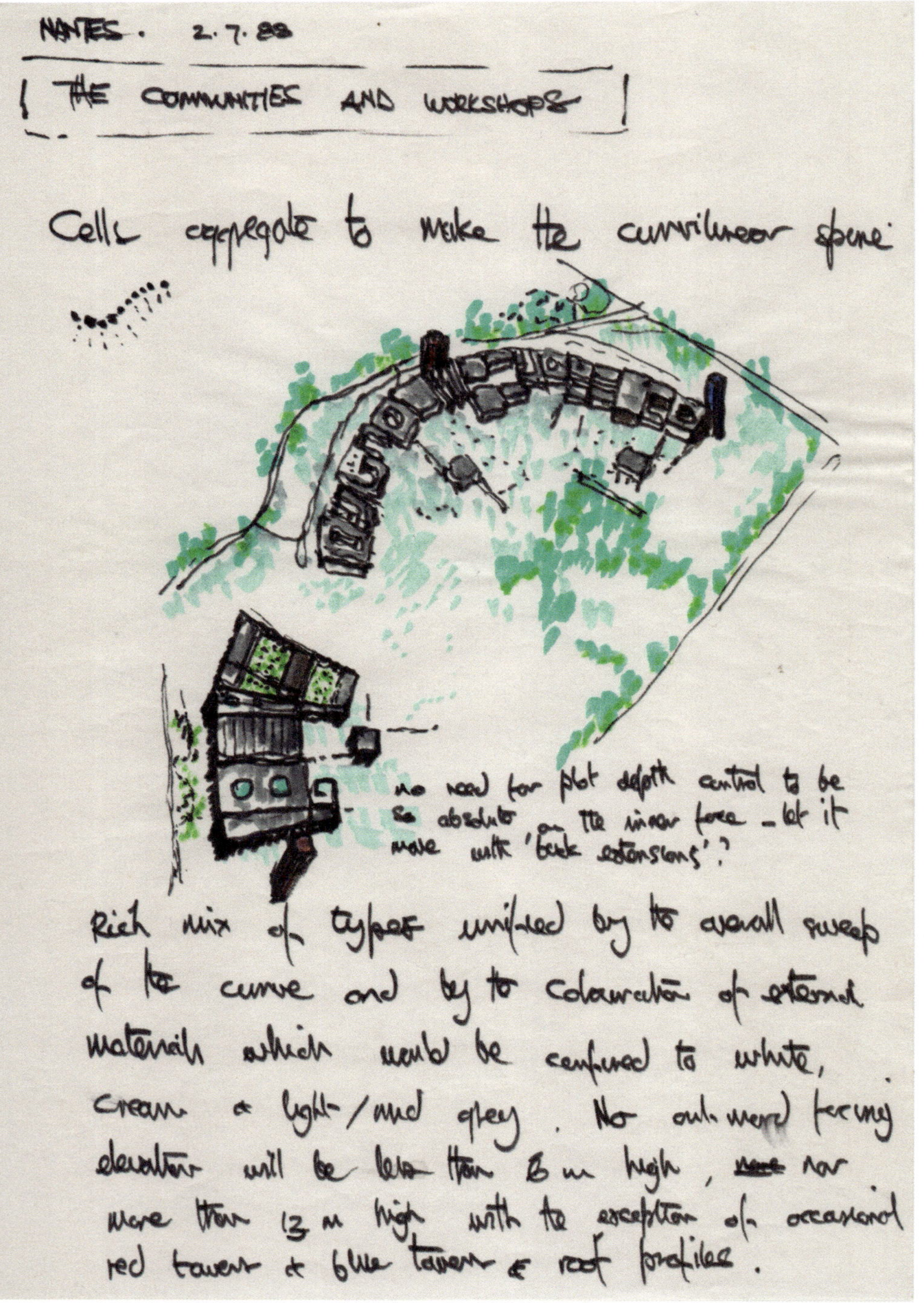

no need for plot depth control to be so absolute on the inner face — let it move with 'back extensions'?

Rich mix of types unified by the overall sweep of the curve and by the colouration of external materials which would be confined to white, cream & light-/mid grey. No outward facing elevation will be less than 8 m high, nor more than 13 m high with the exception of occasional red towers & blue towers & roof profiles.

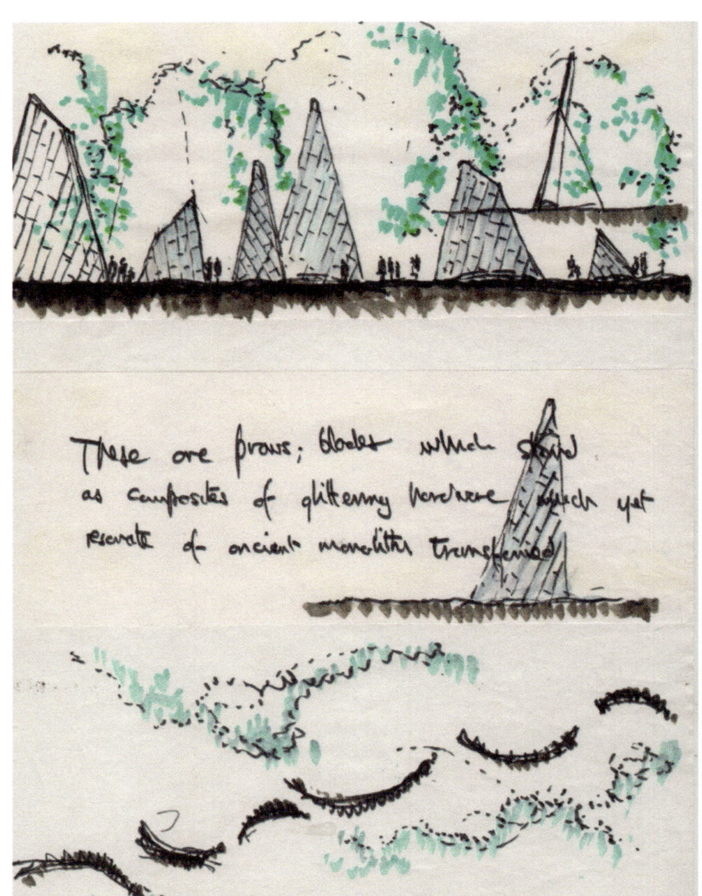

These are prows; blocks which stand as composites of glittering hardware which yet resonate of ancient monoliths transformed

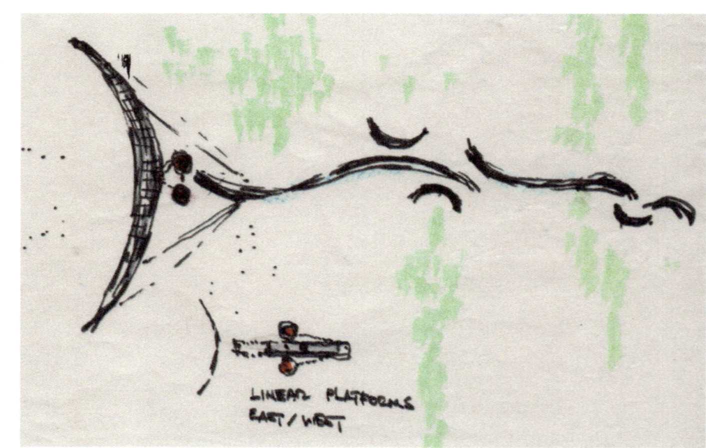

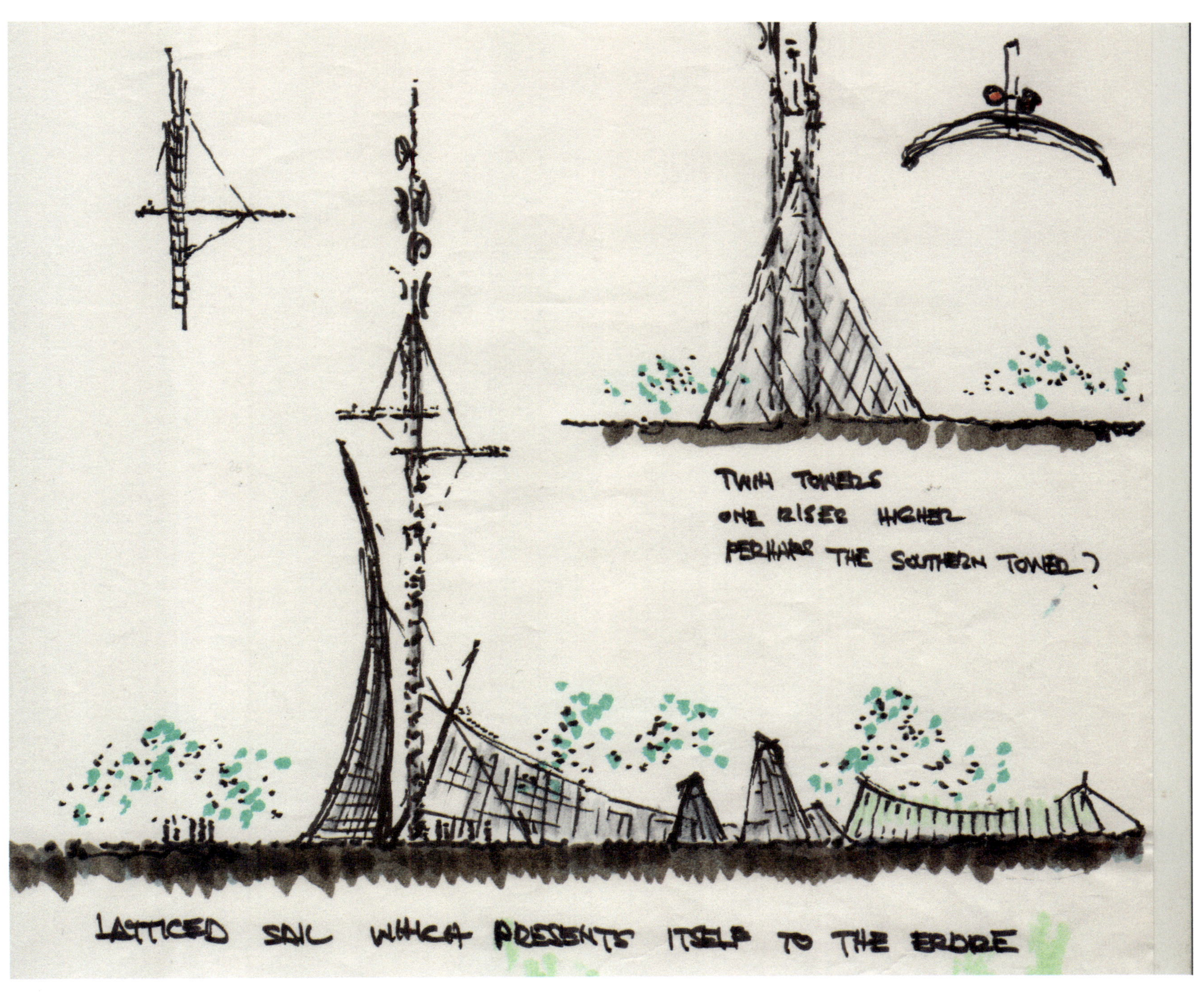

Lattice-structured towers provide feature elements within the landscape and support a range of functions, some specific and others ambiguous.

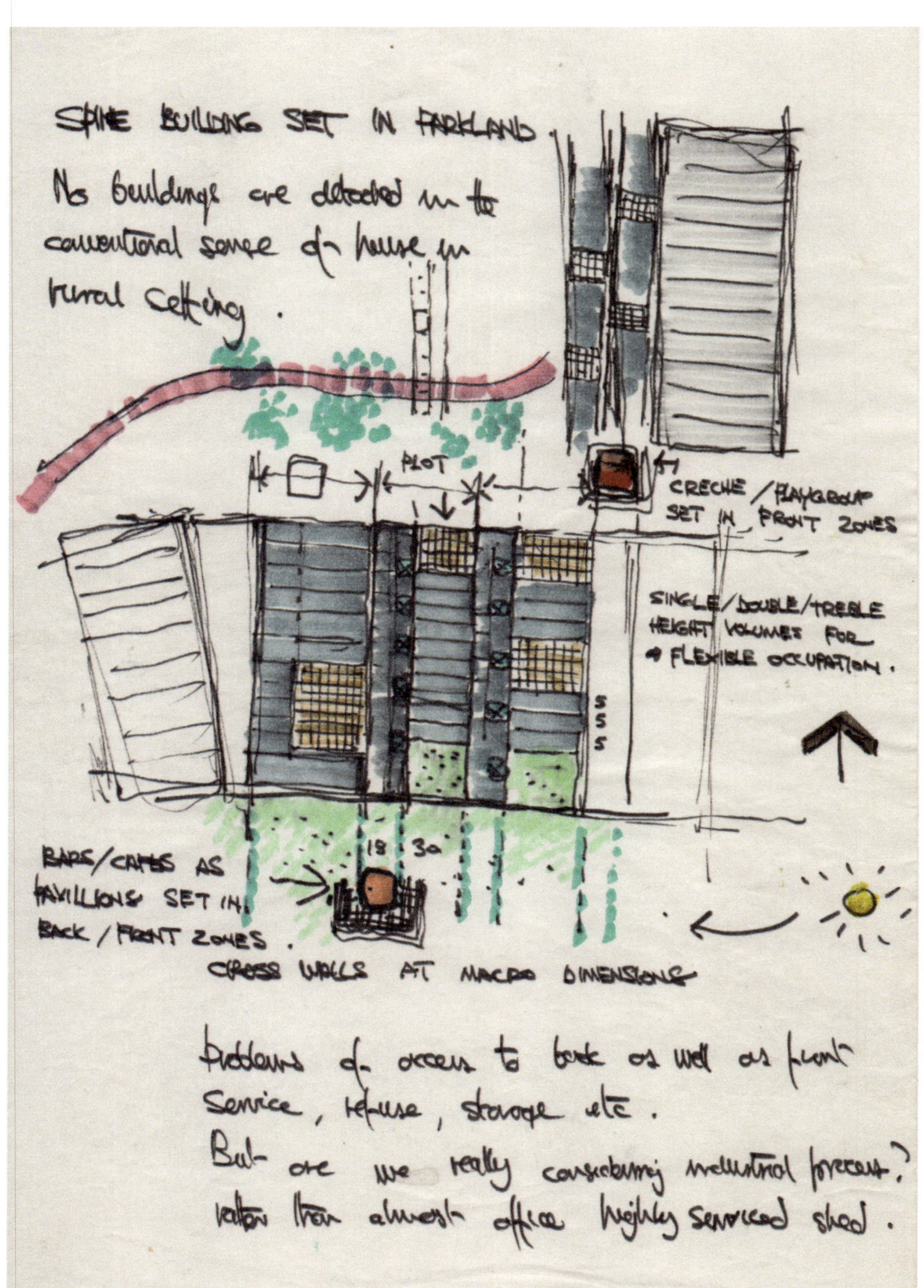

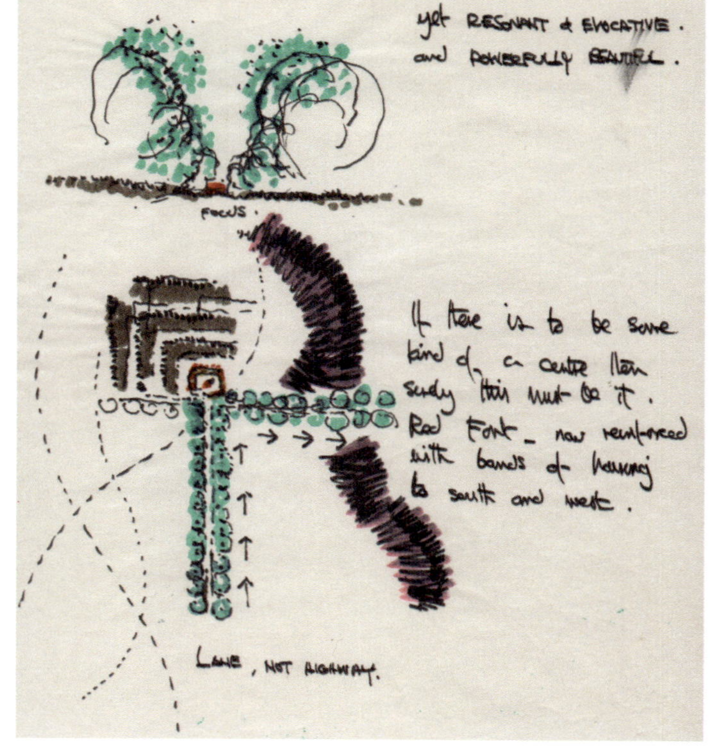

*Exploratory sketches for an
idea for a 'spine' building that
could accommodate a
variety of research and
development functions.*

These drawings are typical of a number of quickly-done, minor projects that would come our way over the years.

As we had carried out projects at Manchester University's Whitworth Art Gallery, and had worked on a proposal to extend the university's John Rylands Library, we were also invited to come forward with ideas to help announce and improve the control of the Burlington Street entrance to the campus.

We proposed a glazed pedestrian canopy, vehicle barriers, a cabin for security personnel and alignments of new trees along the access road. So far as I was able to establish, nothing came of any of the submissions. It seems to be in the nature of projects that some come and go without ever materialising.

1994

First thoughts for a marker structure to signpost the entrance to Manchester University's urban campus.

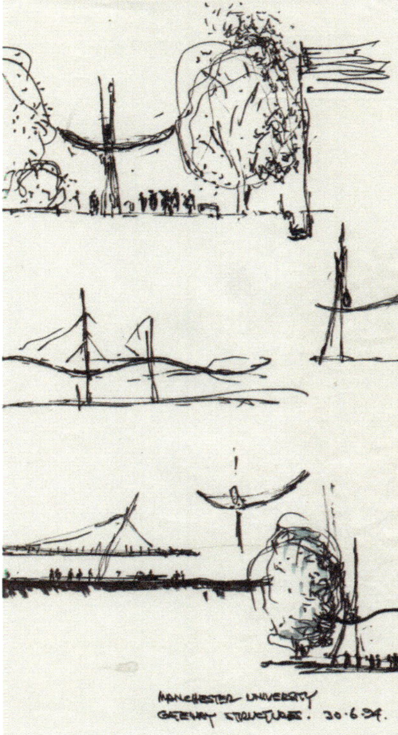

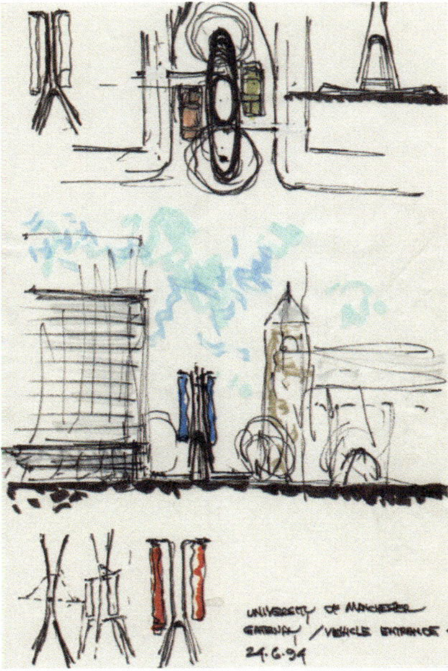

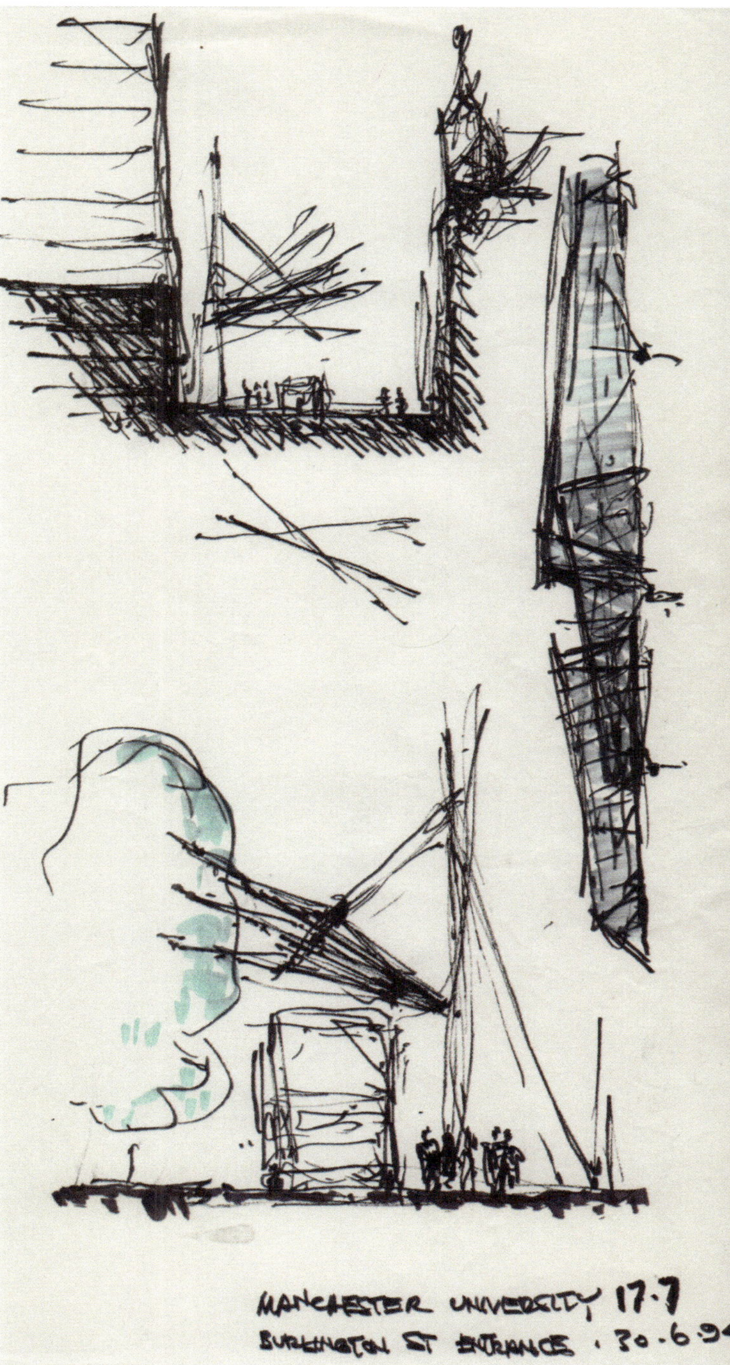

Canted pylons supporting canopies that shelter bus drop-off and pedestrian routes.

I made these sketches following a visit to the University of Aberdeen to see the site designated for a new library, with its steeply rising embankment along one of the two adjacent roads. We proposed an L-shaped plan with a glazed roof over the sheltered court, making provision for communal areas such as the lecture theatre and refectory at ground and basement levels, and a suitably-placed zone for a future extension. This, we thought, was a clear and appropriately low-key response to the brief.

The project included finely worked ideas-in-principle for externally-mounted shading comprising hardwood screens on the sun-oriented glazed facades. We had worked on ideas for energy-saving facades over a period of more than 30 years. Earlier examples include the automatic external blinds for the unbuilt Post Office headquarters building in the City of London, while a similar arrangement was brought to fruition at WH Smith's regional headquarters in Swindon. Later examples include the externally-mounted screens at Techniquest in Cardiff and the Civic Offices in Tralee, Ireland.

2005

The University of Aberdeen sought an architect to design its new flagship library. The international competition was won by Danish architect Schmidt Hammer Lassen.

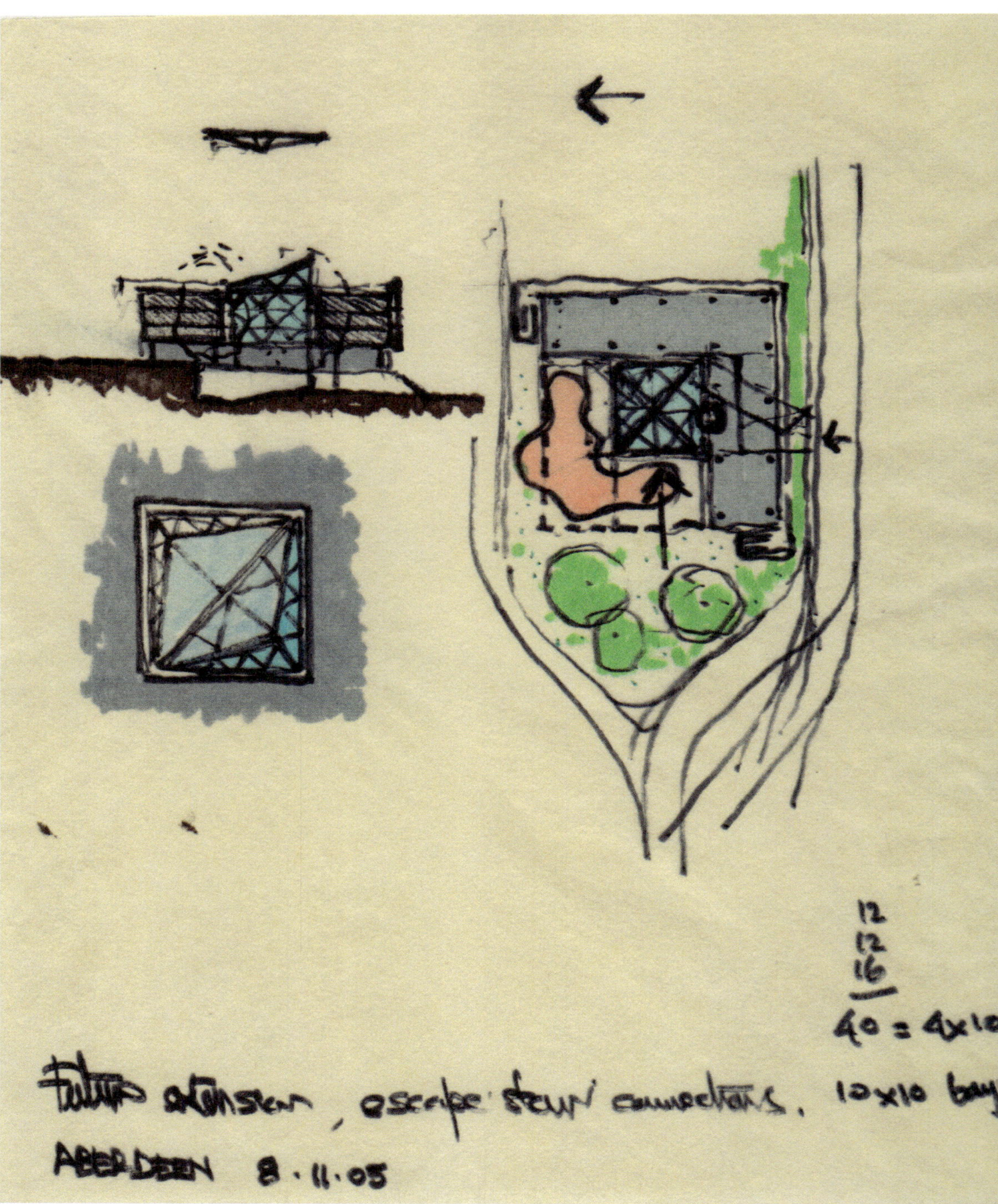

An L-shaped plan form shelters a glazed court that provides the organisational focus for the library project.

River Douglas Bridge

This competition entry is for a bridge across a rural stretch of the River Douglas in Lancashire that was intended not only for pedestrians and cyclists but also, somewhat unusually, for horses.

The selection panel reportedly expressed disappointment with the quality of the designs and, as far as I know, there was no outcome. Although I didn't see the other proposals at the time, I recall having doubts about the viewpoint – it sometimes seems to be a convenient excuse for abandoning a scheme.

Our submitted proposal is shown here along with one of our other early design options for a free-spanning diagrid structure which, if developed and submitted, just might have caught the selection panel's collective eye and avoided their disappointment. Structurally the design bears traces of the curved bays of our schemes for Canberra Bell Tower (1968) and Poplar Bridge (1991).

2008

Lancashire County Council held a two-stage ideas competition for a bridge to cross the River Douglas at Becconsall near Preston.

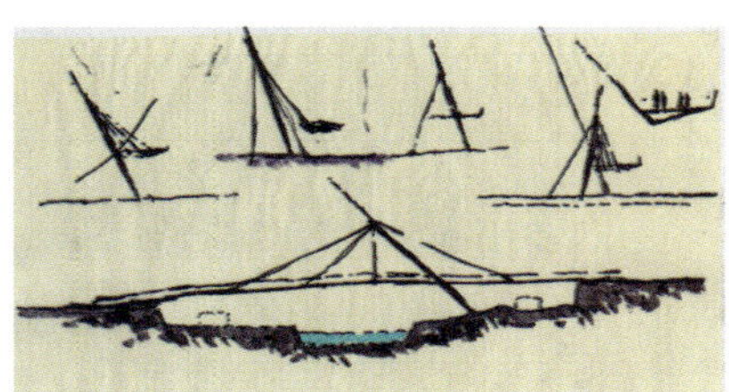

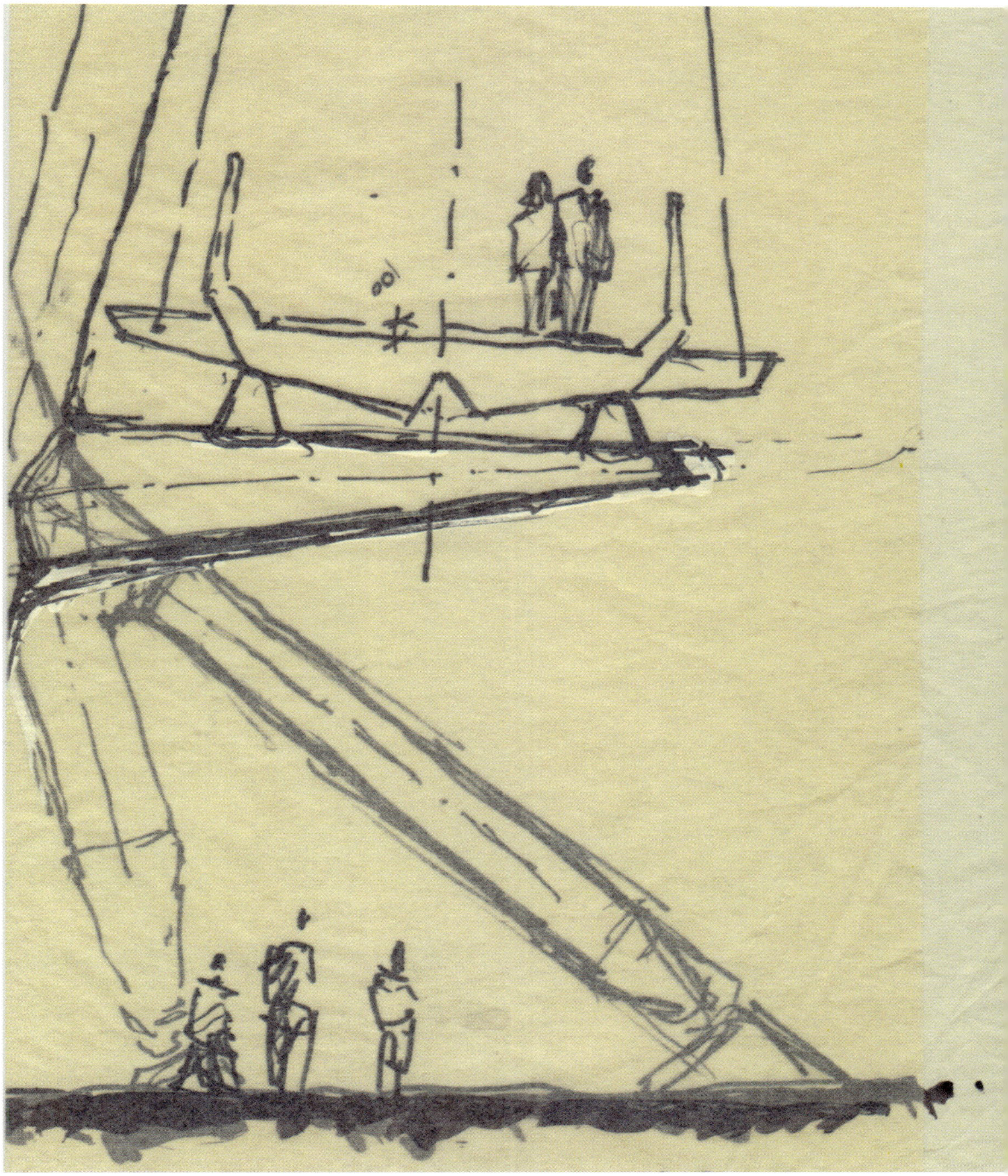

An angled pylon anchored to the adjacent river bank forms a triangulated structure from which the bridge deck is suspended.

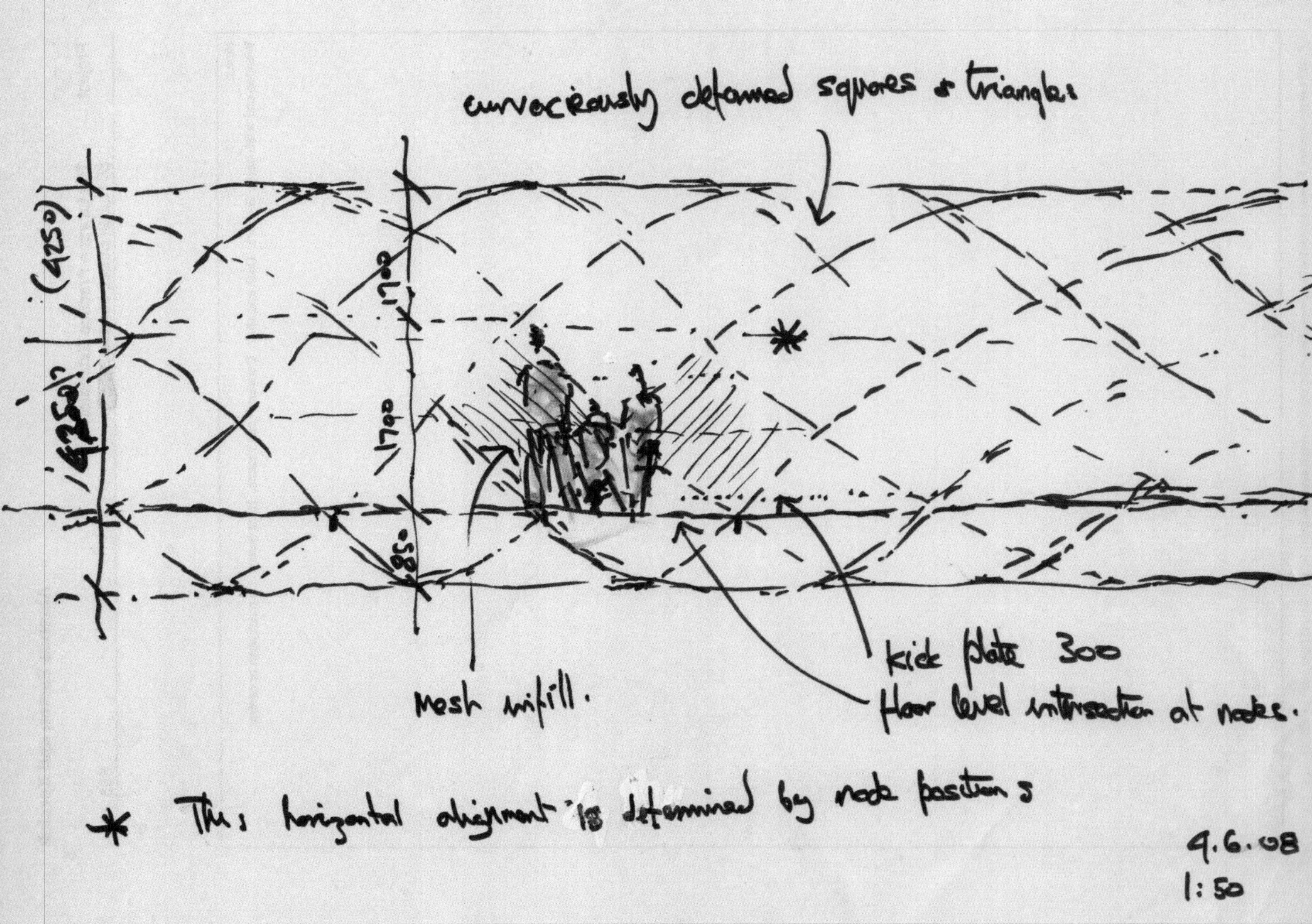

An alternative, free-spanning
tubular diagrid structure.

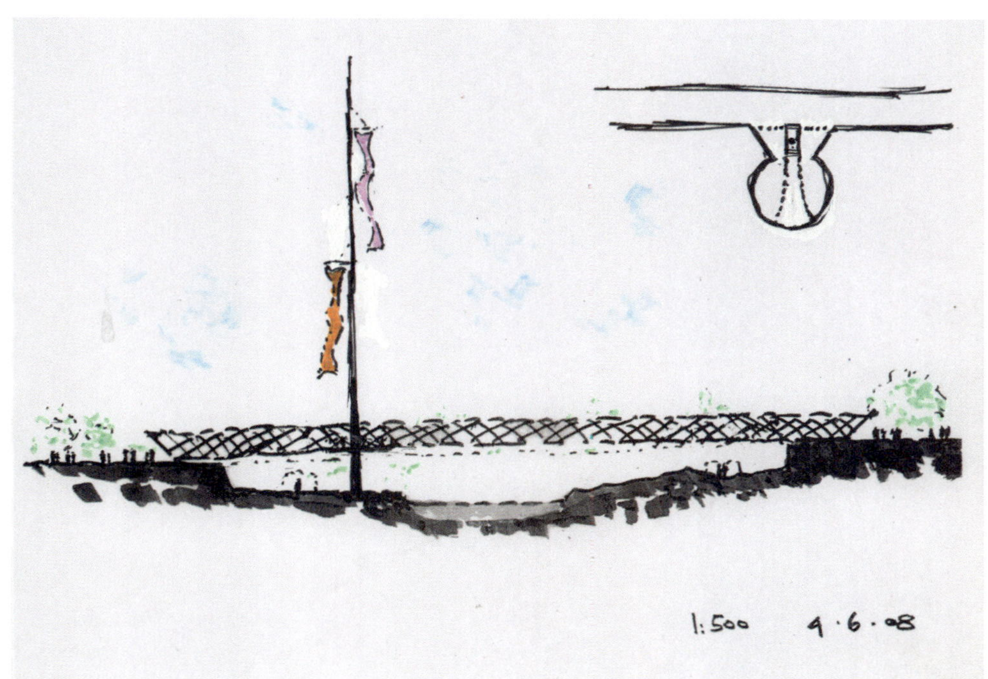

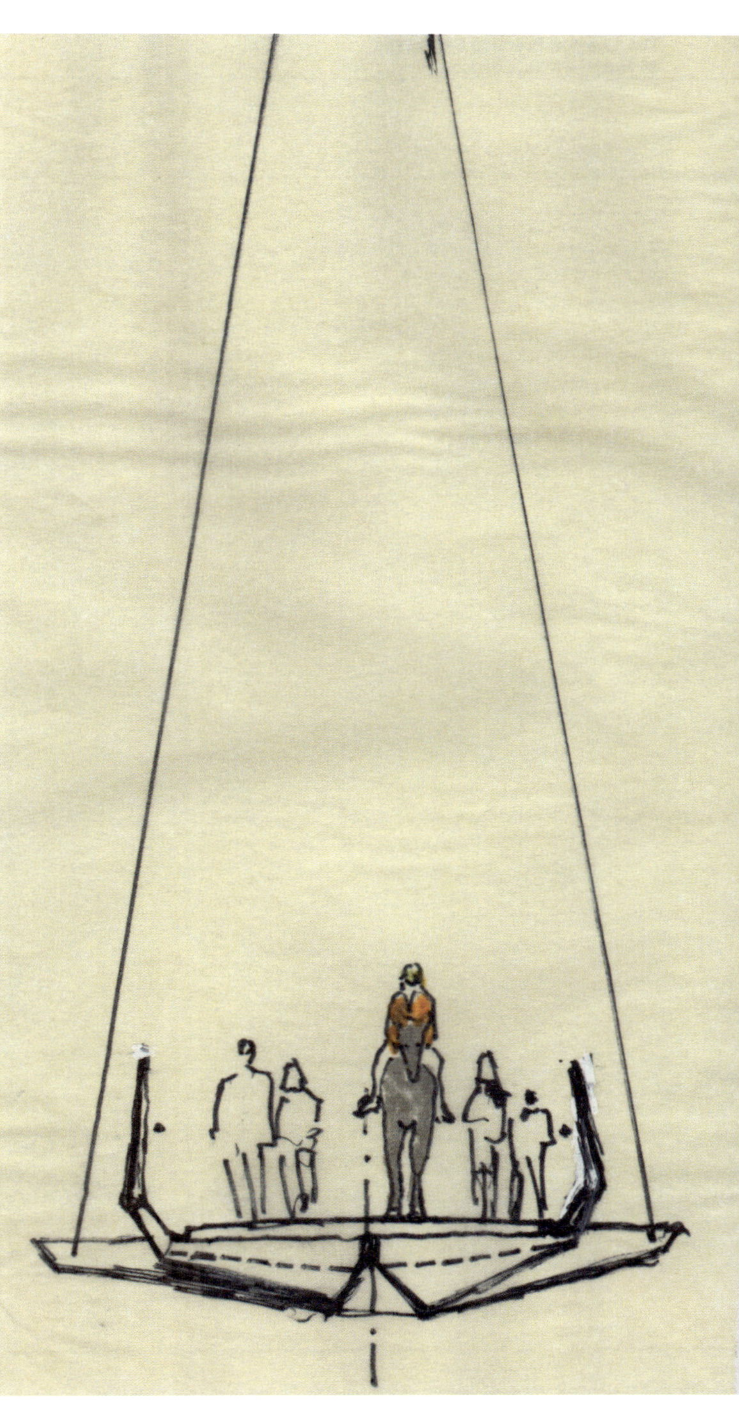

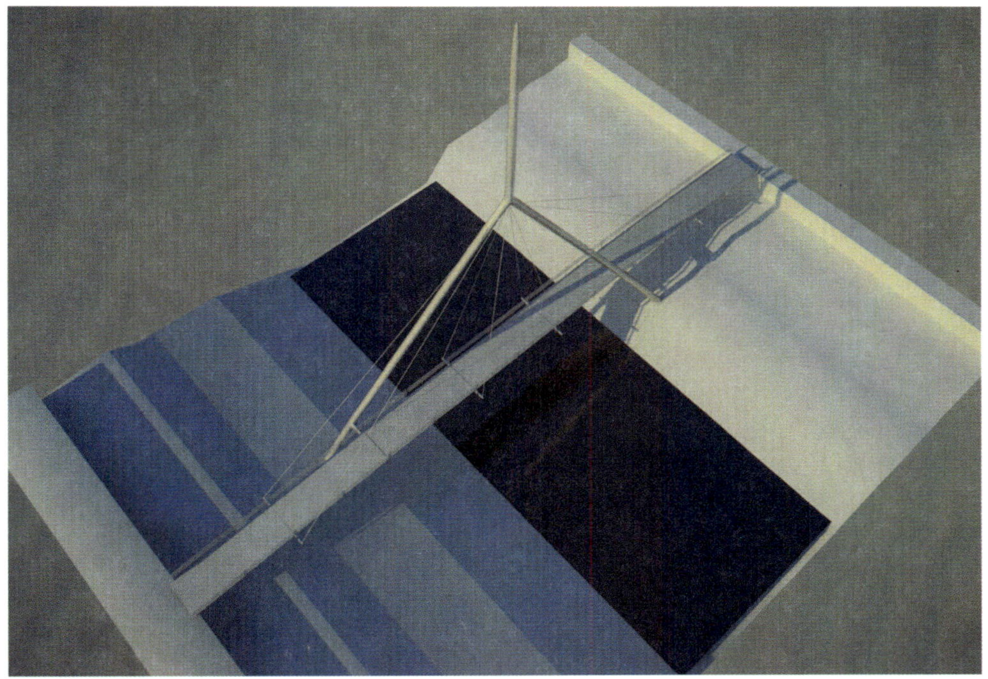

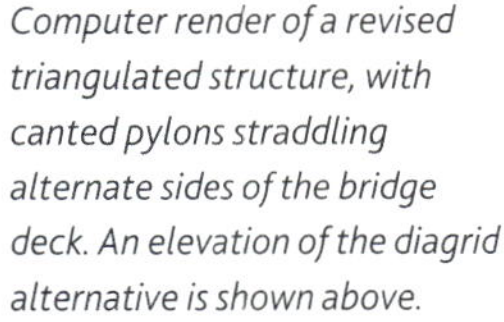

Computer render of a revised triangulated structure, with canted pylons straddling alternate sides of the bridge deck. An elevation of the diagrid alternative is shown above.

Section through the bridge deck with assorted users.

The developer Urban Space Management had pioneered the reuse of shipping containers as buildings, but I never understood how it came to advise Newcastle's Citizens Advice Bureau that such a building would meet its needs.

We had already designed and built USM's Riverside container building at Trinity Buoy Wharf, among other such projects, and were conversant with the particular technical requirements. These sketches show three mini-towers, separated, articulated and slightly misaligned on site boundary angles to form a cluster of square footprints, stepped in heights to break up the building's mass. This formal arrangement was intended as a response to the diversity of building types in the neighbourhood.

A planning application was to have been made, for a site in Gateshead's north-facing slope down to the River Tyne, but the project was halted in its tracks with the onset of the global financial crisis.

2006

Developer Urban Space Management asked ABK to prepare ideas for an office building in Gateshead using shipping containers.

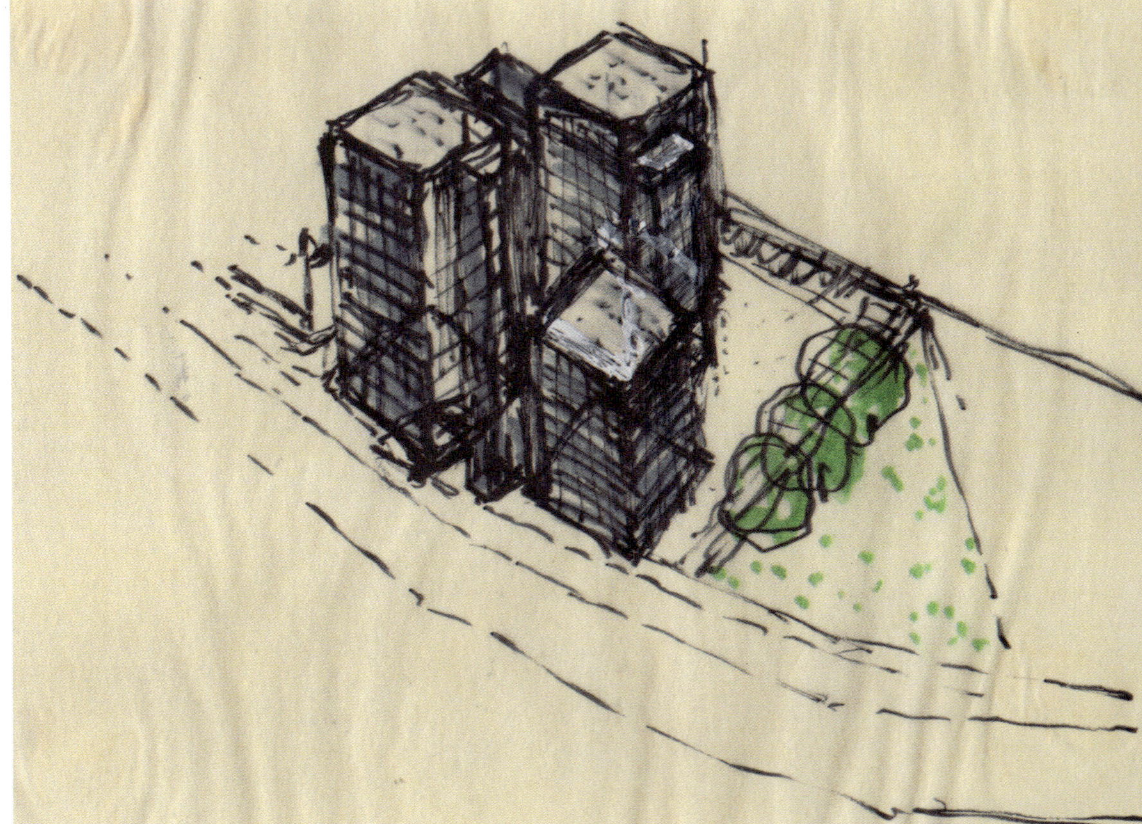

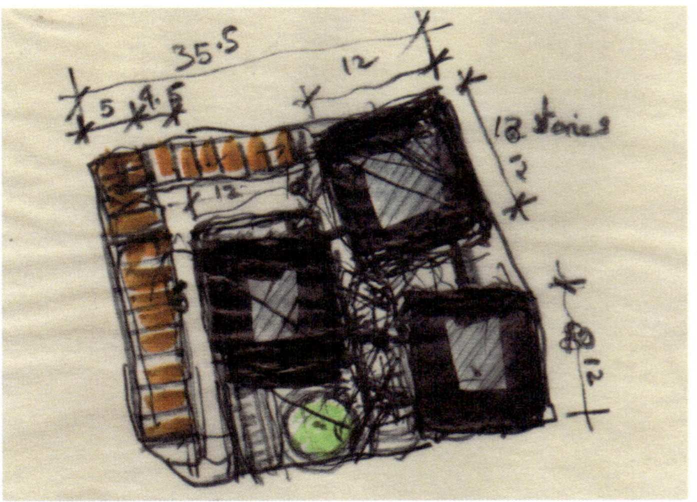

The containers are stacked to form a cluster of three towers, each aligned to the nearest boundary so as to create non-orthogonal interstitial spaces that contrast with the modular regularity of the components.

Here, the interest lay in 'finding', by design, a way of adding a new layer of quietly distinguished modernity to the university's clear idiom of 1960s architecture. We hoped to achieve this by bringing the 'earth and environment' concerns of the department into the formal arrangement and language of the new architecture. We therefore developed a glazed 'breathing layer' between the new and existing buildings and investigated a variety of facade treatments to establish the technology and economy of a well-tempered environment.

Our commitment to and experience of environmental design was manifest from the early 1970s in projects such as the Post Office headquarters in the City of London, WH Smith in Swindon, the Techniquest visitor centre in Cardiff Bay and Civic Offices in Tralee. Both the brief and our initial design of this building on this campus offered an optimistic further opportunity.

2003

The University of Leeds sought an architect to extend and upgrade its School of Earth & Environment building.

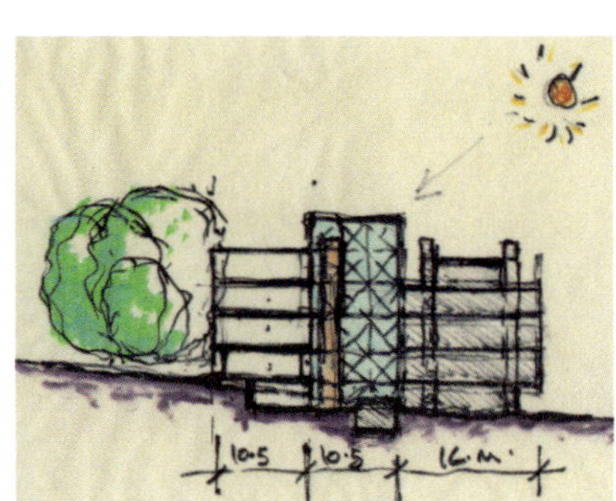

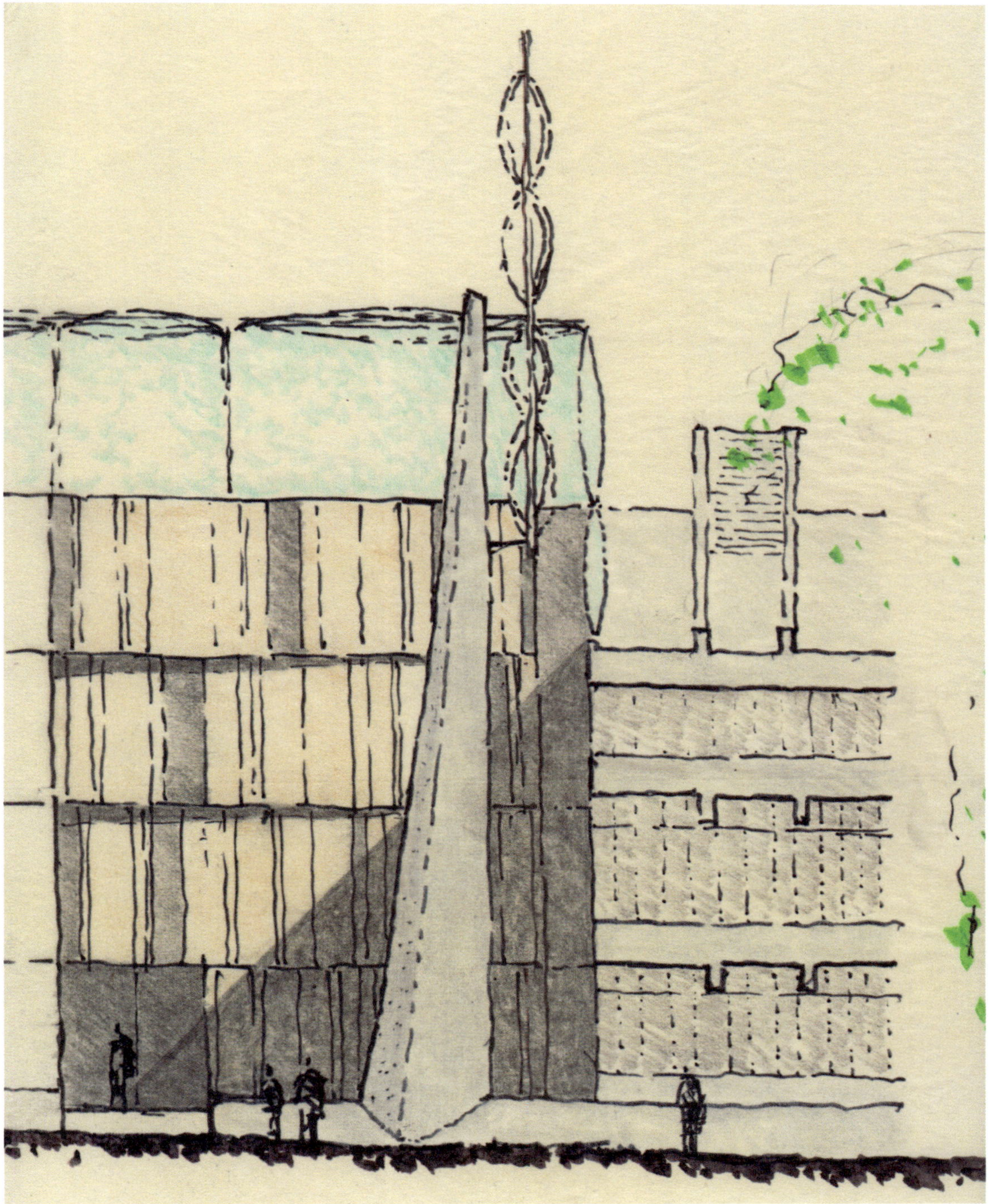

Earth & Environment, Leeds University

Facade study with a helical wind turbine to symbolise the environmental concerns of the faculty's teaching within.

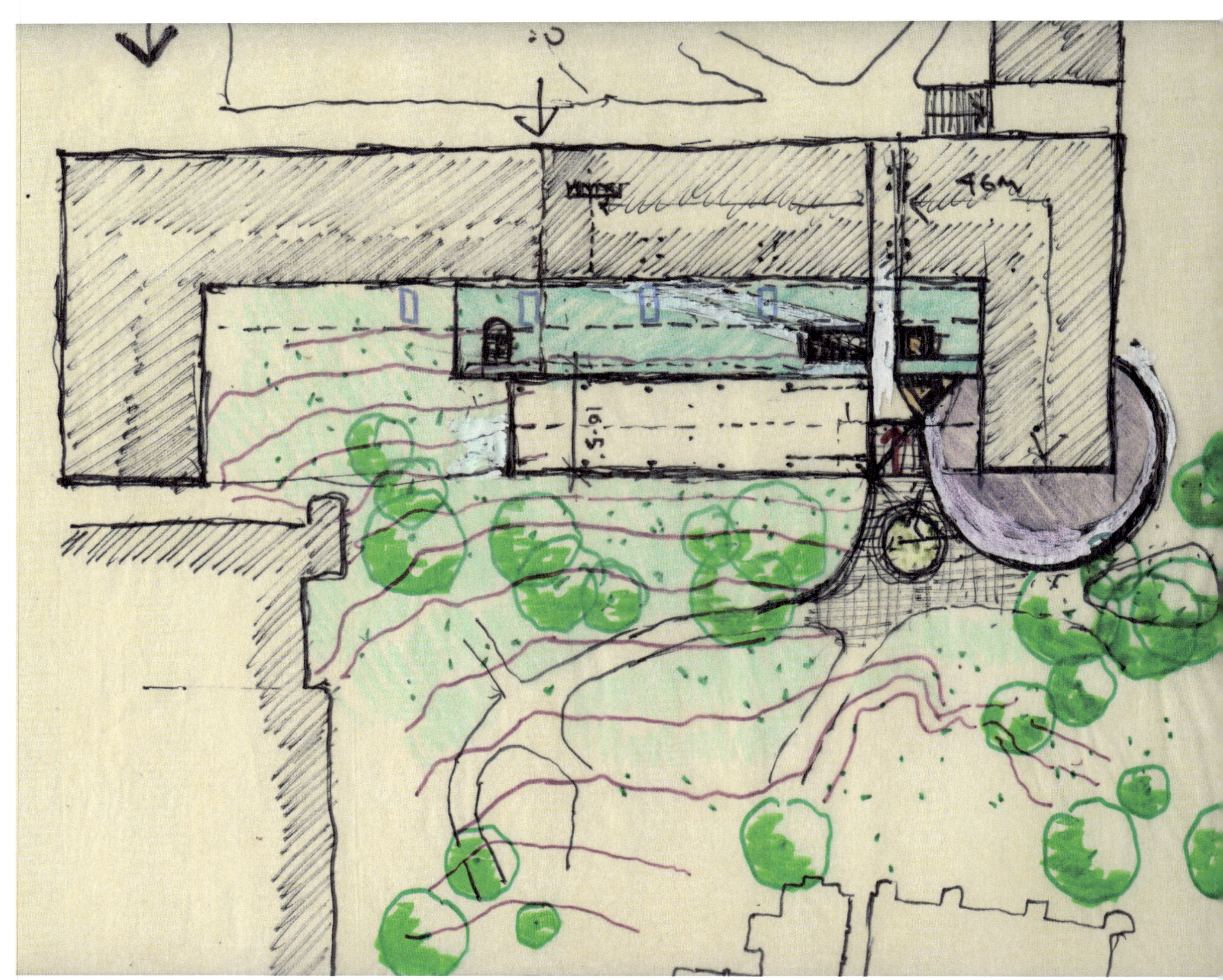

The campus contains a range of
distinguished 1960s buildings
designed by Chamberlain Powell
& Bon. These plans explore ways
of adding to the existing buildings
so as to prolong their useful life
and upgrade their efficiency while
respecting the integrity of the
original structures.

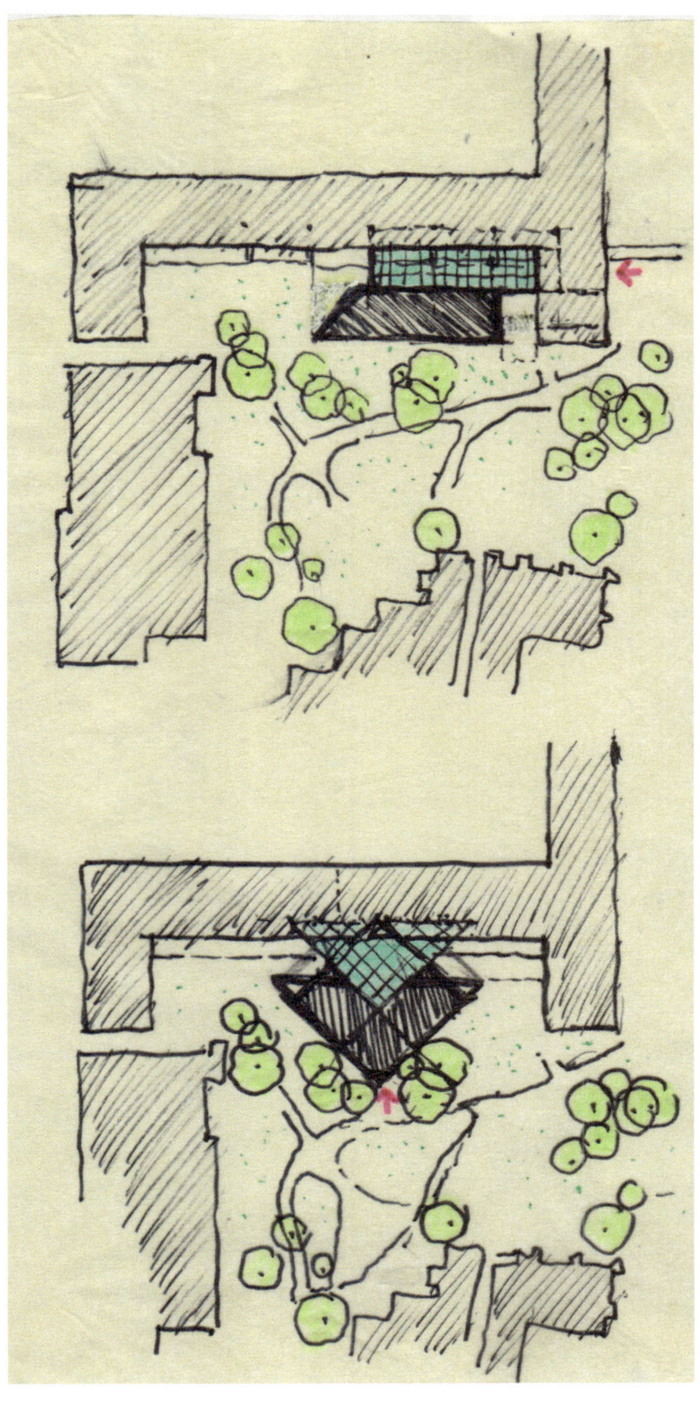

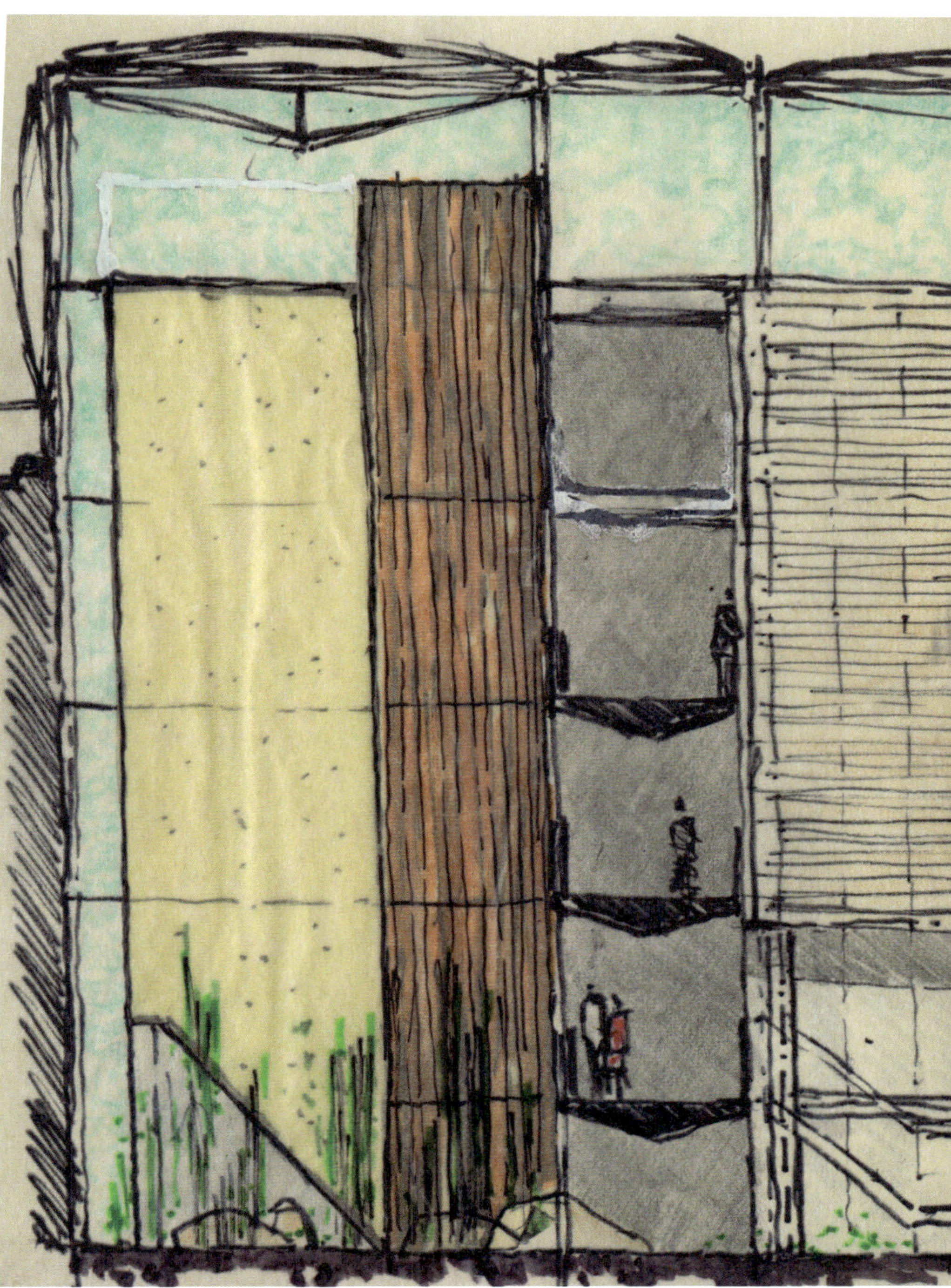

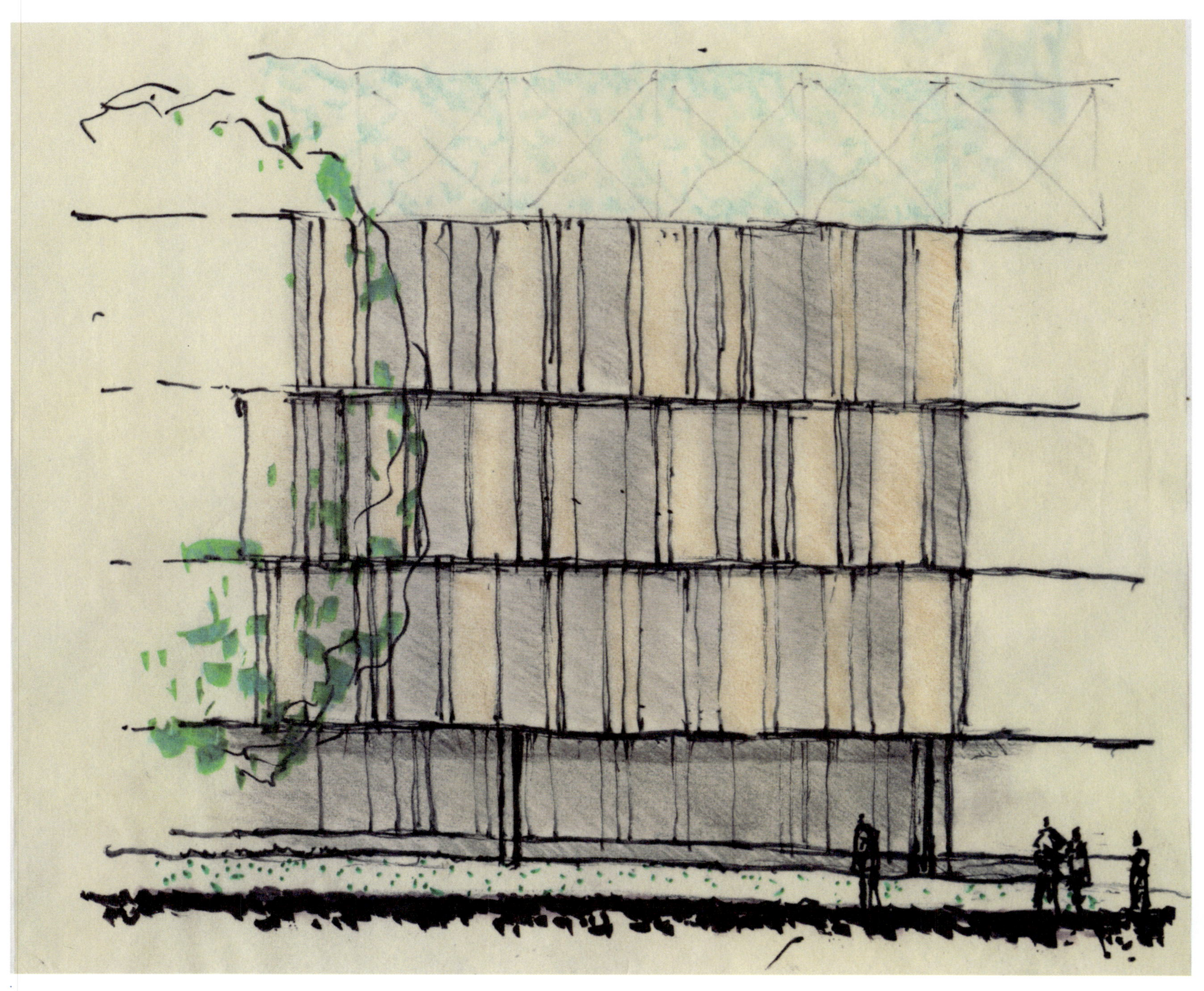

*Elevational study with
syncopated spacing of mullions
to add interest and variety.*

Two years after South Africa's liberation, the ANC government was invited to exhibit at the 2006 Venice Architecture Biennale. So it was that, in the aftermath of my involvement with the UK's Architecture Against Apartheid group, I was invited to comment on the design content that was to be carried out – or rather was it that, in not having been invited, I did so nevertheless?

The sketches shown here had no formal status but rather reflect my interest in, and pursuit of, a project formulated during my attendance at the ANC's first international conference in February 2004. They led later to proposals for a major planning study of 'Post-Apartheid Cities' – a project to address possible future plans for the country's townships that had come into being as a result of the National Party's apartheid policy. The formulation of fresh strategies for these 'bipolar' cities should be, I suggested, the most important subject for the Venice exhibition. This was not done; the opportunity was missed.

2006

A 'missed opportunity' with South Africa's exhibit at the Venice Biennale.

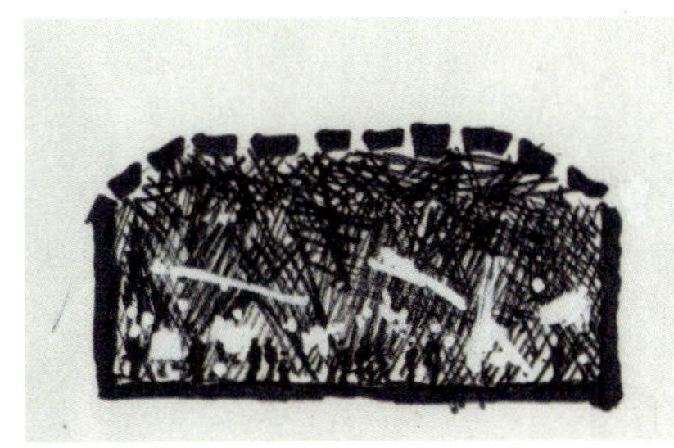

Post-Apartheid cities –Venice Biennale

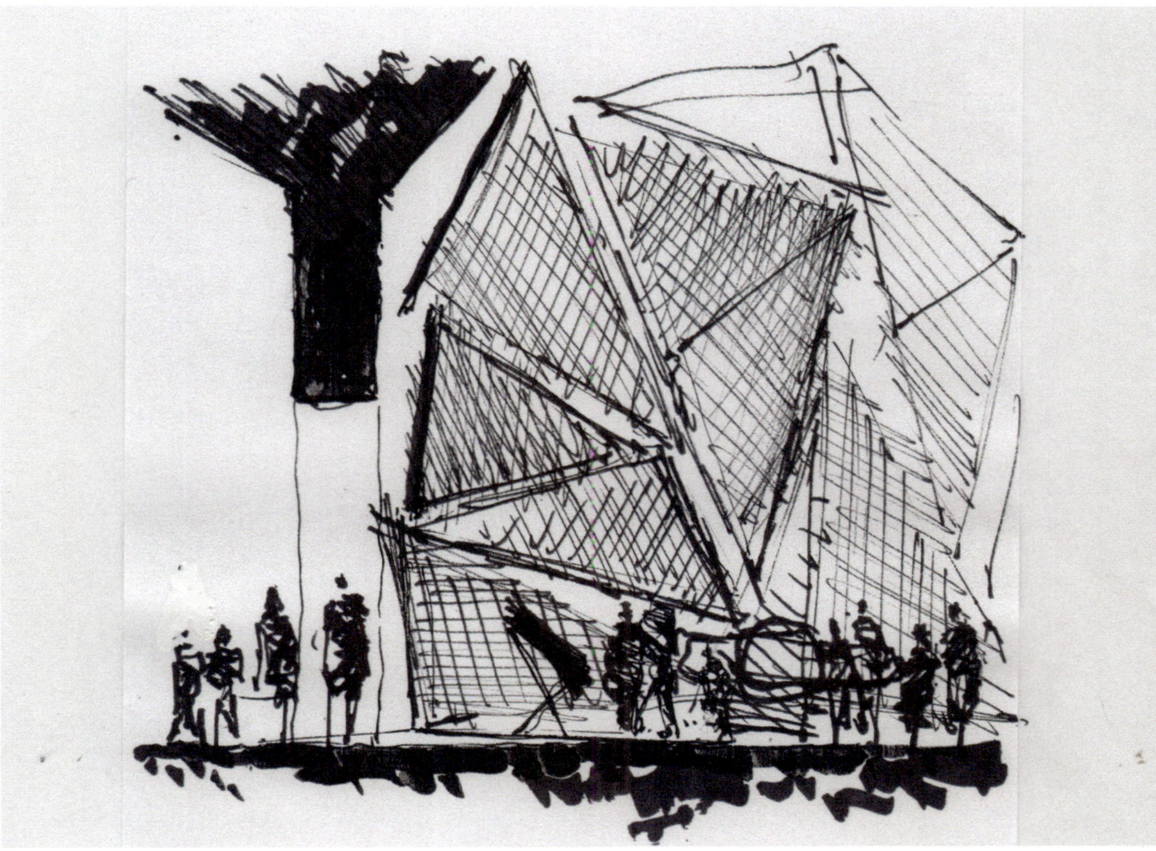

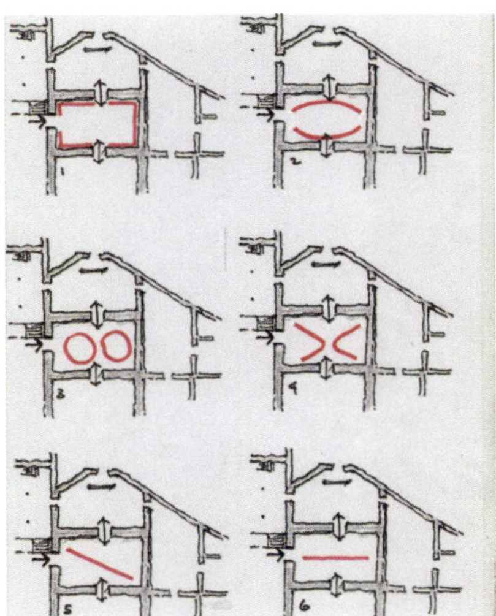

Alternative options for an exhibition display at Venice.

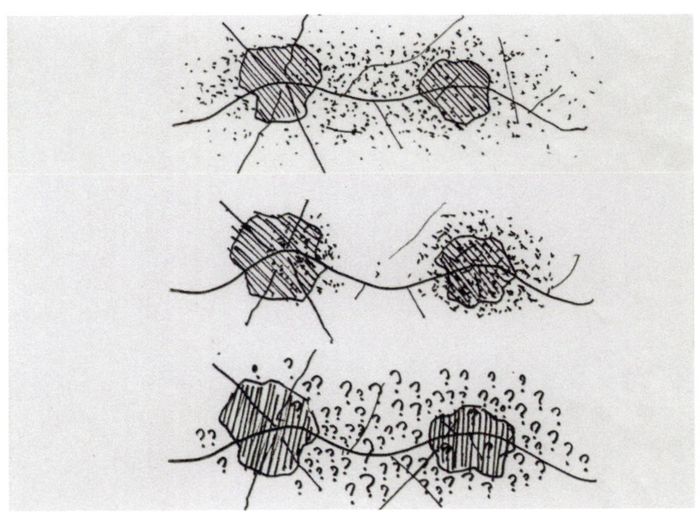

How South Africa's towns and cities might be replanned so as to mitigate the consequences of apartheid-era segregation policies is among the key issues facing the country.

These sets of sketches relate to design ideas for two separate schemes in Stockport, one following the other in 2002 and 2003.

'Designs on Democracy' was a well-organised national competition for new civic offices in three towns in England. I was pleased that we were shortlisted as, when travelling by train to the Whitworth Gallery in Manchester, I'd enjoyed Stockport's urban topography, especially when seen obliquely from the great viaduct as it crossed the River Mersey on the approach to the station.

In the upper part of the town the characteristic Victorian town hall was to be retained, as was an adjacent typical 1960s office block. We proposed to add two new wings so as to define an enclosed civic space, largely sheltered by an over-sailing glass roof, with a curvaceously-formed freestanding library and conference centre building forming a new focal element, and a bridge-like connection to the existing building.

We were selected as the winning team for the first Stockport scheme but as time passed by with further meetings, correspondence and phone conversations, it became evident that the funds for the project would not materialise. Such policy decision changes tend to fade away rather than coming to a clear halt and, being ever hopeful, it can take a while to read the signs.

By contrast, our next scheme for Stockport was a response to an open invitation to come forward with ideas for urban improvements to a lower part of the town centre. I doubt whether the council had anticipated such radical interventions as high-rise buildings but, among our other urban-scape and low-rise housing ideas, that is what we chose to do.

Considering Stockport's proximity to Manchester, we envisaged introducing something of a big-city scale and character to the more local urban scene. The high-rise tower, with a plan based on an asymmetric two-centred oval geometry, was to accommodate a hotel, offices and penthouses. Such a vertical element, we suggested, would establish a positive formal dialogue with the horizontally functional emphasis of the not-too-distant Victorian viaduct. But, it transpired, this was not what Stockport regarded as an appropriate response.

2002/03

Two successive design competitions in the Lancashire town of Stockport.

Stockport: Designs on Democracy

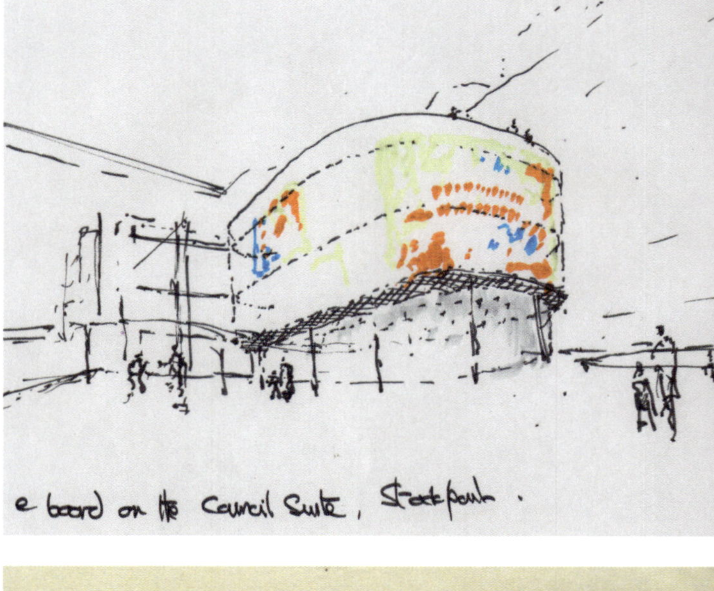

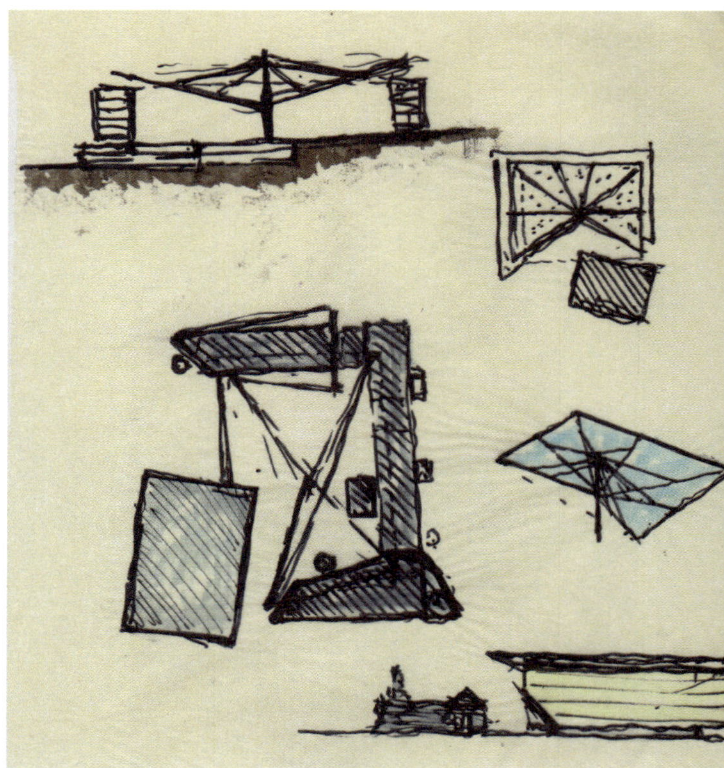

A large, covered public forum seemed to best suggest an open and accessible democractic system of council governance.

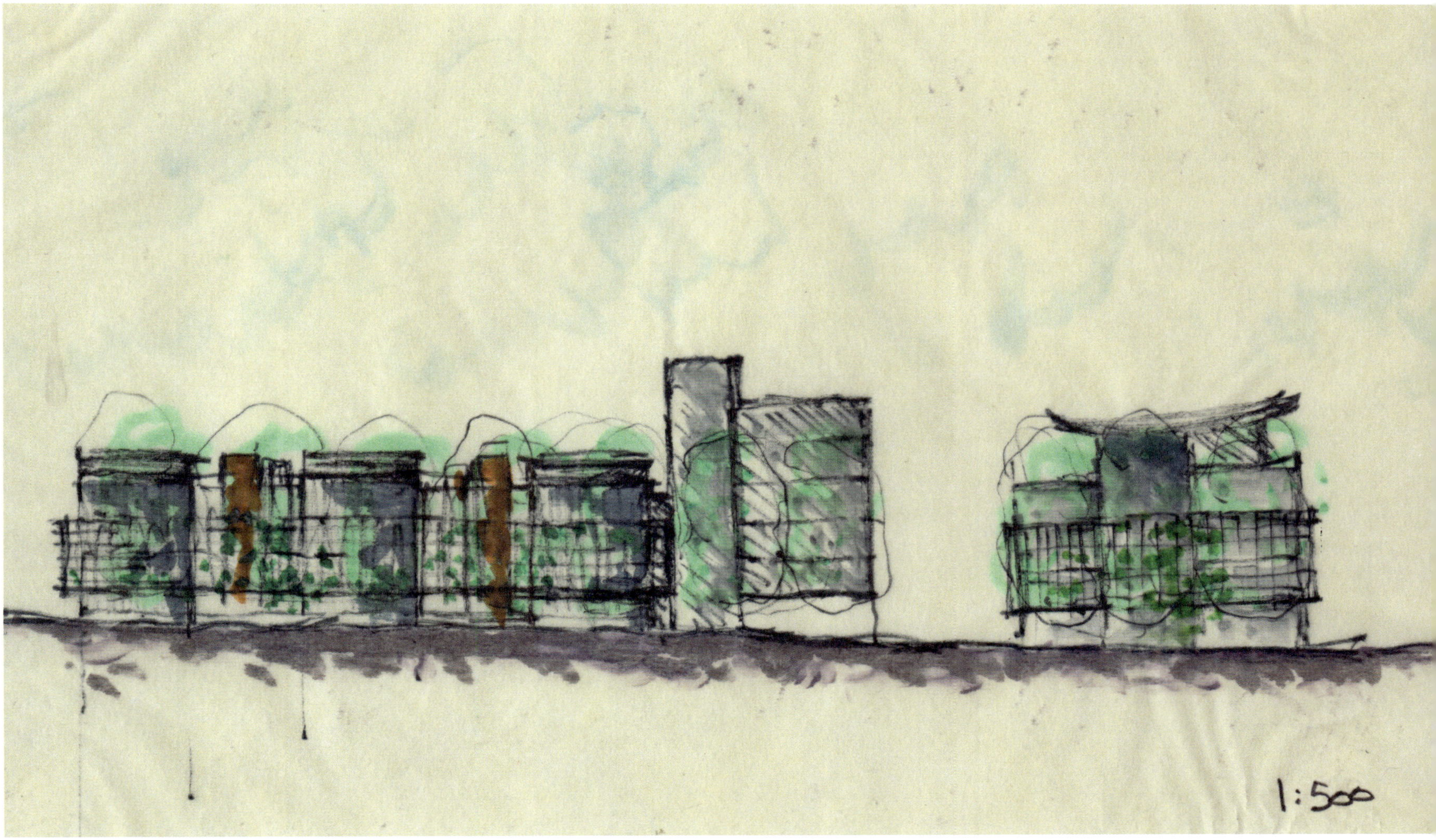

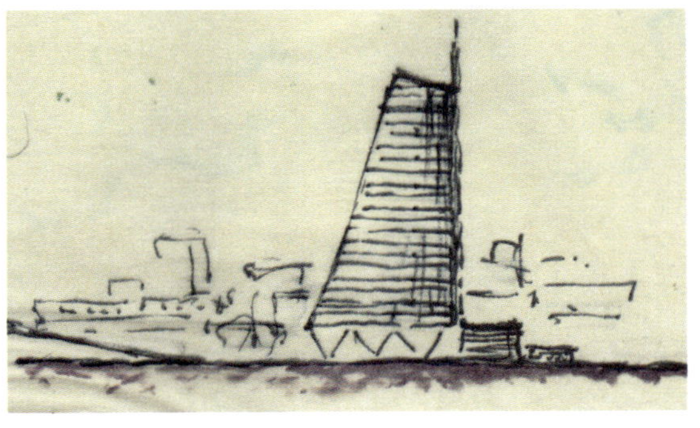 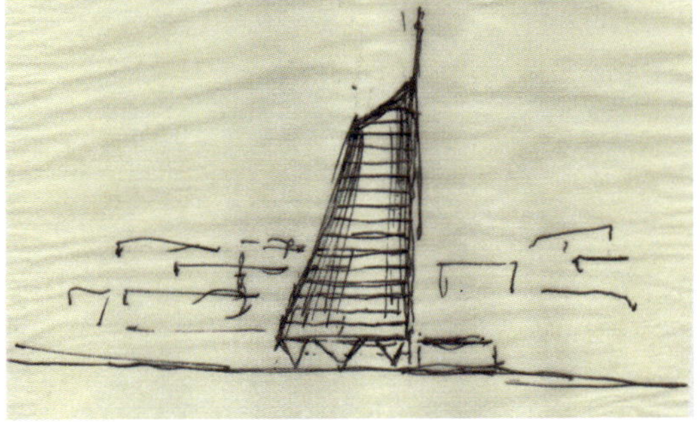 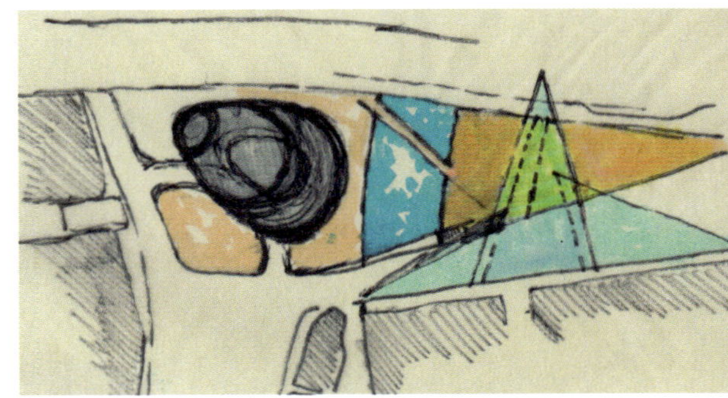

A high-rise mixed-use proposal for offices and a hotel in Stockport town centre. The elevation study above is for a residential project.

In the mid-1980s, soon after the cancellation of our commission for the National Gallery extension, the London Docklands Development Corporation appointed ABK to prepare designs for the 12 stations then being engineered to extend the Docklands Light Railway eastwards from Poplar to Beckton.

Soon thereafter we were also asked to prepare a development plan for a freely-briefed mixed development on Poplar High Street, just west of what was later to become the station's Poplar Bridge. The sketches illustrate an idea for an office building that unfurls from a dense encirclement around a tight court or atrium, extending curvaceously westwards as it steps down in height to become a relatively modest neighbour to the existing Peabody-type housing.

The circular element is sited in turn within the three wings of a rectangular 'urban container' that respects the alignments of the high street and neighbouring boundaries, to form an interstitial public open space. Even then I recognised the formal similarity with our 1970s Keble College scheme, thinking that, like siblings, time-lapsed reinterpretations can be positive. In any case, they're never quite the same, are they?

1985

The LDDC asked ABK to prepare 'design studies' for appropriate development within its demise on Poplar High Street.

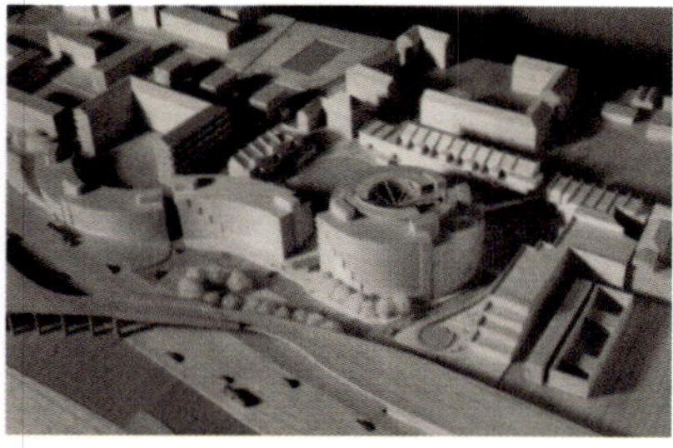

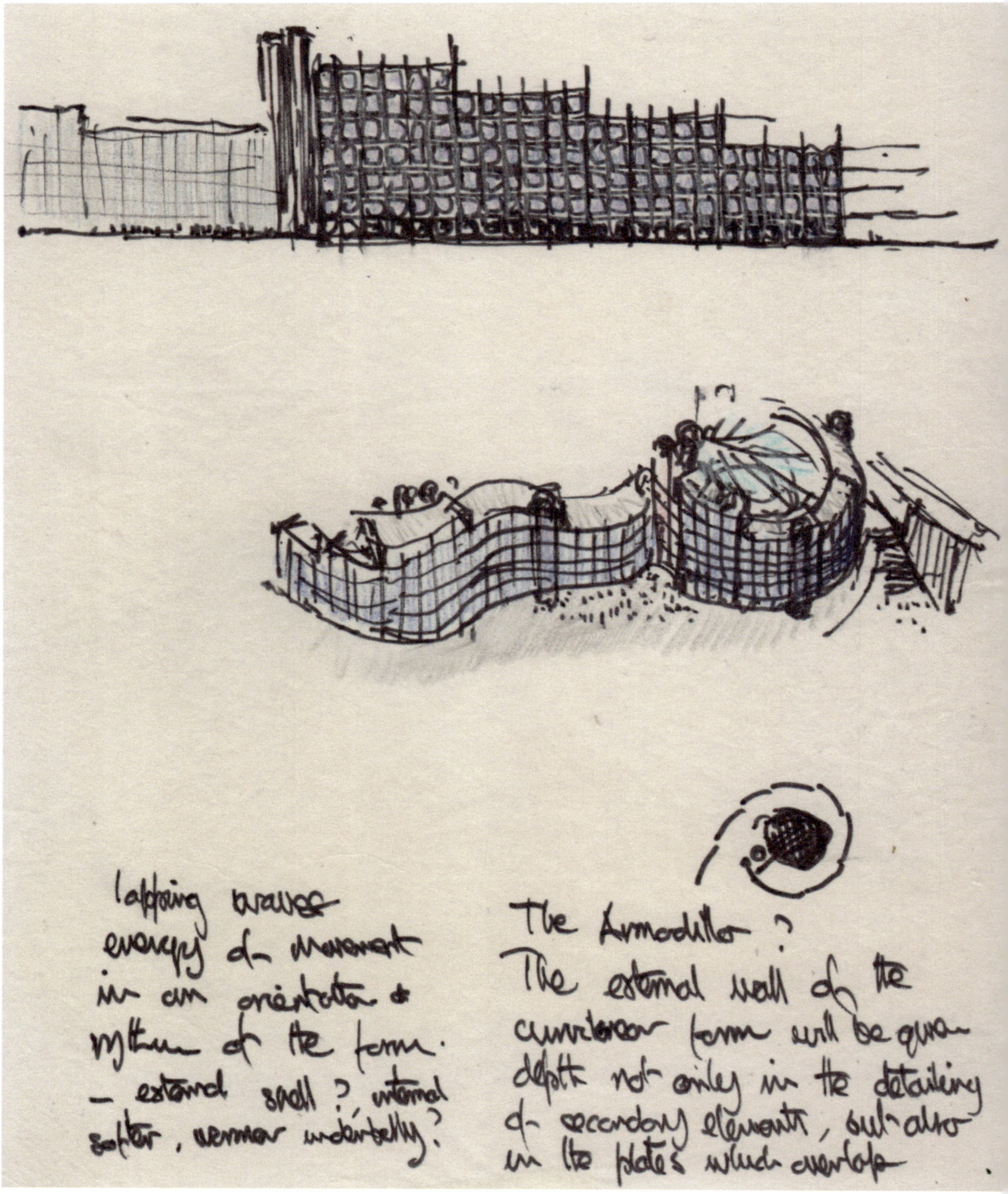

The formal combination of a 'head' and 'tail' is a theme that resonated within ABK's work over several decades. Here, the curvilinear shapes are contained within rectinear perimeter blocks, defining an unfolding series of public spaces.

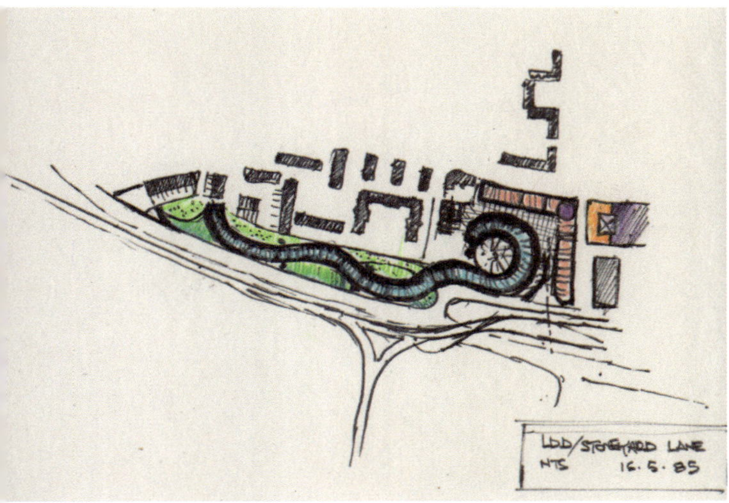

LDD/STONEYARD LANE
NTS   16.5.85

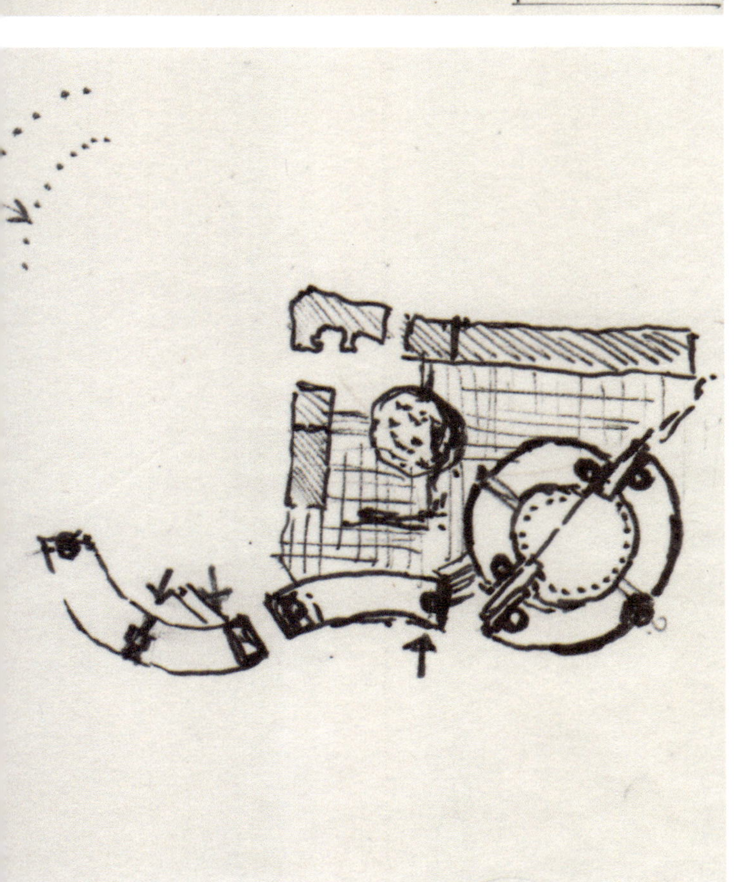

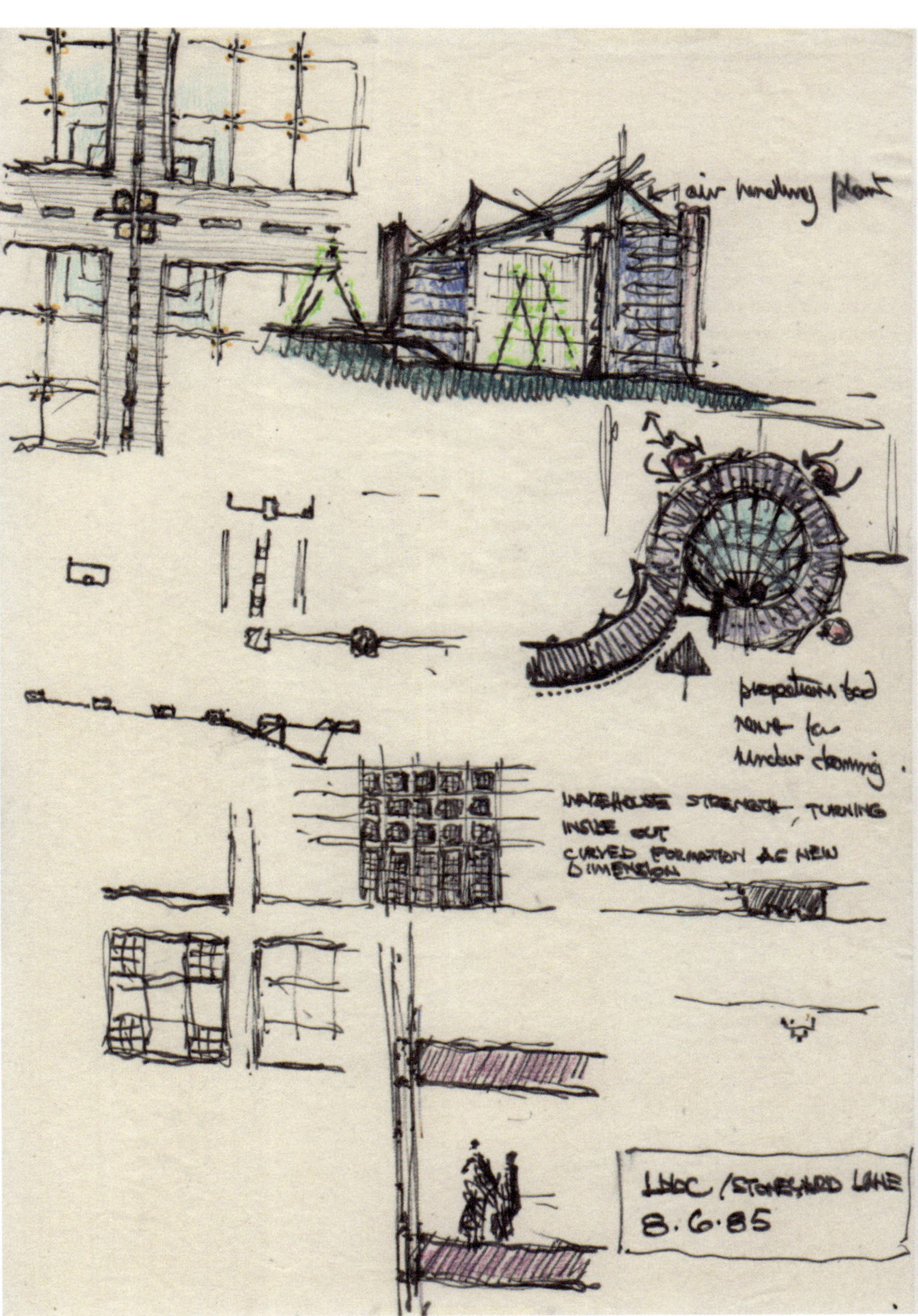

air handling plant
proportions too
narrow for
window drawing
WAREHOUSE STRENGTH, TURNING
INSIDE OUT
CURVED FORMATION AS NEW
DIMENSION
LDDC /STONEYARD LANE
8.6.85

The London Docklands Development Corporation invited us to design the 12 stations for the second stage of the Docklands Light Railway line, extending eastwards from Poplar to Beckton. The first stage of this new overground line, from Bank to Island Gardens via Canary Wharf, had been an evident success, so it was interesting and to some extent frustrating to join the project after the civil engineering design had been completed, and miss the benefits of collaboration.

Most of these outlying stations were to be situated in the recently-vacated dockland zones where, at the time, there were but a few scattered areas of housing. I recall standing at the site for our prototype station and platform structures, beside the desolate Royal Victoria Dock, feeling a lonely sense of the loss of community. While there was a positive anticipation of new lives to be made, I wondered what had become of the communities that had so evidently been uprooted and, with this, the almost tangible absence of the energy of the historic working docks.

The brief, for the design of a kit of parts, was interesting and fundamental. To some extent it was absolute in its requirements – canopy lengths, for example, were to be extendable by small increments. And, given the initially isolated settings of some of the stations, our questions about security led to a general recognition of the need for openness, and subsequently the extensive use of glass.

1987

Stations along London's Docklands Light Railway line helped to open up previously disadvantaged parts of the capital.

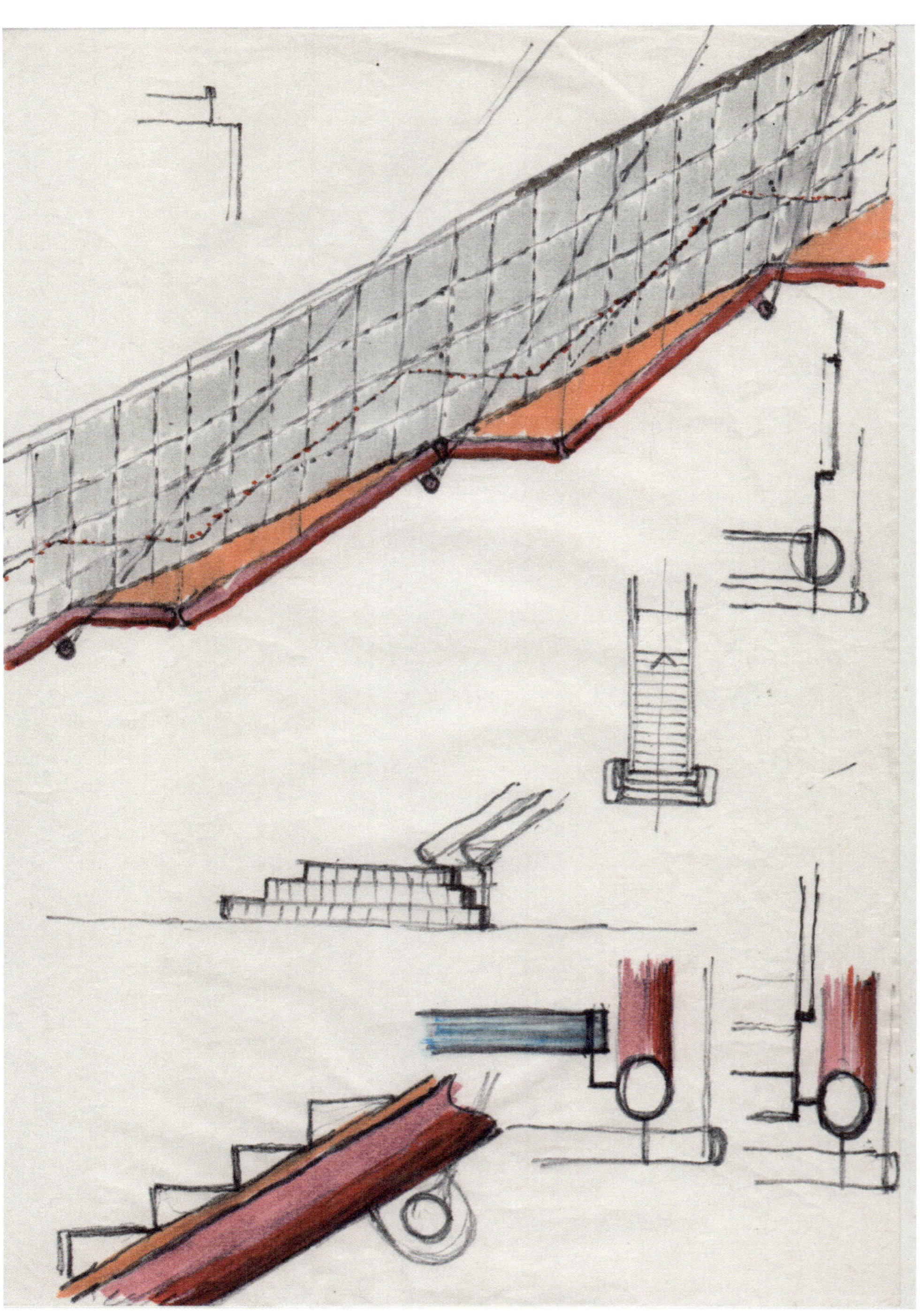

Design studies for access staircases. Many of the stations were raised significantly above ground level, so the stairways naturally became key elements in their design.

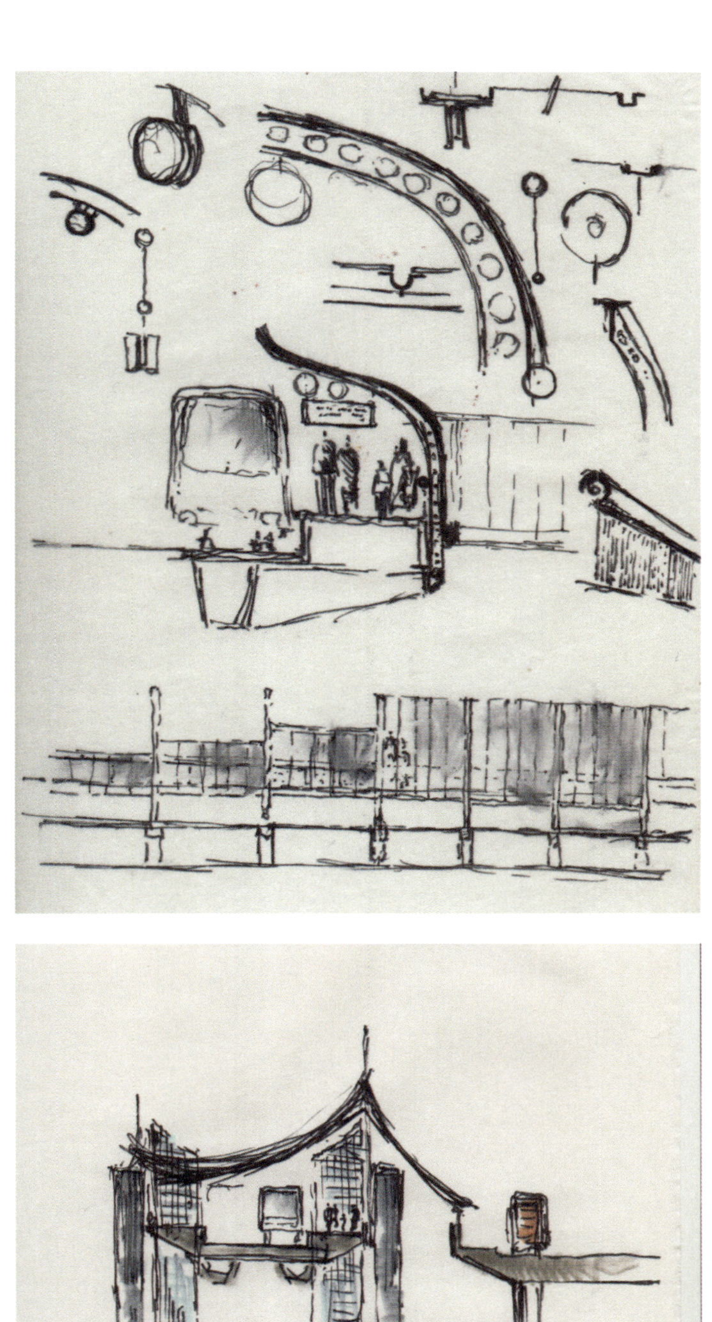

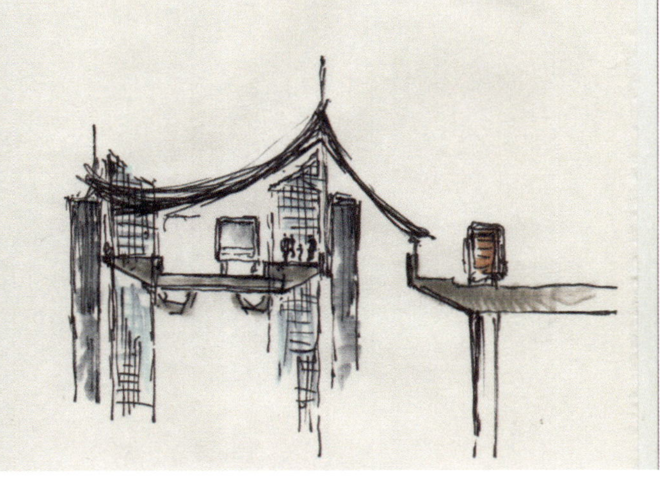

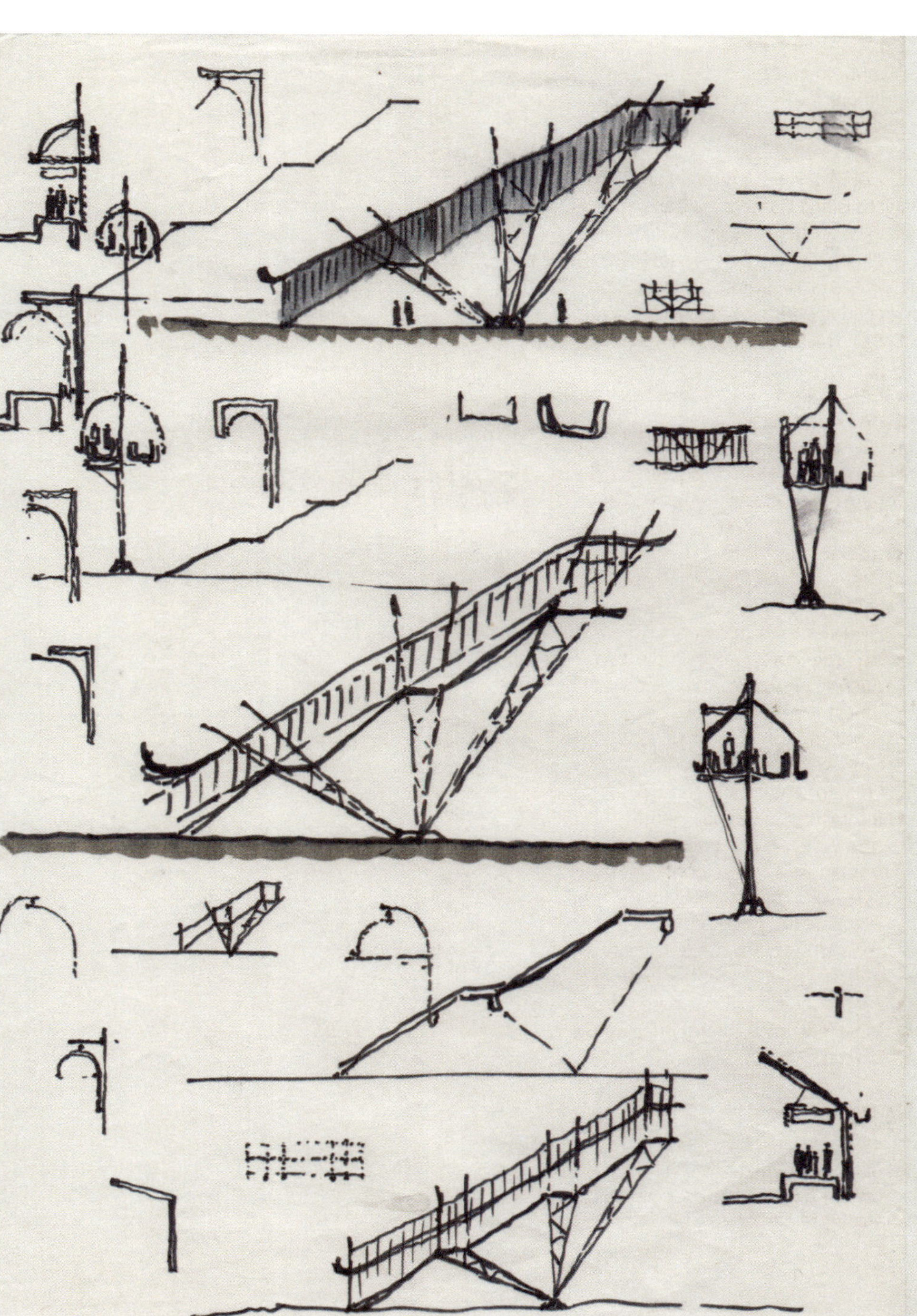

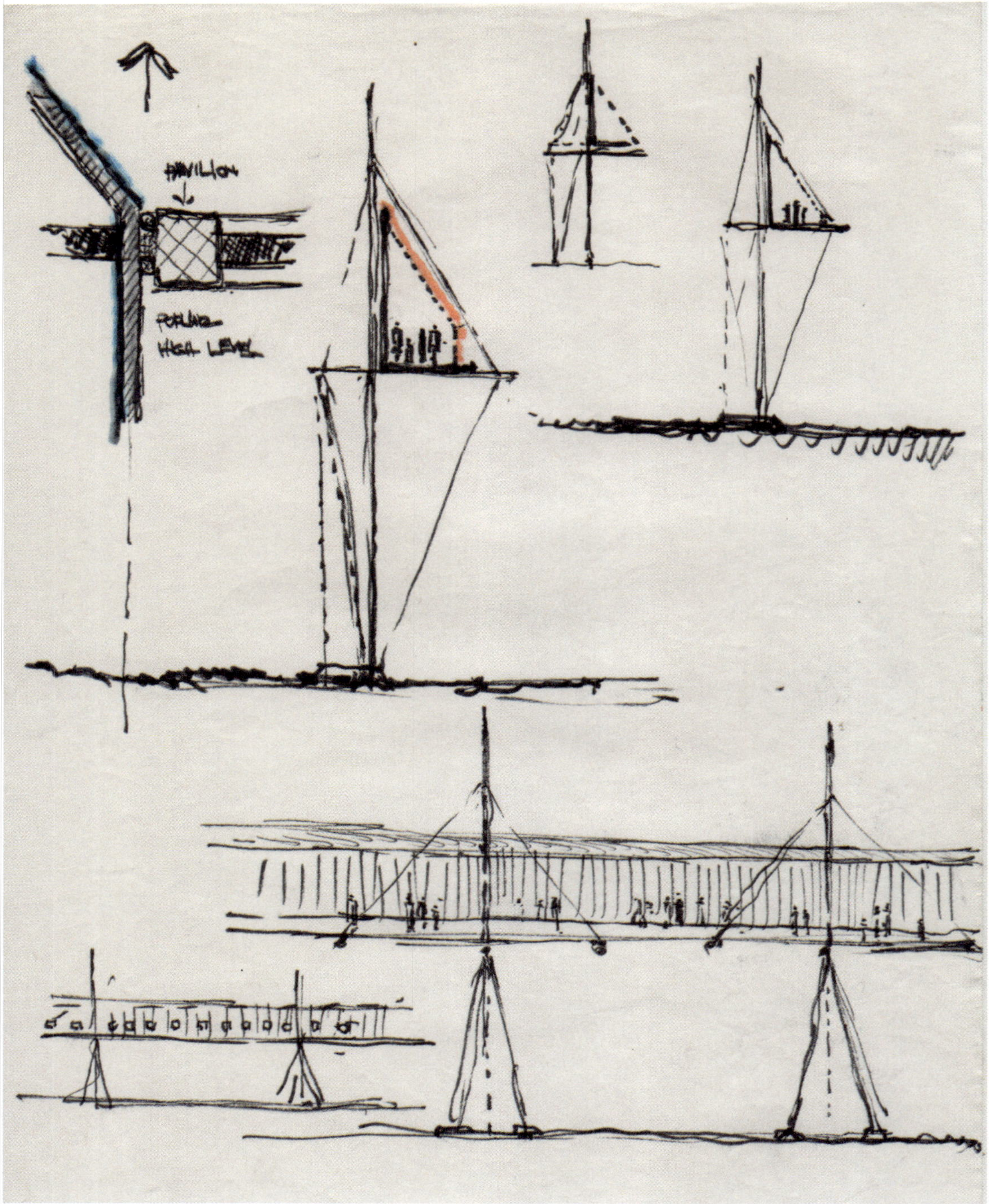

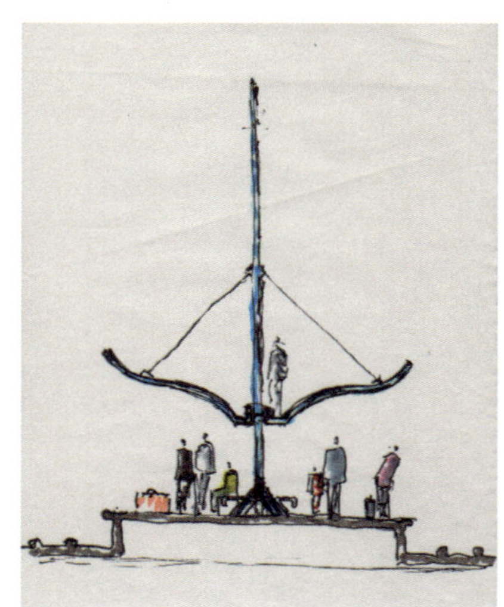

*Bridge elements suspended from
triangulated support structures.*

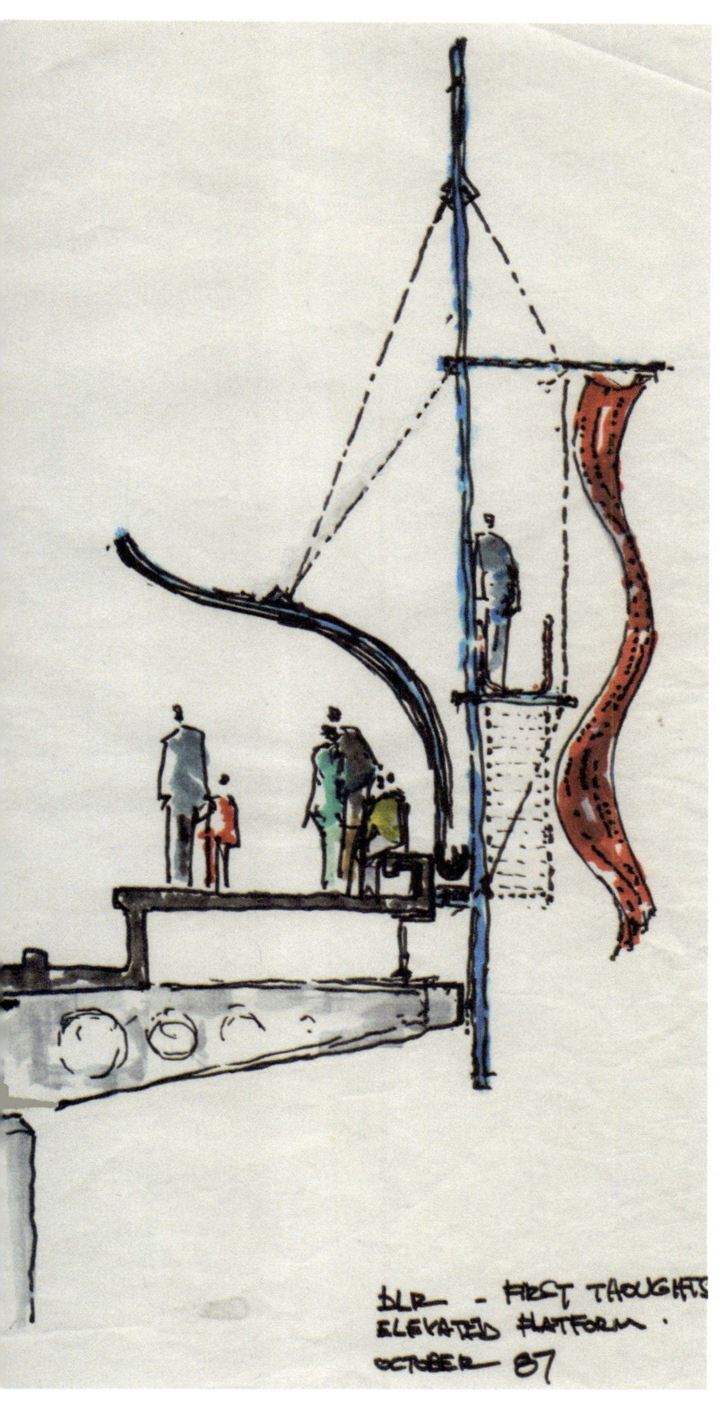

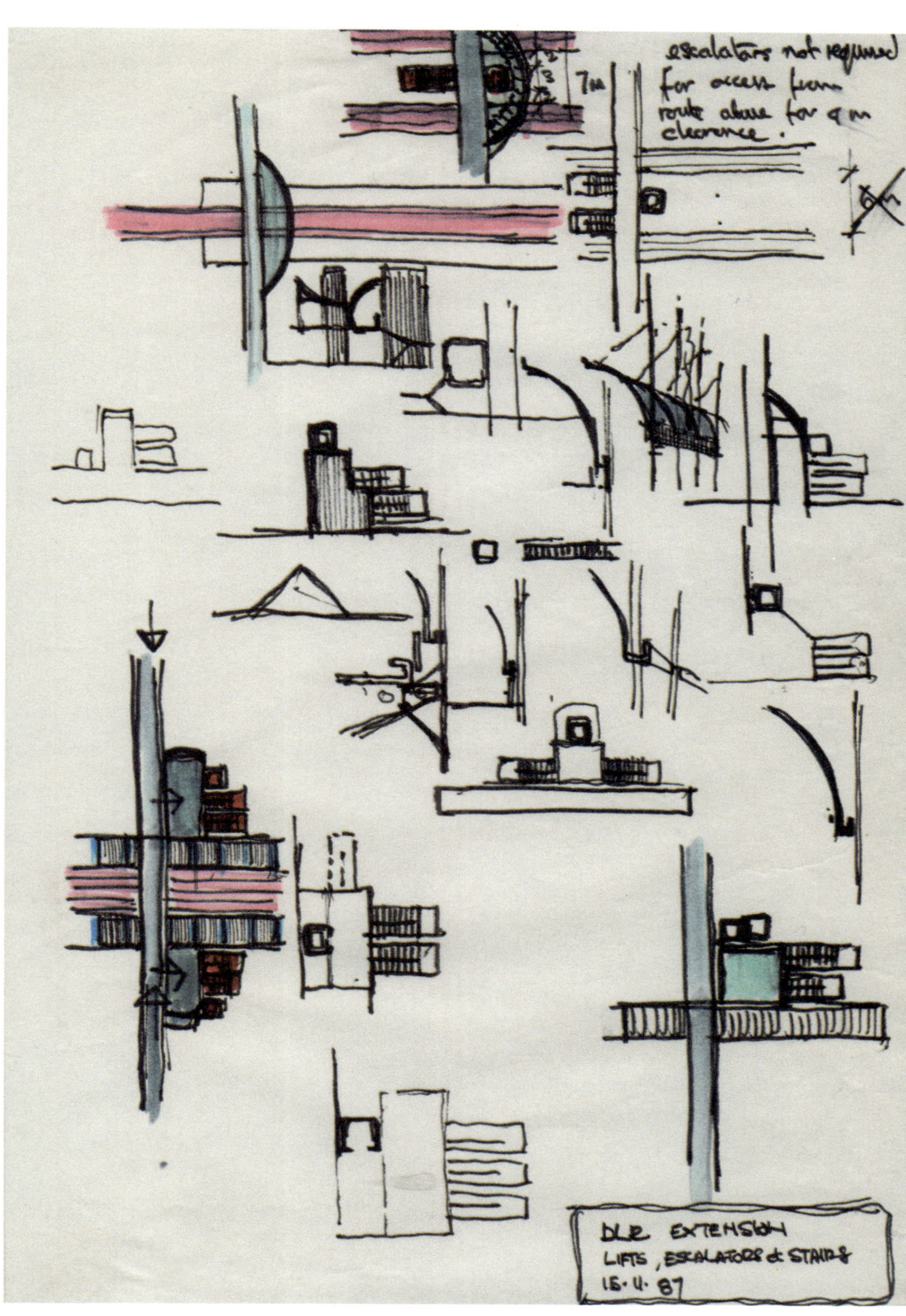

A particular aim with the station designs was to try to achieve 'more with less', by making the structures work hard and satisfy a wide range of requirements, combining loading, safety and security, shelter and signage.

This is a set of design options for the development of the headland at Sliema, on the north-east coast of Malta, embodying the historic Fort Tigné and to include a marina.

I can't recall quite how this opportunity came our way, nor how things developed thereafter – if at all. However, I'm now helped and to some extent intrigued by a questioning of the notes that accompany my sketches: references to Henry Moore's 'Helmet Head' sculptures, Valletta's urban block as a comparative model, incarceration (the fort and its meanings, then and now?) and the geometries of circles and angularities….

1988

Planning redevelopment proposals for Tigné Point, site of the former British barracks in the prosperous town of Sliema.

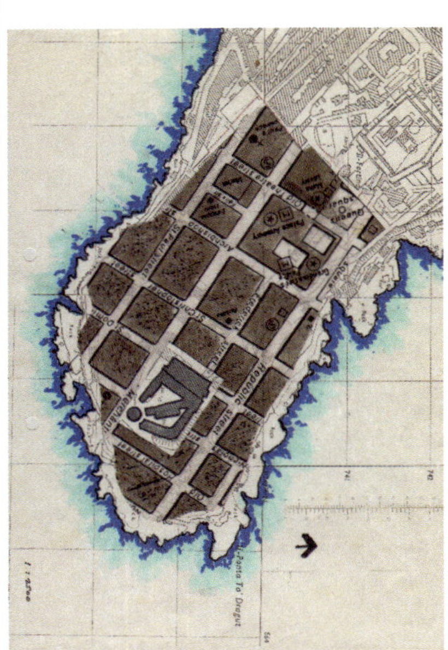

Sliema is located on a peninsula of land facing across the water to Valletta. Fort Tigné, sited near the end of the peninsula, was built by the Order of Saint John in 1795 and remained in military use up to 1979. Recently restored, it forms a focal point in redevelopment plans for the area.

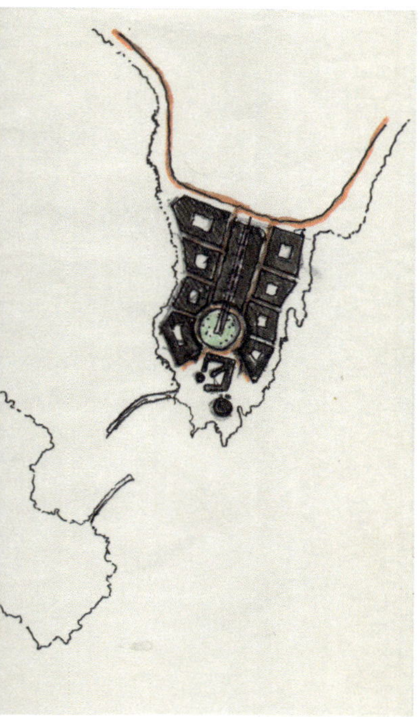

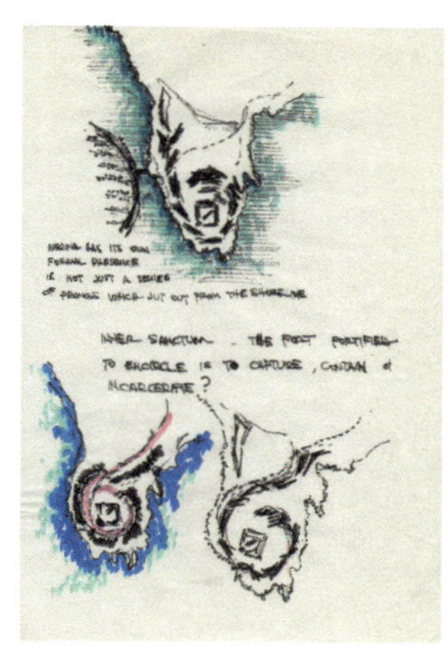

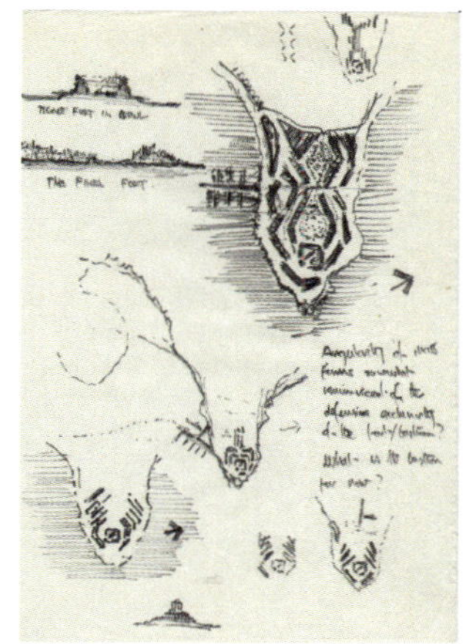

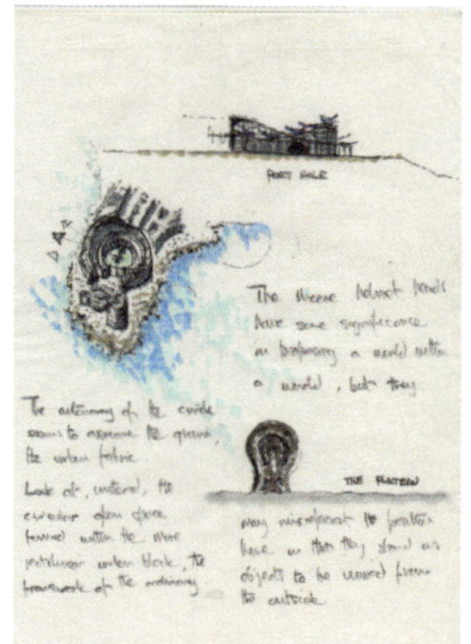

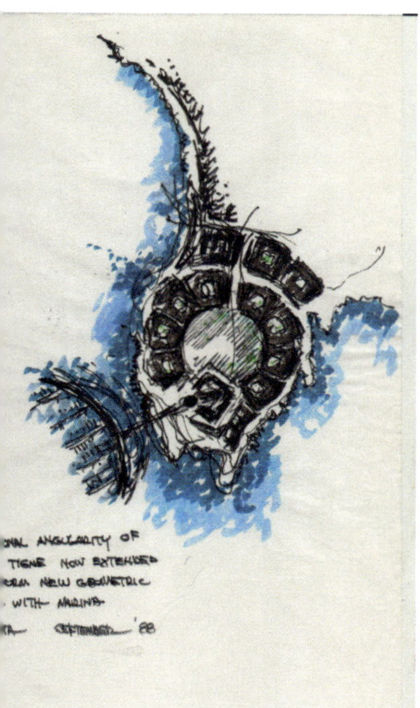

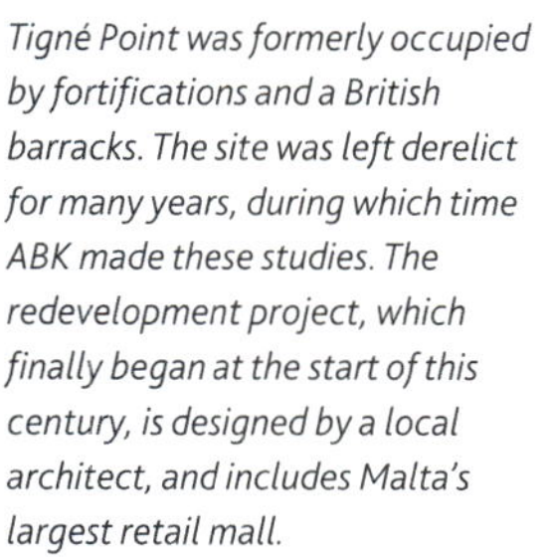

Tigné Point was formerly occupied by fortifications and a British barracks. The site was left derelict for many years, during which time ABK made these studies. The redevelopment project, which finally began at the start of this century, is designed by a local architect, and includes Malta's largest retail mall.

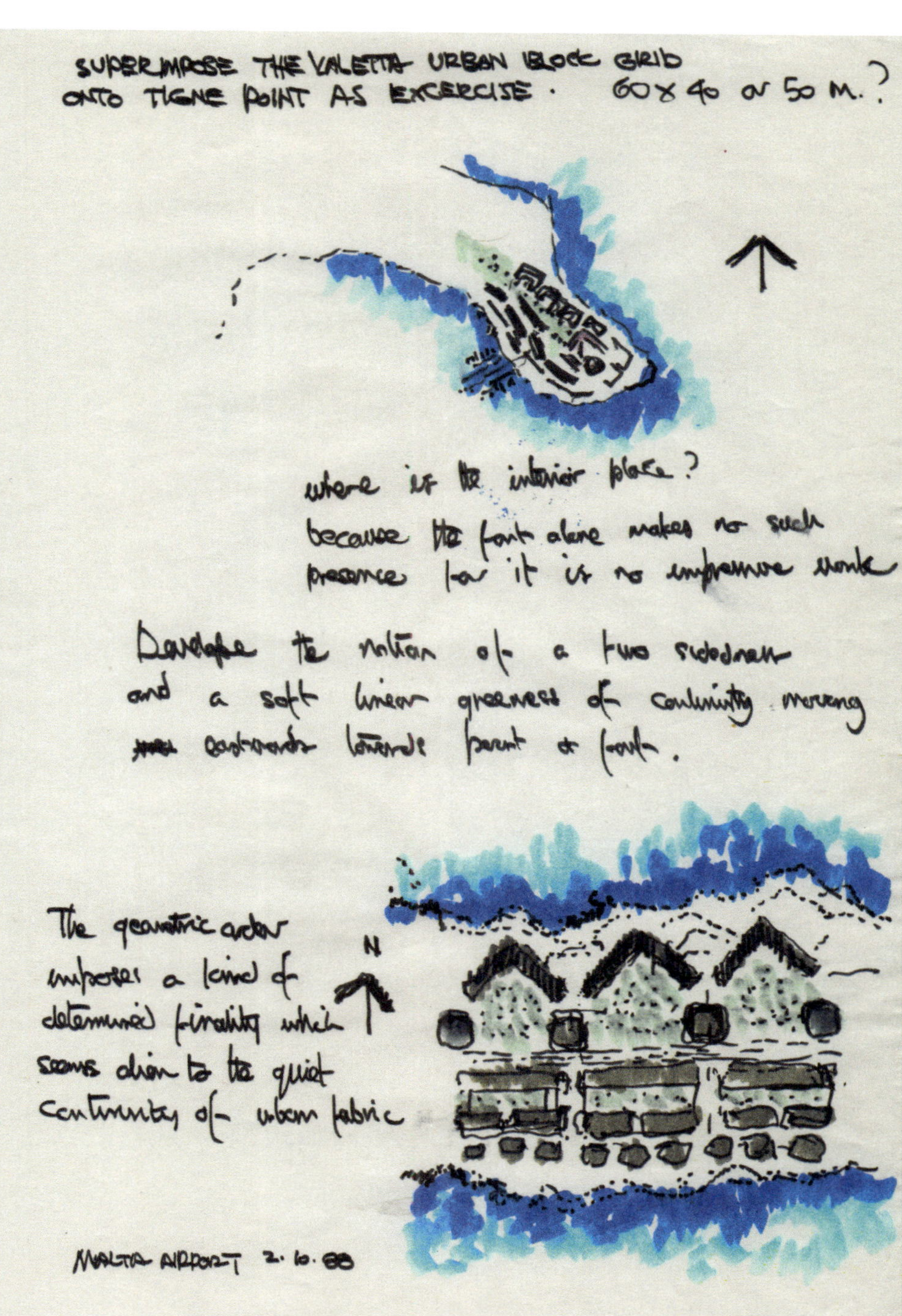

Analysis of local urban precedents informed the design process.

Was it, I now wonder, the opportunity to consider these then unknown stretches of the Thames at Brentford that first drew us to this planning brief? Twenty years later, without documentation of either the brief or our final submission, I find myself frustrated in my search to find a way back to a coherence of ideas that, no doubt, would have been apparent to me at that time. Instead, with a sense of some relief, my post-hoc laziness prevails, offering permission to leave the sketches to be no more than themselves, alone on these pages.

1996

Redevelopment of this prominent site on the Grand Union Canal in west London has been subject to lengthy deliberation, but work is now finally under way.

Brentford Lock urban design competition

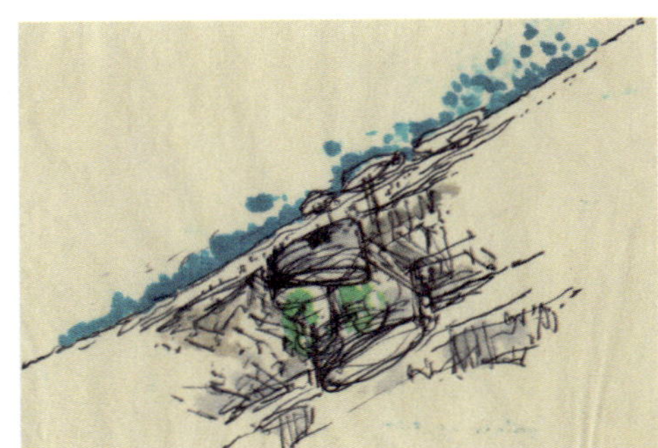

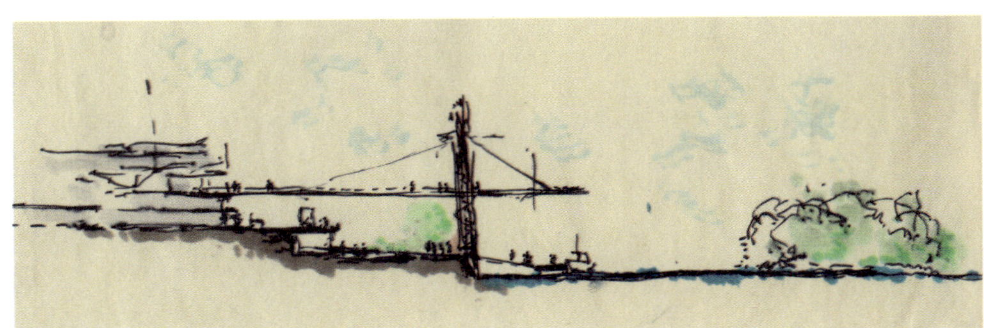

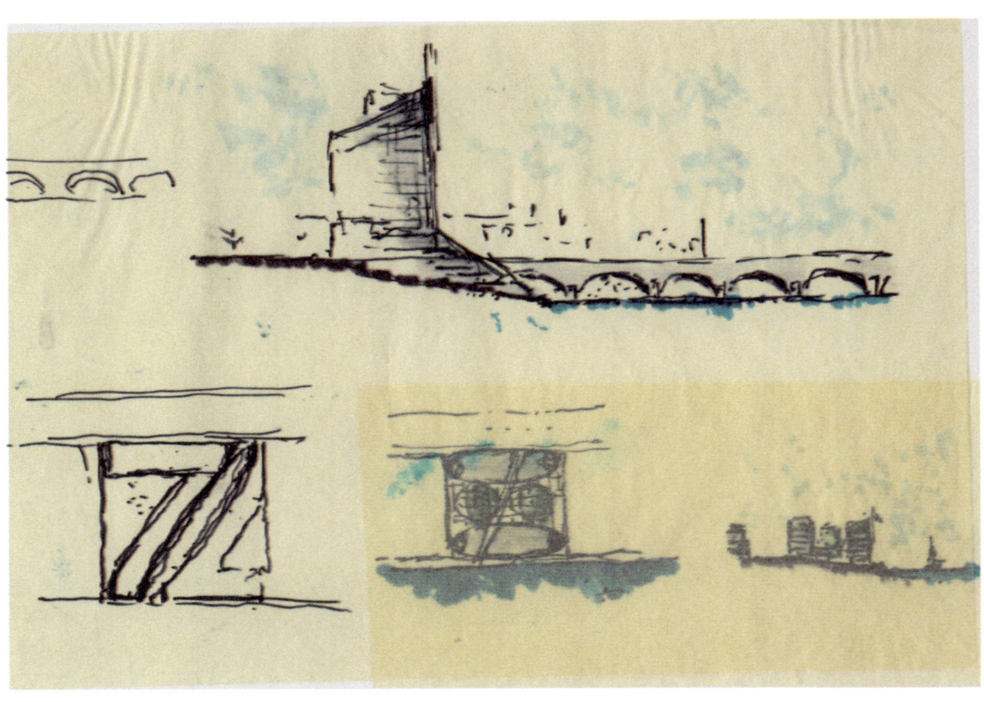

A variety of different options and approaches are explored in these sketches, from high-rise residential blocks and landmark bridges to lower, linear buildings defining green waterside parks.

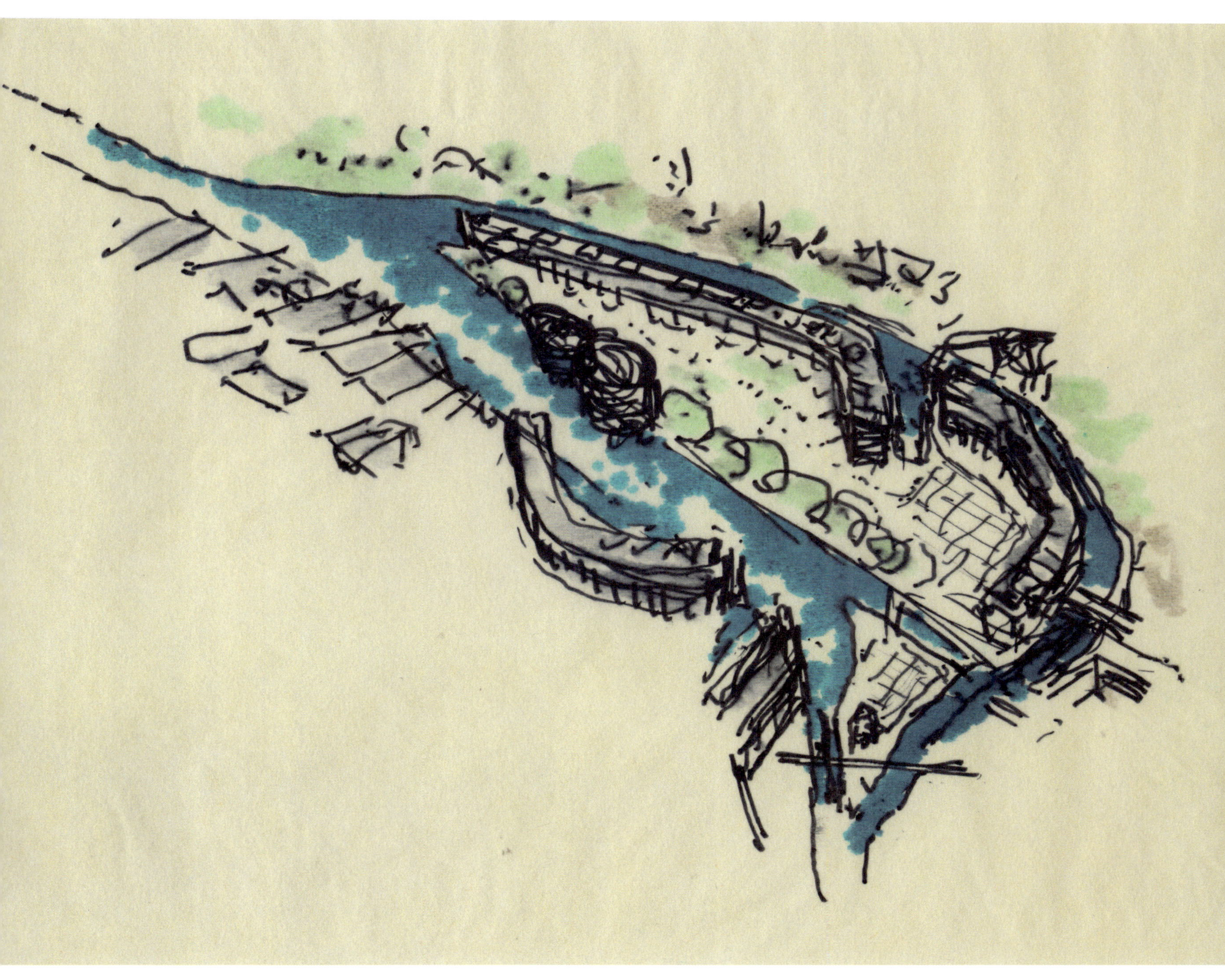

Looking through this bundle of sketches again, I've become aware of the amount of design energy that architects invest in every outline planning consent to help ensure that, if built, the project would have the expected character and coherency.

In this case, where perhaps London Underground may have required no more than a planning sufficiency for an outline approval (eg zoning of elements such as entrances, platform canopies, lifts and stairs), we went much further, as part of a compelling drive to make it well, enhancing the weight/mass of a historic brick-arched viaduct by a contrasting lightness of new modern elements.

Later, when permission is granted, you can find that a different development agency has been appointed with a new architect; so you question what it's all been about. Is it, perhaps, that the production of a surplus of design energy, wastage and consequent redundancies are inherent in the frameworks of tick-box competitive procedures?

1993

Station design options for a planned extension to the East London rail line, now part of the capital's 'Overground' network.

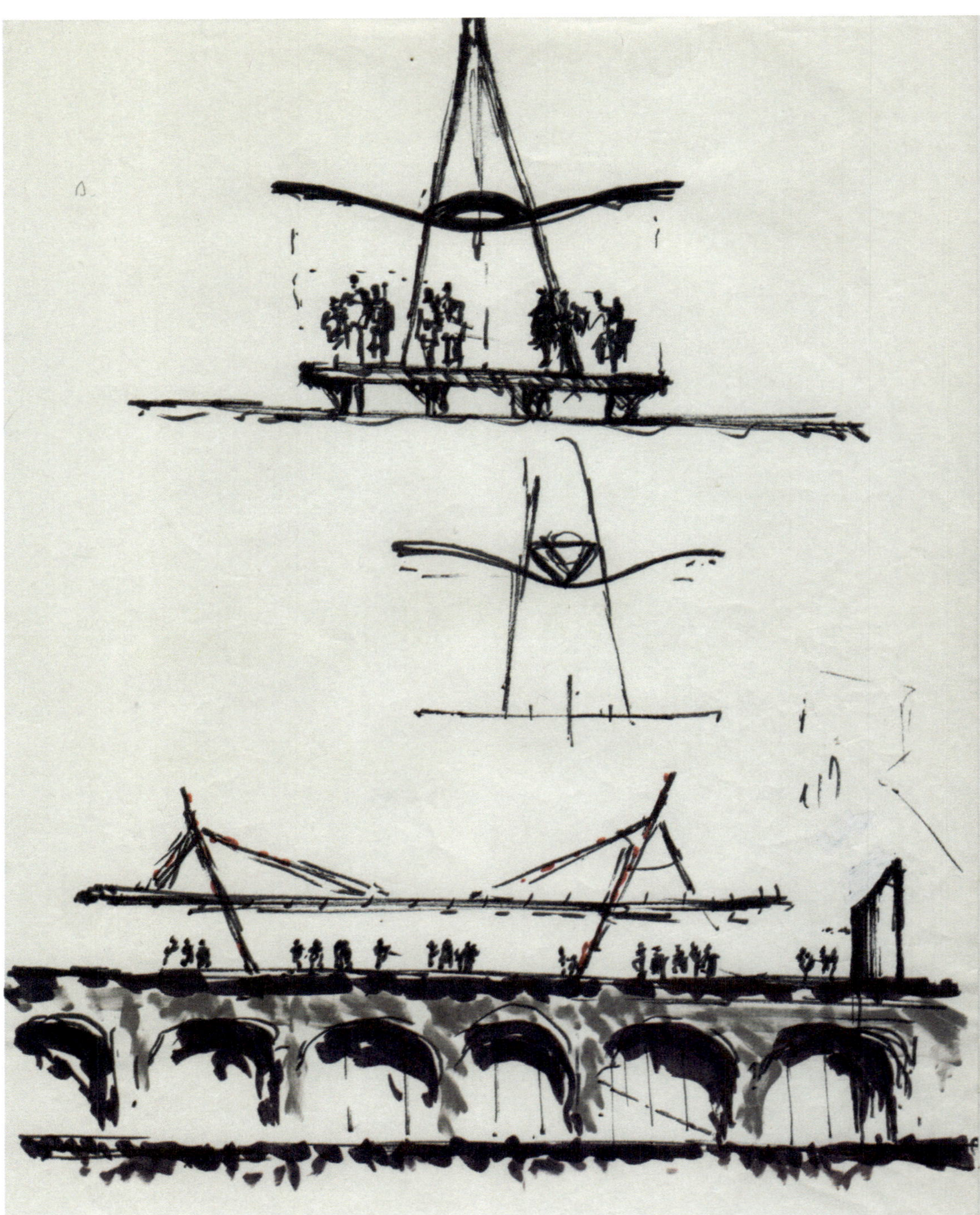

The 1993 plan – one of several made since the 1980s to extend the East London Line – proposed a route from Whitechapel to Dalston Junction, with new stations at Bishopsgate, Hoxton and Haggerston. Construction was due to begin in 1996 but this project was put on hold in 1997.

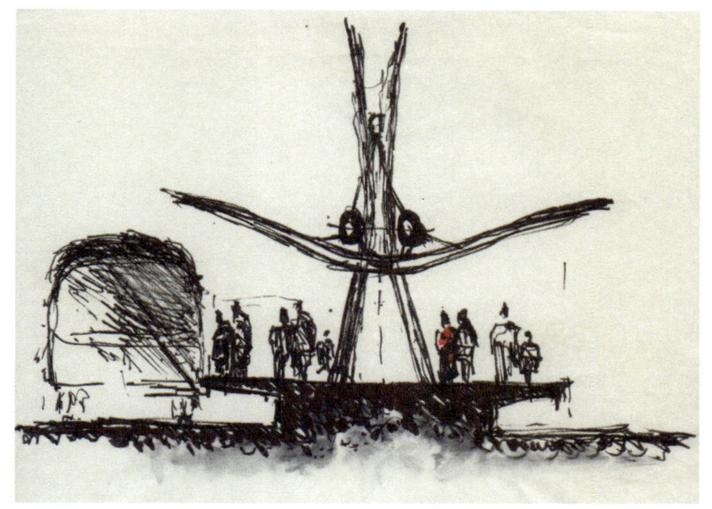

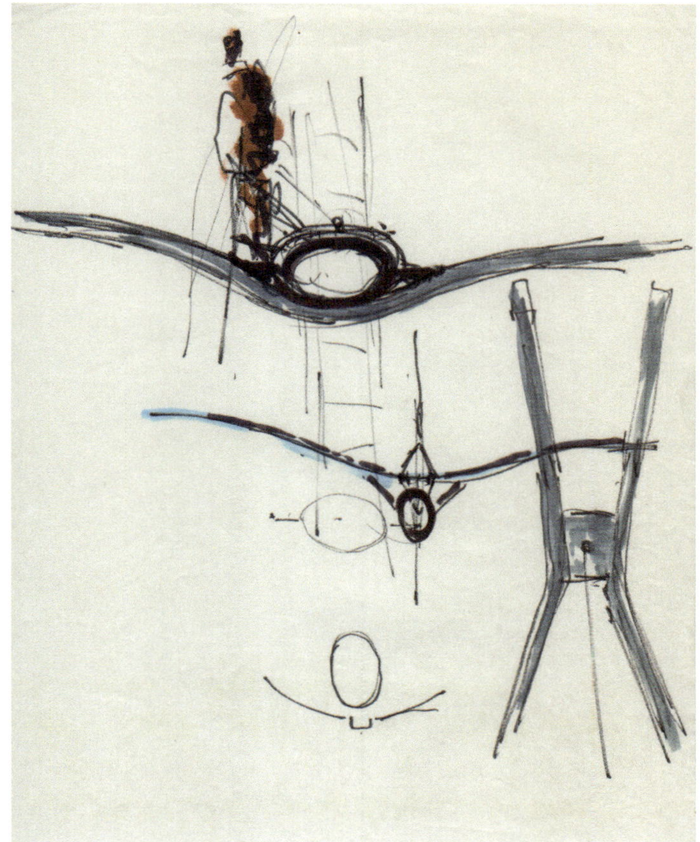

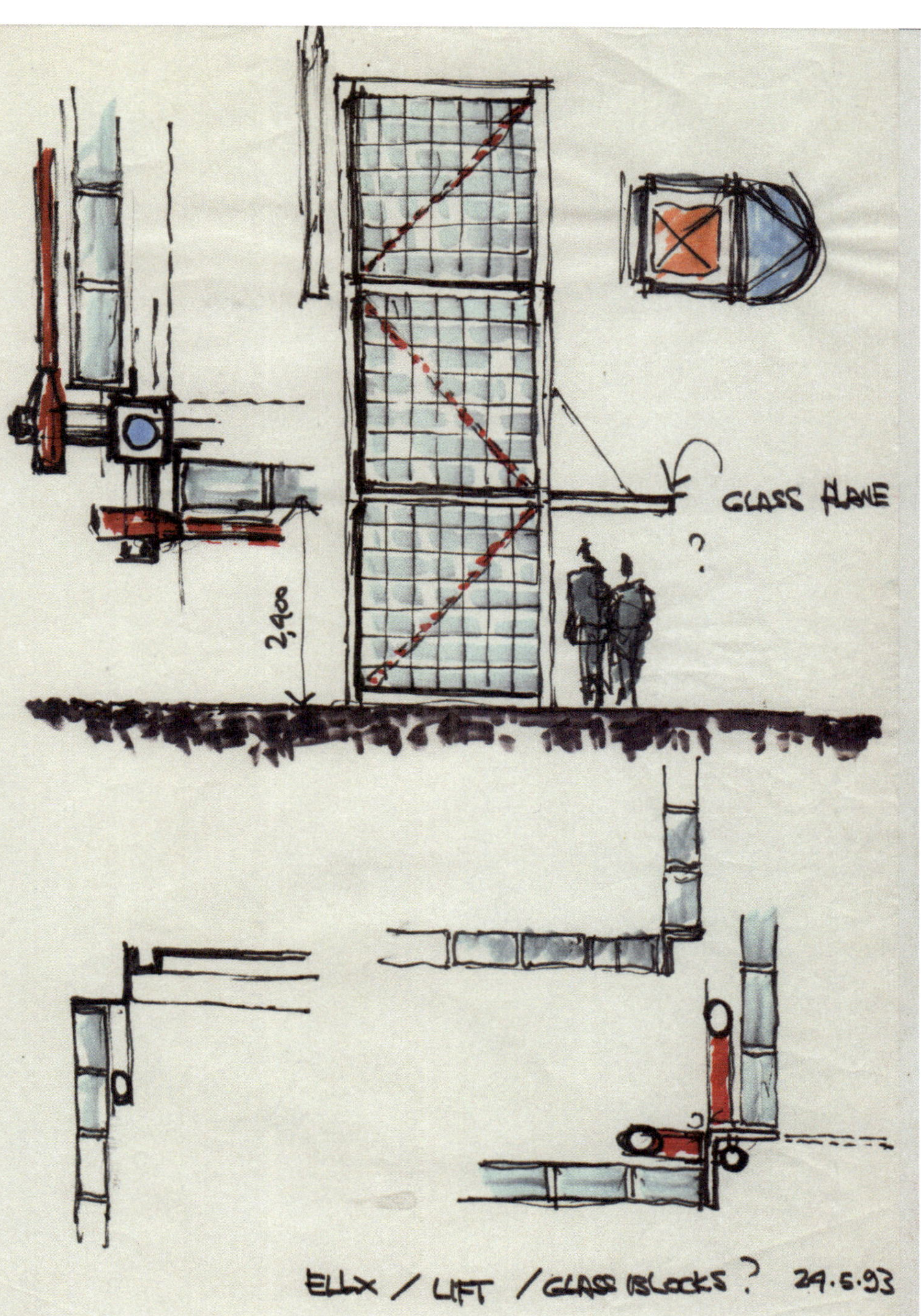

GLASS FLANE
?
2,400
ELLX / LIFT / GLASS BLOCKS ?   29.5.93

These few sketches were intended to be no more than a quick response to a passing remark made by a friend, Dan Darin, who for some years was the deputy mayor of Tel Aviv. I first came to know Dan when he was a student at the Architectural Association where I taught for a while in the early 1960s. We met occasionally over the years, once in Tel Aviv when he'd spoken in passing of a dream-plan for an offshore development, a new outrigger to the city's beachline. Crazy, of course, but I thought it was worth sending it on to him to give form to the idea – a gesture of two interweaving road alignments with buildings placed as chevron-like punctuations along them.

In later years I found myself recalling these thoughts when our ideas for the high-rise alignments for the Leven Road scheme, situated beside the River Lea south of the Olympic-Park-to-be, first came to mind.

1994

An idea, in passing, for a feature offshore from Tel Aviv's Mediterranean coast.

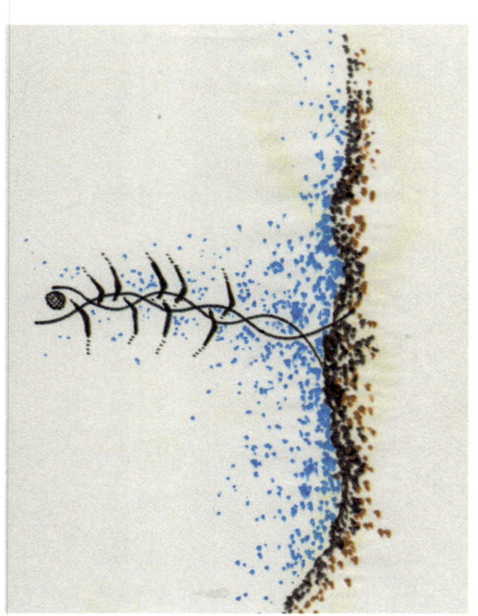

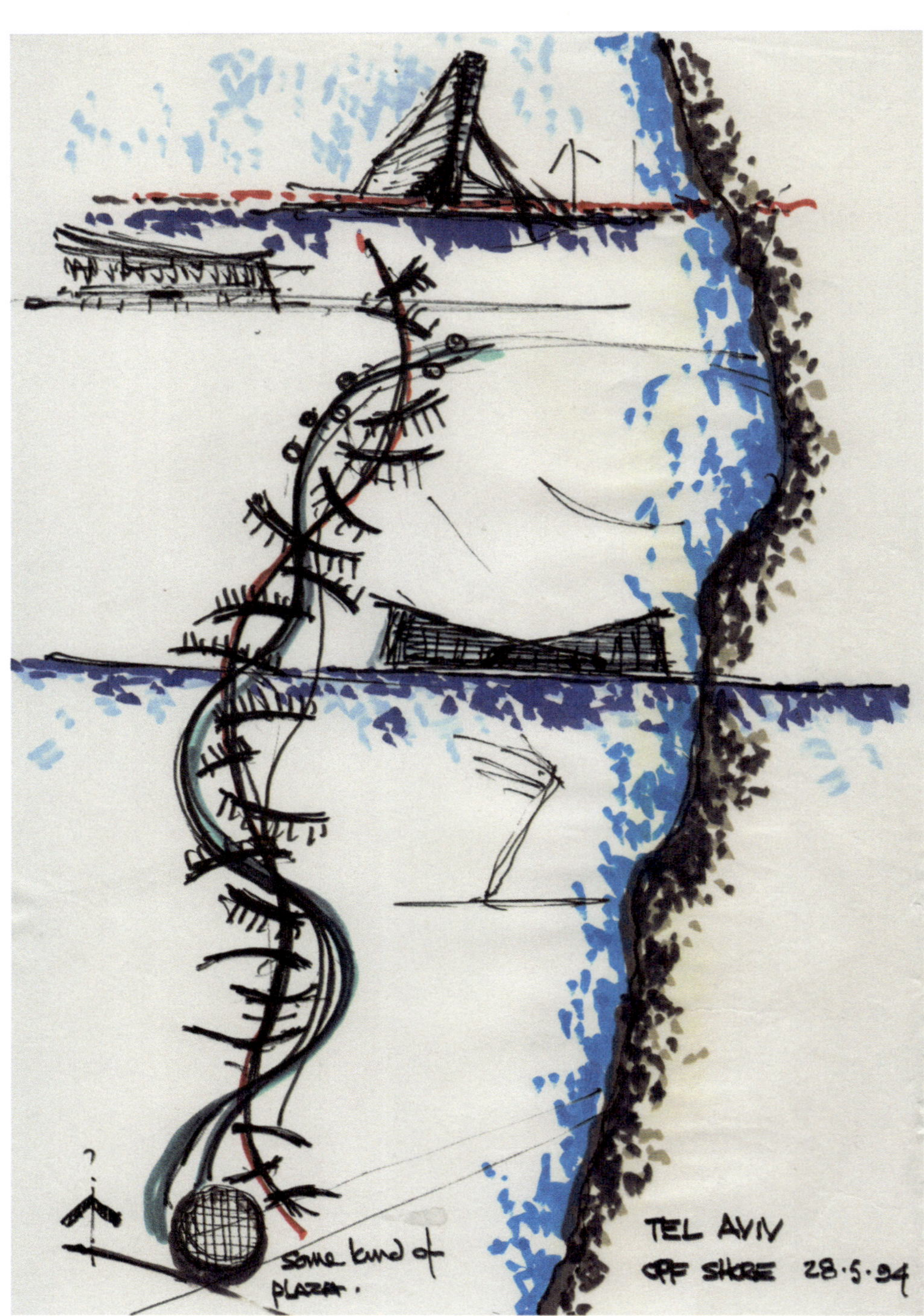

The meandering pier structure, punctuated by multi-storey buildings of different heights, would terminate in a seaward plaza, a destination for perambulation.

This was an interesting competition which, I later learned, culminated in a selection procedure which had an unusual twist.

I took to the brief's rich mix of elements and a site that benefitted from a narrow green, a former canal running along the inner faces of the buildings on Peckham Hill Street. This suggested an opportunity to make a new street-related community building that would enjoy the open space lying along its inner face; an accessible street/garden linear strip that came to provide the underlying theme for our set of site-arrangement options.

On hearing that we'd narrowly missed out to Will Alsop, I asked the borough architect for feedback. Apparently the selection panel had reached the view that ABK's and Alsop's schemes had equal but very different merits. How, they had wondered, should they proceed? Toss a coin, perhaps?

1993

A high-profile competition for a library for the twenty-first century in the south London borough, won by Will Alsop.

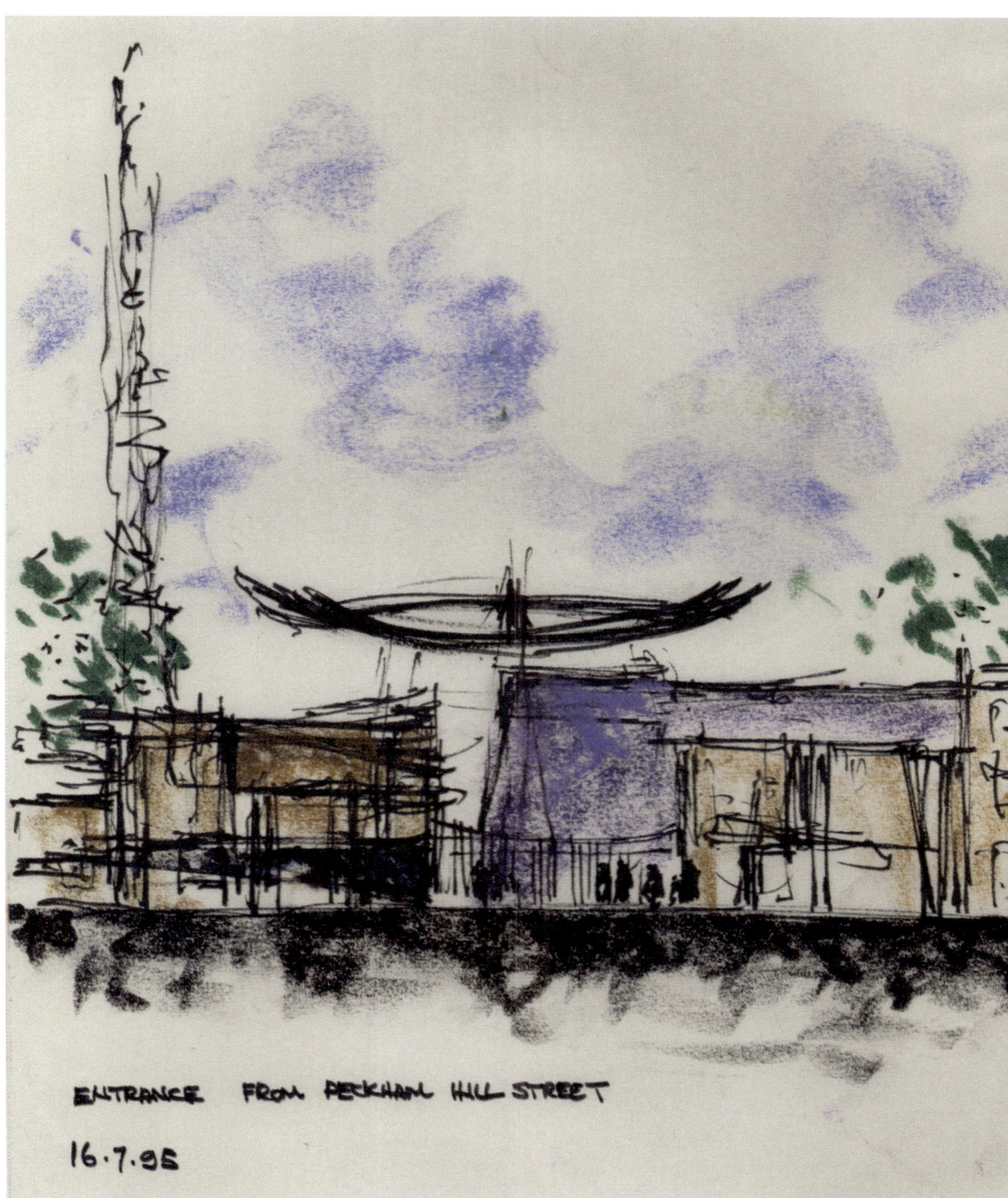

A richly layered collage of building forms and treatments addresses Peckham Hill Street.

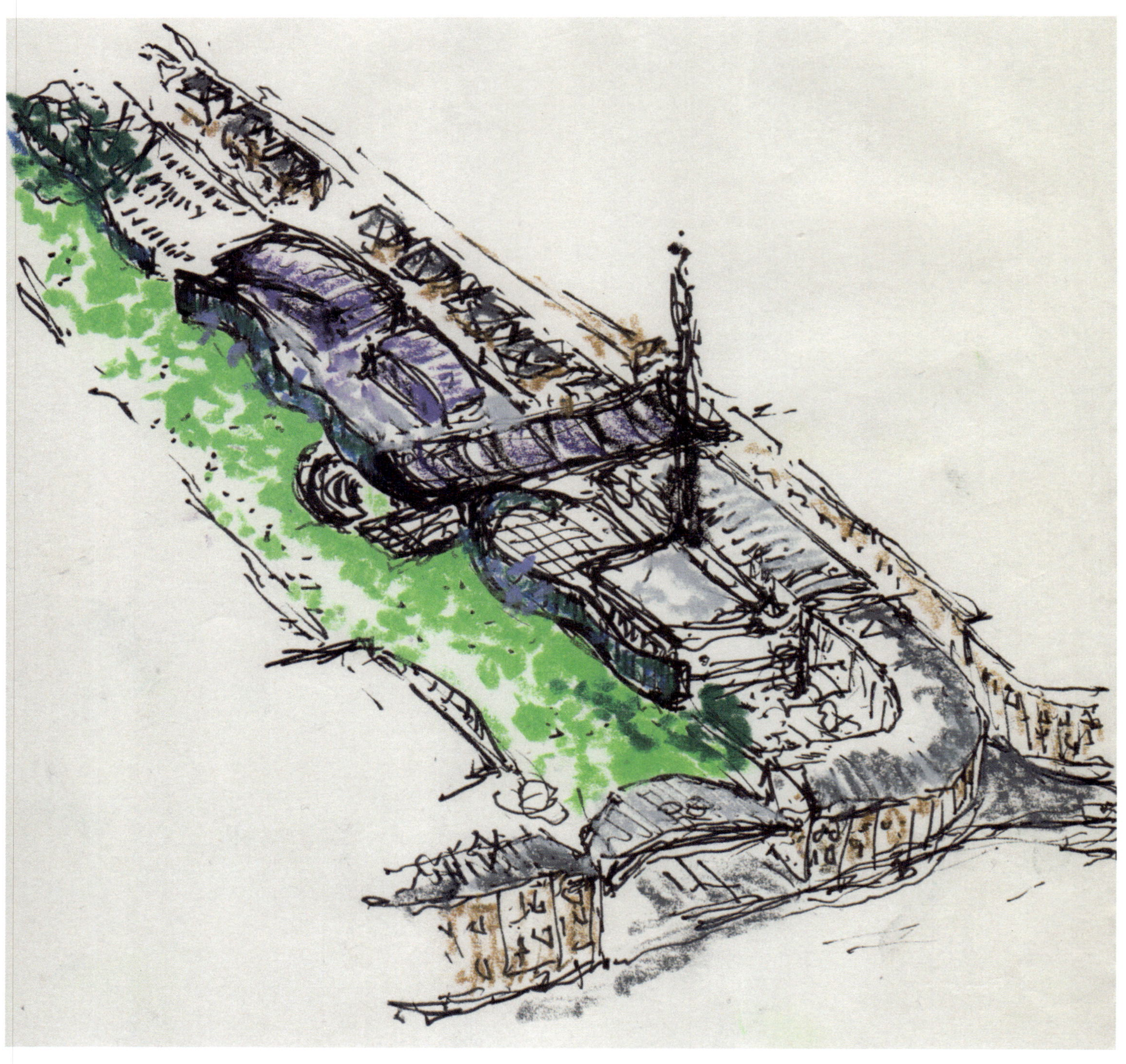

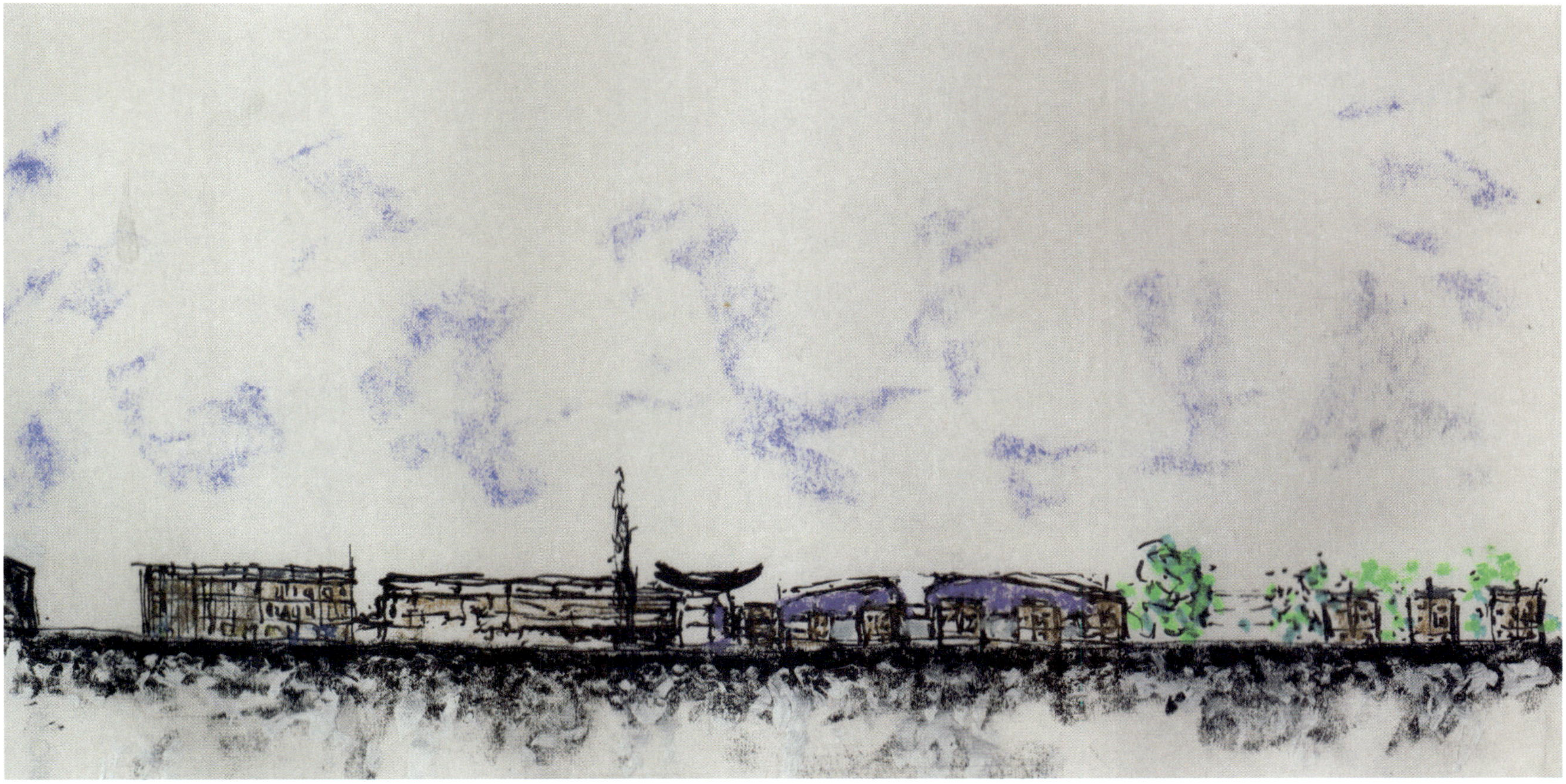

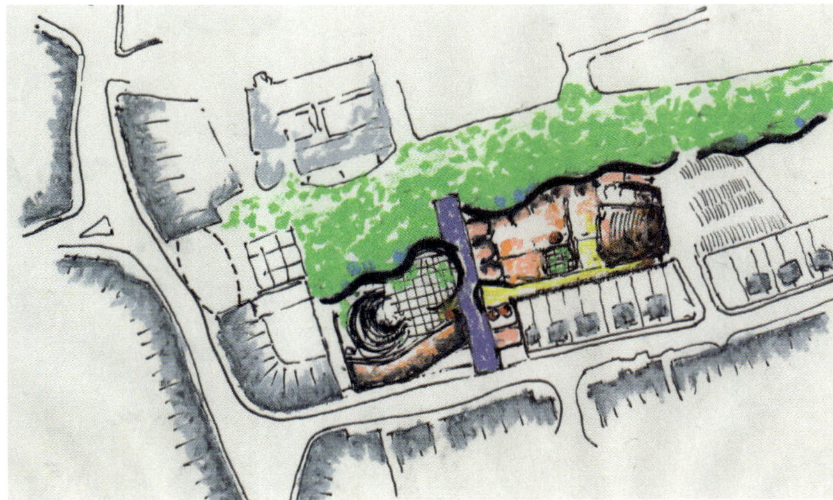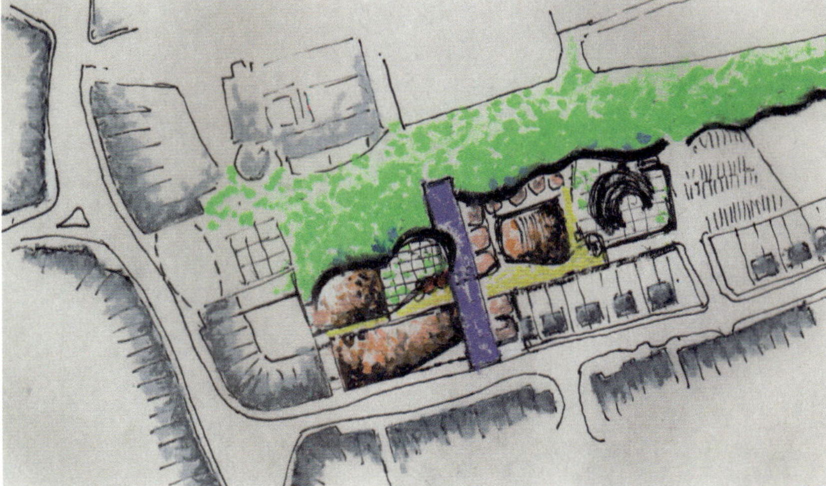

*Elevation study and exploratory
plan alternatives, disagregating the
various elements of the brief into
identifiable architectural forms.*

In the early 1960s, when ABK's team numbered six to eight people, then working on the early design stages of Trinity College Library (later the Berkeley Library) and Chichester Theological College, we opened our first 'real' office on the top floor of a former 'sweatshop' in Carter Lane, no more than a long stone's throw from St Paul's Cathedral. Why there? Cheap rent, at the time. The raised-deck development for the adjacent bomb-damaged Paternoster area was under construction. Not a beauty, but William Holford's scheme tied into the City of London's 'of-it's-time' planning vision of raised pedestrian 'pedways' and traffic-segregated decks that was also implemented further north at the Barbican. Later, in the site arrangement of our unbuilt 1970s' scheme for the Post Office headquarters offices on Newgate Street, we had planned to subvert this policy.

In 1986 Standard Life commissioned us to design a replacement office building on Shaftesbury Avenue. For funding reasons this came to nothing, but the client then asked us to suggest radical improvements to all of its buildings at Paternoster. These sketches touch on our substantial interventions, which envisaged a very different formal and spatial world on top of the 1960s deck. Working on the project, however, I came to think that this approach wasn't radical enough, and that the deck itself should be opened up.

With the enthusiastic support of our client, we began to consider the potential demolition of the whole site in order to make a fresh start. Instead an international competition was set up, but this foundered when Prince Charles saw another opportunity to intervene, wrecking the outcome after the winner was announced.

1988

Commissioned proposals for remaking the 1960s Paternoster district north of St Paul's.

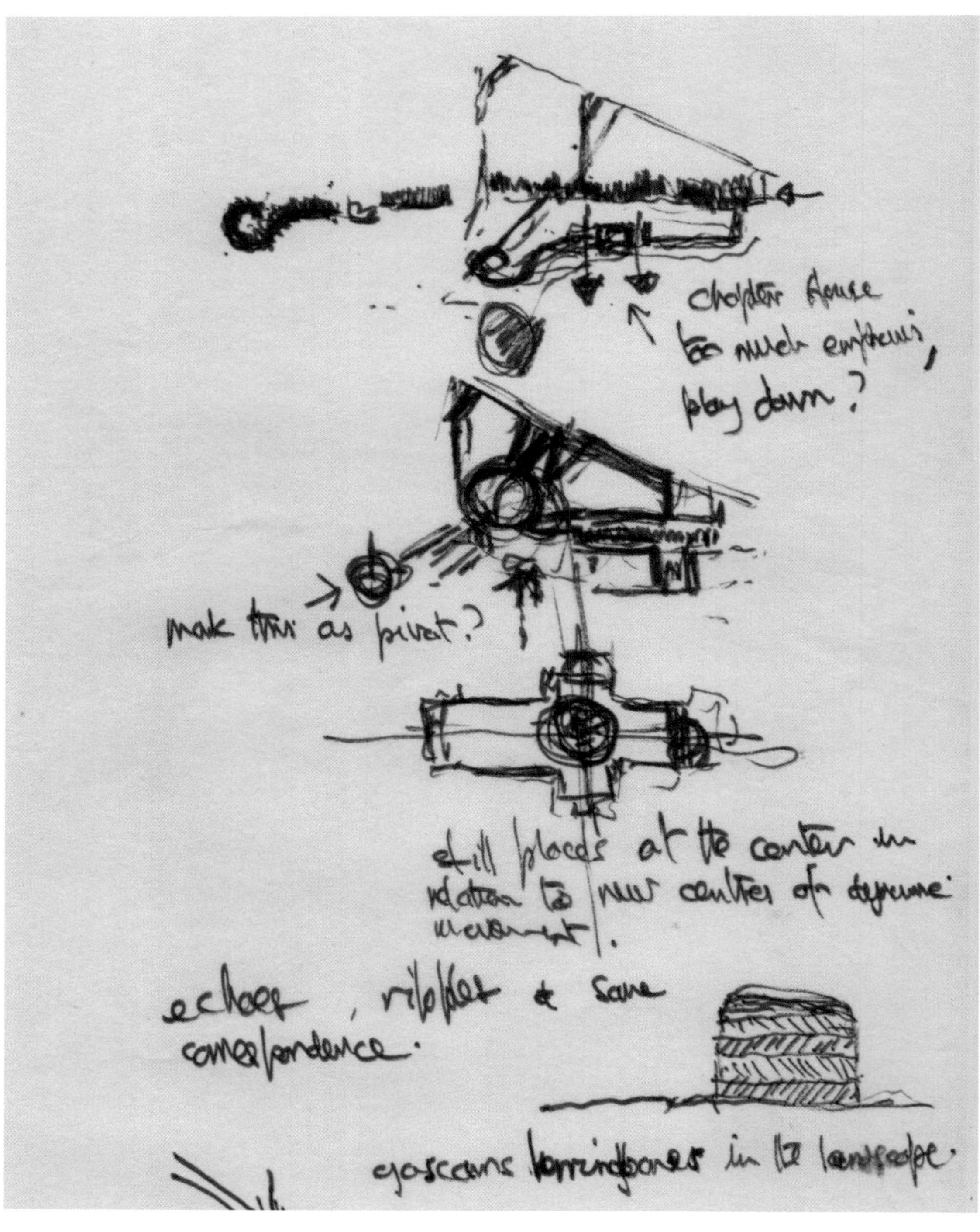

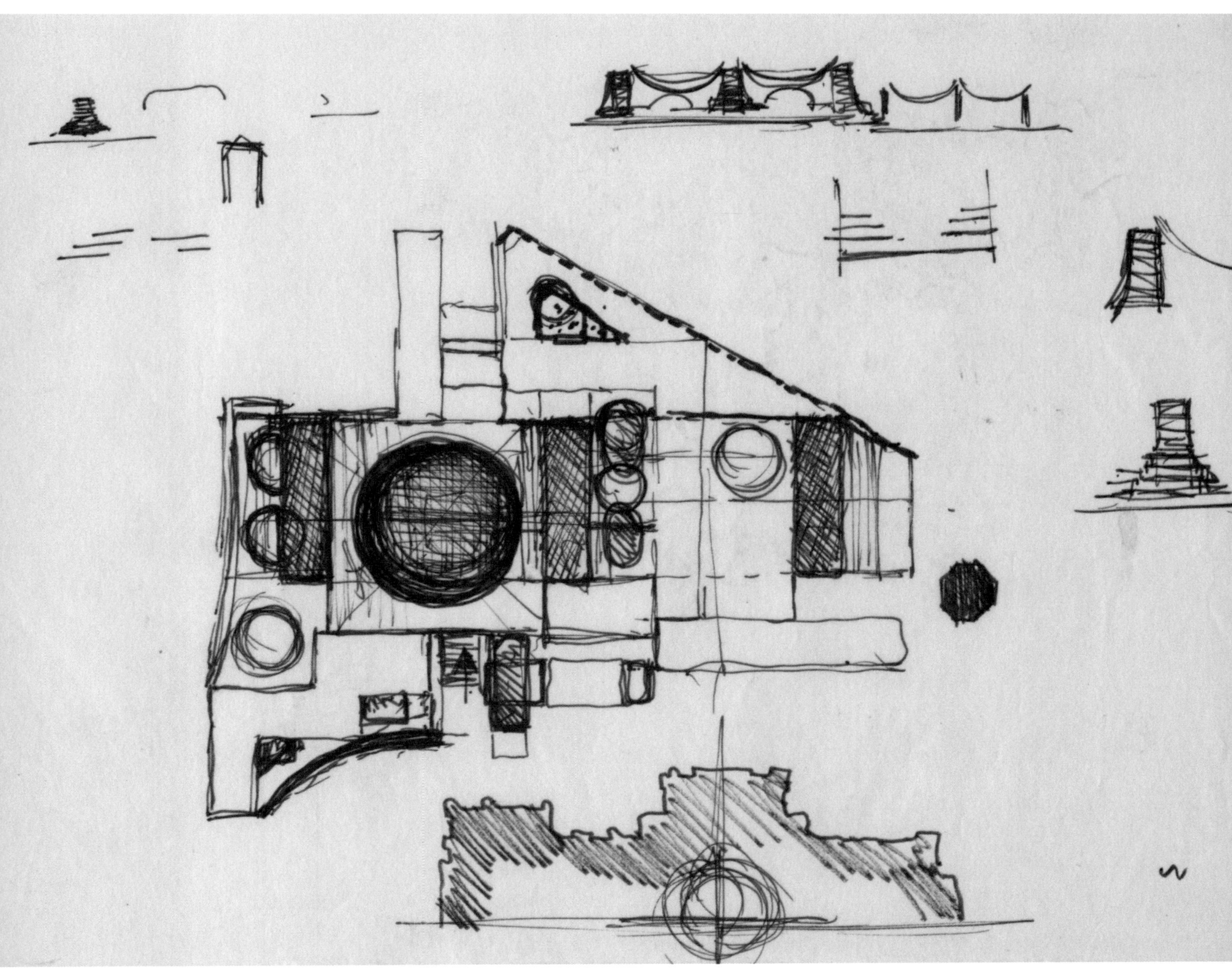

A new arrangement of buildings and spaces, set above the raised deck and woven between the existing office buildings.

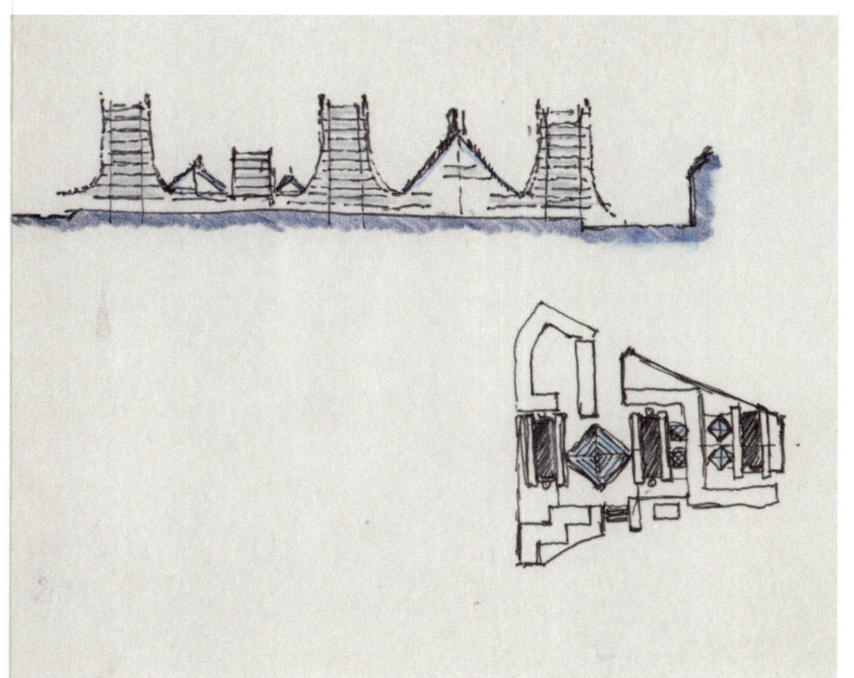

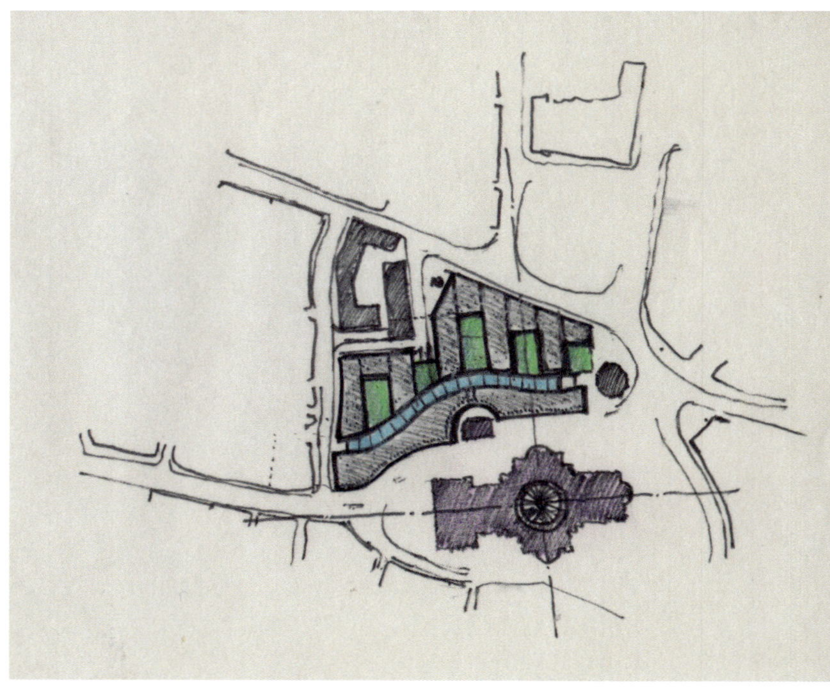

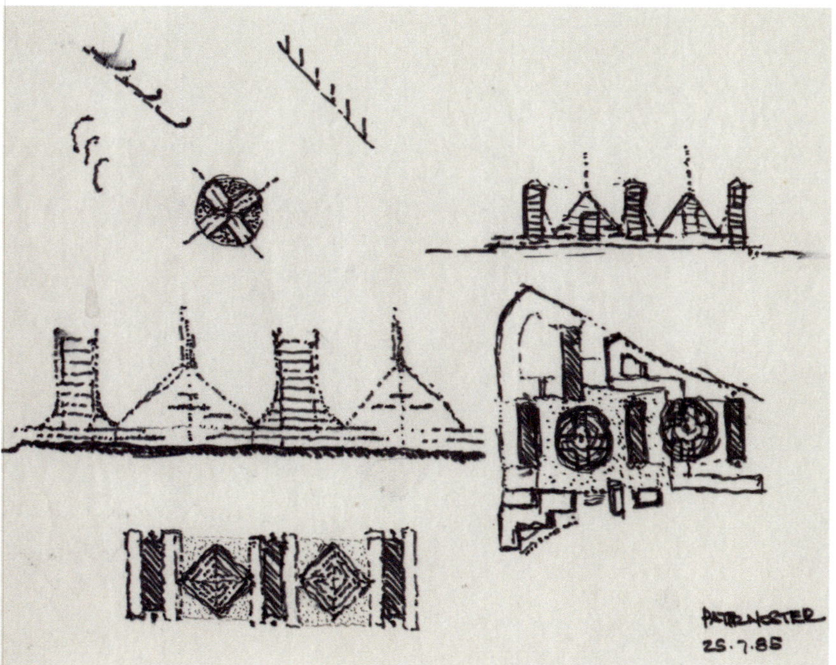

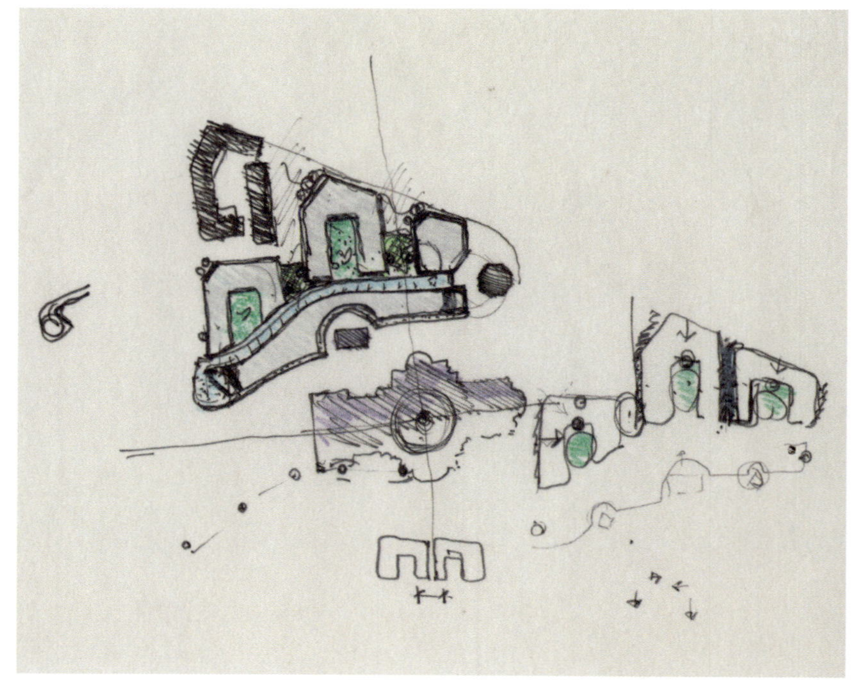

A more radical approach, in
which most of the existing
buildings are demolished to be
replaced by a permeable
development of buildings, courts
and a galleria, together forming a
coherent 'edge' to St Paul's
northern precinct.

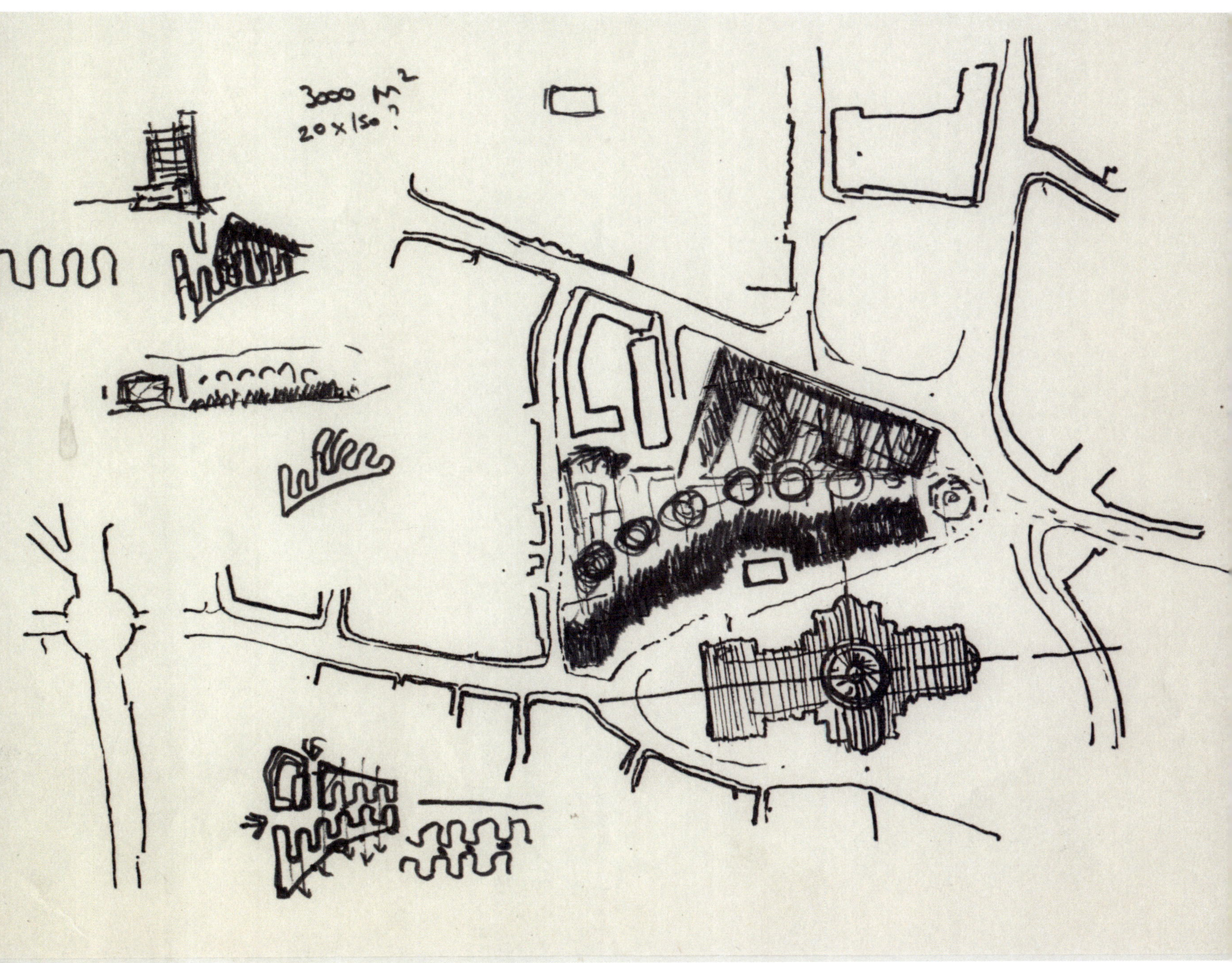

3000 m²
20 x 150 ?

This commission from Dublin City Council provided us with an opportunity to achieve a contextually meaningful mix of retained historic buildings and new architecture on Dublin's Sean McDermott Street. The range of existing buildings included a characteristic example of a Roman Catholic convent that had earlier housed young unmarried mothers and their children. The few remaining nuns needed no more than a small proportion of their buildings; even their chapel had become redundant.

Accompanied by the department's project architect, I visited the convent: the vacant dormitories where mothers had been separated from their children, the laundry – the whole sad story laid bare in a succession of disused rooms. The history was moving, and difficult to deal with, but on reflection it seemed to provide an incentive to make something strong and secular. Retain the chapel building to make of it a local library, we suggested, together with new socially-related office functions which were to take their place here to bring a new and different life.

2000

The last of Dublin's infamous Magdalene laundries closed in 1996 and was given to the city by the Sisters of Our Lady of Charity. Proximity to O'Connell Street made the site viable for development.

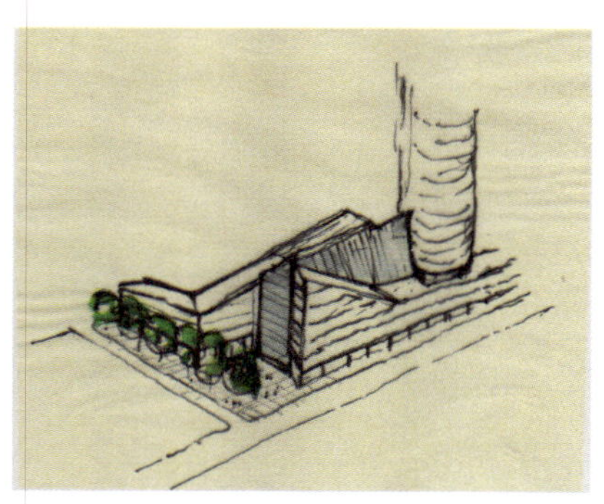

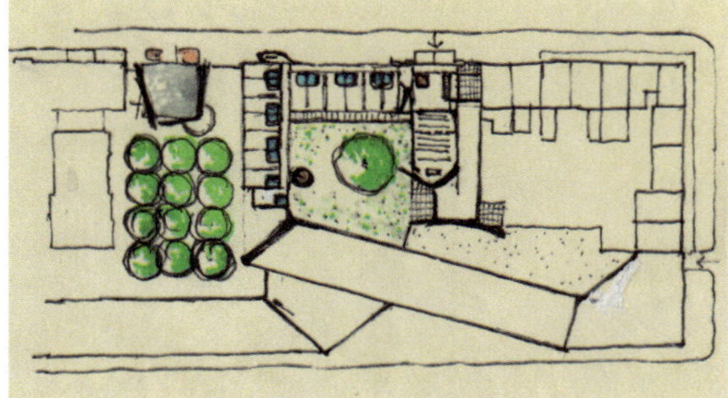

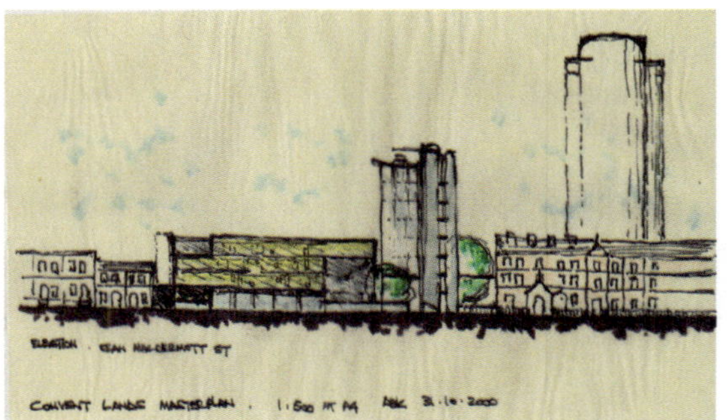

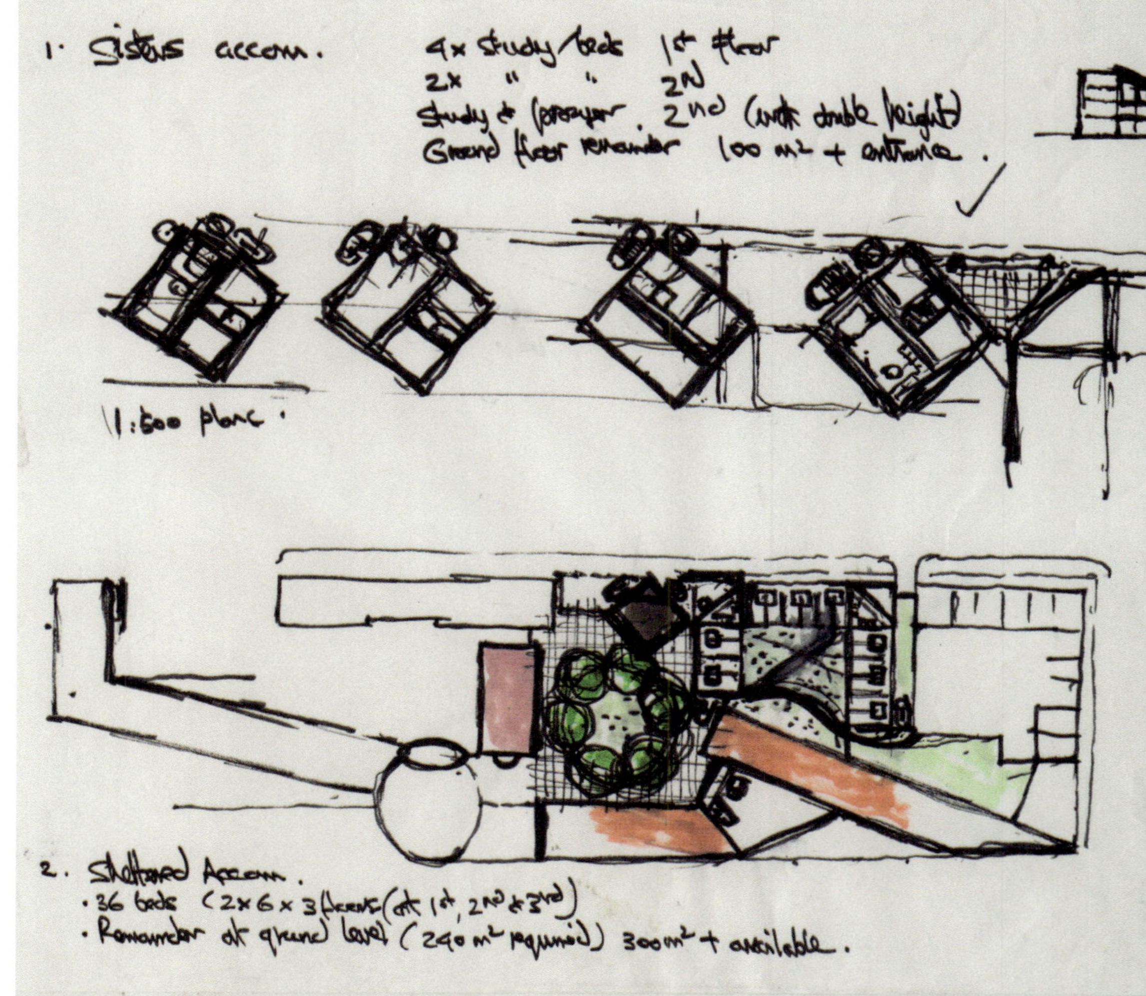

The initial ideas envisaged new interventions woven between retained historic buildings so as to form new public spaces across the site.

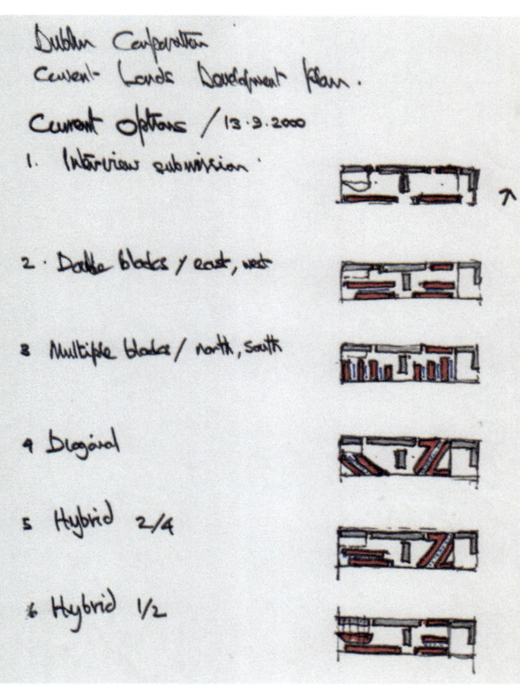

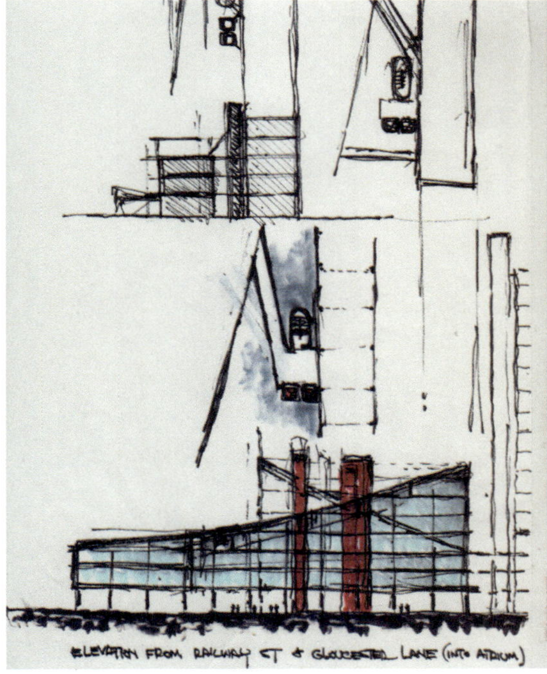

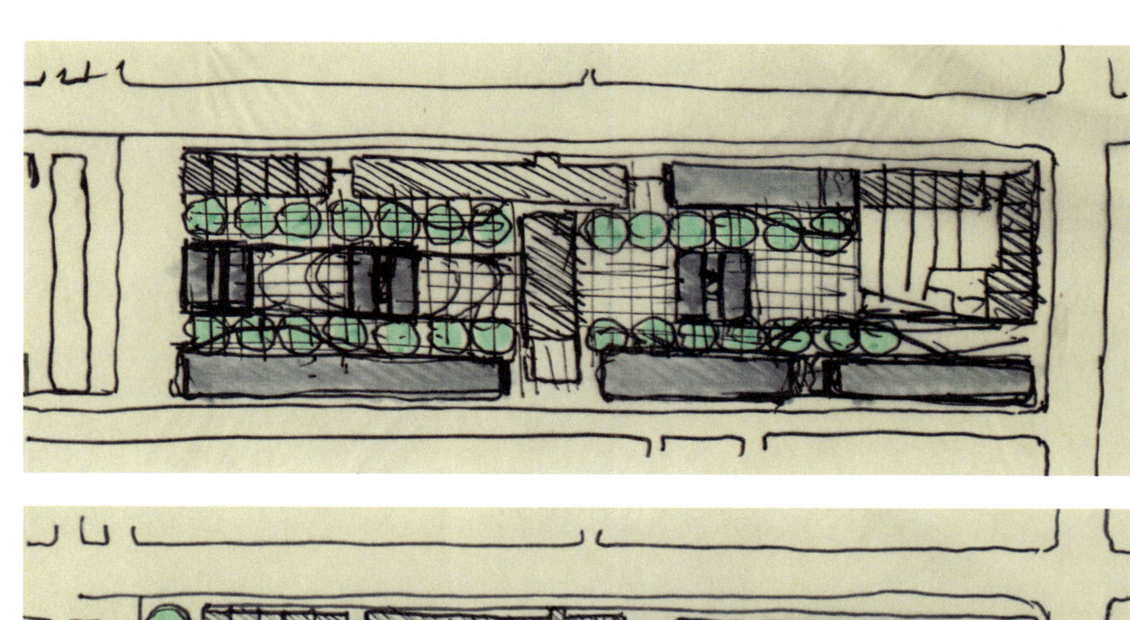

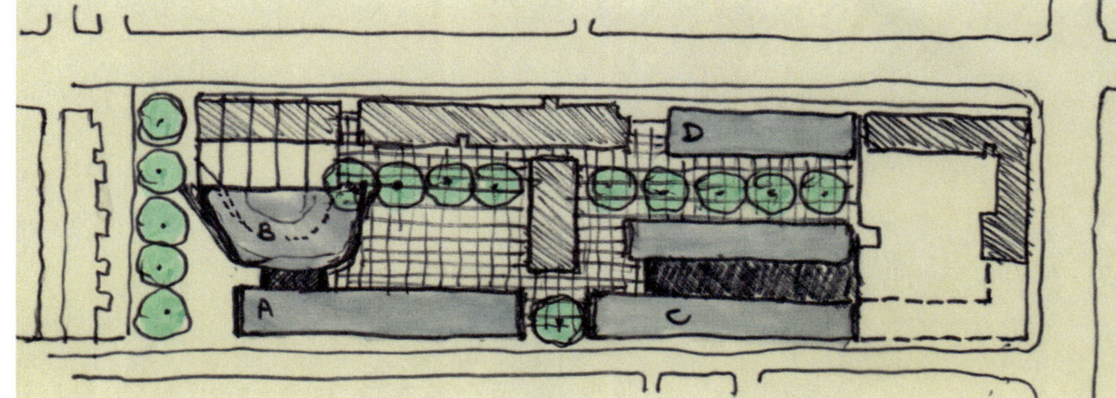

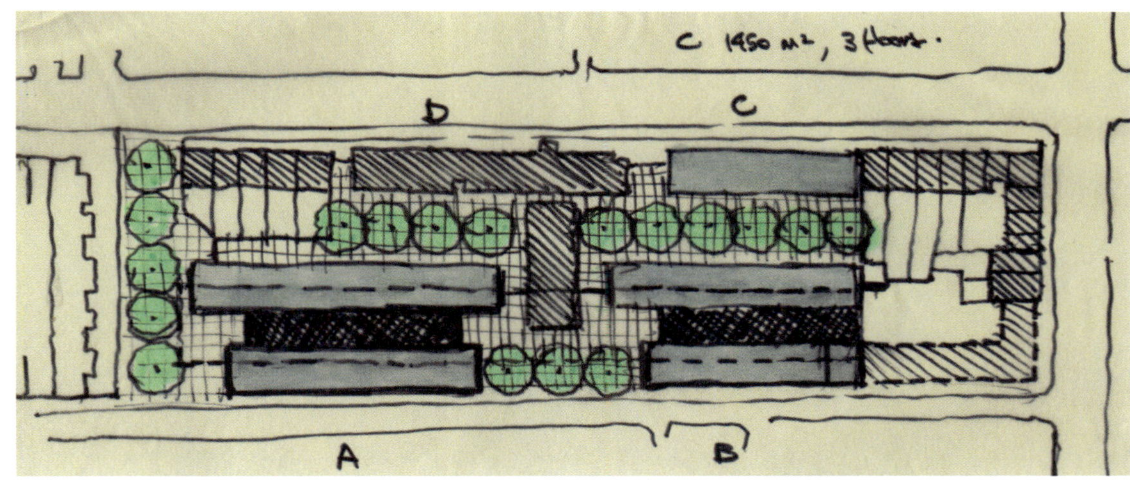

Alternative site planning options aimed to form a series of courtyards within, and routes through the site.

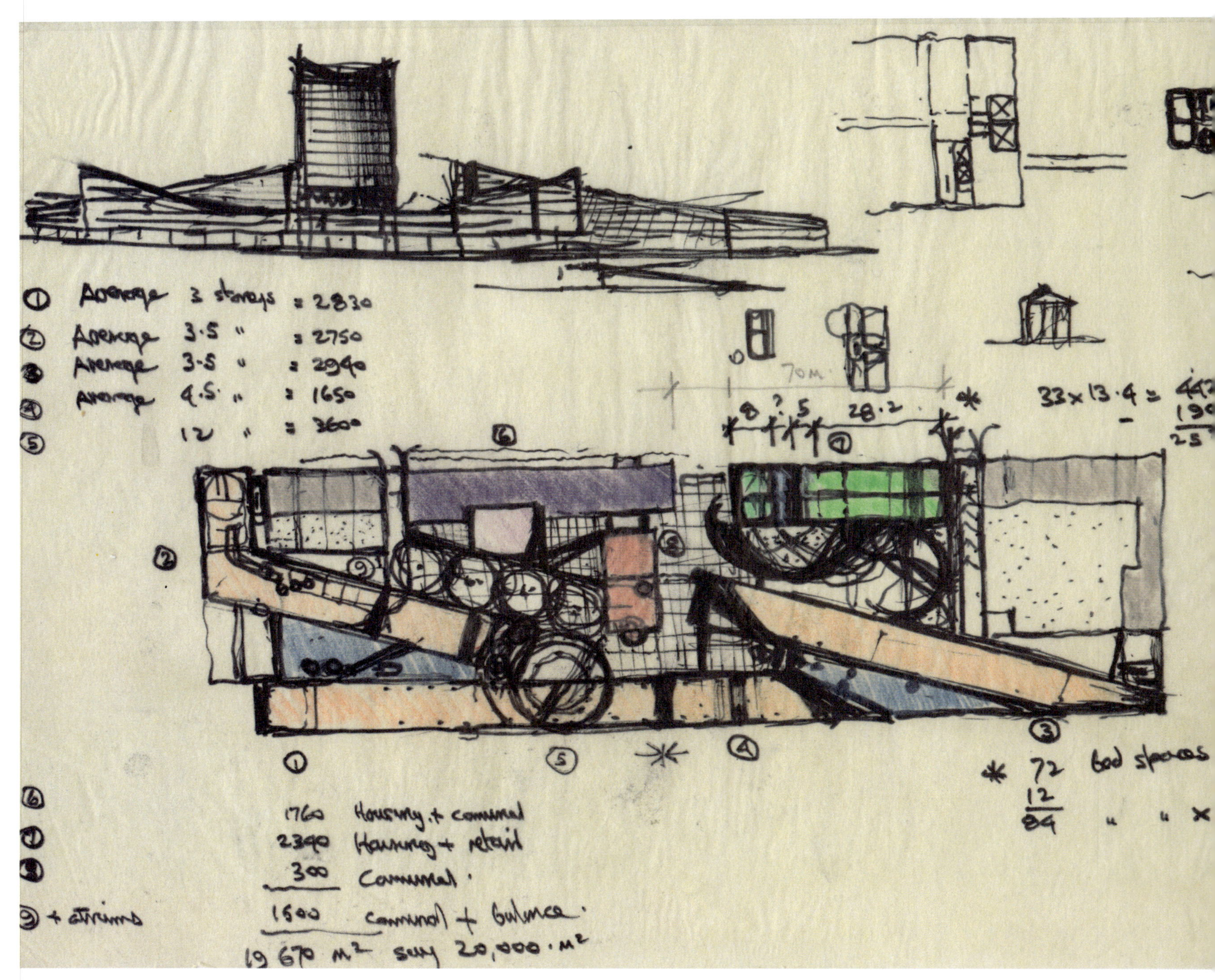

*Diagonally arranged
intermediate buildings with a
range of profiles generate a
dynamic urban district.*

For some years I chaired the UK Architects Against Apartheid group, which provided support to those who sought the end of apartheid in South Africa. In October 1987 we joined 60,000 others on a march from Hyde Park, through Mayfair and on to Trafalgar Square. These were ideas for the banner; probably over-ambitious for what might need to be a low-cost over-night production job?

1987

Ideas for a banner for the Anti-Apartheid Movement rally in London, calling for prime minister Thatcher's government to impose sanctions on South Africa.

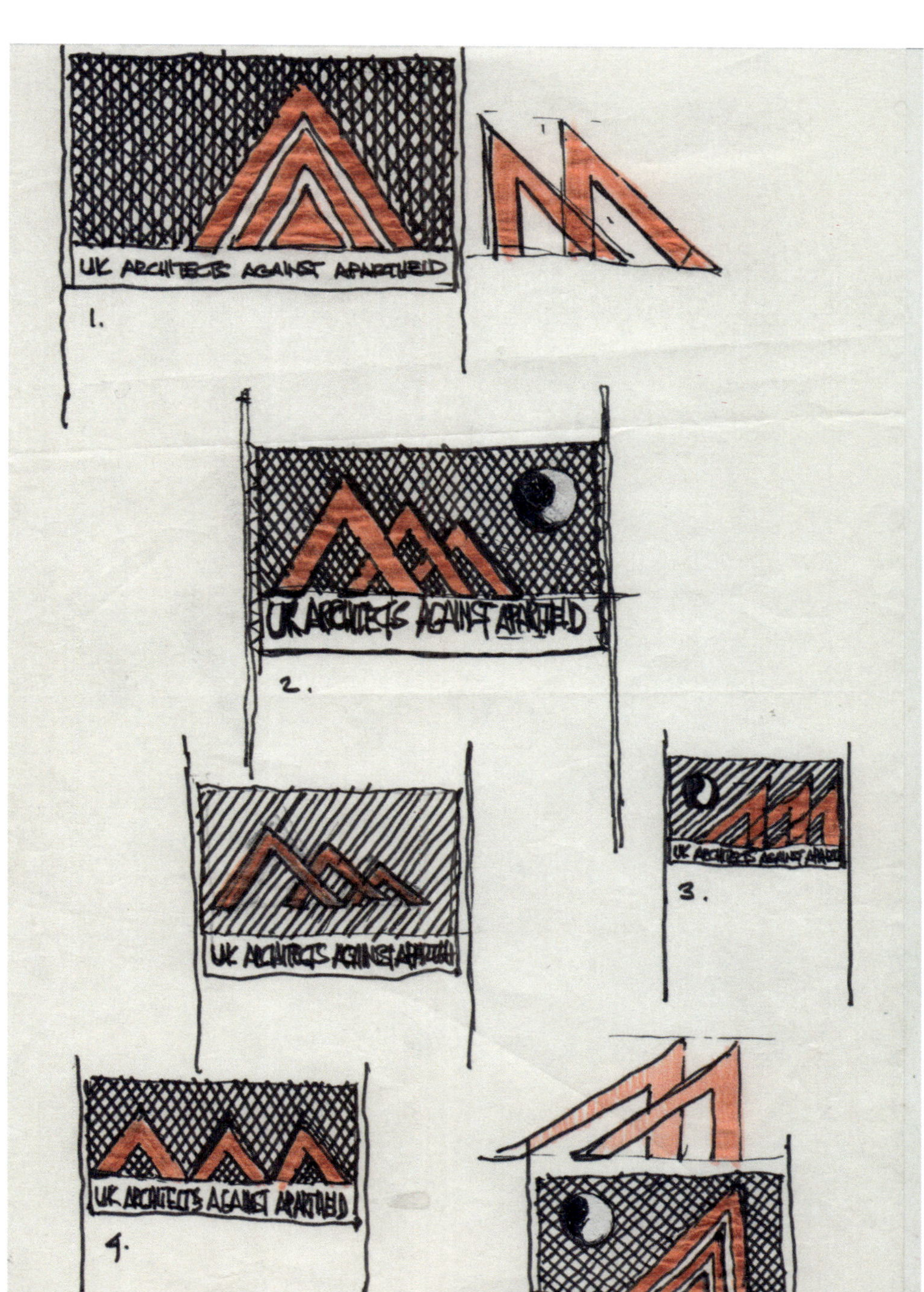

When my daughters were at primary school, I was invited to talk to a class of young people about architecture. I did so with much pleasure, particularly as at the time we were building a new school for Leicestershire's progressive department of education. The evening before, sat at our dining table, I made a basic model of parts of our project, which with the childrens' enthusiastic participation I was able to reassemble in the class.

Thirty-five years later, Big Arts Week invited me to run an architecture-related workshop over a period of several days at a primary school near our office in Primrose Hill. Having looked around the school premises I chose to situate a self-build 'construction' in a colonnaded undercroft beside the playground.

Reusing cardboard boxes collected from Camden market we put together two multi-storey crescent-like built forms to enclose a communal gathering space and provide each child with their individual box-territory. In the days that followed, having selected their 'place' by discussion and negotiation, each student would go on to make and show their own designed objects – a personal display situated within the structure of the whole. During the closing afternoon we all gathered to enjoy presentations of what they'd made, and why. I never spoke to the class specifically about architecture but they had, each in their own way and with their own hands, contributed to a live exercise of designing and making a model of modern urban life.

2003

Introducing architecture, design and planning through making to school children for the Big Arts Week programme.

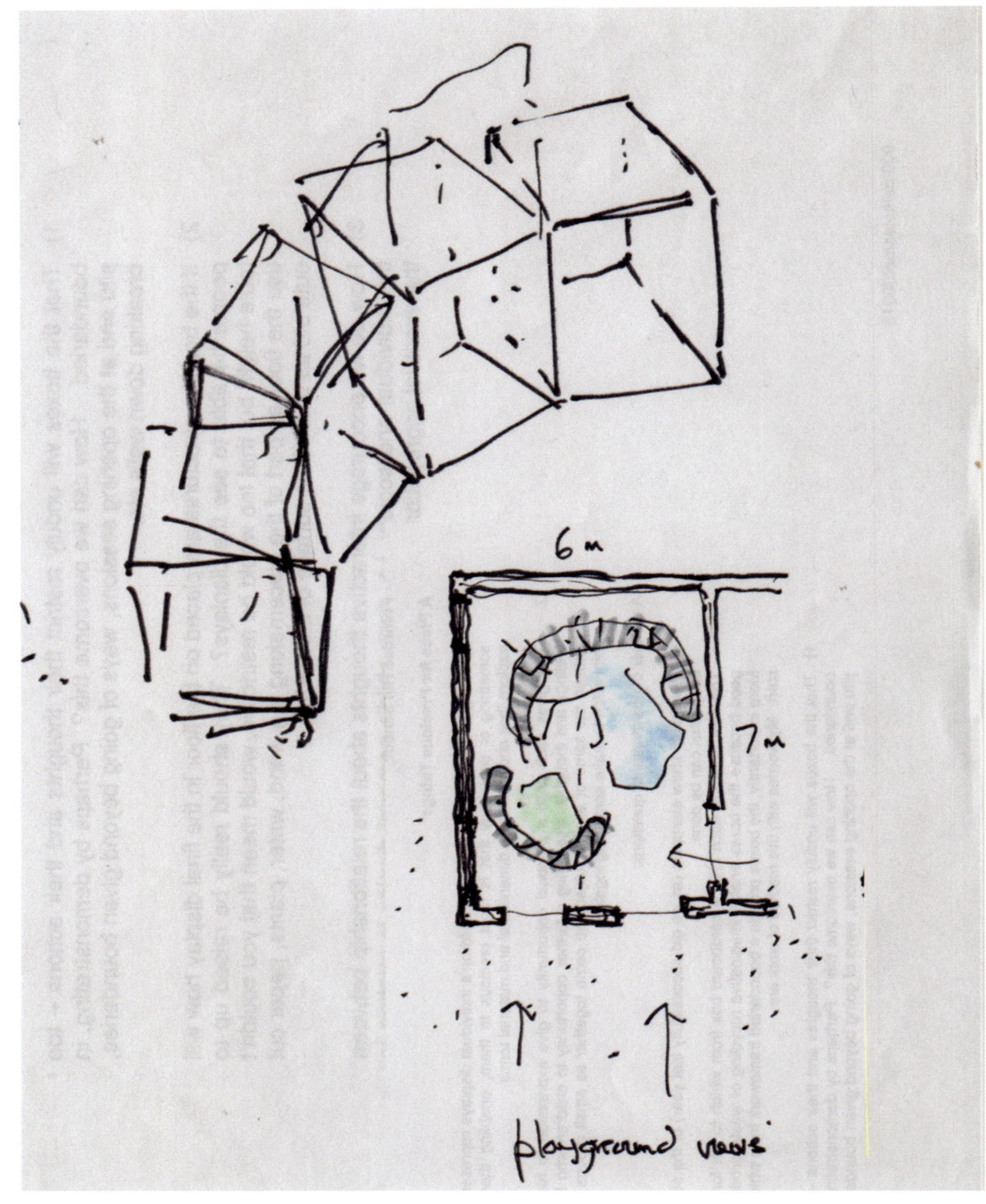

Furniture design

During periods of designing and making buildings, several opportunities arose to also design pieces of furniture. In our early 1960s' work for the Berkeley Library in Trinity College, Dublin, parts of the furniture were made of white concrete, matching the material used for the structure and much of the building's interior. Later, we designed a selection of furniture for WH Smith's Regional Headquarters in Swindon as well as the new campus of Ireland's Institute of Technology in Blanchardstown.

2000

Ideas for a boardroom table and other furniture suggest a site-specific, contextual approach, much like urban design.

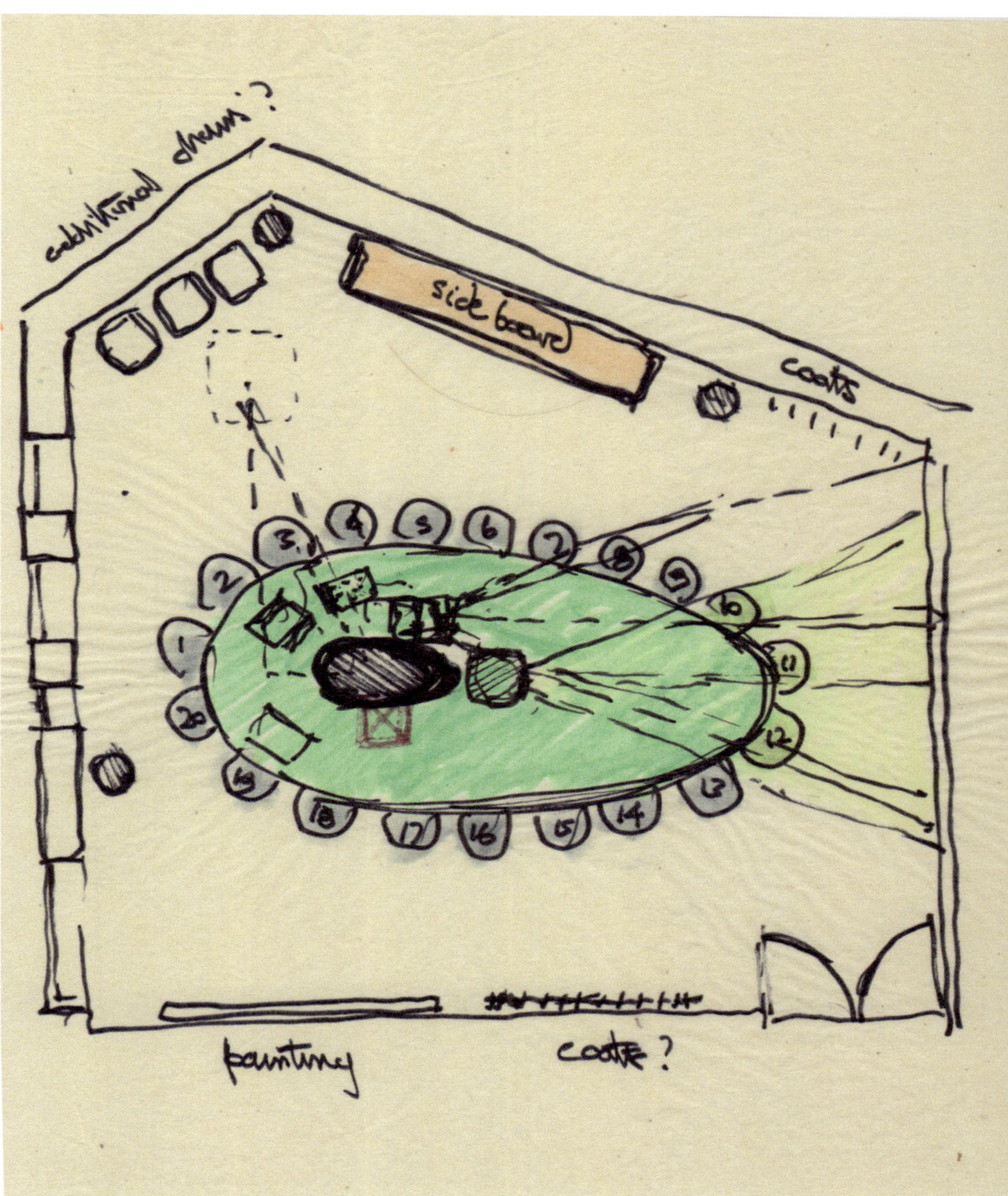

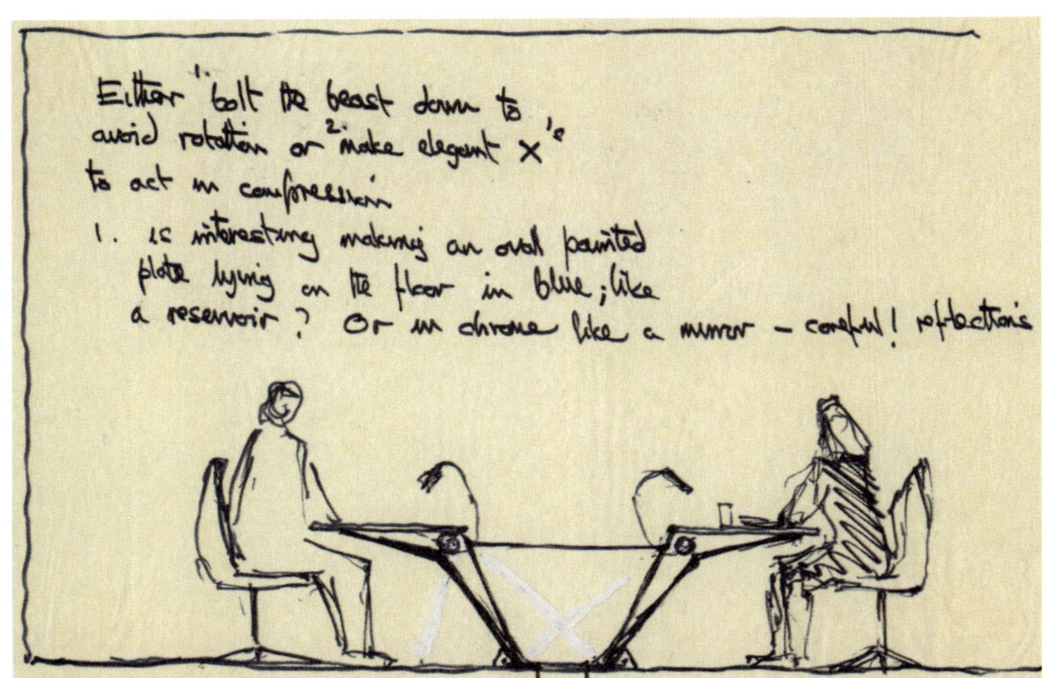

Either 'bolt the beast down to
avoid rotation or 2. make elegant X's
to act in compression
1. Is interesting making an oval painted
plate lying on the floor in blue; like
a reservoir? Or in chrome like a mirror — careful! reflections

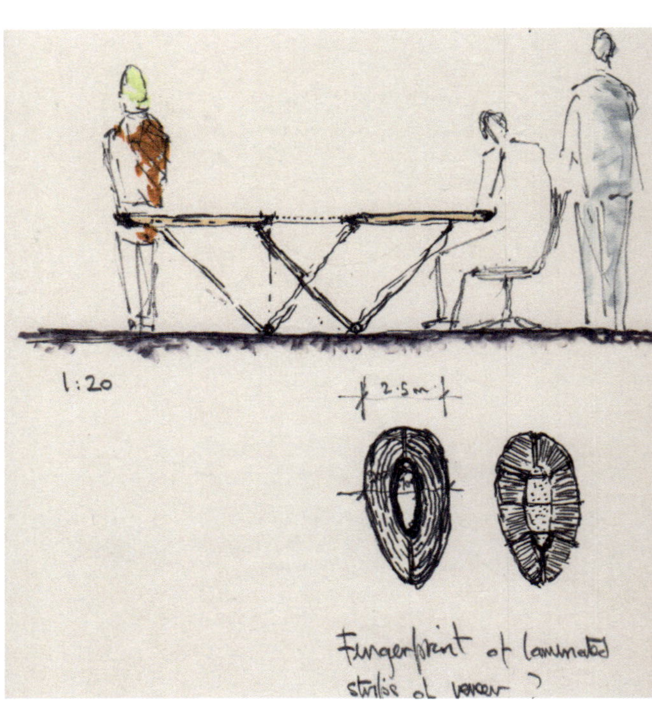

1:20
2.5 m
Fingerprint of laminated
strips of veneer?

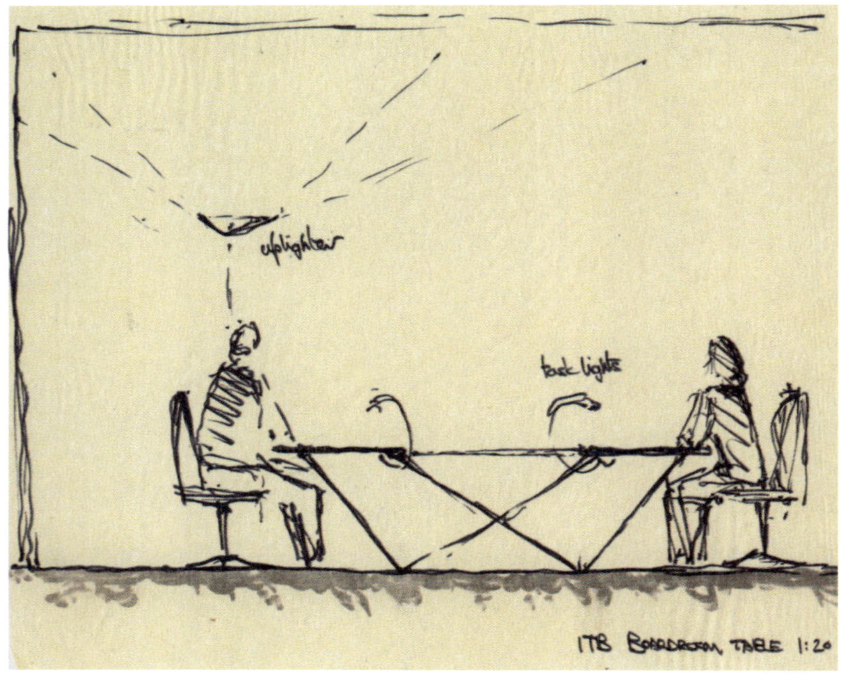

uplighter
back lights
ITB BOARDROOM TABLE 1:20

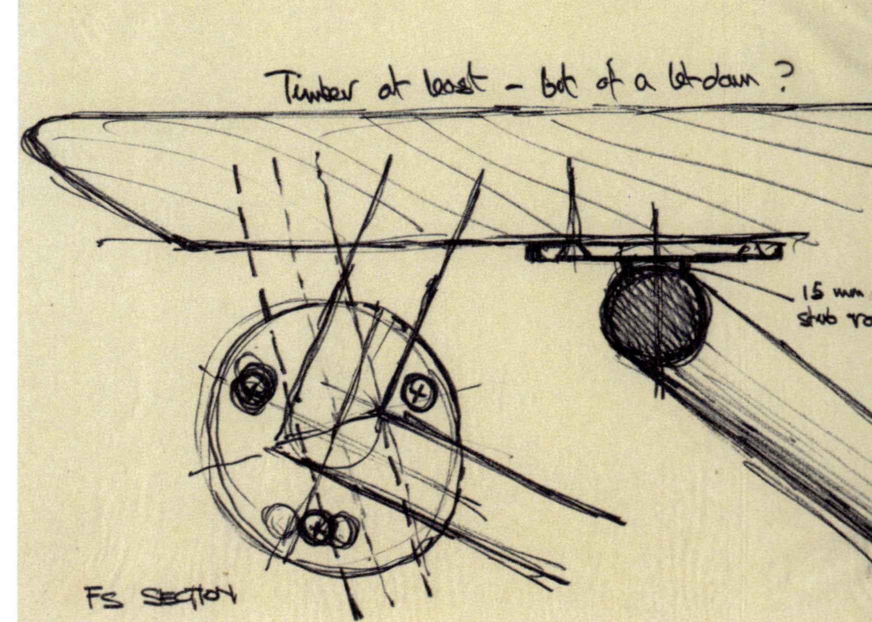

Timber at least — bit of a letdown?
15 mm
stub row
FS SECTION

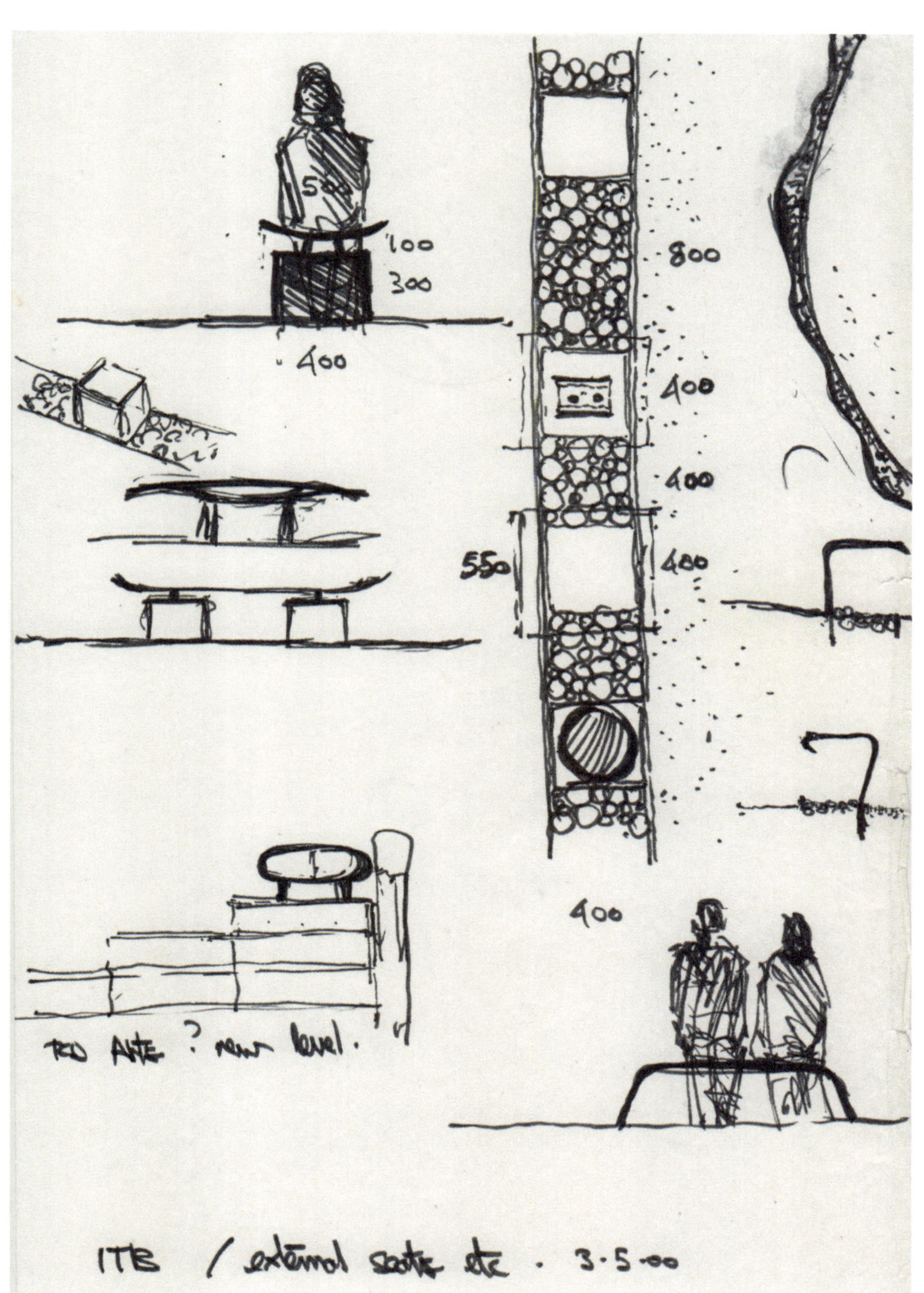
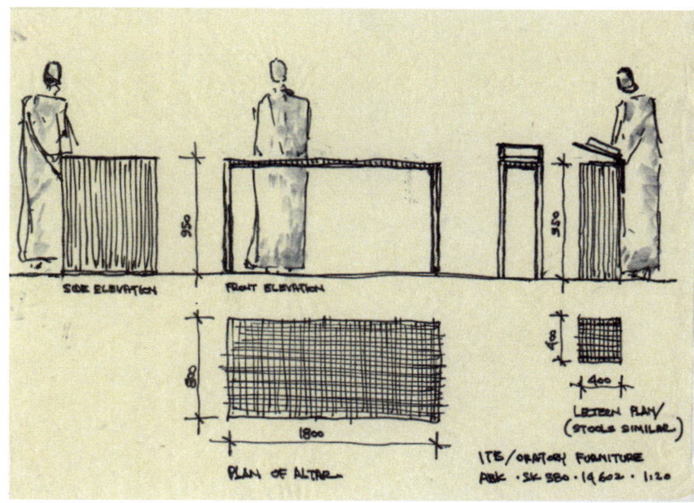
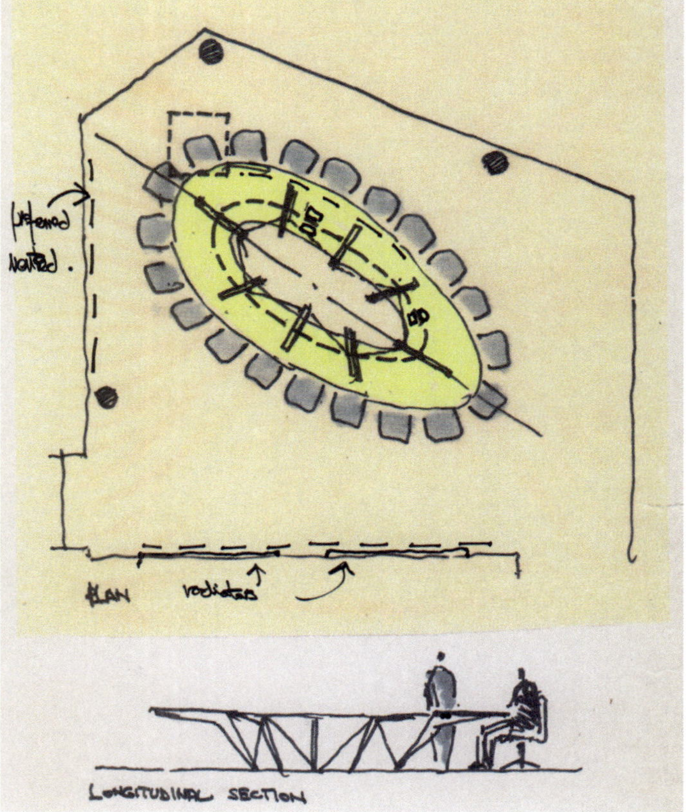

Consideration of the human dimension pervades the design process, from concept through structural design to components and constructional detail. Built furniture included a boardroom table and external seating.

At the turn of the millennium we had discussions with the Royal Institute of British Architects about putting together an exhibition to mark the ABK's 40th anniversary. This would be complemented by the institute's Annual Discourse, a formal lecture which we were to be invited to present the following year.

In the event neither the exhibition nor the lecture progressed – directions change and plans dissolve. These sketches show some of the design options for the exhibition layout, using black and white printed banners suspended from a grid installed just below the ceiling.

2001

Initial ideas for an exhibition layout in the first-floor gallery at RIBA's Portland Place headquarters.

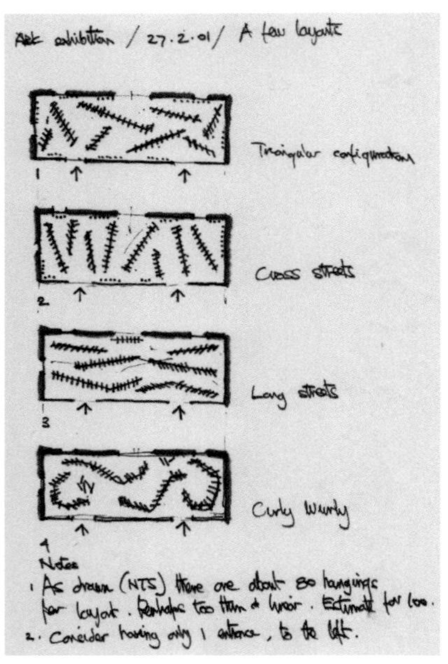

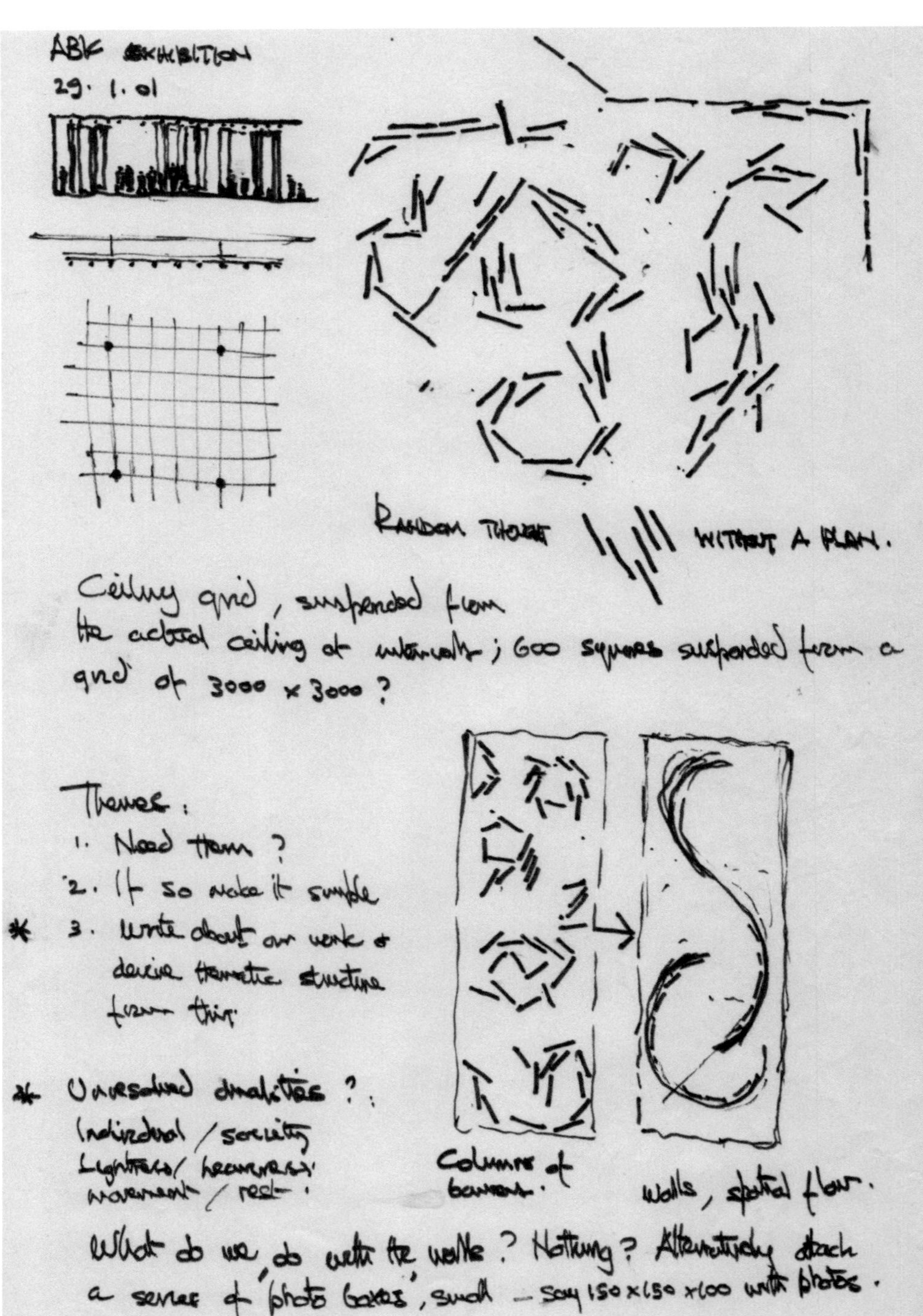

The people-centred approach to configuring an arrangement of exhibition screens is seen in much the same way as designing for an urban situation.

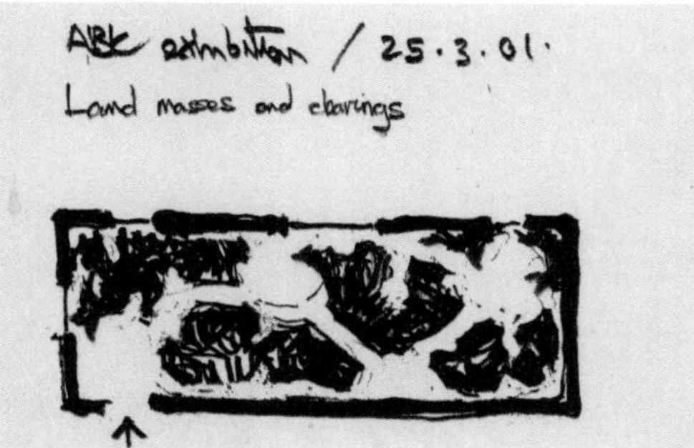

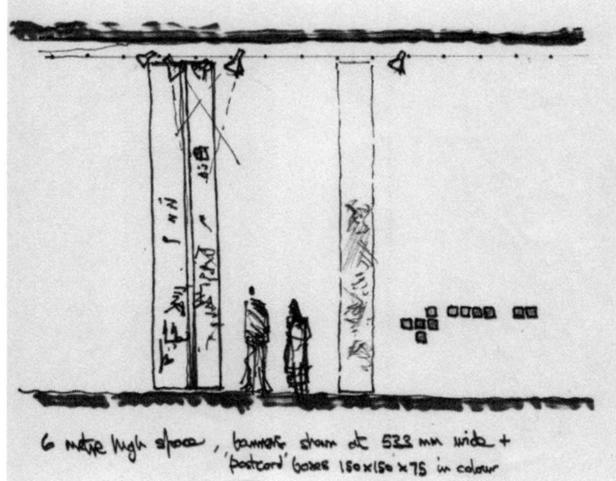

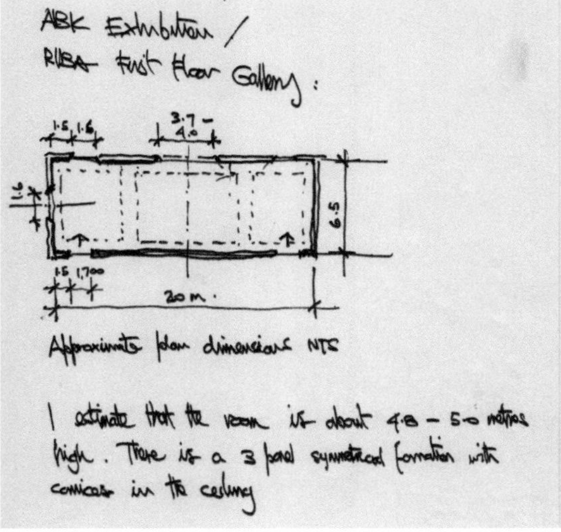

Finish printing the estimated 200 banner images
in say mid October, 3 months i.e. 60
working days to print i.e. 1 image over 3 images a
day! Start printing no later than mid July.

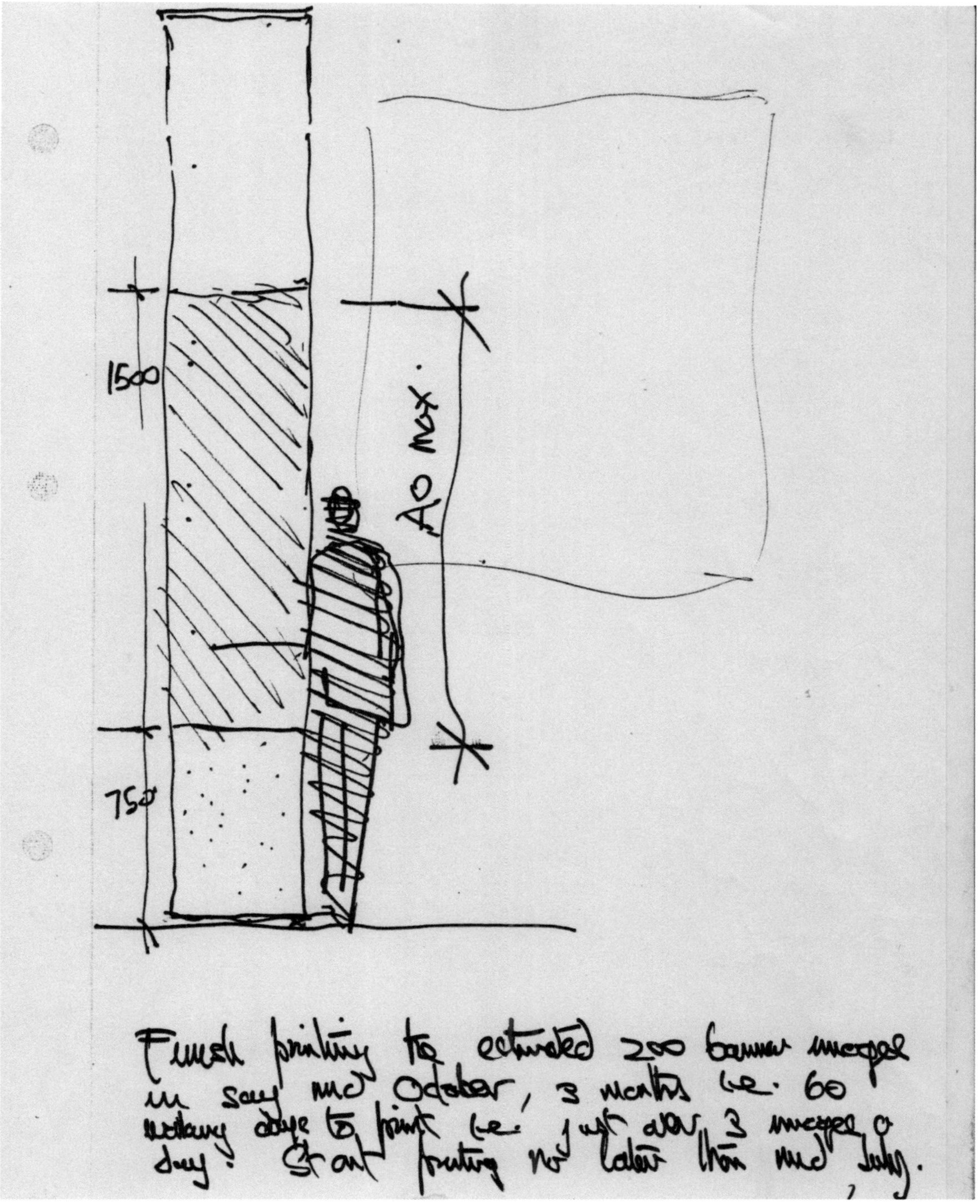

These sketches were made for a competitive interview for a residential and mixed-use scheme at the edge of Dublin. The brief included a hotel and retail accommodation on a fine green and open site beside the M1 motorway, not far from the airport and adjacent to a typical low-rise outer suburb. Concerning ourselves with contextual matters relating to the character of the city's pre-war suburbs, and the dissociating effect of adjacent motorways, we looked at a number of site layouts, two of which are shown here.

2006

Layout options for a large housing, community and commercial development in north Dublin

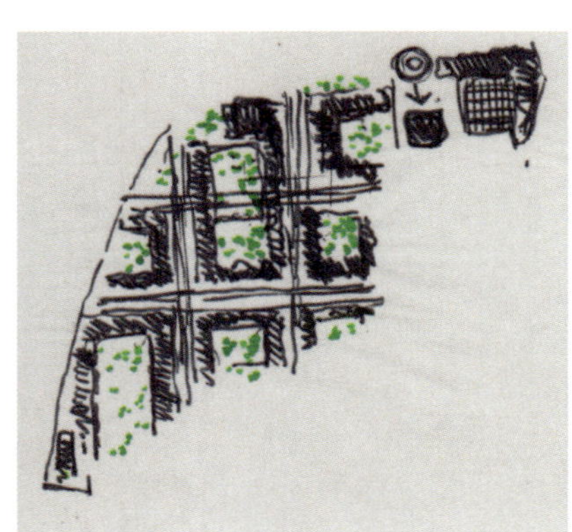

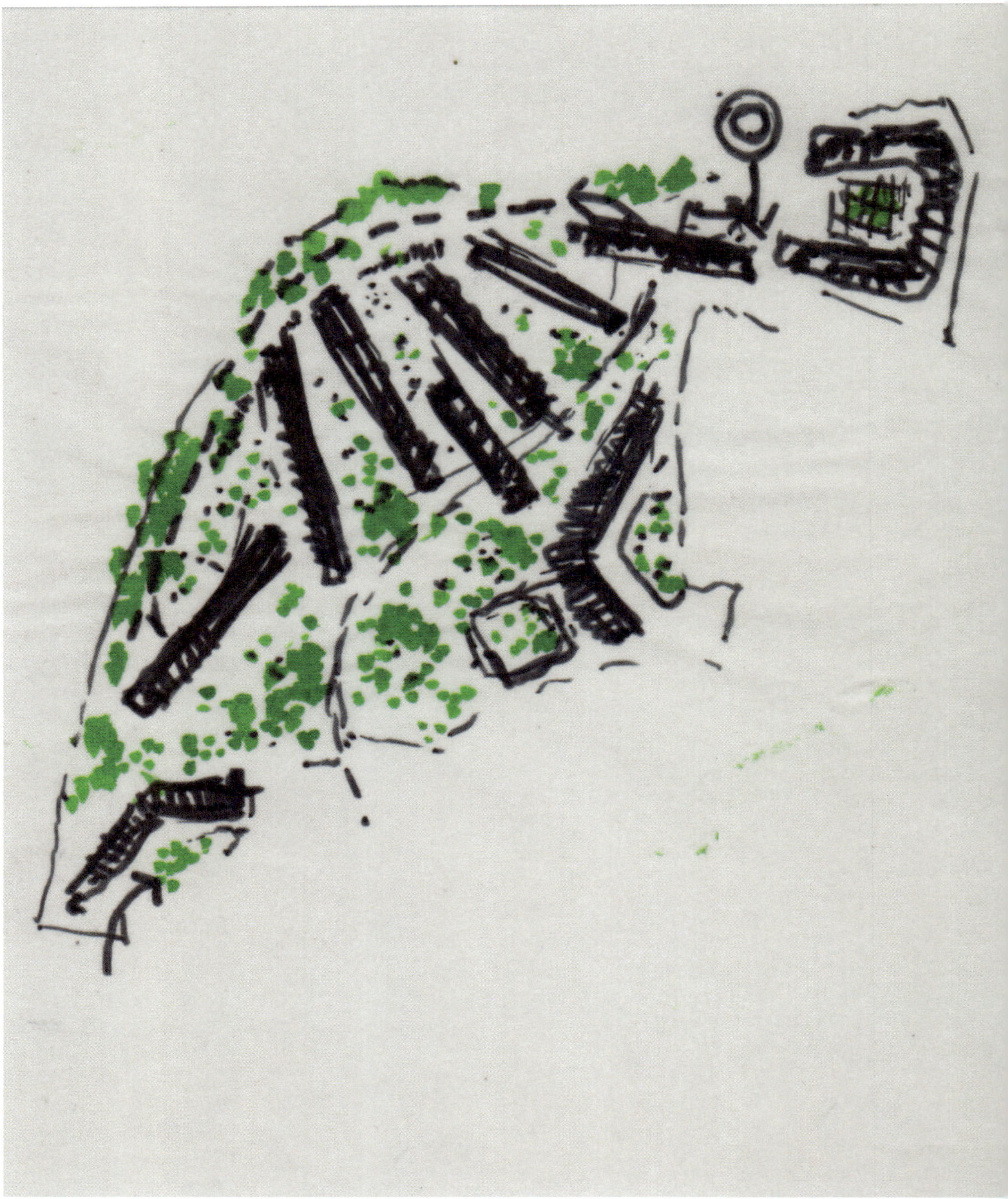

Oscar Traynor Road

Two very different approaches to urban design are apparent in these alternative options: linear blocks informally arranged in the parkland, and perimeter blocks adhering to an urban grid.

We were commissioned by British Rail to design the architectural aspects of two Eurostar train sheds, to be built on a long, narrow site beside the westbound mainline out of London. One was for complete rail-set routine servicing, the other for engine repairs. With our experience of planning large-scale industrial buildings, we sought to bring a level of functional and environmental excellence to this nationally-significant infrastructure enterprise. We wanted to make an efficient, good place in which to work, even though the building would only be glimpsed by the public through train windows at speed.

Our proposal was approved with enthusiasm, and was achieveable within both time and budget constraints. Work was proceeding well when, at a late stage in the detail design period, a newly-appointed management contractor, unbeknown to us, had recommended an alternative 'design and build' contract procedure. This, the chief architect told us, was to lead to the 'honourable' abandonment of our scheme. Nonsense, of course, for our scheme could have been both economical and elegant.

When all was said, done and dusted, I wondered whether such corporate contractual routes would come to make good architecture. Later, speeding by on the train to Oxford, I saw what had been built, and I thought not.

1989

A west London depot for Eurostar cross-channel trains during its period of operation from Waterloo International. An alternative design & build project was built.

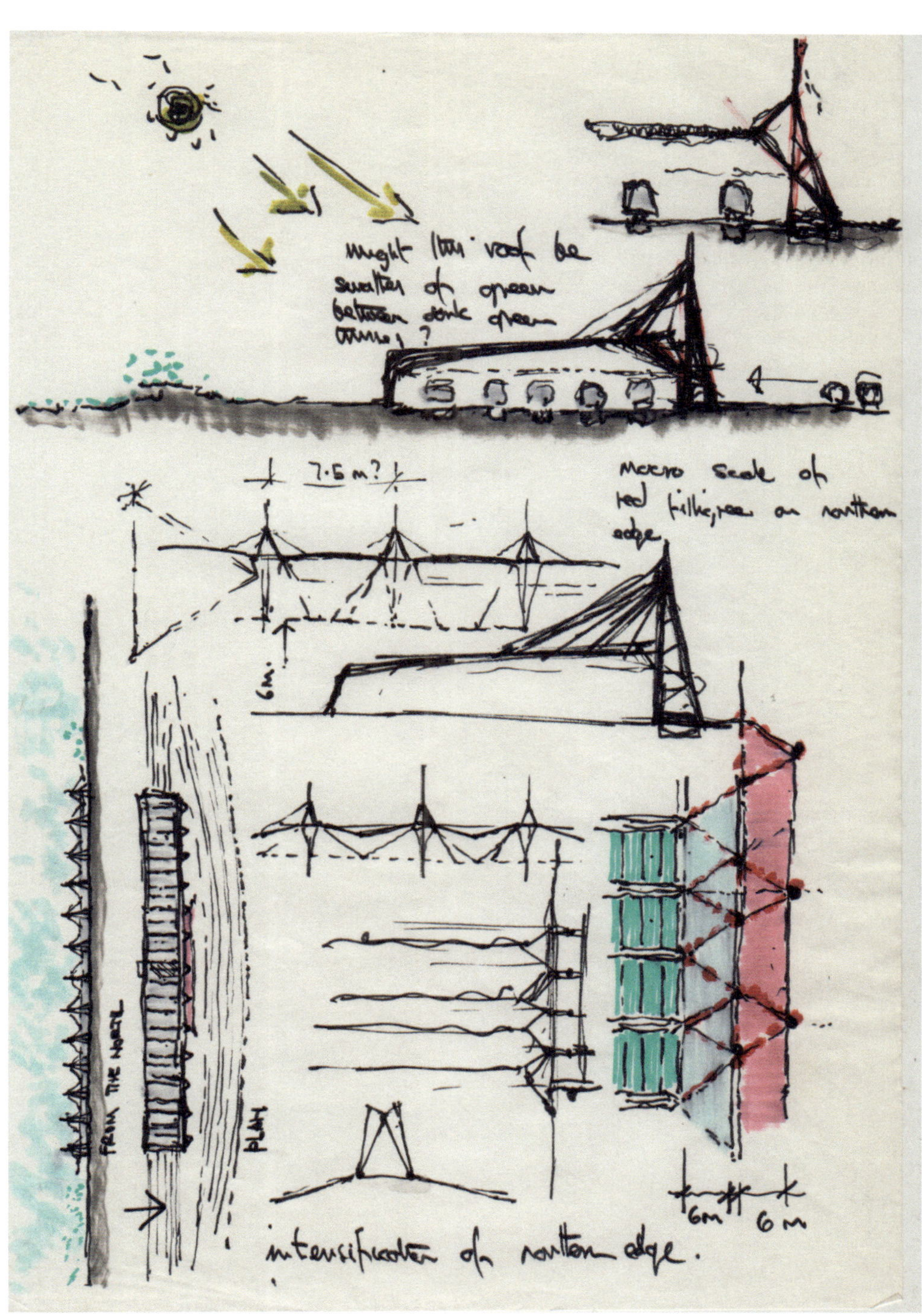

The North Pole was to be used by Eurostar as the London depot for its fleet of trains from 1994 until 2007 during the period Waterloo International was in operation.

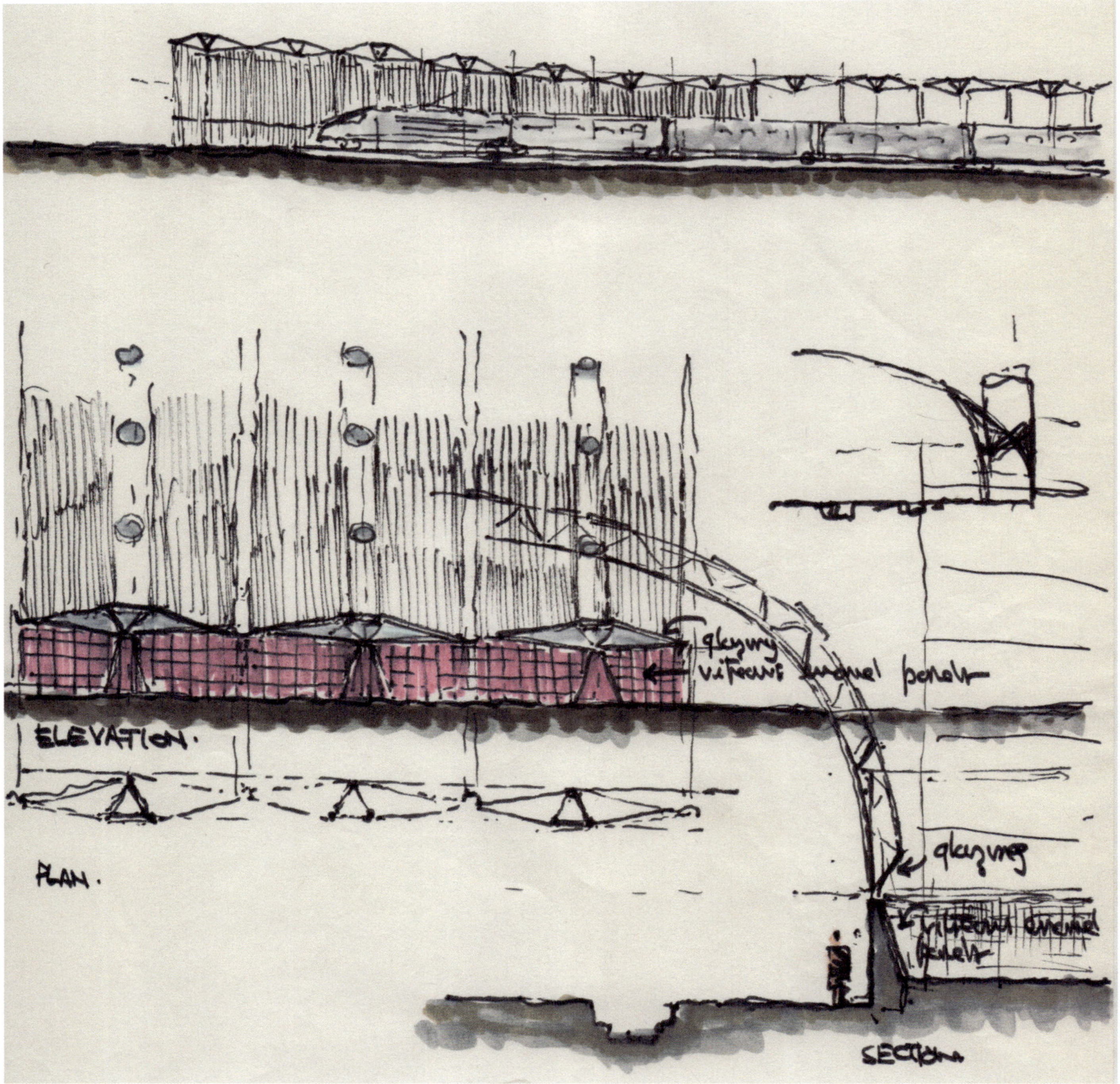

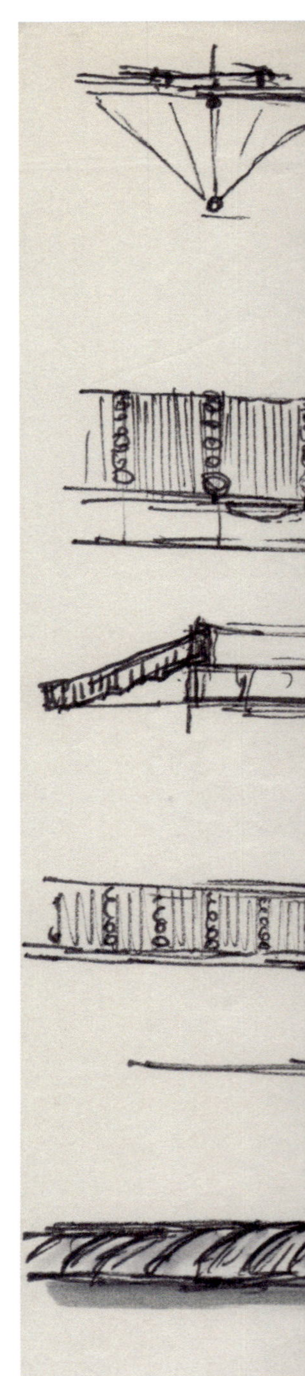

The project was particularly unusual because the completed building would be seen by many thousands of people, but each only for a fleeting moment.

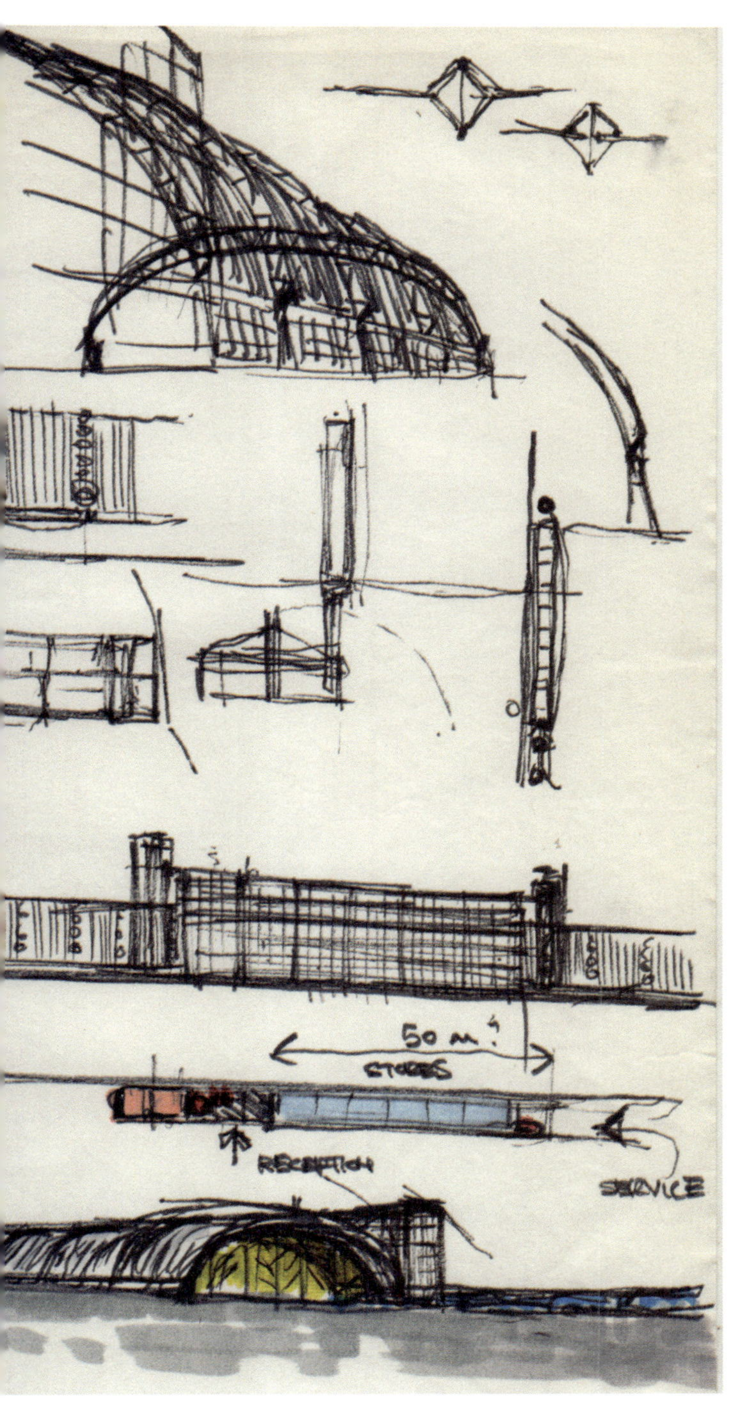

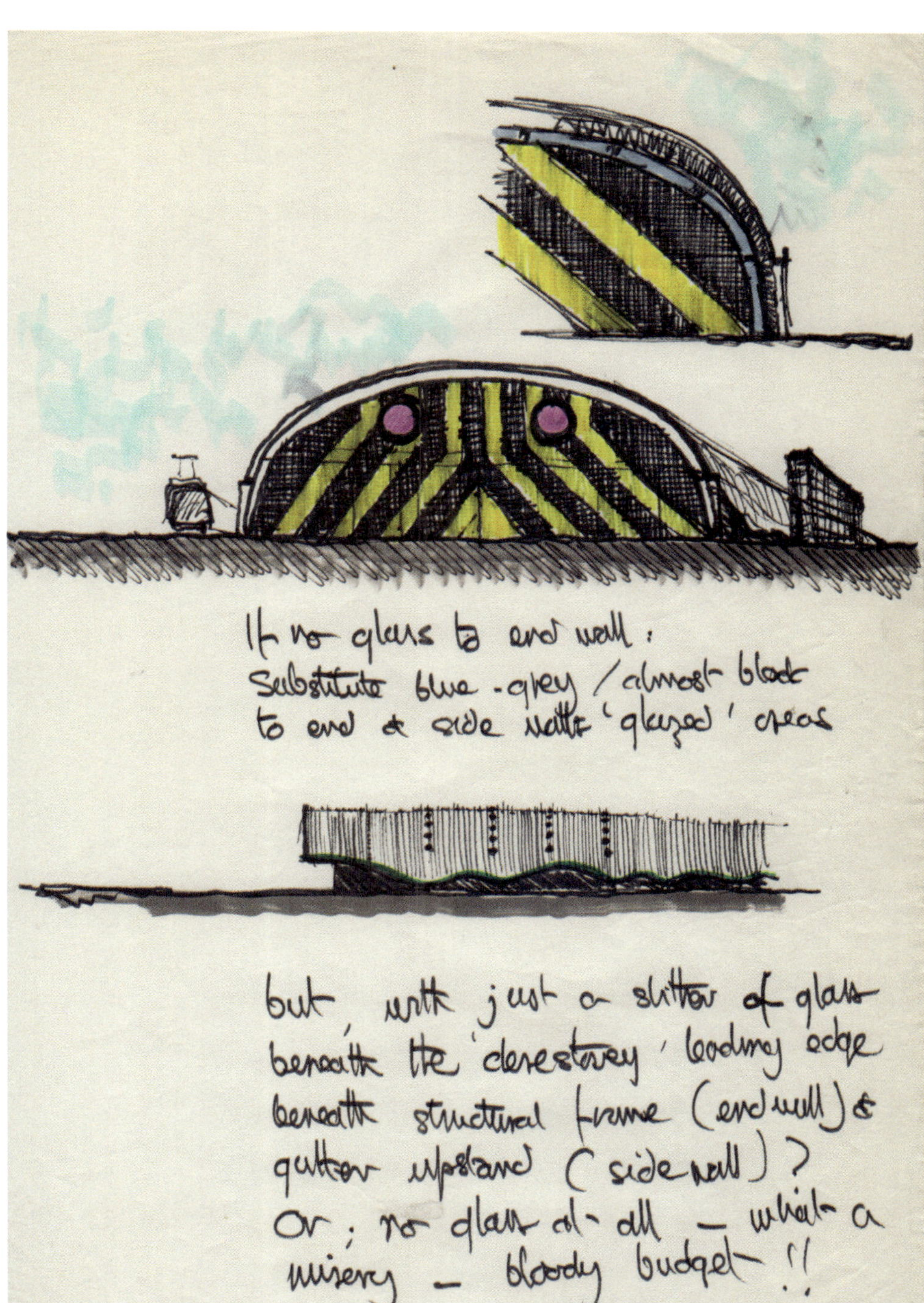

If no glass to end wall:
Substitute blue-grey / almost black
to end & side walls 'glazed' areas

but, with just a slither of glass
beneath the 'clerestorey' loading edge
beneath structural frame (end wall) &
gutter upstand (side wall)?
Or; no glass at all — what a
misery — bloody budget !!

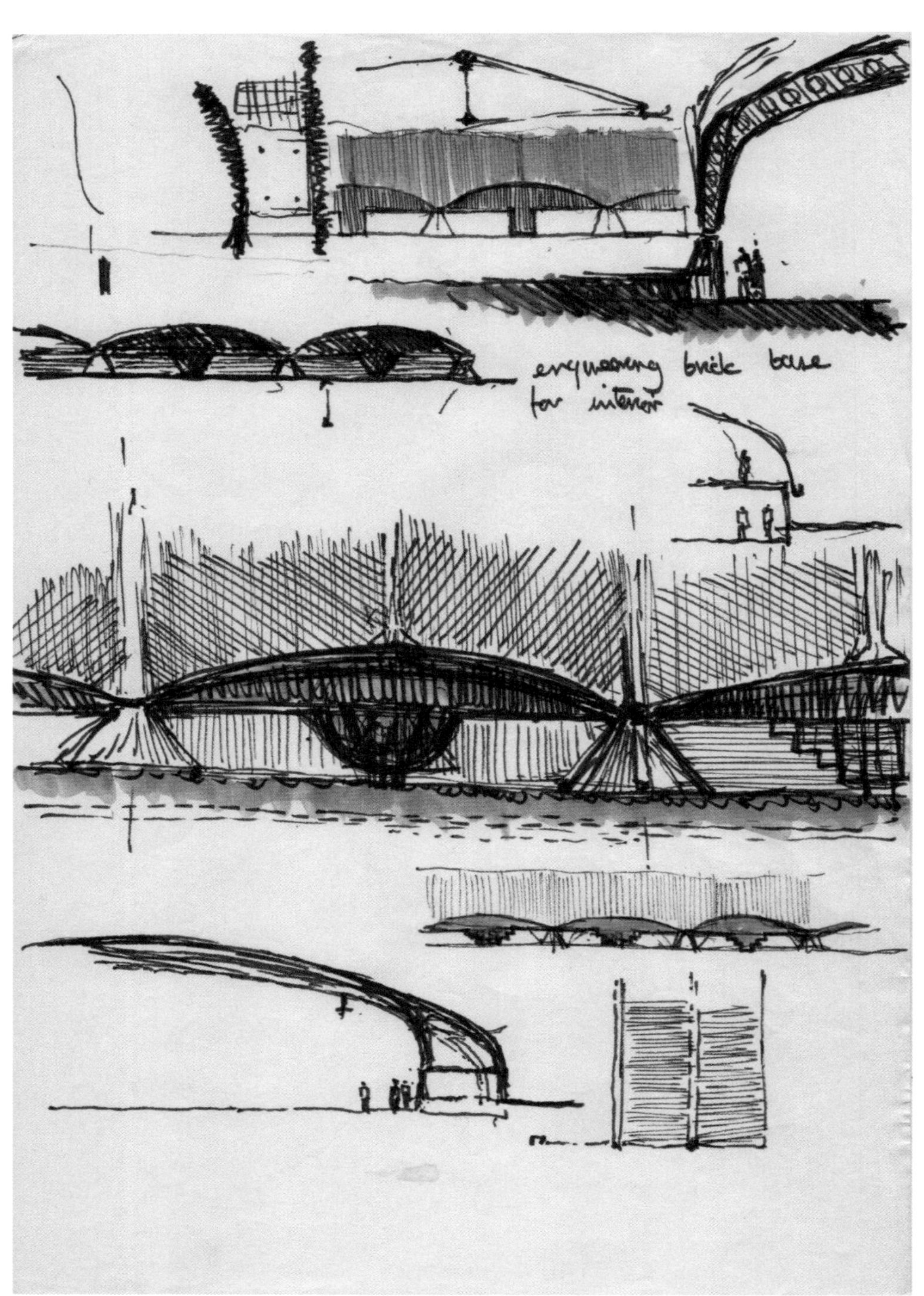

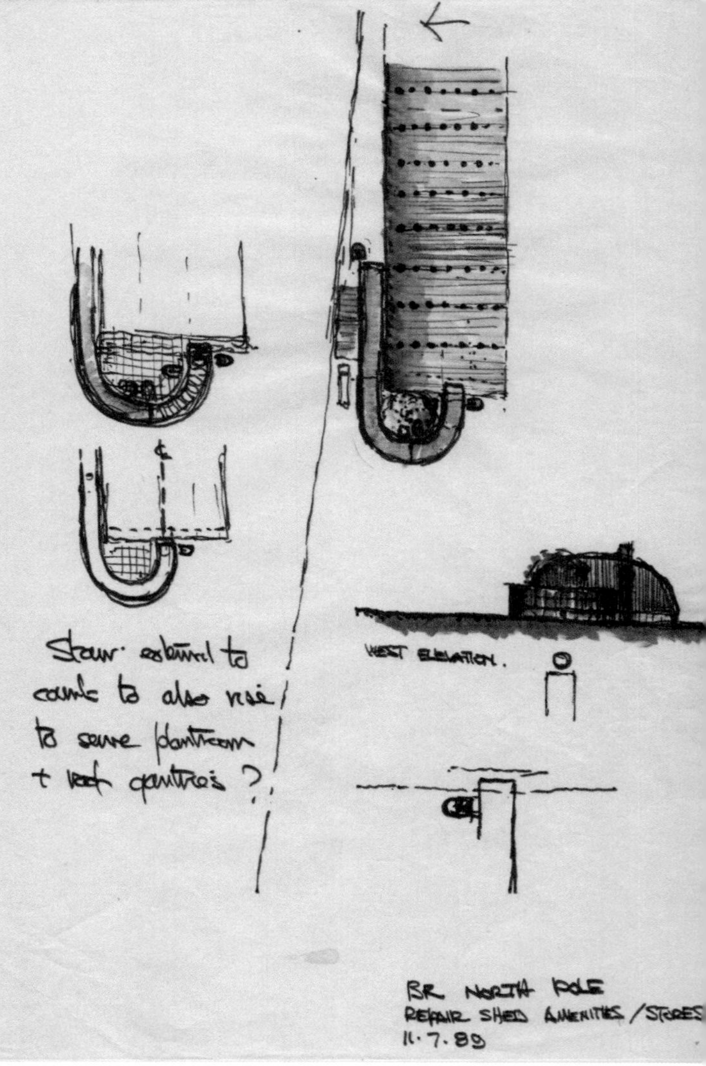

*The design process oscillates
between consideration of the
plan, section, structural
technique and construction
materials, as well as perspectival
views of the end result.*

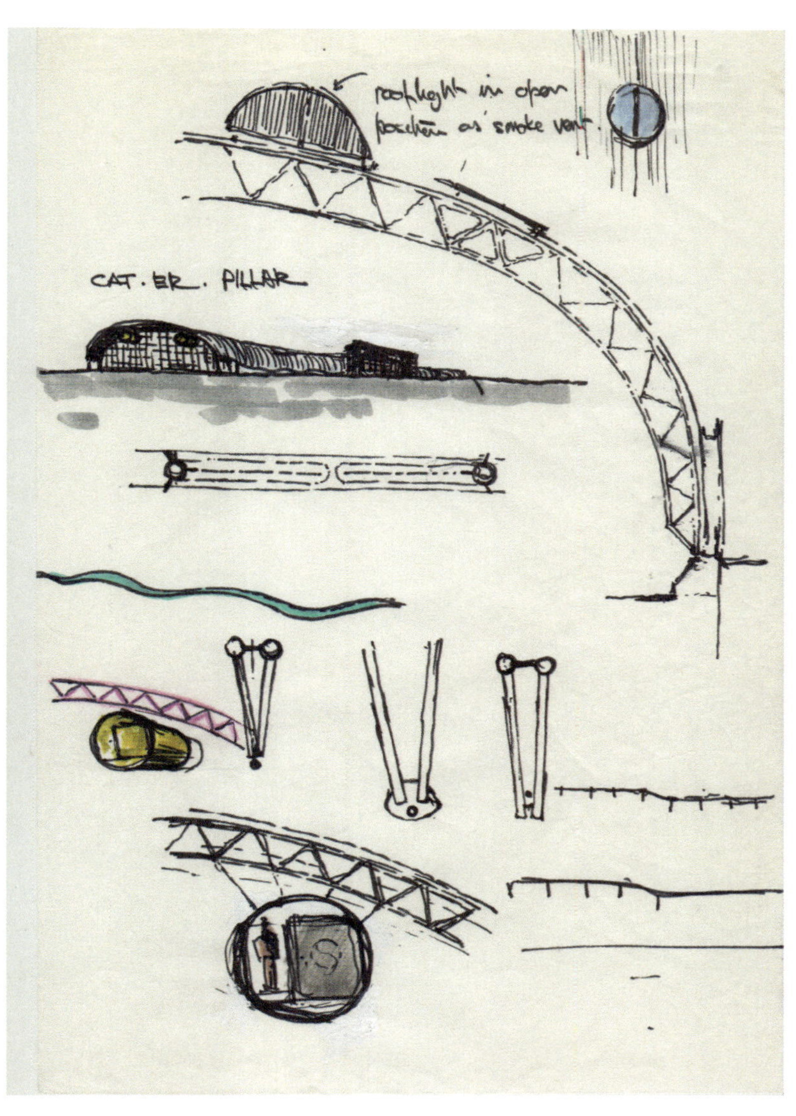

roof light in open
position as smoke vent
CAT · ER · PILLAR

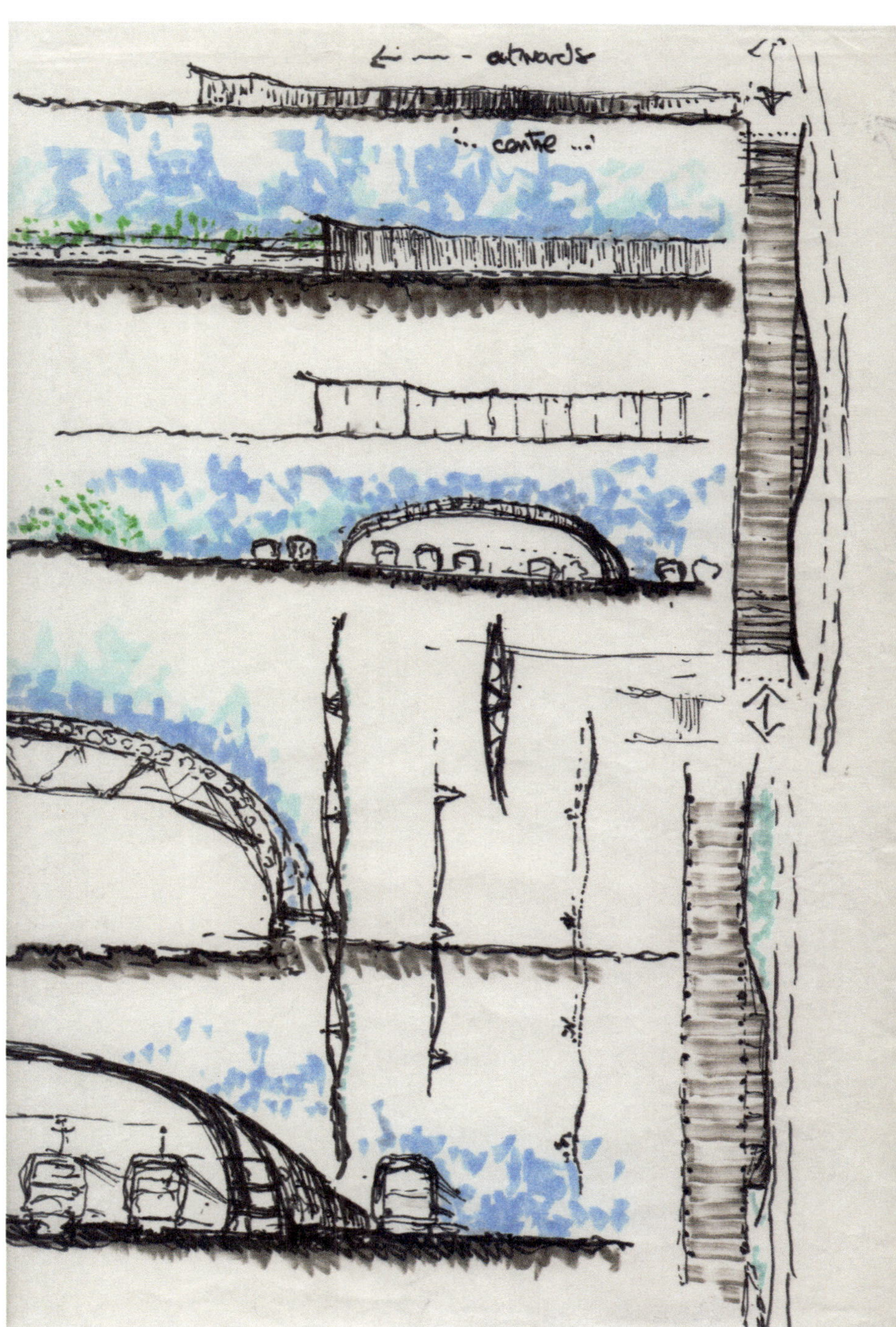

in — outwards
'... centre ...'

You might wonder why a major new museum should be built so close to the pyramids at Giza, rather than on a less sensitive and more accessible site close to Cairo's city centre. Nonetheless, this open competition was always likely to attract hundreds of entries. No chance of winning, I thought, and so it was. But then, after working on the project for a while, our ideas seemed interesting.

Sometimes, looking back at early-stage drawings, it's clear that they were just the beginnings of an idea, even though it might have grabbed you at the time. Coming upon these sketches now, the story we were exploring seems a bit thin and raw, not yet together.

At the time, however, we stayed with it, knowing that things move on and gain in depth, feeling that the initial ideas described an interesting reading of what the place could become.

So here's a selection of sketches based on our central premise that the overall plan-form and the built mass should, so far as practical, settle deep into and meld with the natural rise of the site's topography. The large, low-lying roof spans over and beyond a series of geometrically offset floorplates, each stepped in a spatial sequence of reduced floor areas and activating a grand volume that contains and describes the form of the whole museum.

2002

The competition for the Grand Egyptian Museum, to be sited two kilometres from the Giza pyramids, attracted 1557 entries from 82 countries, making it the second biggest architectural competition to date. Heneghan Peng was selected as winner.

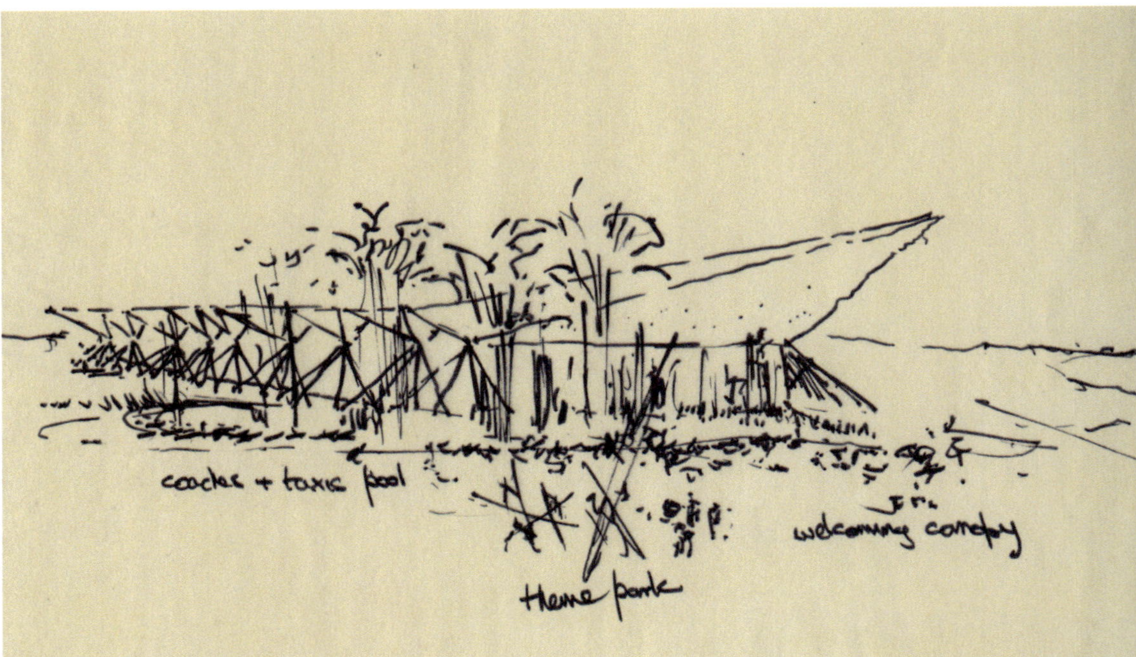

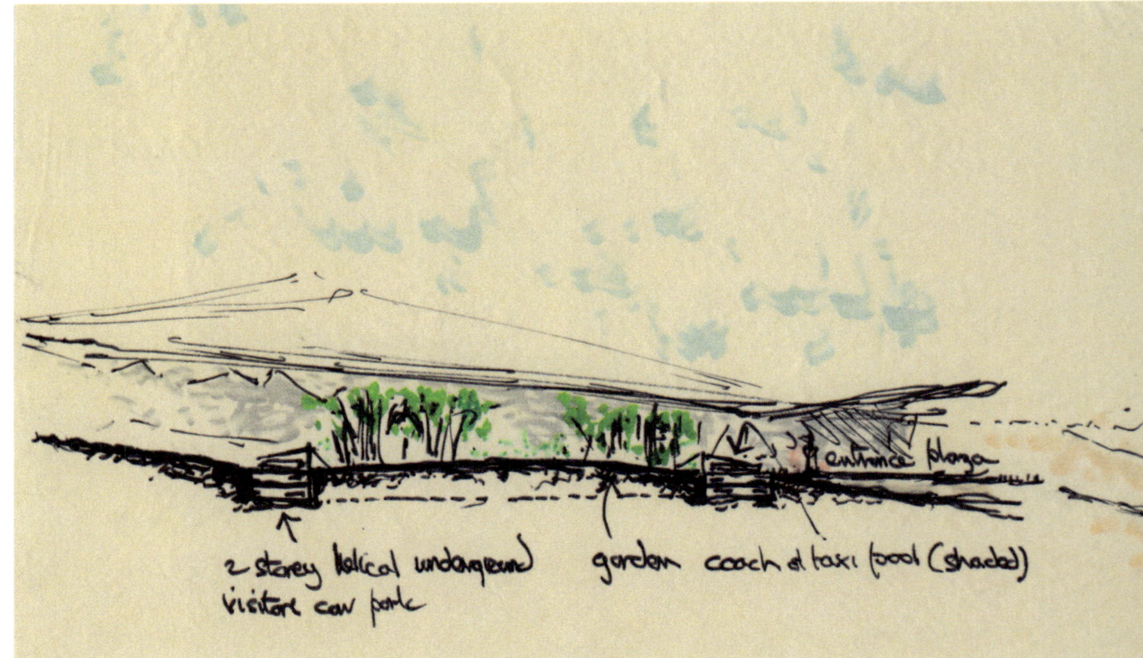

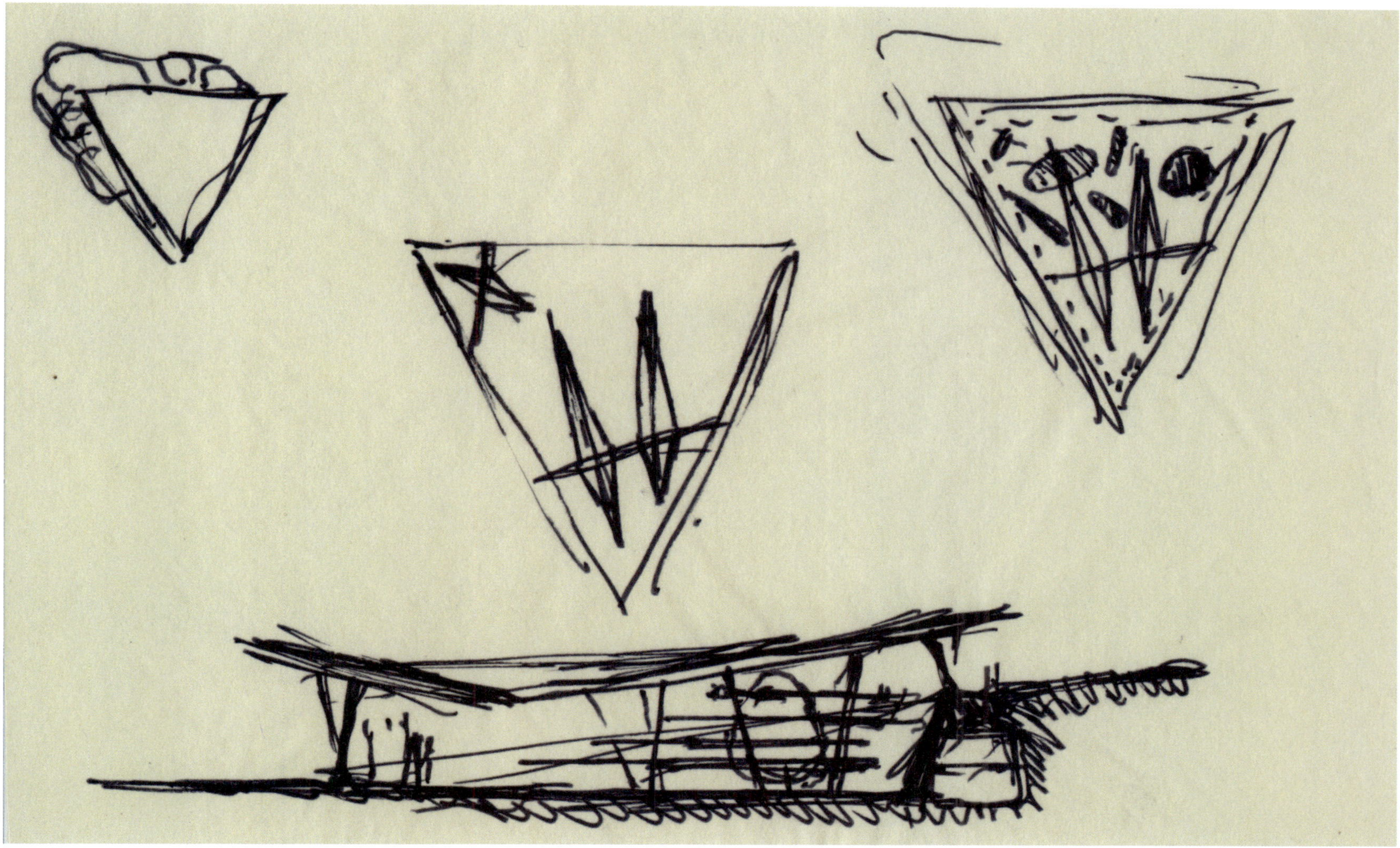

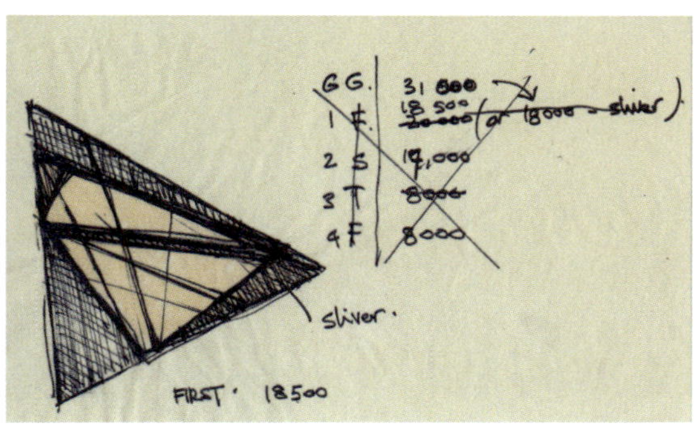

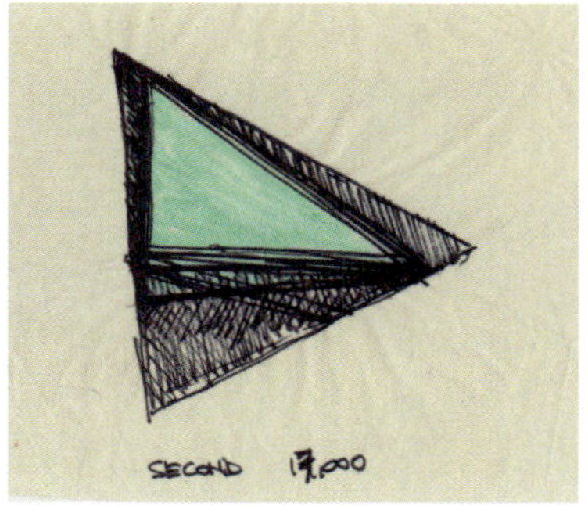

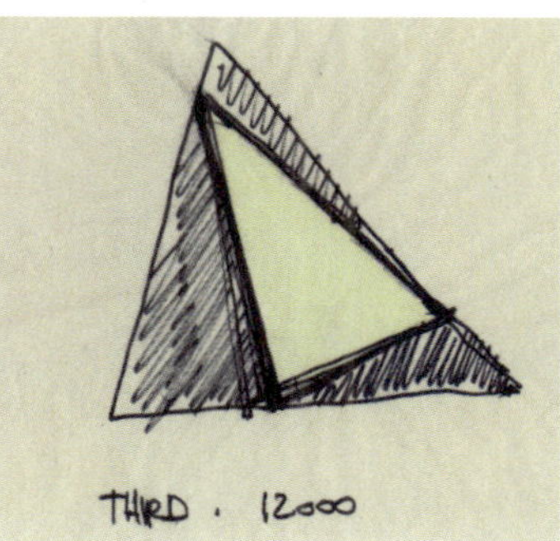

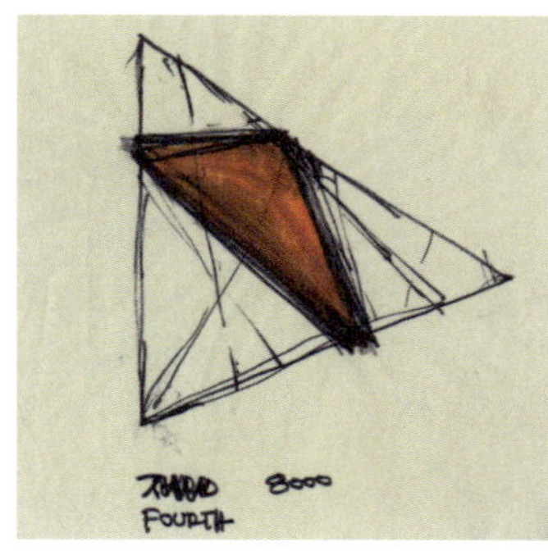

A triangular plan form was envisaged, enclosing terraces of floor plates beneath a canted and overhanging roof.

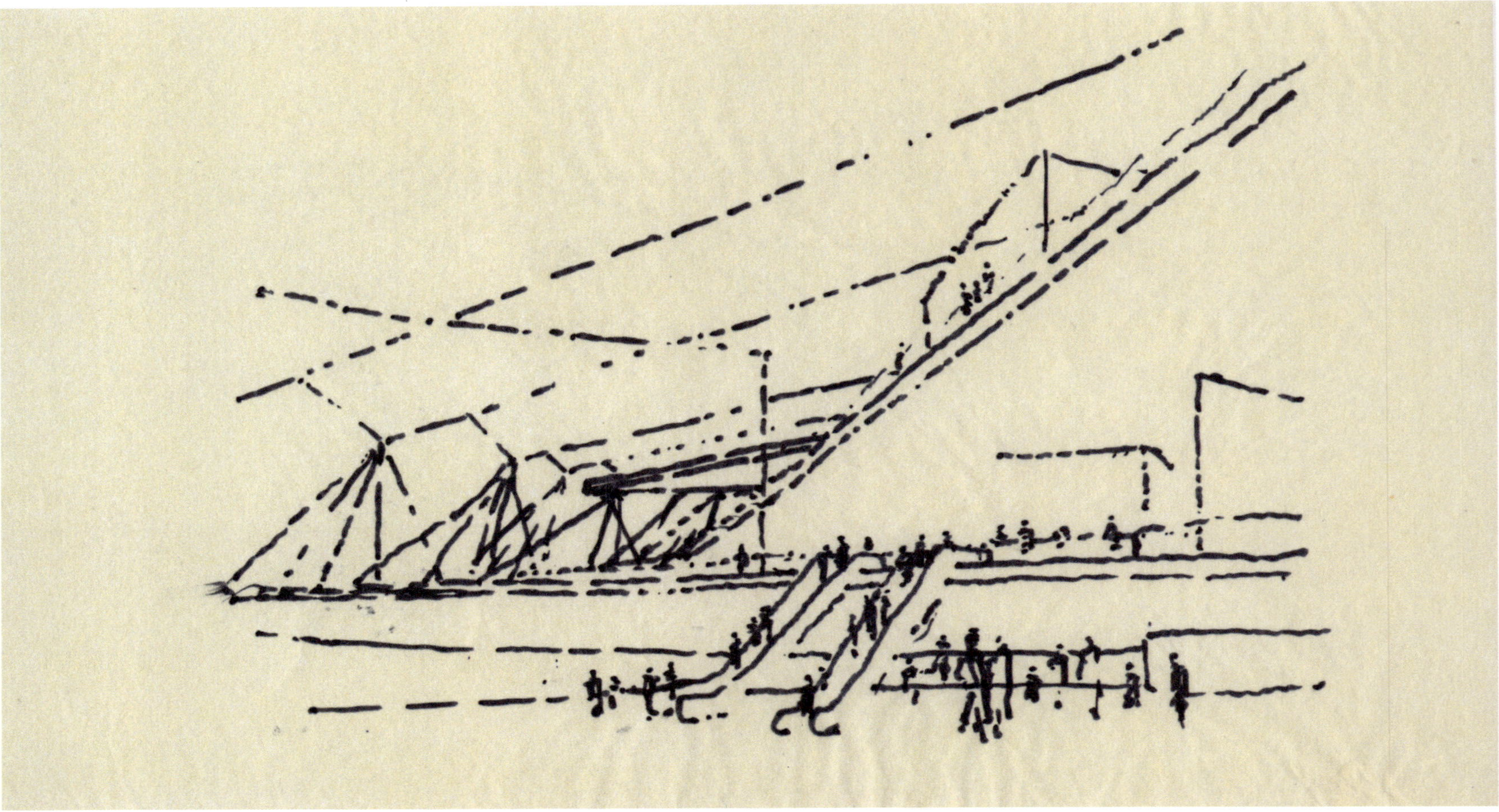

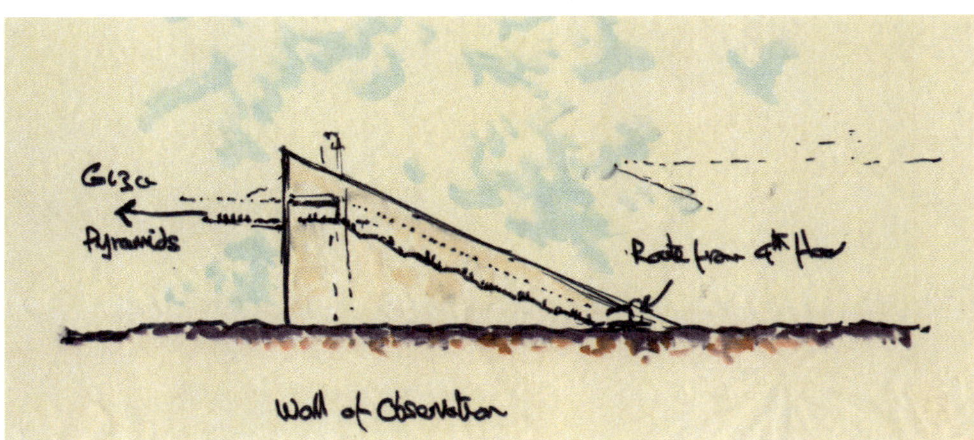

Giza
Pyramids
Route from 4th floor
Wall of Observation

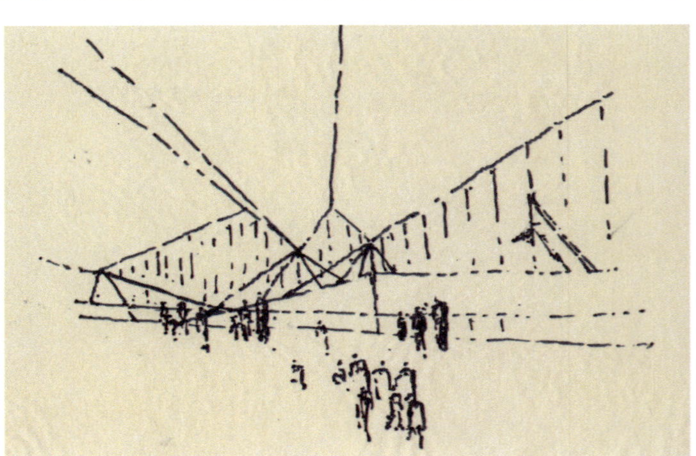

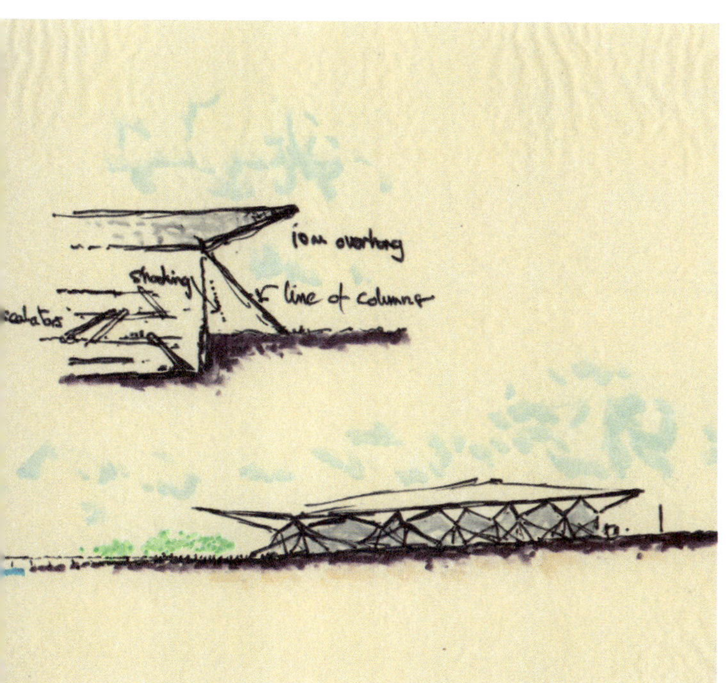

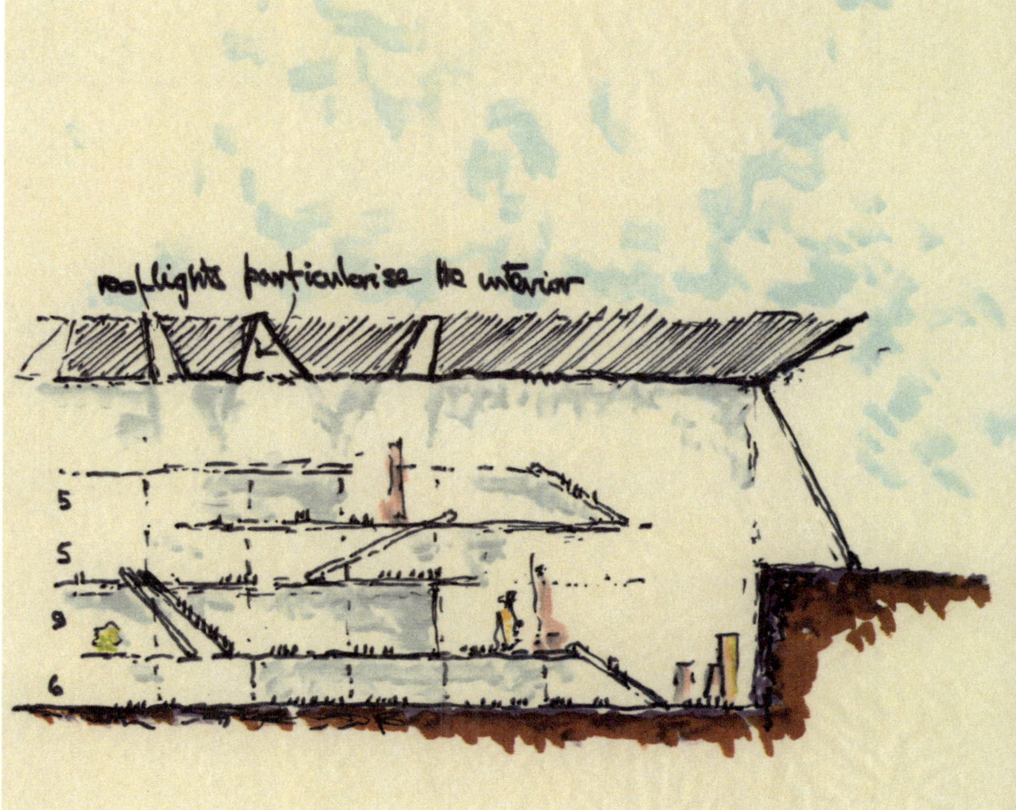

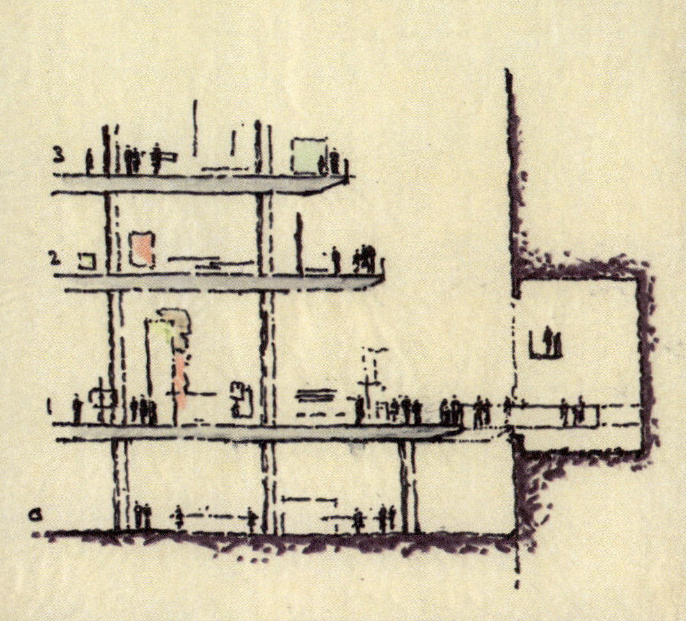

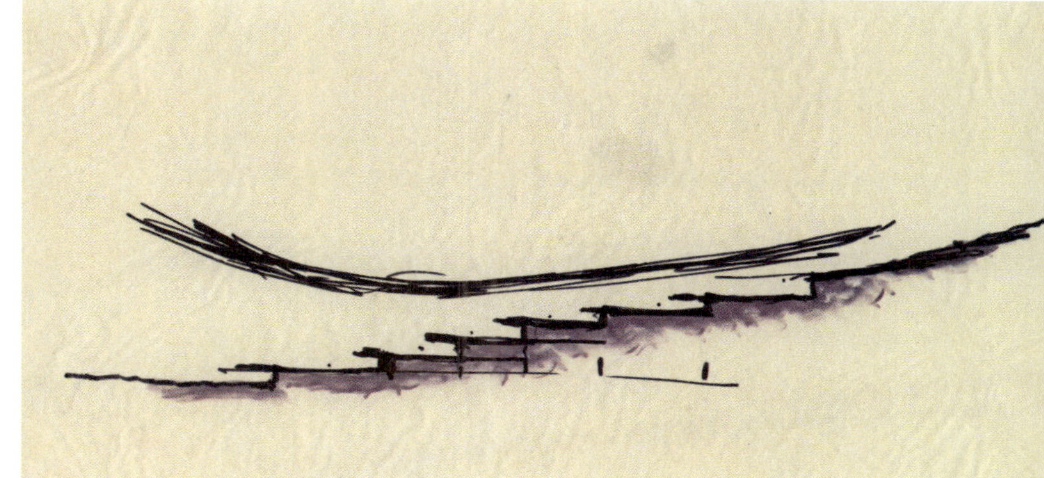

Tiered interior terraces, accessed by way of paired escalators, provide extensive and flexible exhibition spaces beneath the embracing roof canopy.

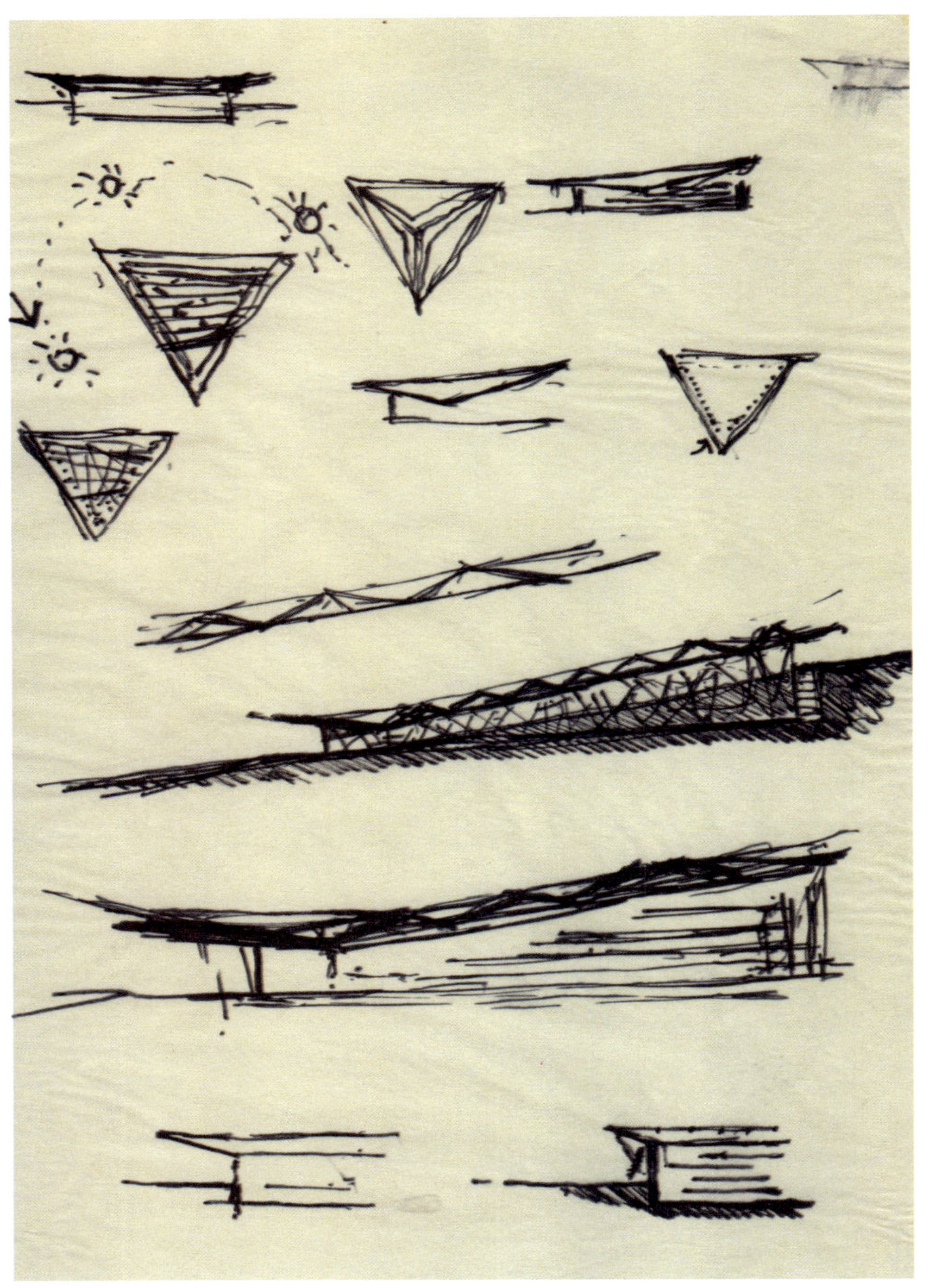

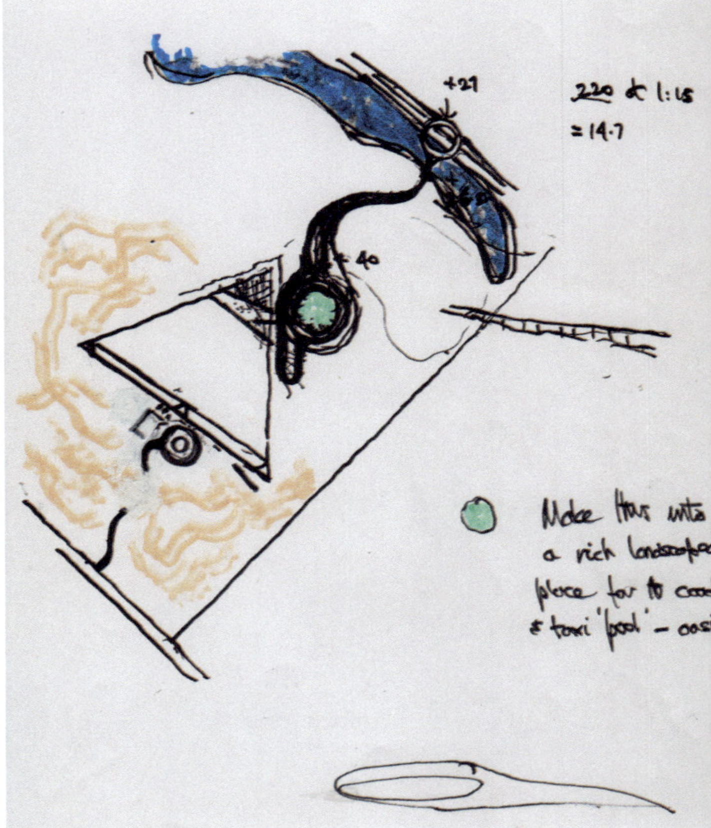

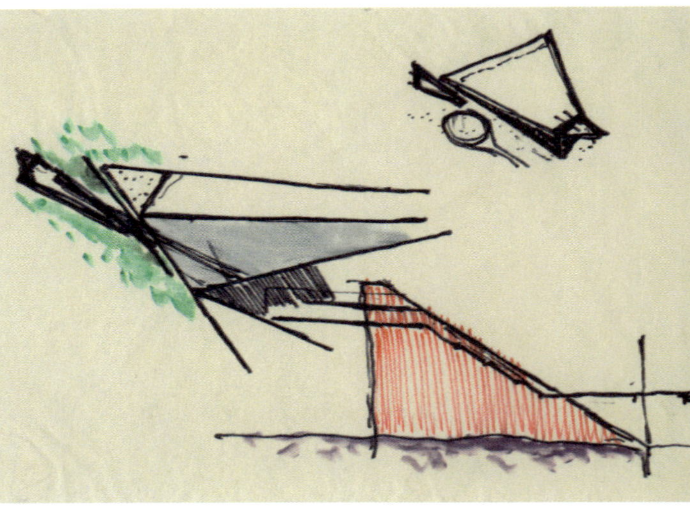

The slope of the roof follows the site topography, nestling into the hillside to diminish the apparent scale of the building. Other options are partially buried below ground, as if part of a latter-day archaeological excavation.

The site for the Grand Egyptian Museum (GEM), also known as the Giza Museum, is west of the pyramids, near a motorway interchange. Initial sketches suggest an appropriately-scaled geometric forms that are tempered by melding with the site's topography and natural landscape.

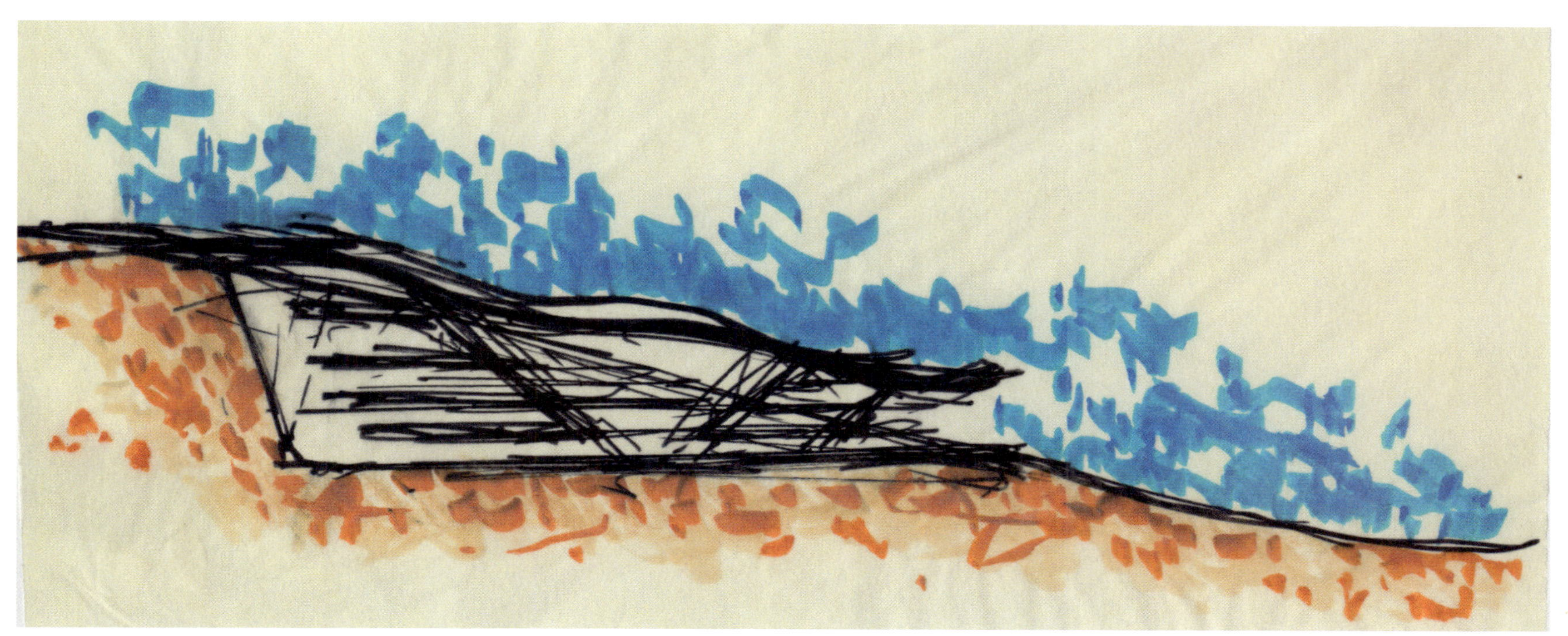

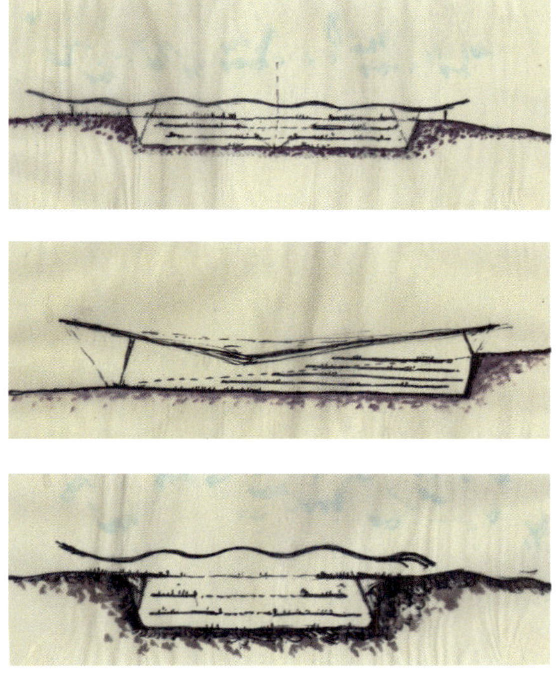

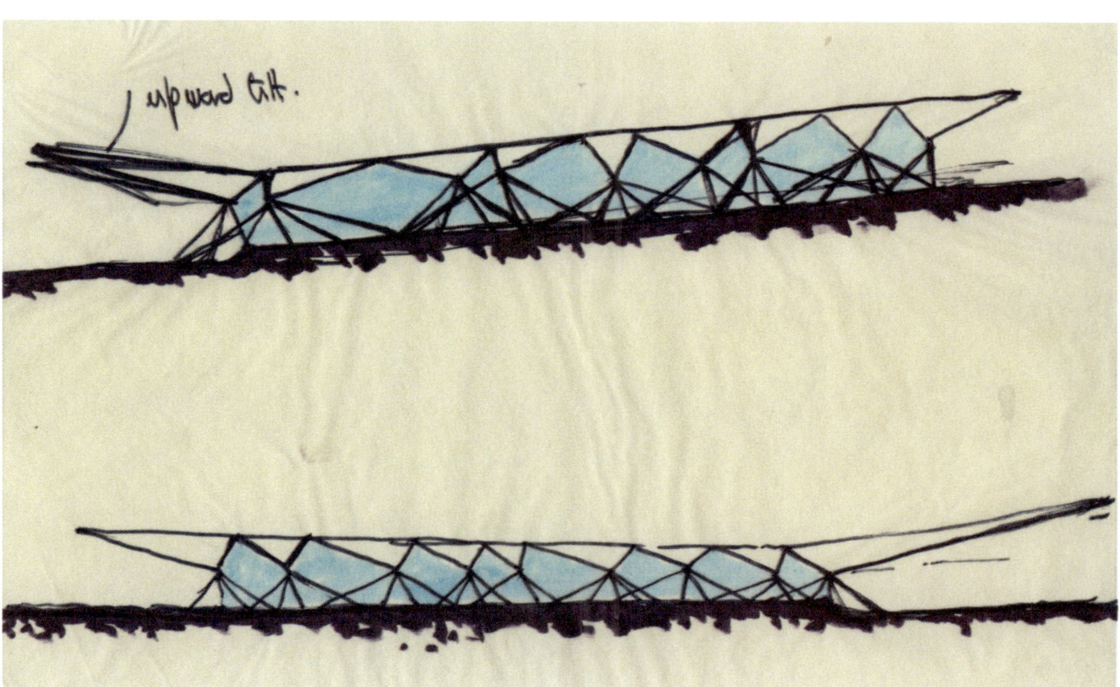

Irregular triangulated structural
systems suggest a contrast with
the platonic geometry of the
nearby pyramid forms.

In the mid-1990s, the law faculty at the University of Oxford launched a competition to design a major extension to Leslie Martin's fine, quietly strong St Cross Building, which opened in 1964. I would have wished for no better outcome than for the university to commission Martin himself for the project, but unfortunately he had retired from practice some years earlier.

With the clarity of the three courtyarded arrangement of Martin's library in mind, preceded by the generous external entrance stair (together they form a complete story), it seemed obvious that the original matrix pattern should not be simply extended in the new plan.

A separate entrance was required, bringing with it the opportunity to form a new south-facing forecourt, a physical onset and connection with the idea of suggesting an internal vector routed towards the eastern boundary, where the waters of the Mill Stream flow between pleasant green banks. Now, 20 years later, it seems obvious that this arrangement would also have supported a destination coffee bar, tablets and all.

We drew eight variations, but none were deemed of sufficient interest, it seemed.

1996

A competition to update and extend Leslie Martin's much-lauded St Cross Building. Foster & Partners' proposal was selected and built in two phases.

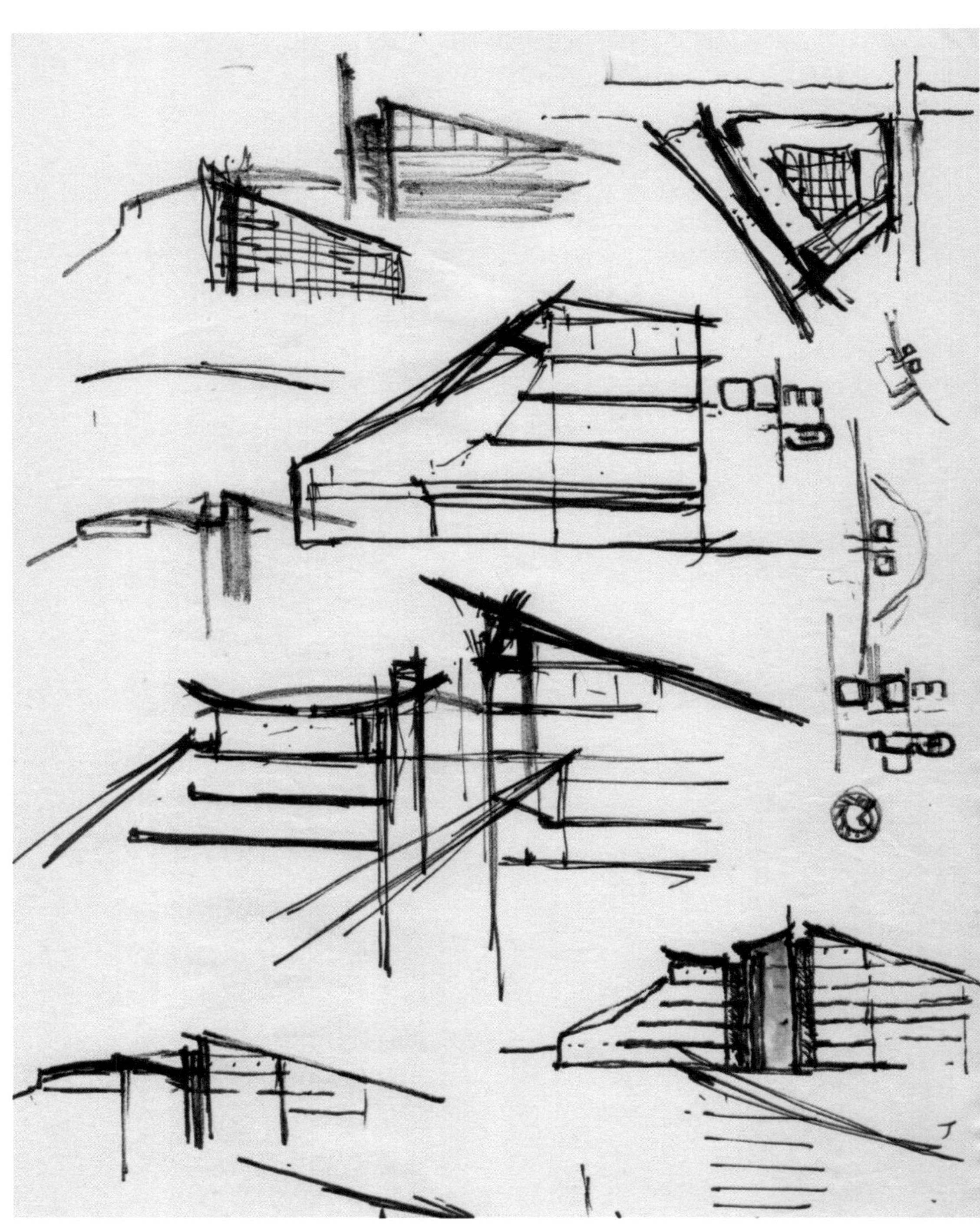

The approach was to design a sympathetic neighbour that complemented Leslie Martin's original building.

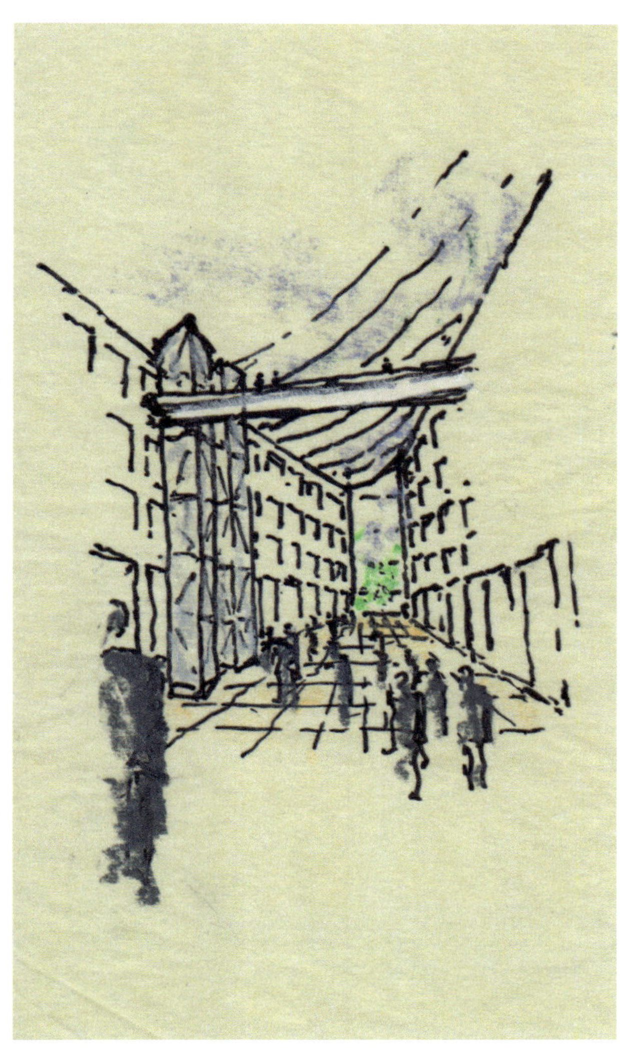

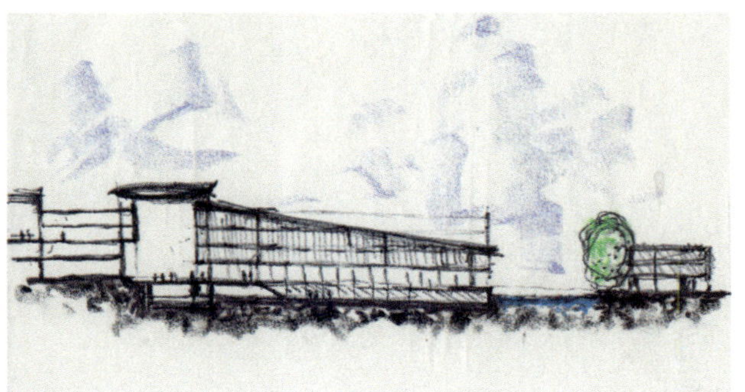

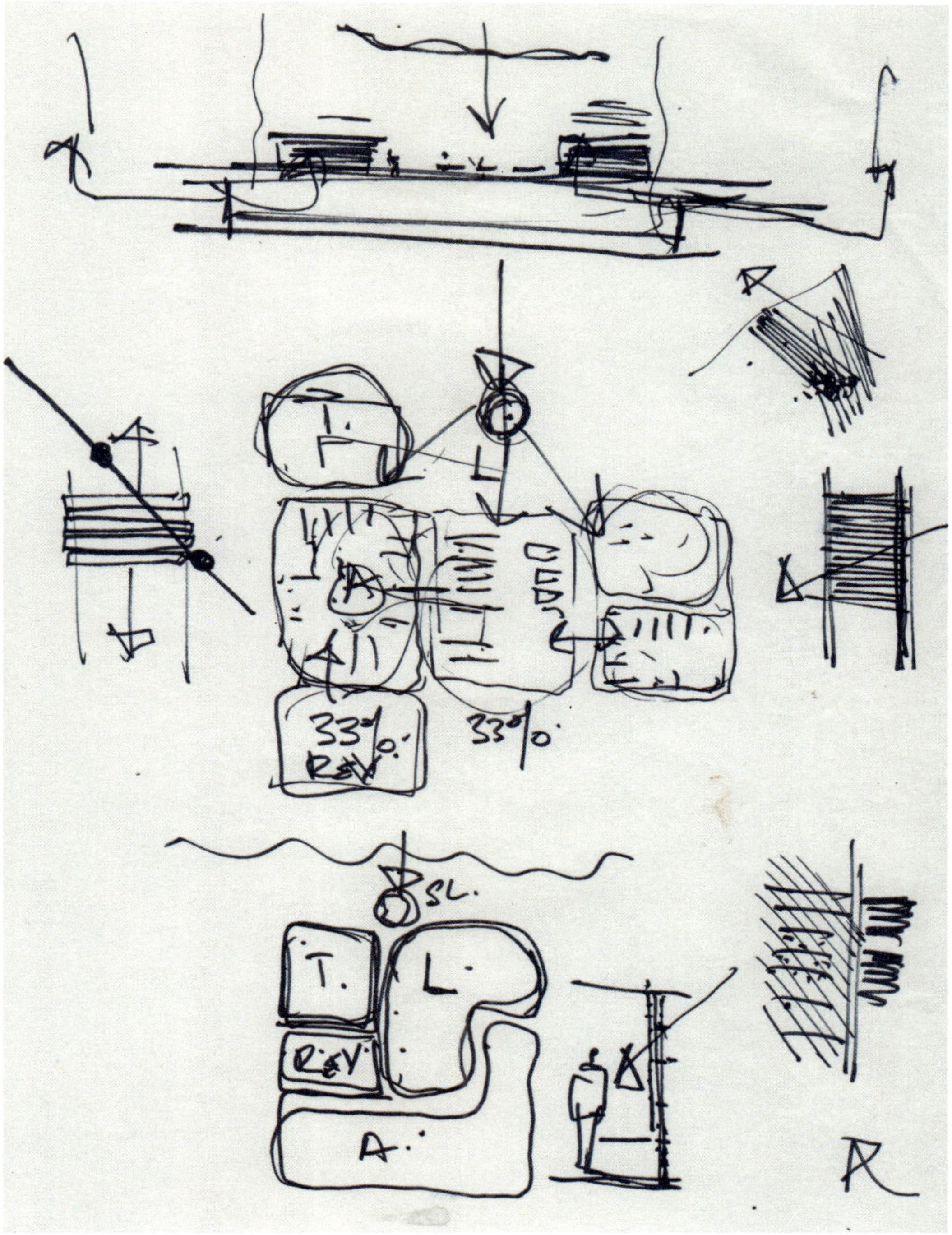

*Sketches reveal the complex
nature of the library as a building
type, requiring a variety of areas
to study, as well as access to, and
security for, their contents.*

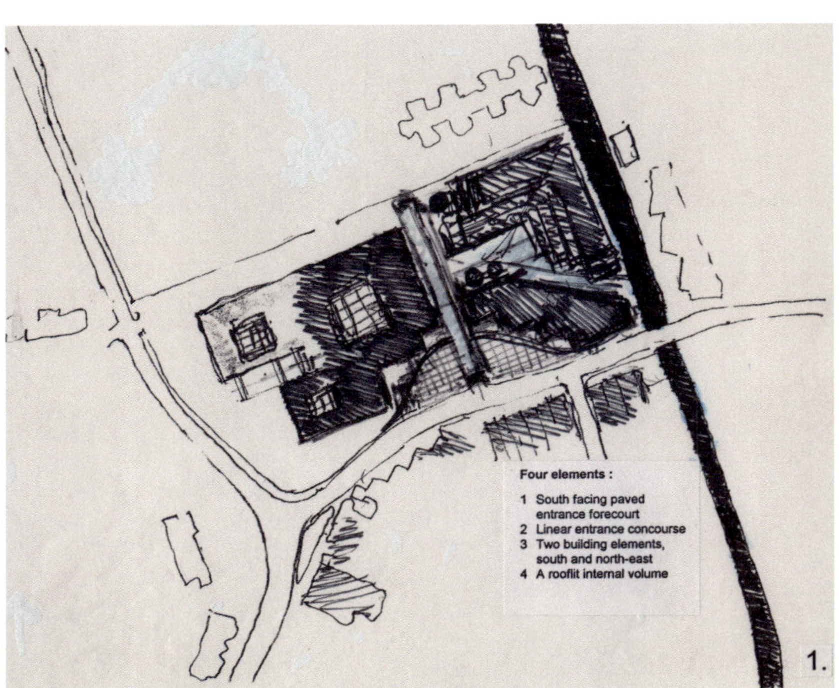

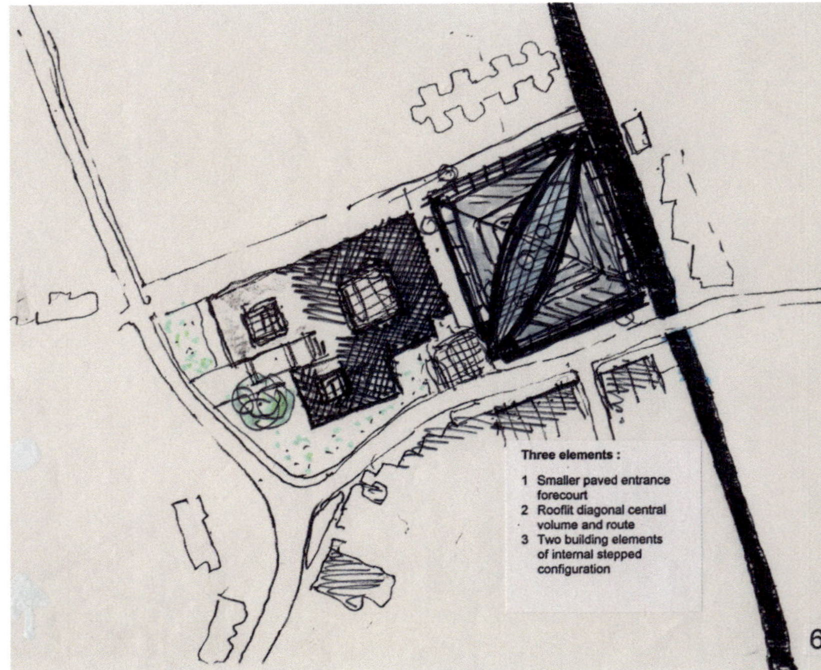

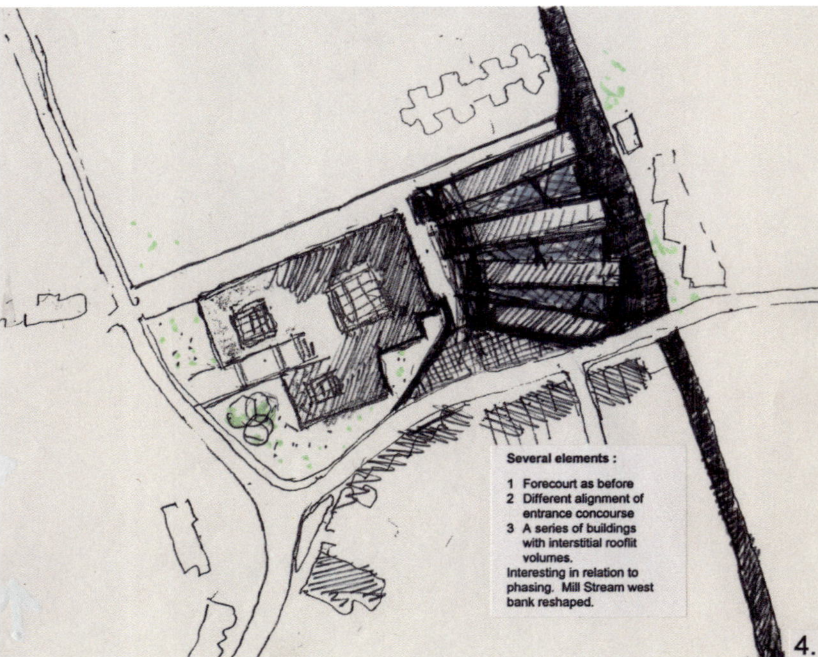

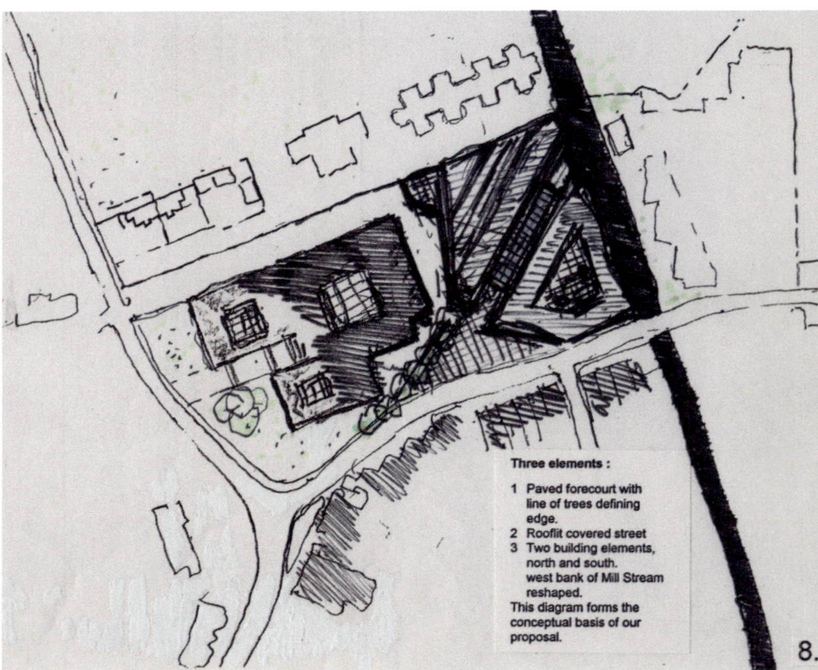

Four of the options developed for the extension, on a site to the rear of the existing building. All of the arrangements seek to establish a south-facing entrance plaza that engages both the old and new buildings.

· Planning: in layers; perhaps load distributing from west to east?

Entrance, Make something that has # an urban stature and a presence equivalent to the St Ovies building entrance.

Make a quite grand sweeping urban place, facing south – a place to linger in its sun, to drink coffee and meet friends when the weather is fine.

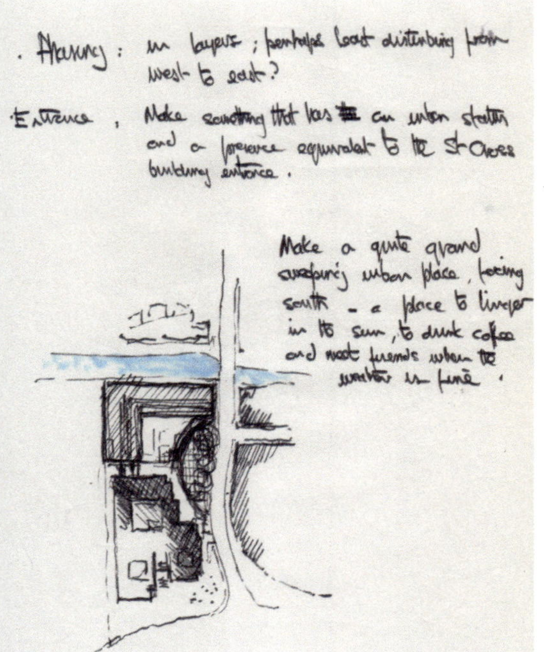

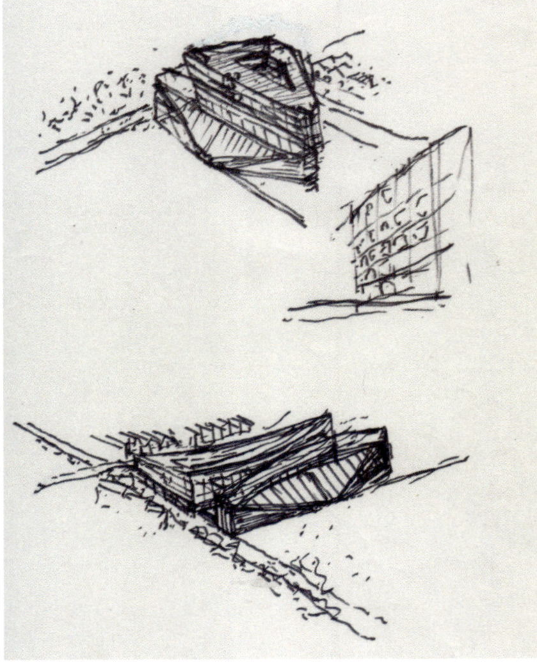

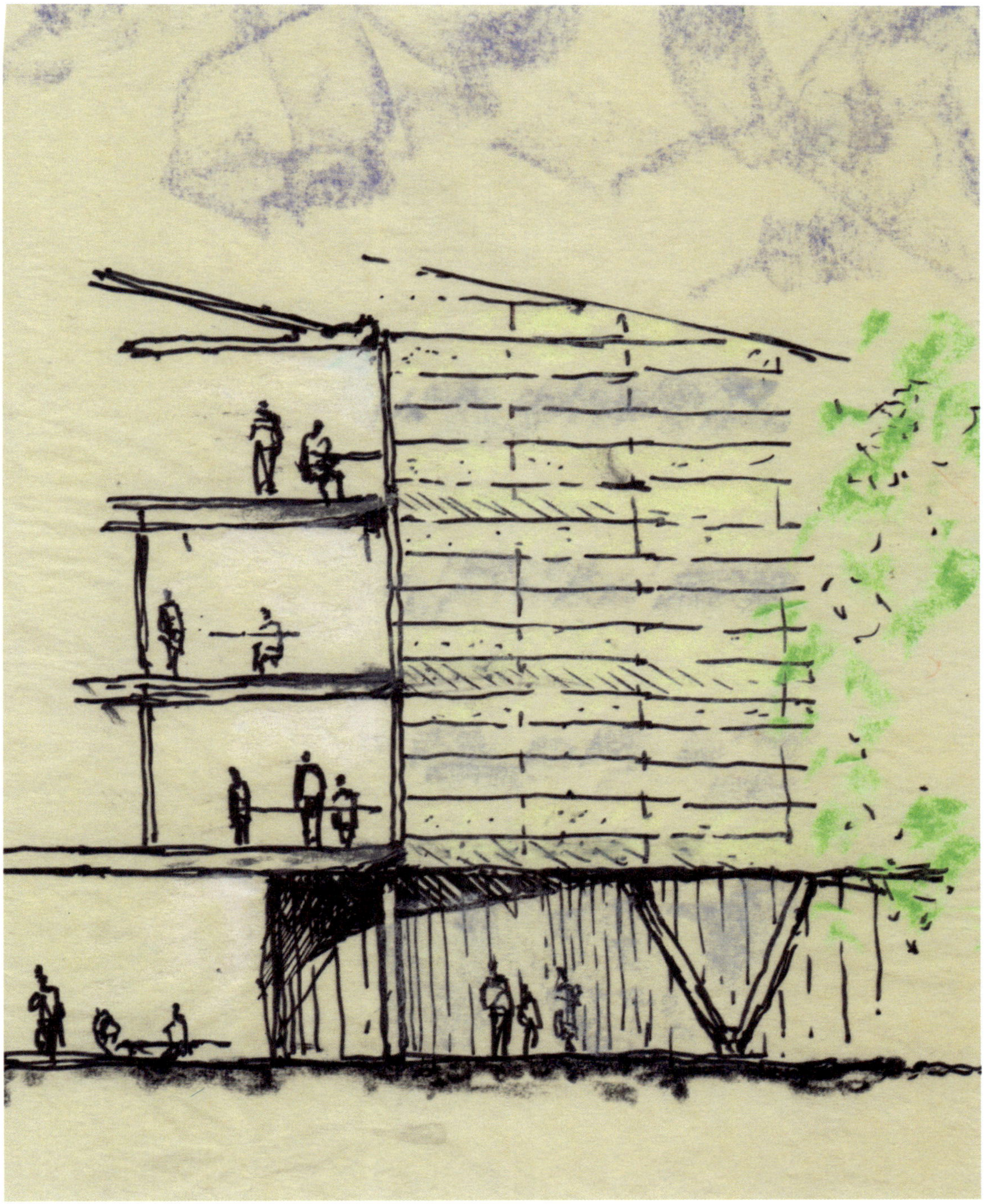

I hesitate to write this, for in going through some of the sketches made for our final design for the National Gallery extension, prepared after we'd won the competition, I'm reminded about it's troubled and messy ending.

We worked closely with the institution, responding to its difficult demands for ever more gallery space while recognising its obviously conventional views about the arrangement and spatial character of these galleries. In parallel with the design development, however, we encountered a growing unease amongst some of the trustees; it seemed that something was afoot. And so it proved, for soon after the planning inquiry inspector had published his generally favourable report about our design, Prince Charles put in his royal boot, effectively killing off the scheme.

Design competitions are renowned for occasionally producing mangled outcomes, and this one – inflamed by royal interference and fanned by the media – turned out to be a prime example. The root of the issue lies in the fact that, in design competitions, architects and clients are denied the opportunity for creative dialogue during the briefing and design stages. For prominent competitions such as this one, strong and undivided clients who are determined to 'go with' and support imaginative design are essential for successful outcomes. As we know, this doesn't always happen.

1984

ABK was asked to reconsider its competition-winning scheme to extend London's National Gallery, working with the gallery over a number of years before the project was derailed by Prince Charles.

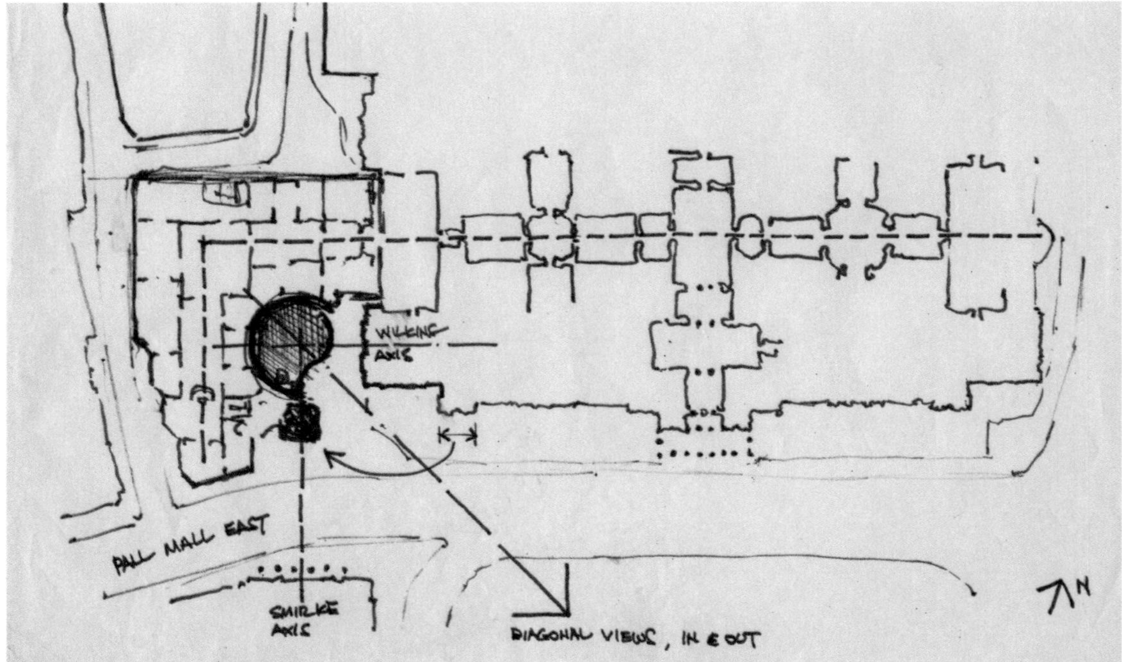

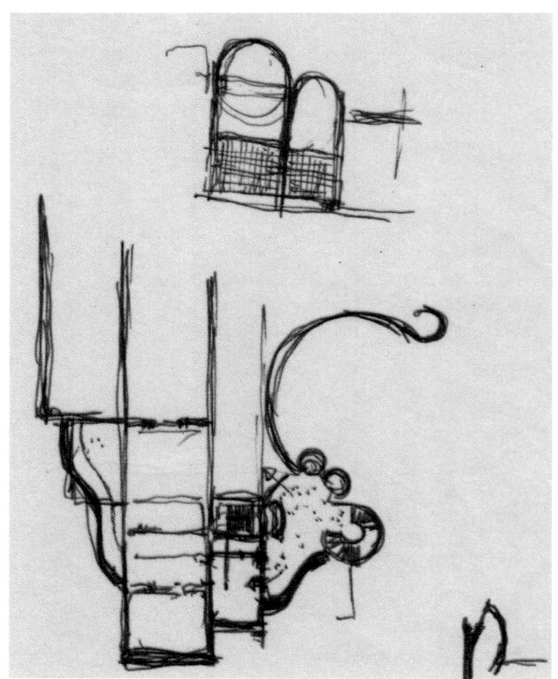

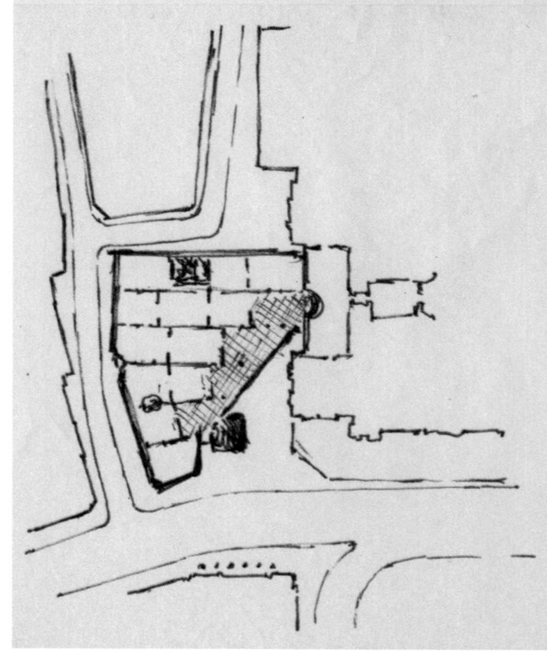

Urbanistically, the scheme envisaged an external sheltered court nestled into the extension and articulating its relationship with Wilkins' original National Gallery building.

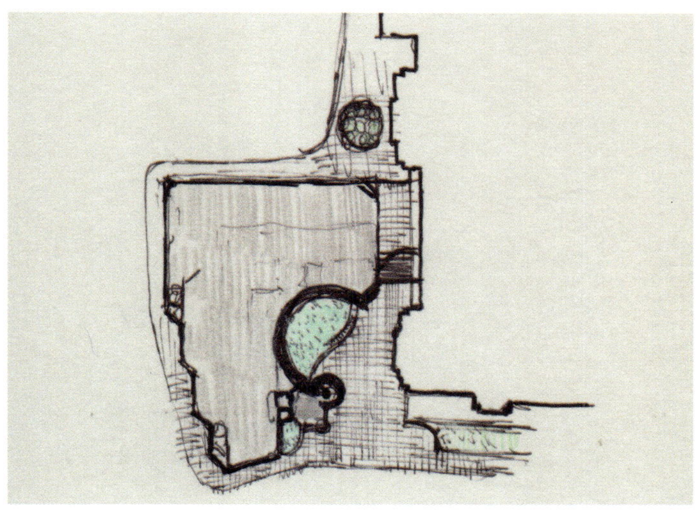

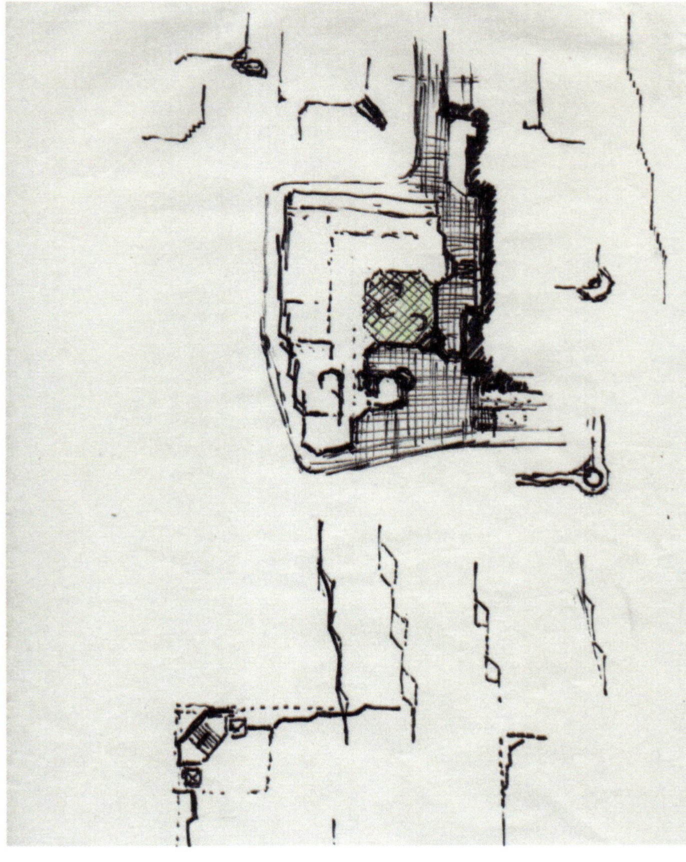

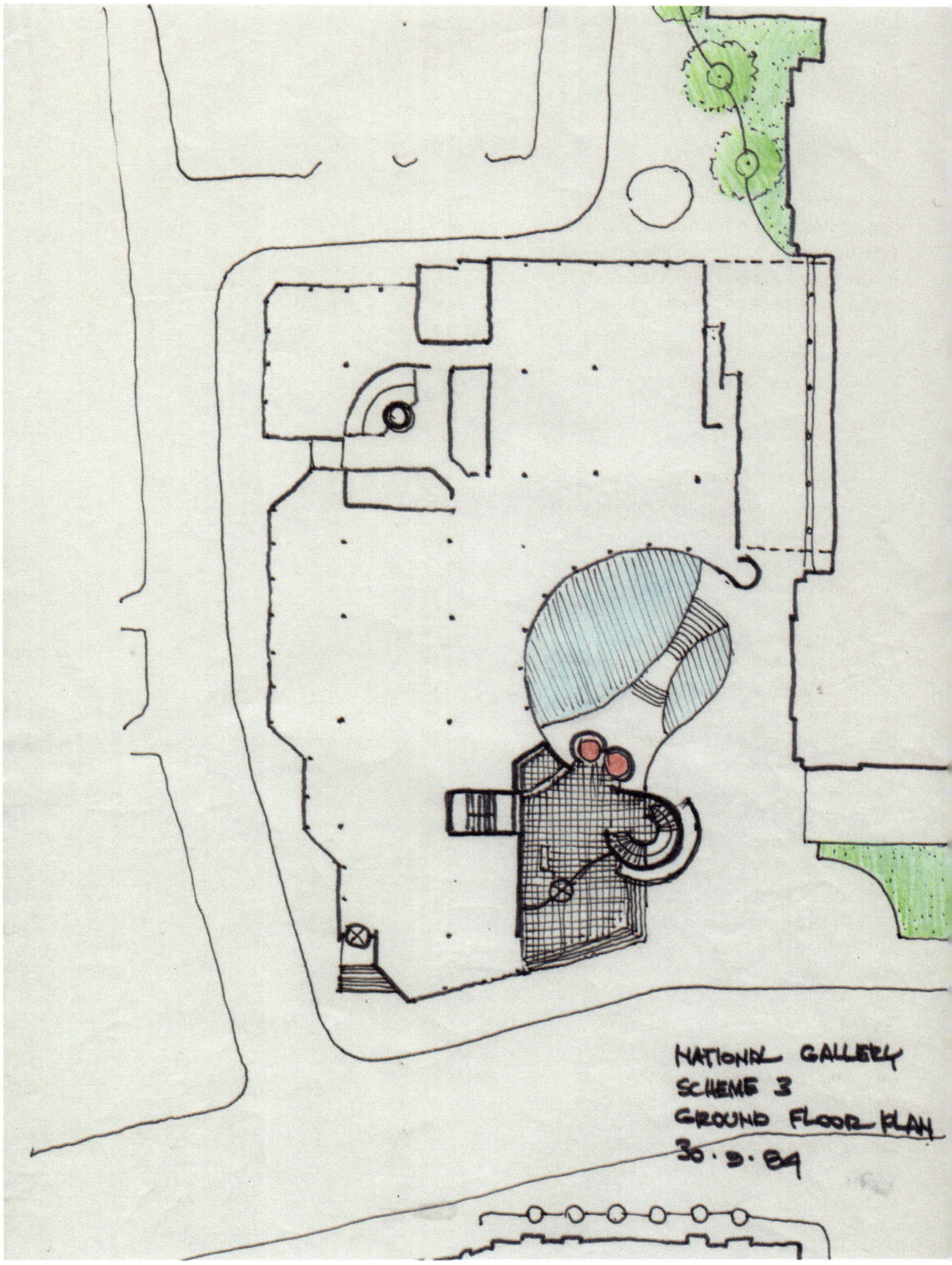

The brief for the so-called Hampton site extension envisaged rentable office space on the ground floor with new gallery spaces above. Eventually, following a further competition, a design by Robert Venturi and Denise Scott Brown was built, with no commercial provision.

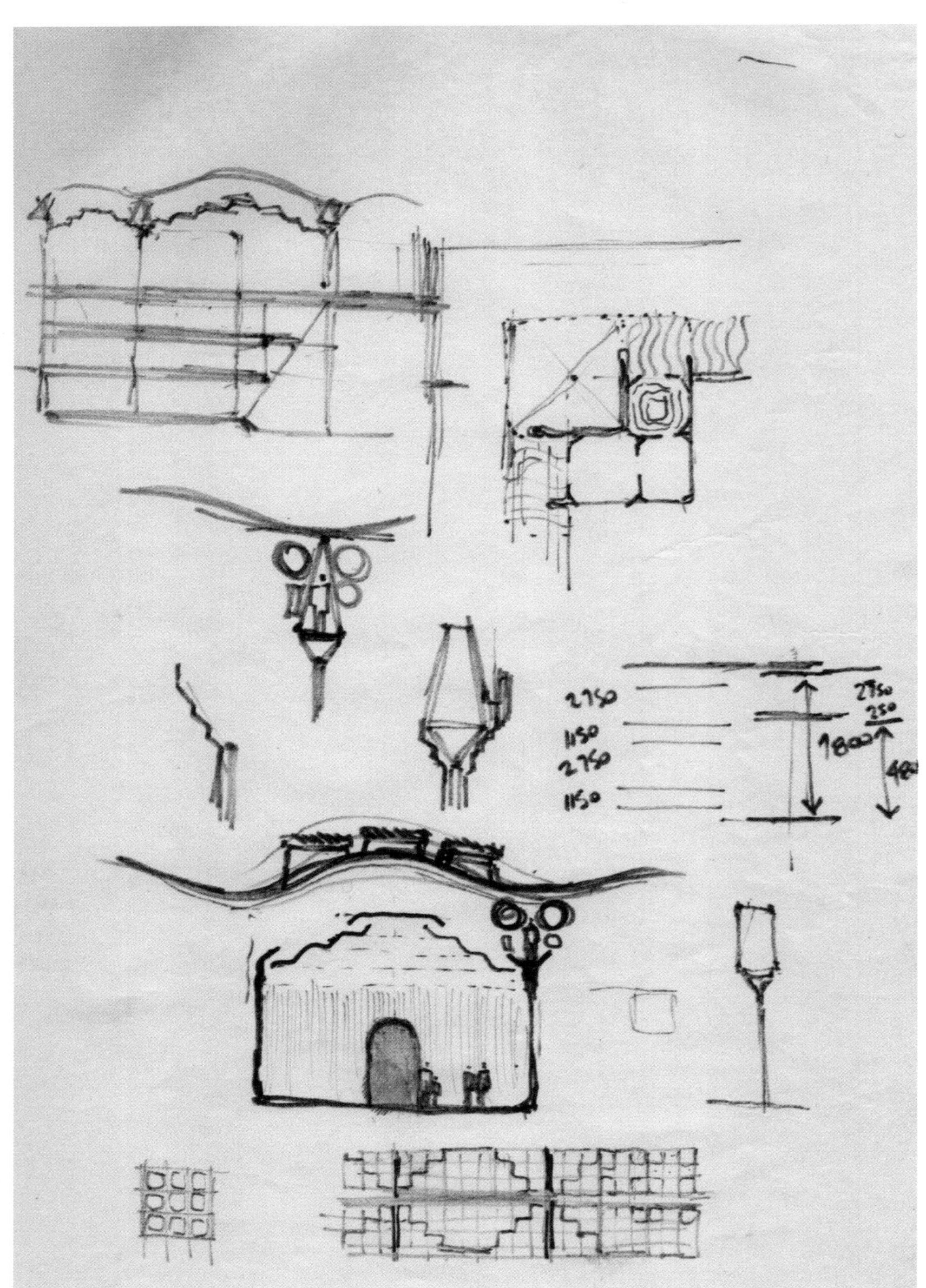

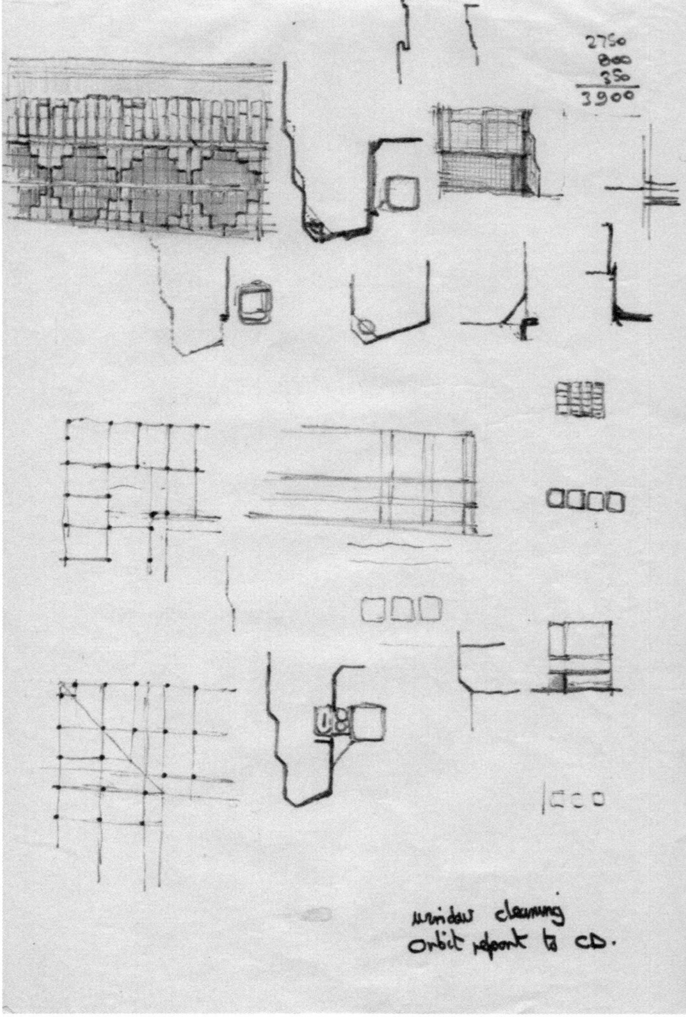

*Gallery cross section and flooring
pattern studies.*

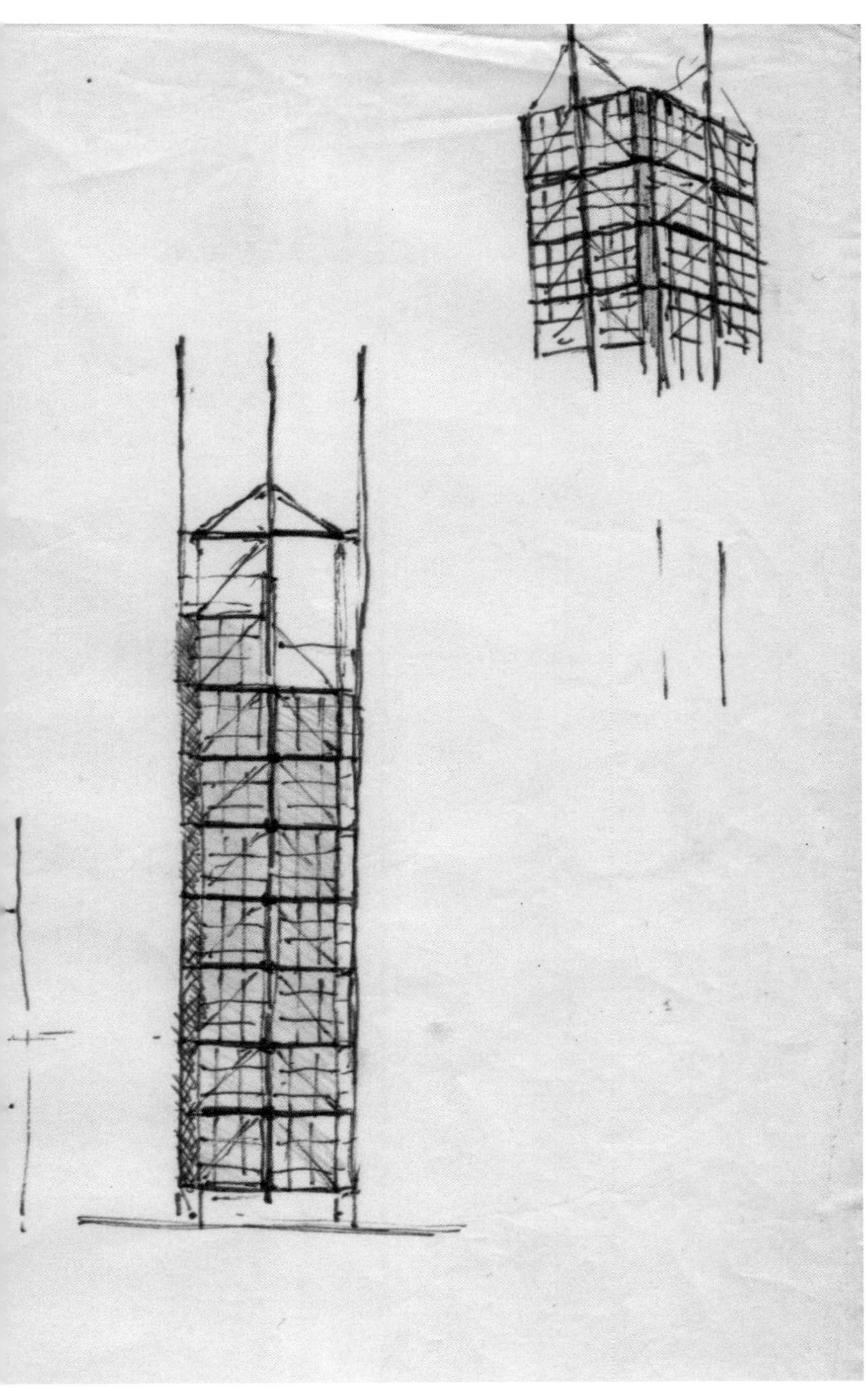

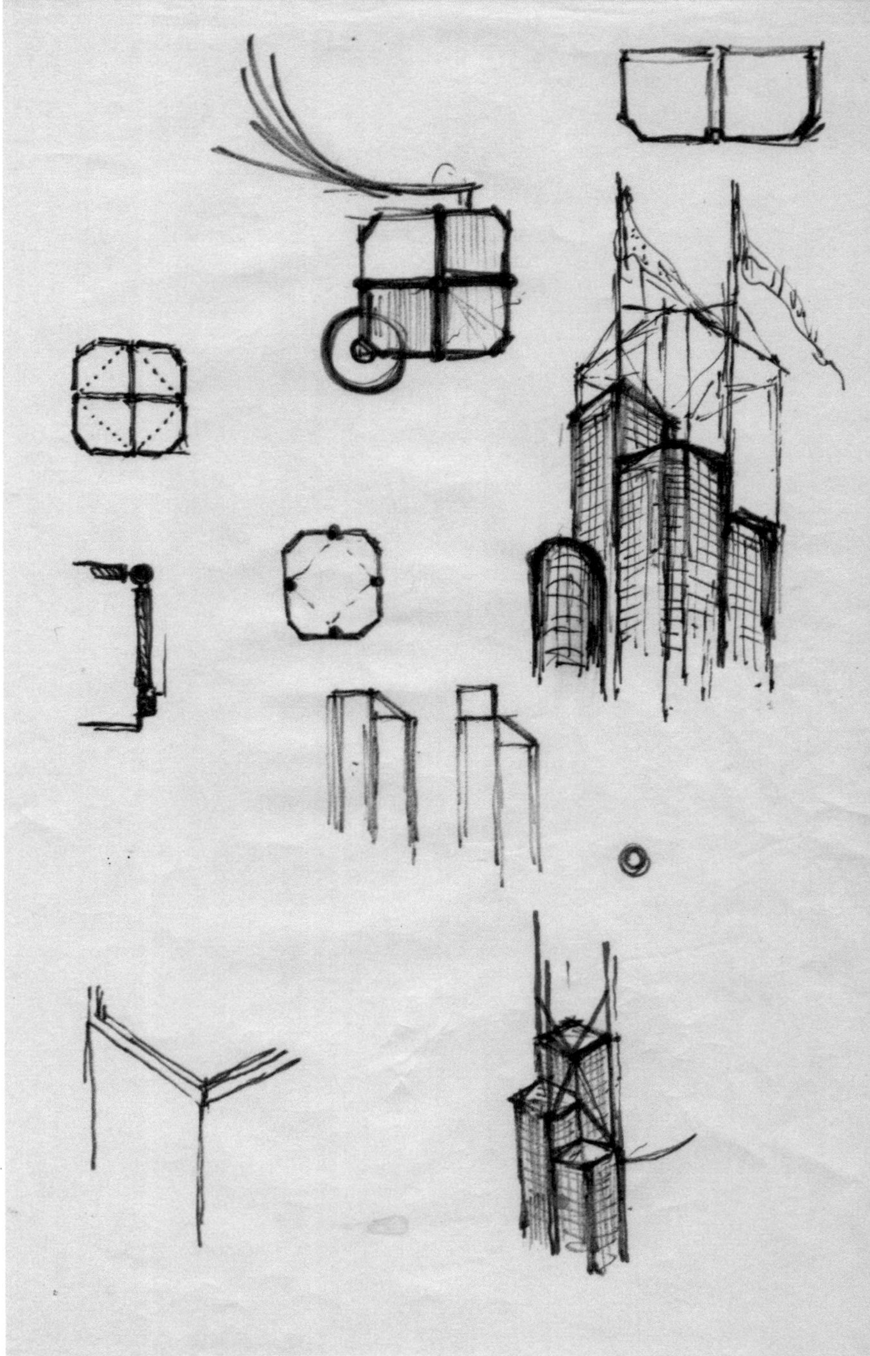

The new extension was marked by a contemporary counterpart to the historic towers in the vicinity of Trafalgar Square, as well as its focal centrepiece, Nelson's Column.

I'm pleased to include these sketches for a low-rise housing competition for a site at Ballymun, on the north side of Dublin. Pleased, because much of ABK's earlier work had been in the field of housing, ranging from private houses in Devon and the Wicklow mountains, Richard Burton's house in north London, a group of six houses at Old Headington near Oxford, two large-scale housing schemes in Basildon and Warrington, the high-rise staff accommodation at Moscow's British Embassy, and an unrealised development plan of mainly low-rise housing for 20,000 people in the Langdon Hills, south-east of Basildon.

Here in Ballymun, on a site that was also part of the masterplan's open space strategy, the competition brief was admirably clear, with a requirement to form continuous frontages along the streets. Having studied a number of layout options we came to favour one that included a type of embedded horseshoe close; a curving layout designed to form a small but particularly centred urban character within the given pattern of street blocks.

1997

An invited competition entry for housing at Ballymun, part of a major regeneration programme at Dublin's northern periphery.

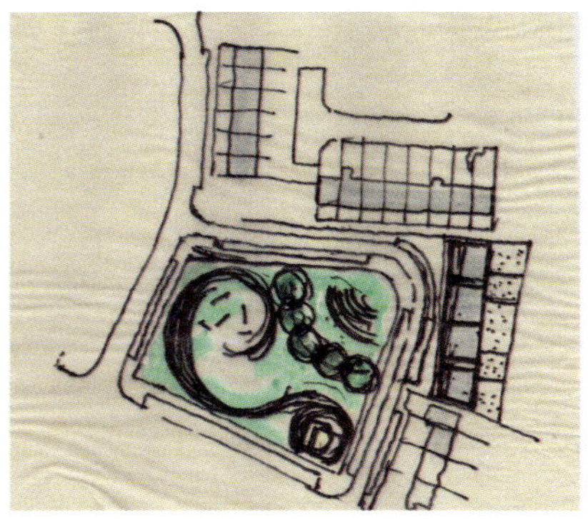

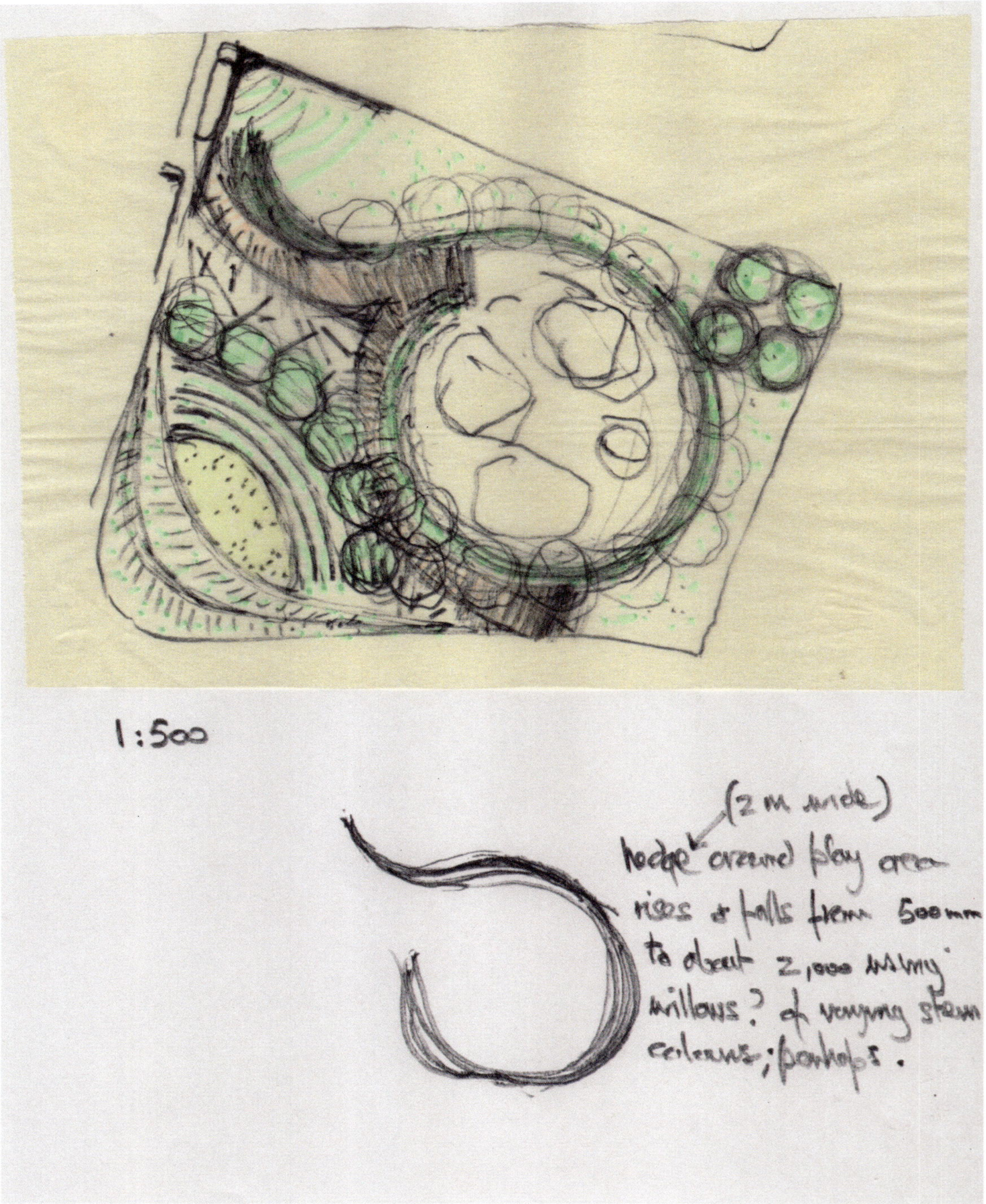

1:500

Exploring options for residential terraces that allow an urban density while also accommodate shared green space.

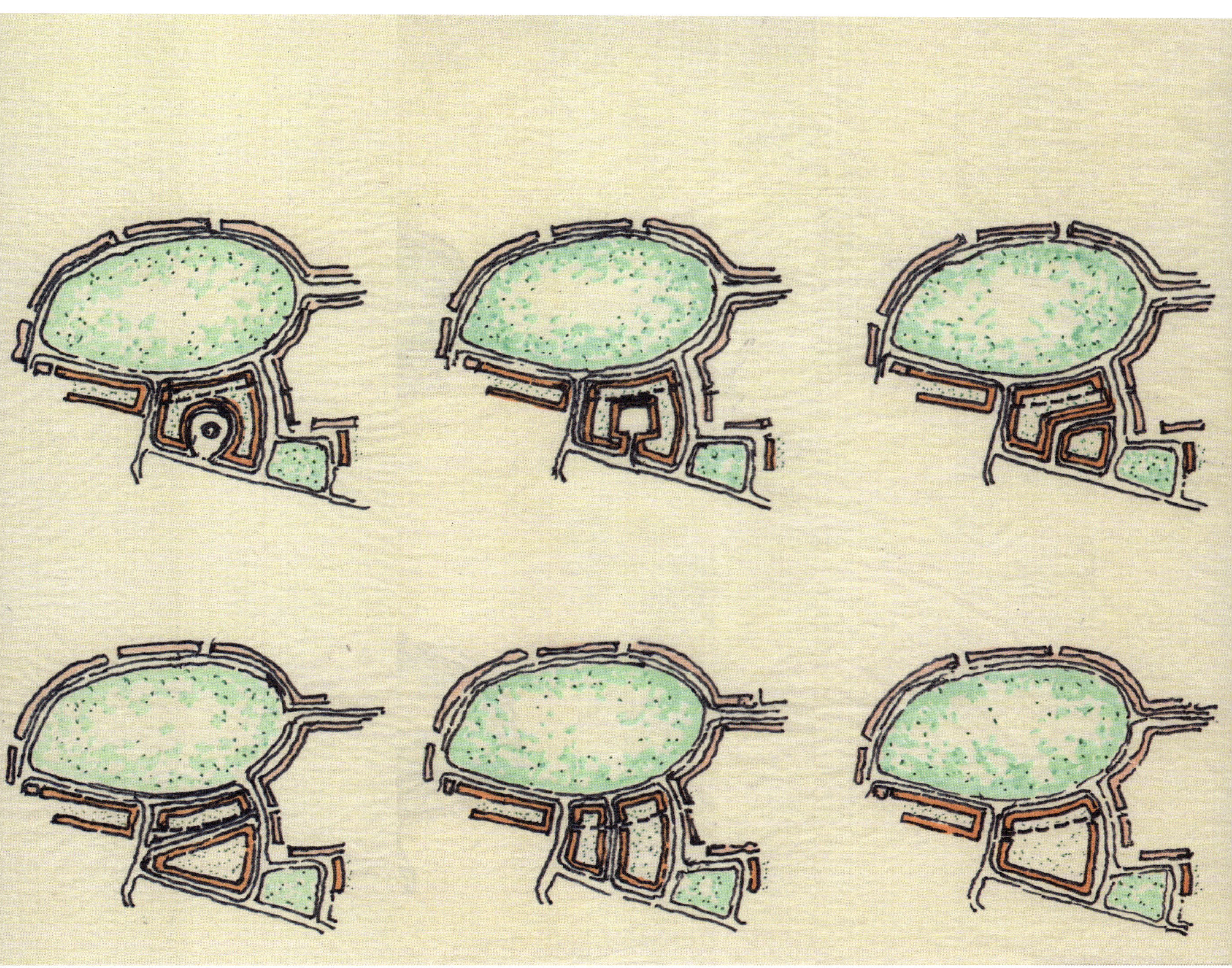

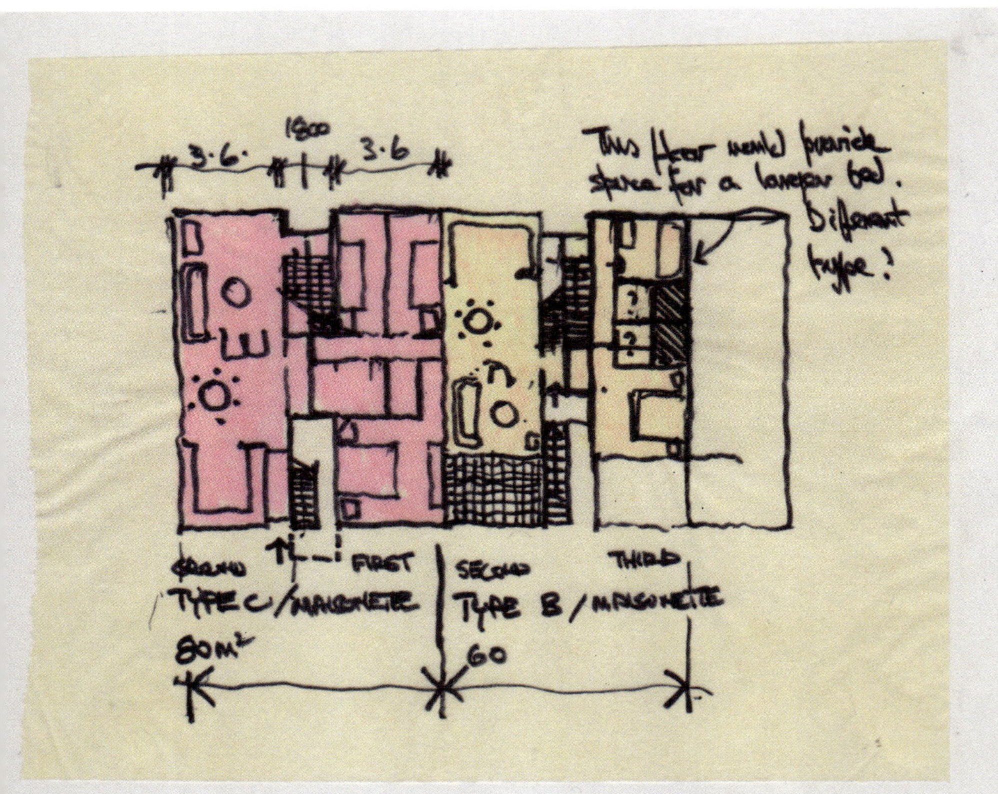

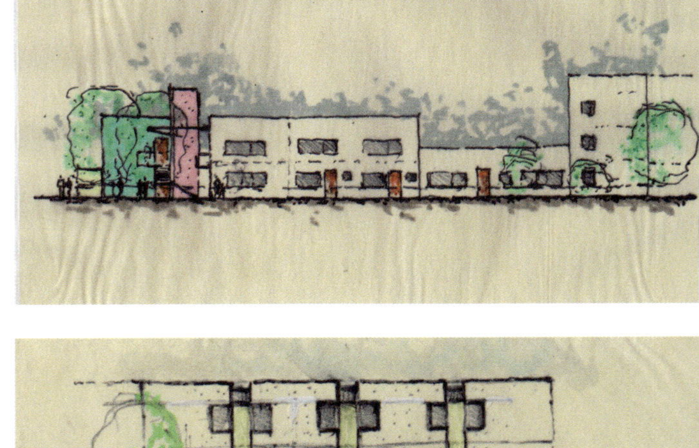

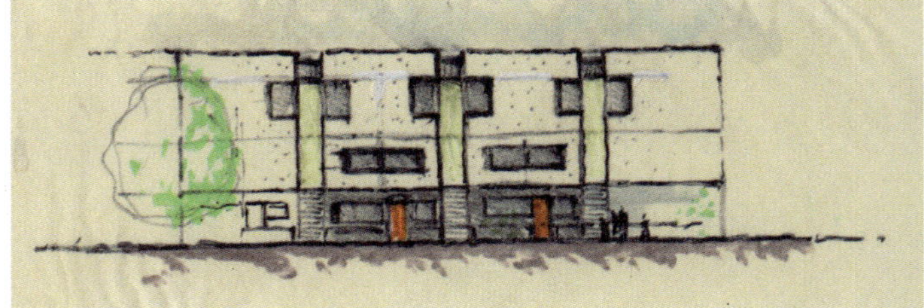

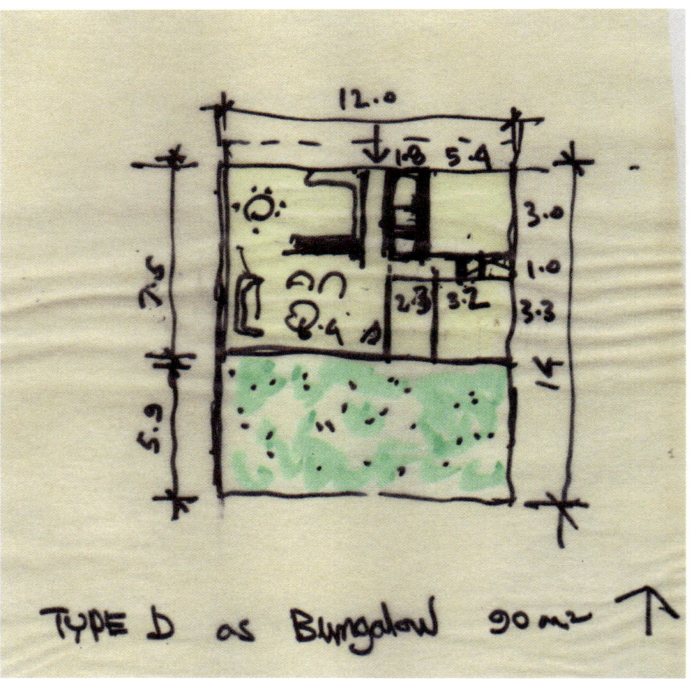

- Alternative Type C layout planned as a maisonette with Type B maisonette above i.e 4 storey building with a narrower footprint
- The plan also considers a more economic use use of the circulation zone for 'external' and internal access.

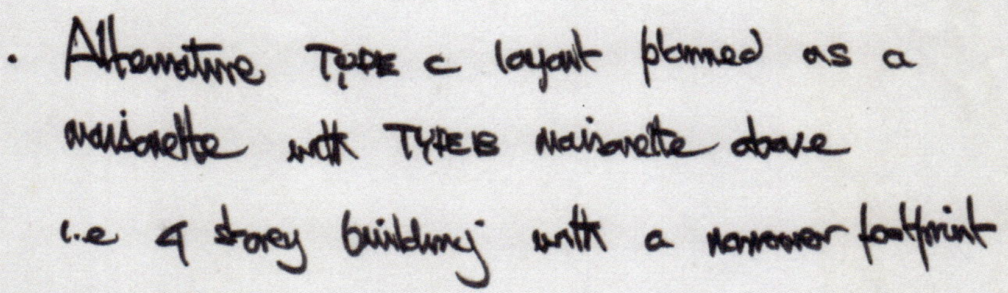

About one third of a century after we built the Berkeley Library at Trinity College, Dublin, the college launched a competition to extend the building southwards onto a vacant site.

The college's Fellows Square (previously the more exclusive Fellows Garden) is largely surrounded by a range of libraries in a variety of buildings, historic and modern. We had been fortunate to be the architect for two of these buildings (in the 1960s and 70s), which were sited along the eastern and southern sides of the quad. So when in 1997 the college launched a competition for a substantial extension to our Berkeley Library, we were keen to have a go – unsuccessfully, as it turned out.

The process, however, was interesting. In the early 1960s we had worked as a close-knit group on Paul Koralek's competition-winning scheme to develop the design. Working on ideas for an extension more than 30 years later, Paul and I found that there was no question in our minds of doing more of the same. Instead Paul came up with the radical and somewhat crazy idea of digging up much of the grassed Fellows Square to form an extensive subterranean, roof-lit reading room in order to contain the mass of the new extension. We explored this for a while but soon moved on to different ideas, some of which are shown here.

1997

ABK revisited its 1960s library at Trinity College Dublin to compete in a limited competition for the design of an extension.

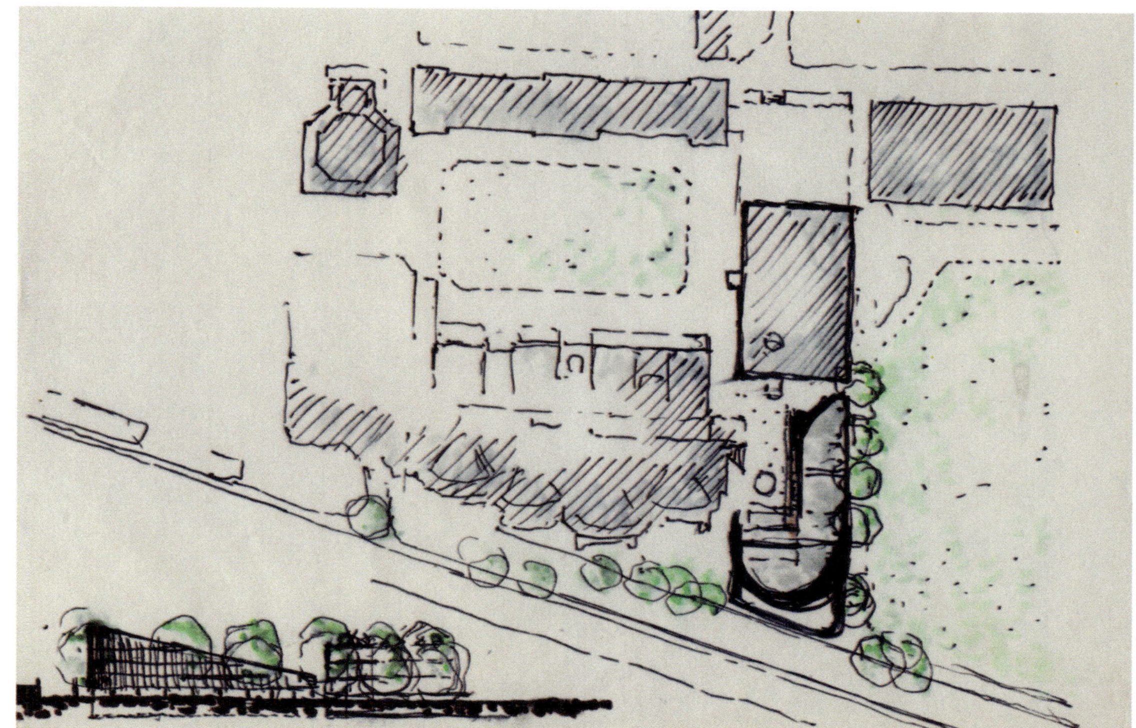

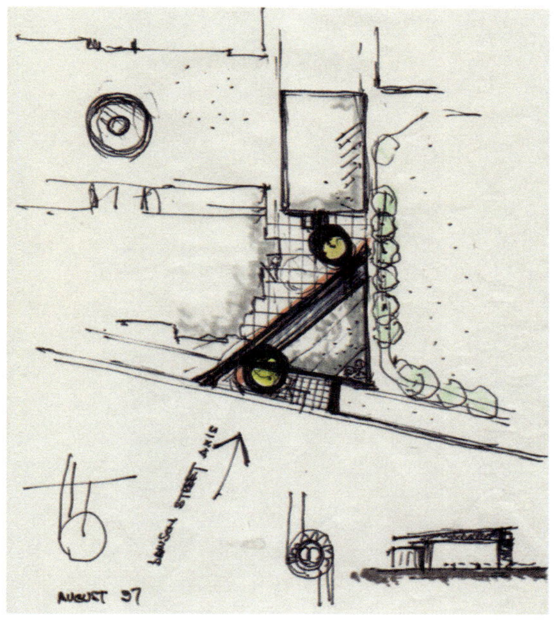

The new building was to be sited adjacent to ABK's earlier Berkeley Library, facing onto Nassau Street. The competition was won by McCullough Mulvin Architects and KMD Architecture, and the building – the James Ussher Library – opened in 2003.

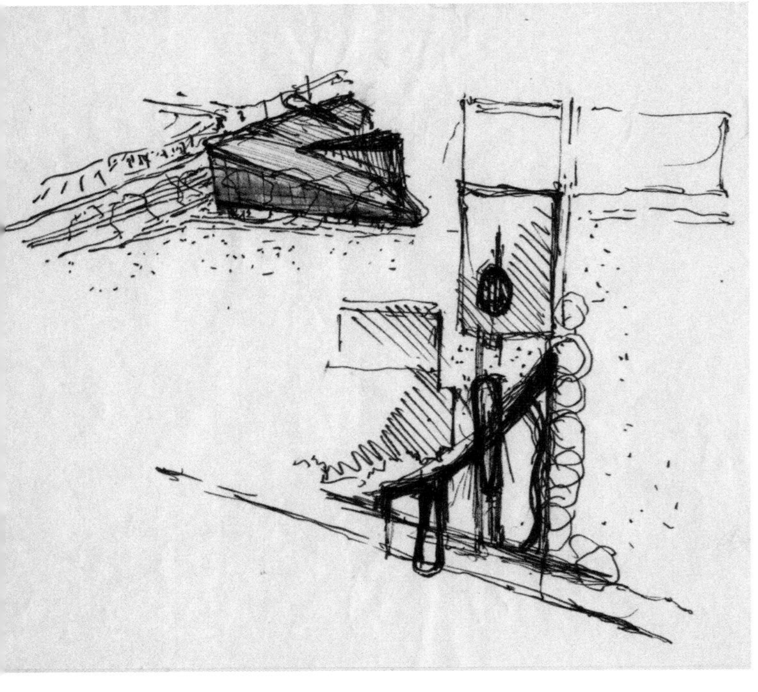

Agde, Tuesday 26th   Fax N° 00.04.67.21.20.36

Paul,

I hope that you had a good break and that all is well on your return. A few thoughts about the library extension:

1. Might it be possible and interesting to slope or step back the upper floors in relation to the slope of the glazed wall?

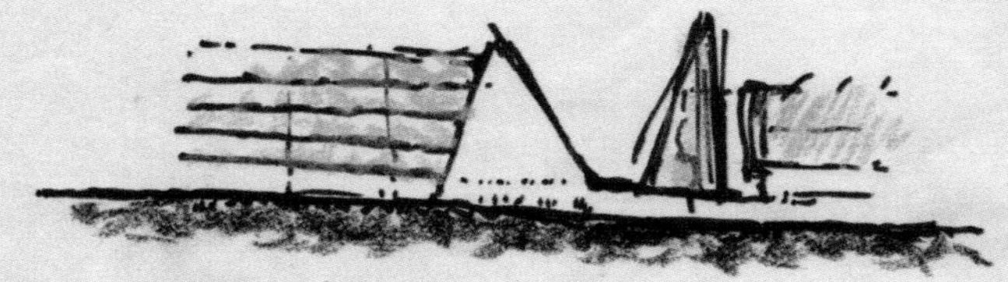

2. To some extent in relation to this but also thinking about the make-up of the materials of the walls of the extension I wonder whether we should make the cladding of the upper floors of bands of white / gray translucent glass (& transparent for 'windows') restricting the granite cladding to the ground floor base and the triangular end wall to College Park.

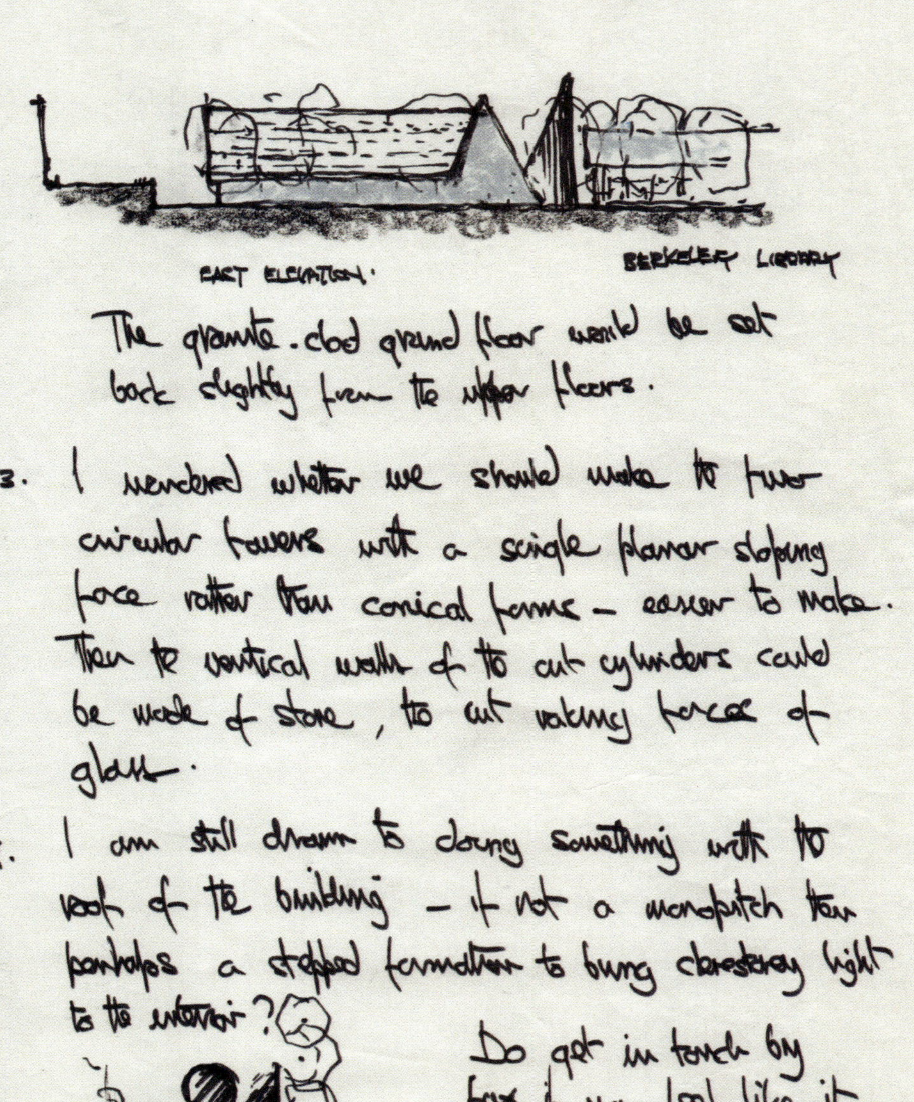

The granite-clad ground floor would be set back slightly from the upper floors.

3. I wondered whether we should make the two circular towers with a single planar sloping face rather than conical forms — easier to make. Then the vertical walls of the cut cylinders could be made of stone, to cut raking forces of glass.

4. I am still drawn to doing something with the roof of the building — if not a monopitch then perhaps a stepped formation to bring clerestory light to the interior?

Do get in touch by fax if you feel like it. Hope all is going well.

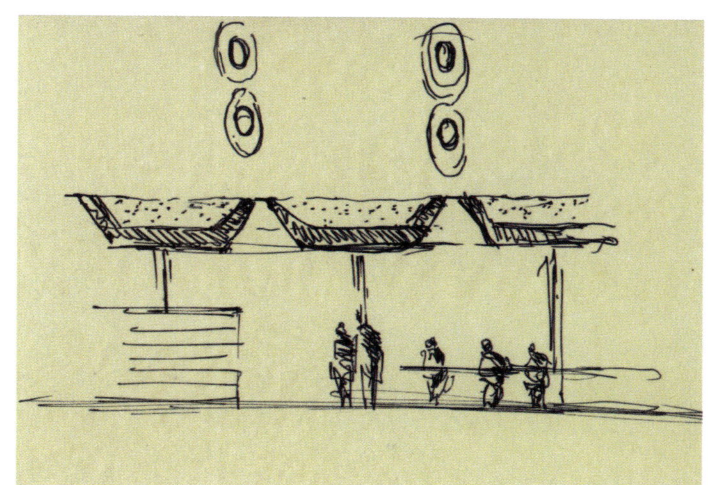

The selection procedure to design a development plan for the new Institute of Technology at Blanchardstown, near Dublin, was by competitive interview. The preliminary brief included not only the development plan but also the first-phase buildings for the greenfield site, just beyond the city's periphery.

The day before the interview, I visited the extensive site, but with some confusion about its precise location. I stood in the all-round greyness of the early winter dusk, looking up at a darkening green rise, hoping that the land mass before me was the right place. Soon I found myself accompanied by a number of friendly ponies who wanted either some recognition or more likely some carrots that I wasn't able to provide. I told them that I hoped to see them again, when we were established as the architects, and set off to my hotel to make a few sketches overnight; not of ponies but of first-response ideas for the interviewing body on the following morning.

Fortunately we got the job, but I never met the ponies again to thank them for their friendly encouragement. Later, during a complex process set up for the development of the brief, we looked at site planning and massing options; some are shown here along with a few other elements. They were positive and responsive clients with whom to work, in parallel with Dublin's architects department.

1998-2002

A competitive interview to plan the 50-hectare higher education campus of Blanchardstown Institute of Technology.

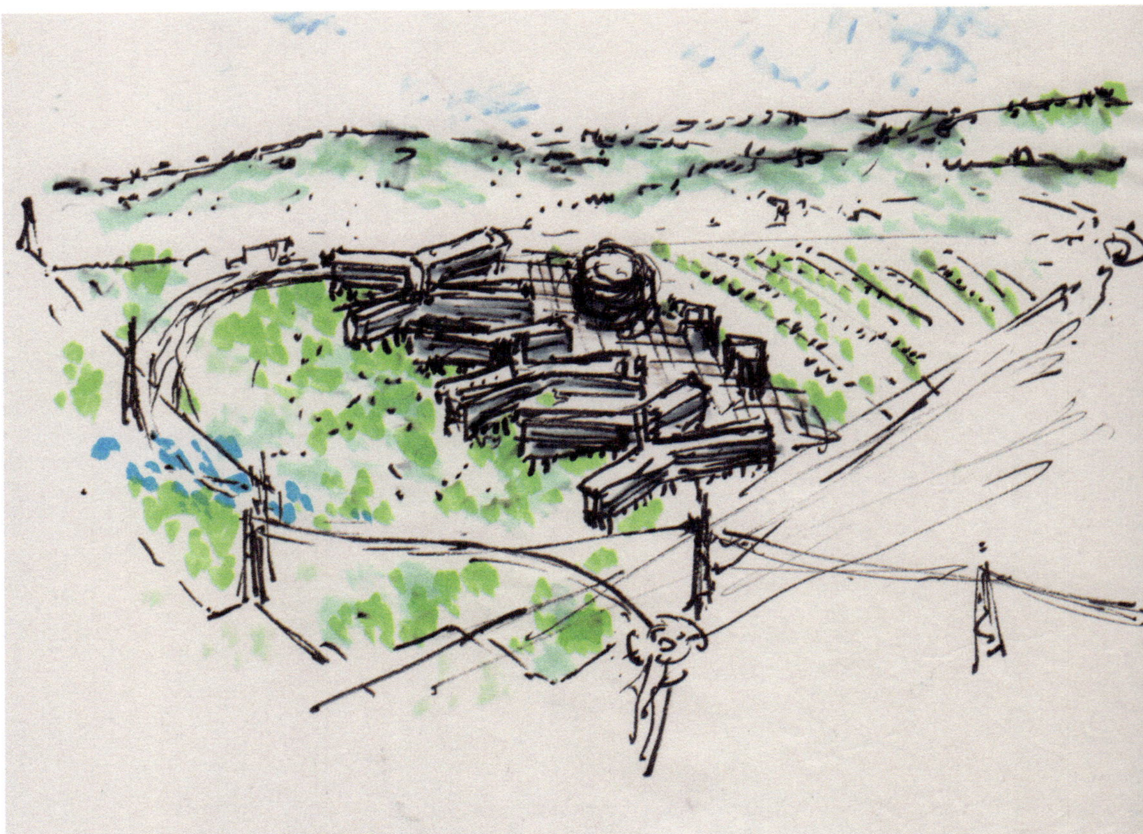

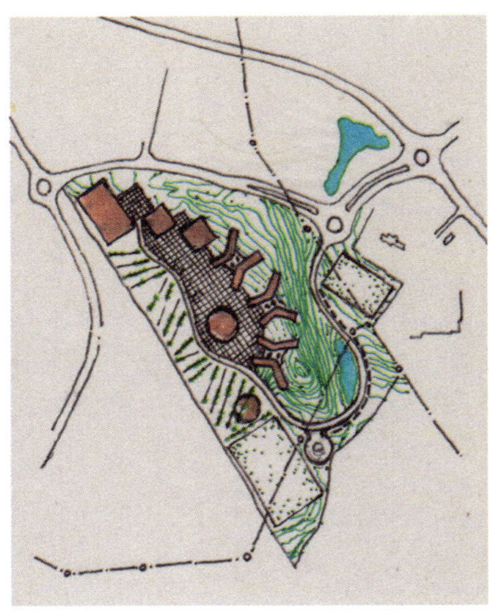

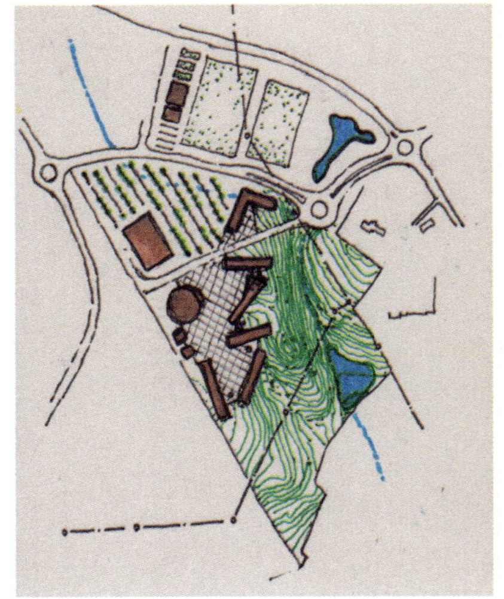

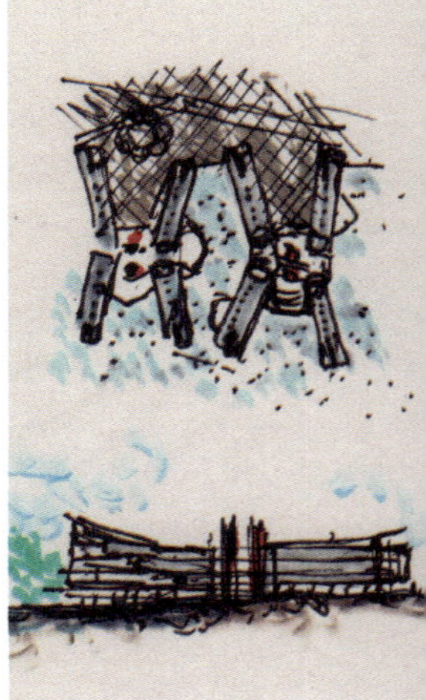

Various options explored the potential of clustered buildings with splayed wings to form a court and take advantage of the prospect across the parkland setting.

The brief for this competition called for the design of substantial new buildings in the vicinity of Herstmonceaux, a listed medieval moated castle in East Sussex, to form a part of a new golf course development, including a hotel.

Looking through my sketches and notes I recall my concern about the ambivalent mix of this proposed new world, offering landed golf and beautiful home-counties riding trails, with the prevailing image of the castle's association with medieval power. This strange ambiguity hovered as a minor disturbance in the mind as I recognised that, say, a proposal by others for a subtly-mannered crumble of soft red brick and pitched roof tiles in a carefully set-aside position might, perhaps, be well received.

No such ideas came to us as we looked at several options. Indeed it was an opposite design position that took hold, in relation to the castle and its south elevation entrance which had been made as if to say 'cross the moat and enter if you dare'. Here, we thought, was an opportunity to make something special: an axially-related landscaped entrance place lying between the new hotel building and the moat, with the crescent form of a green embankment settling gently but notably into the falling contours of the landscape. In its deliberations, the selection panel must have thought otherwise.

1989

A competition for new hospitality and recreational facilities in the sensitive landscape of Herstmonceaux Castle.

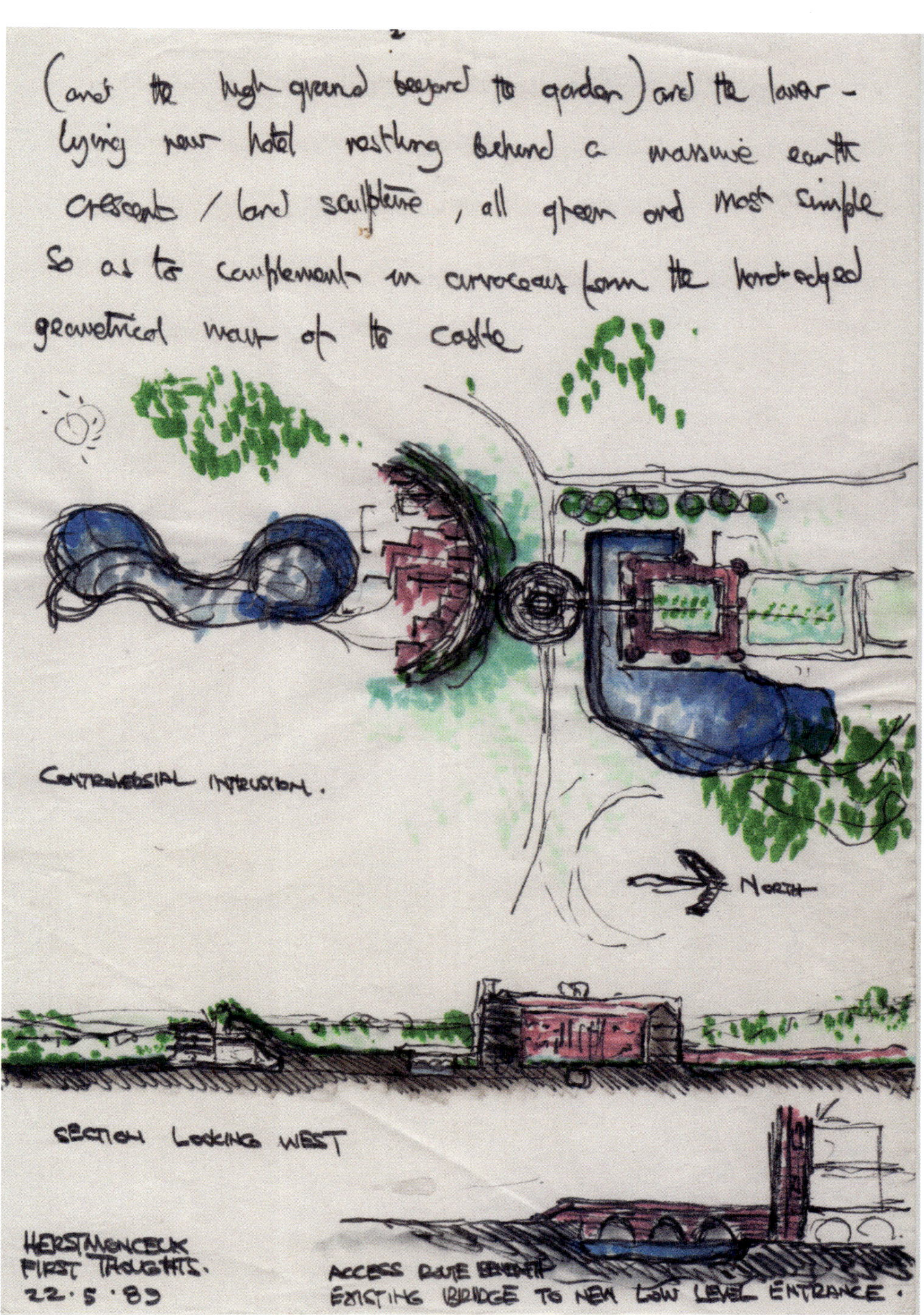

While the proposal sought to embed itself within the precious landscape, it was sited so as to form a clear relationship with the existing castle and bridge.

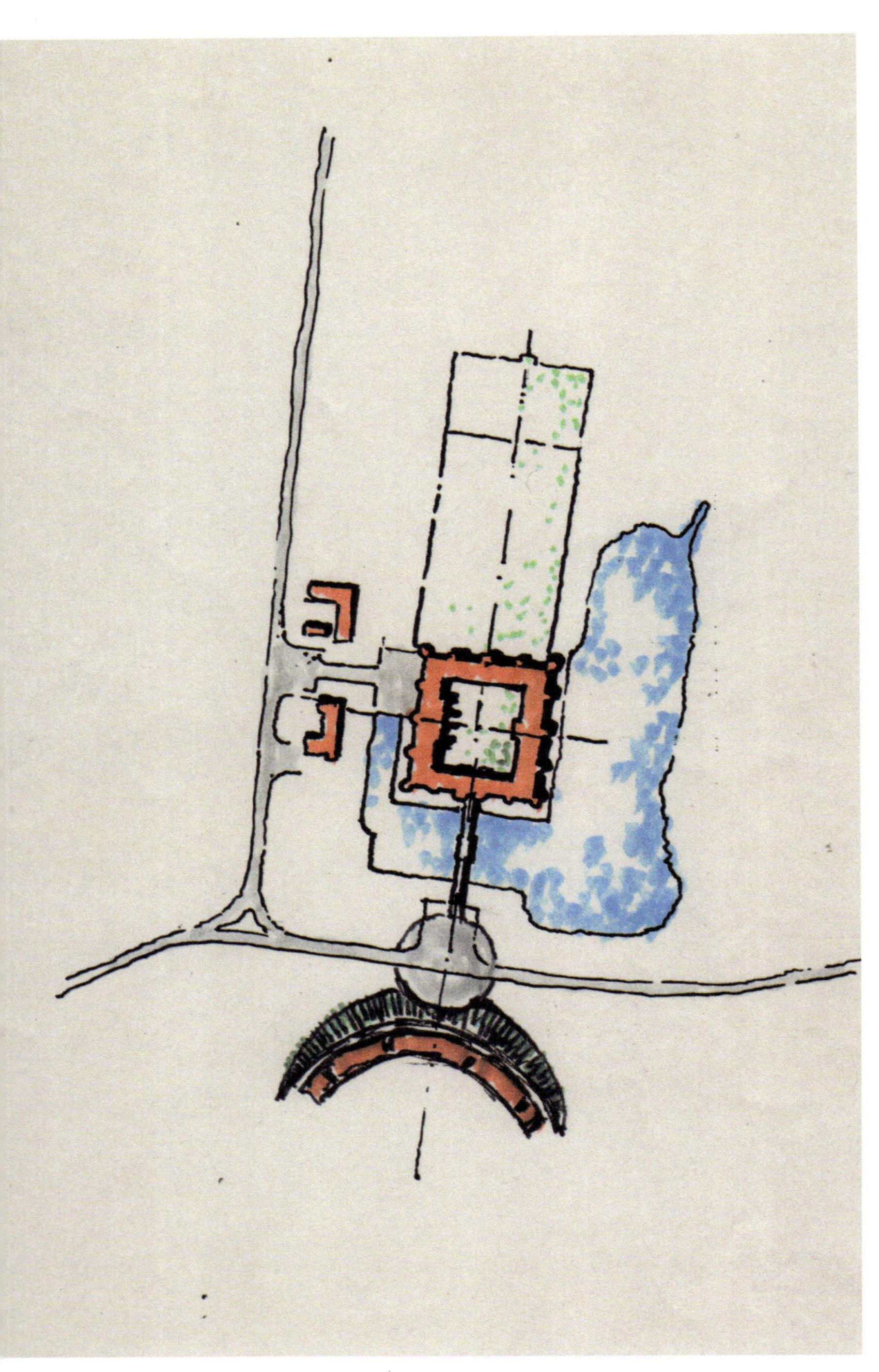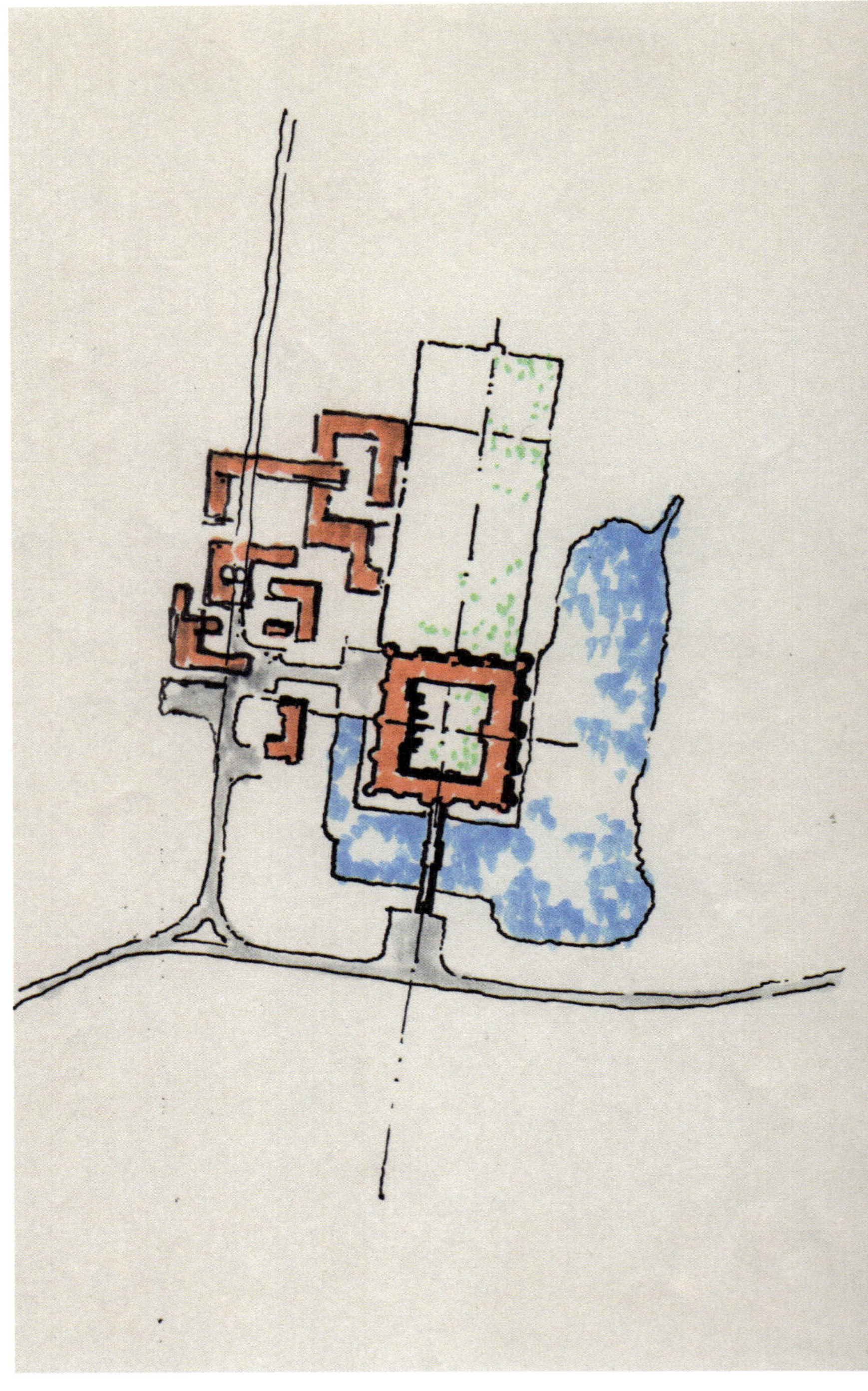

Various options sought to
reinforce the axial alignments
implied by the square castle
building, acknowledging its
primacy within the parkland
setting.

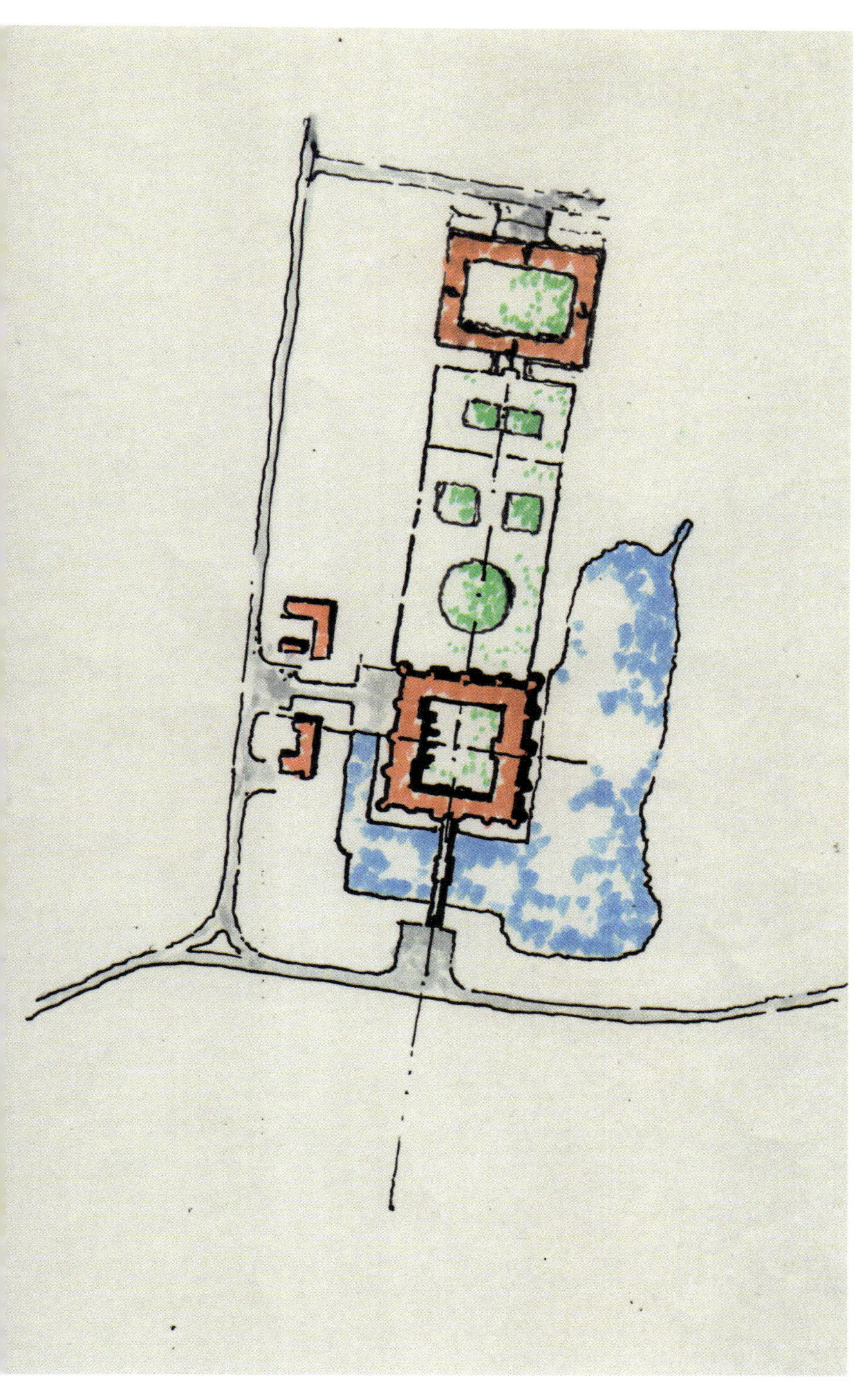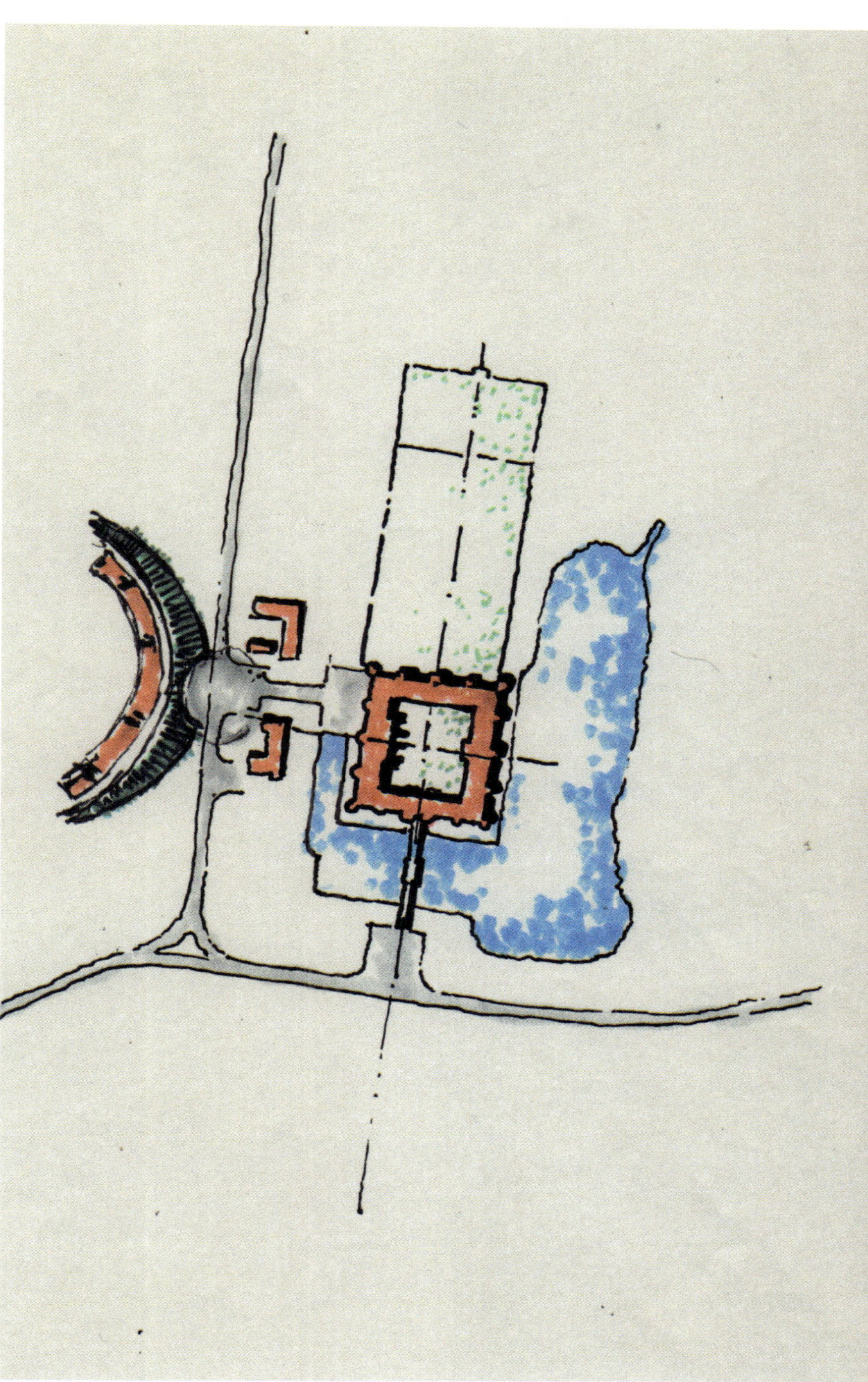

These preliminary sketches are for the design of a building to house the Administration Centre and Building Studies department of Cork Insititute of Technology.

The first plan diagram illustrates two L-shaped parts assembled to form a unifying square; a quad bisected by a diagonal route with entrances and circulation cores situated at alternate corners. Second, and more interesting, is our preferred diagram, again arranged with sets of L-shaped floor plates, but this time held apart to form articulated entrances to the two inset atriums; in turn these are linked and served by shared circulation cores.

I now note that the aerial view sketch is proportionally exaggerated and doesn't engage with the more complex curvatures shown on plan. These curved elevations were intended as a gentle reference to the main facade of the adjacent library, recently built by De Blacam & Meagher, while also adding a subtle emphasis to the asymmetry of the two entrances on opposite sides of the new building. As an initial design idea we enjoyed this arrangement, embodying the duality of the brief within the unifying character of the plan's formal entity.

1989

A competition for the new Bishopstown campus in the western suburbs of Cork.

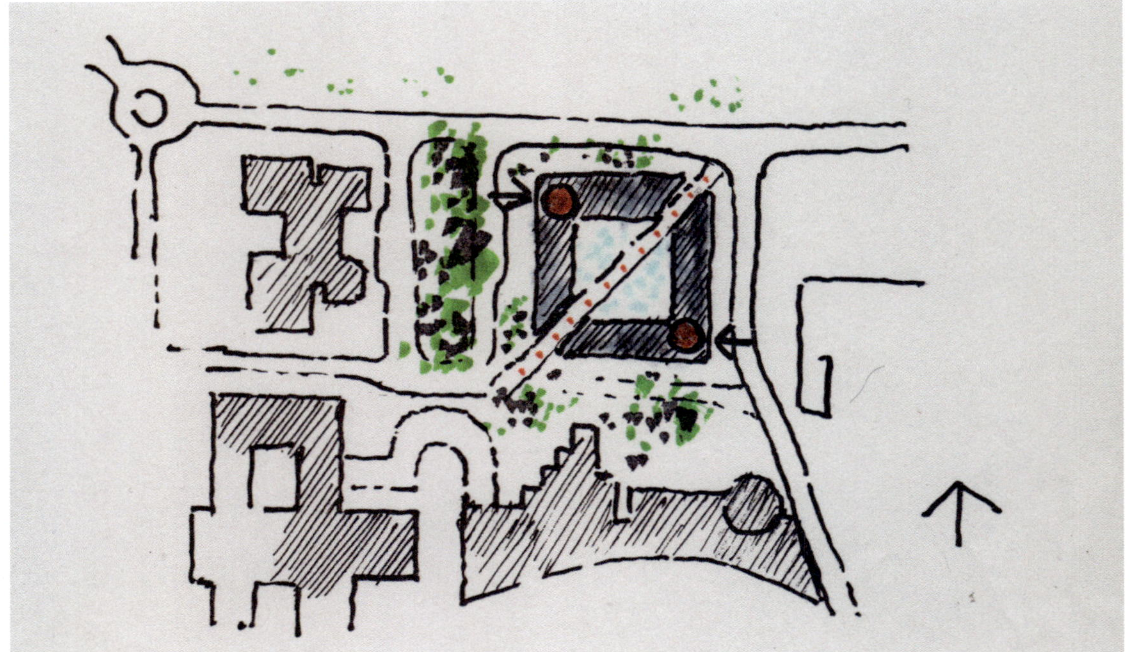

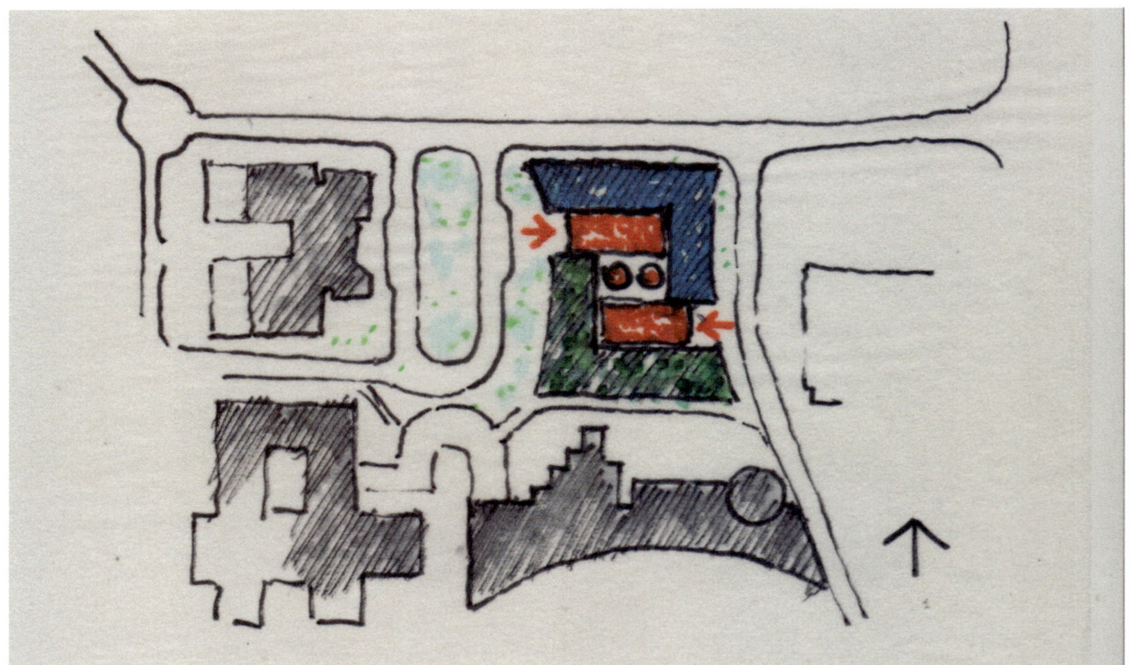

Interlocking built forms allow the building to address issues of access on both the east and west sides, while in part echoing the curved entrance facade of De Blacam & Meagher's adjacent library.

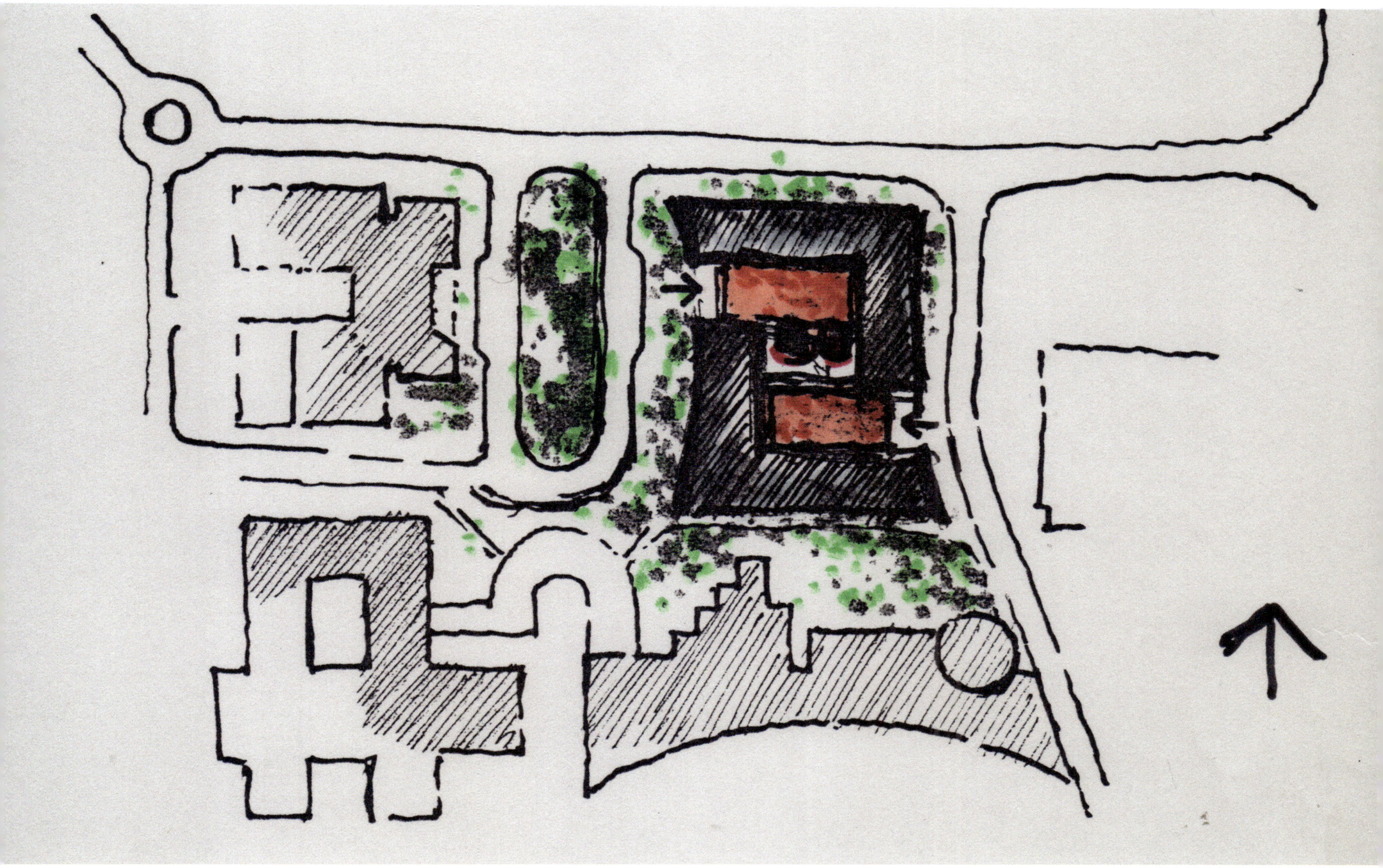

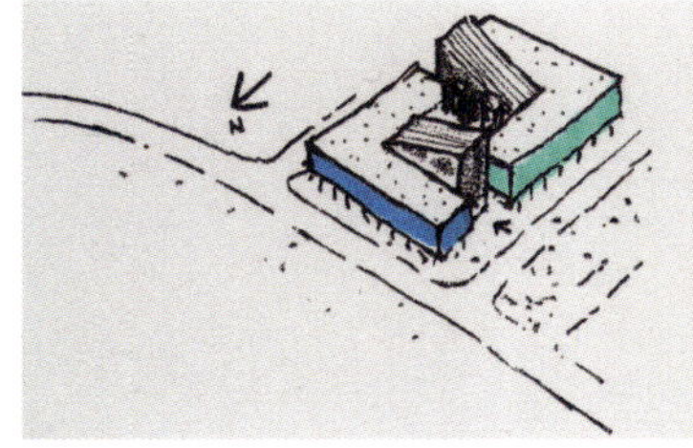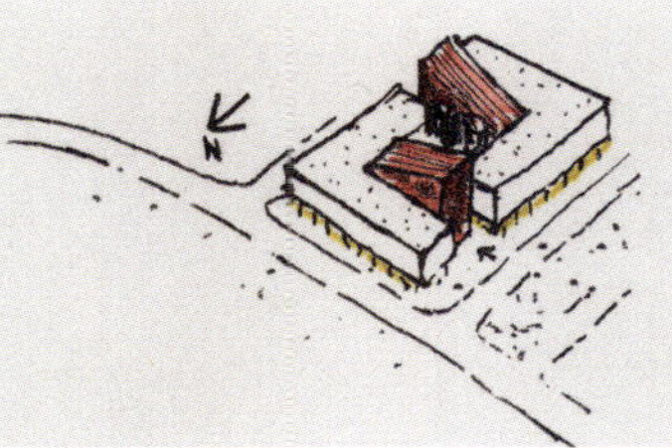

As I remember it, and as some of these sketches indicate, we were originally appointed to prepare an initial design study to accommodate an extension to Manchester University's set of historically distinct buildings that make up the John Rylands Library, as well as a separate graduate school.

As our ideas for possible loose couplings of these elements progressed, the graduate school was removed from the brief, so our focus switched to the design of the library extension alone. We worked on this in some detail, including a curving external wall that would define a new edge alongside a landscaped open space.

The scheme was approved by the university but HEFCE funding was not forthcoming and it went no further.

1990

An extension proposal for Manchester University's main library building on its Oxford Road campus.

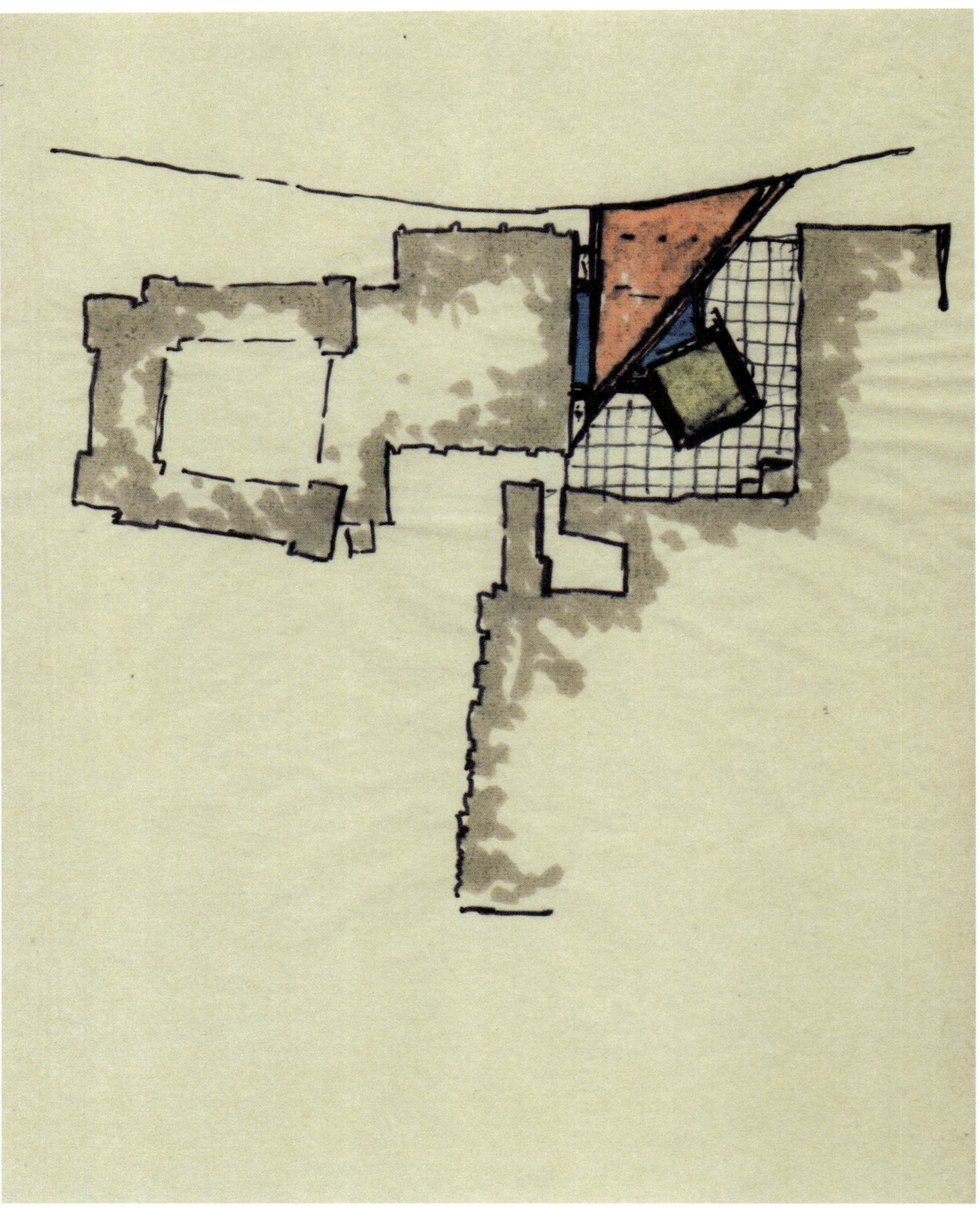

One of only five National Research Libraries in the UK, the existing main building is located on Manchester's Burlington Street. The proposed extension was planned for an adjacent courtyard site.

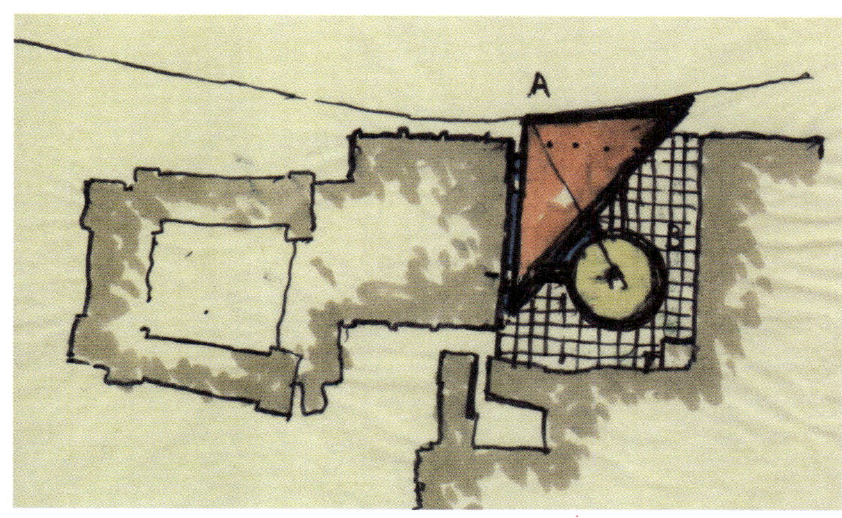

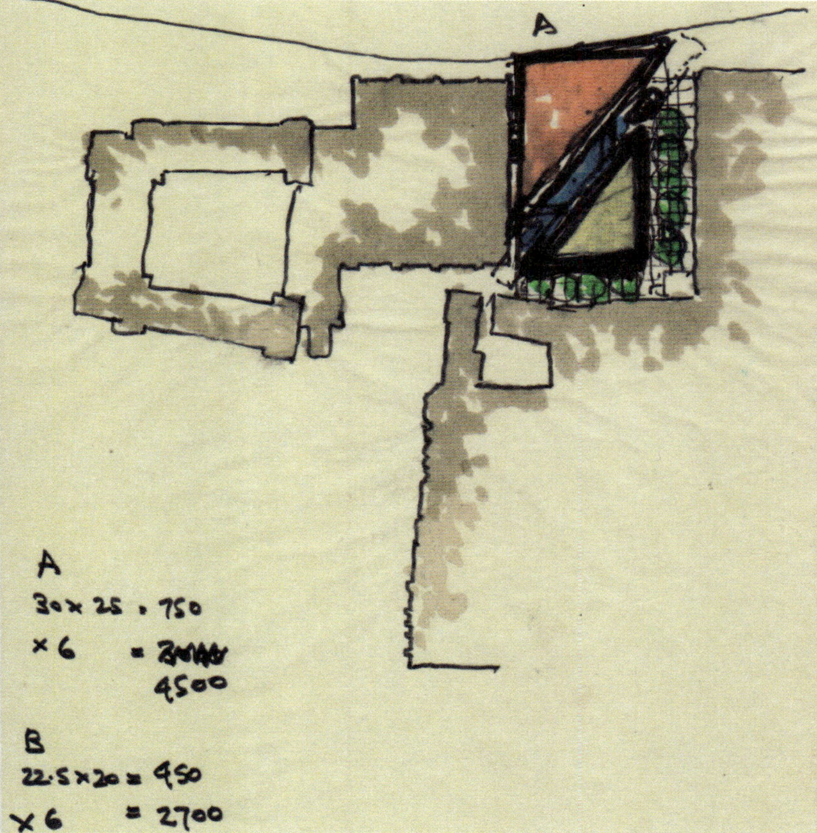

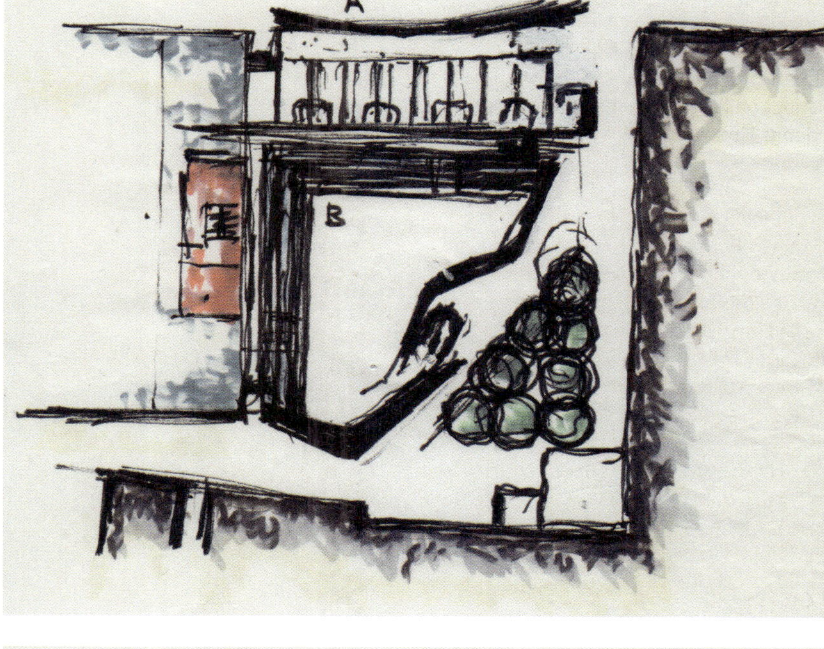

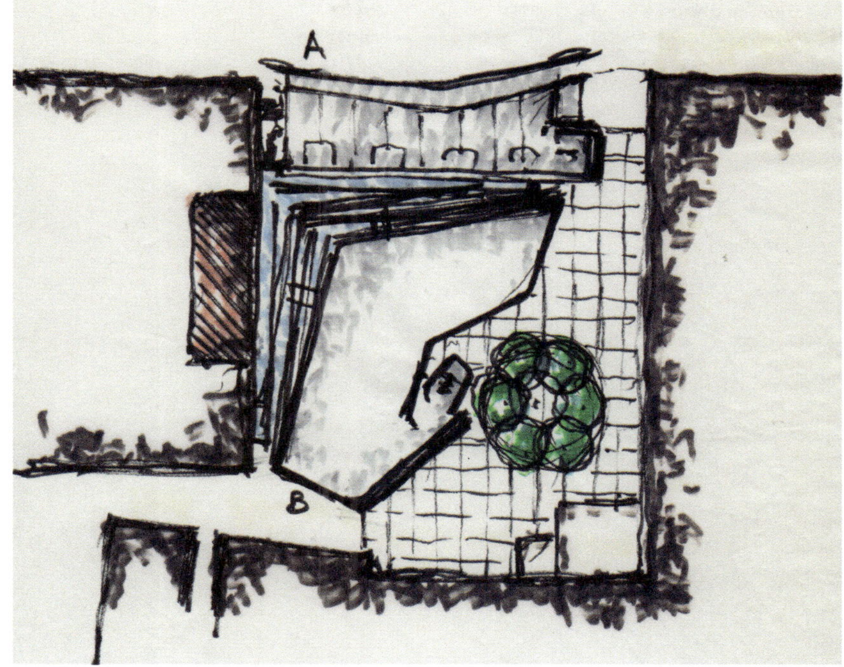

The library's east wing opened in 1936. South and west wings were added in 1953-56 and the Muriel Stott Hall in 1978. A northern extension was added in 1981 by architect Dane, Scherrer & Hicks.

These sketches are for ideas that we worked up in 2008 for a competition for a business incubation centre in Daventry. As it happened, this was the last competition entry that we made before I decided to retire from ABK to pursue other things.

Composed of a series of start-up spaces, an assembly of cubic elements bound together by the linear route of a separated pedestrian way. This comprised a glazed link, running through and beside the building at low level and connecting with the canal and the barge lay-by that we proposed along the boundary.

2008

Designs for a canalside innovation hub at Daventry, Northamptonshire.

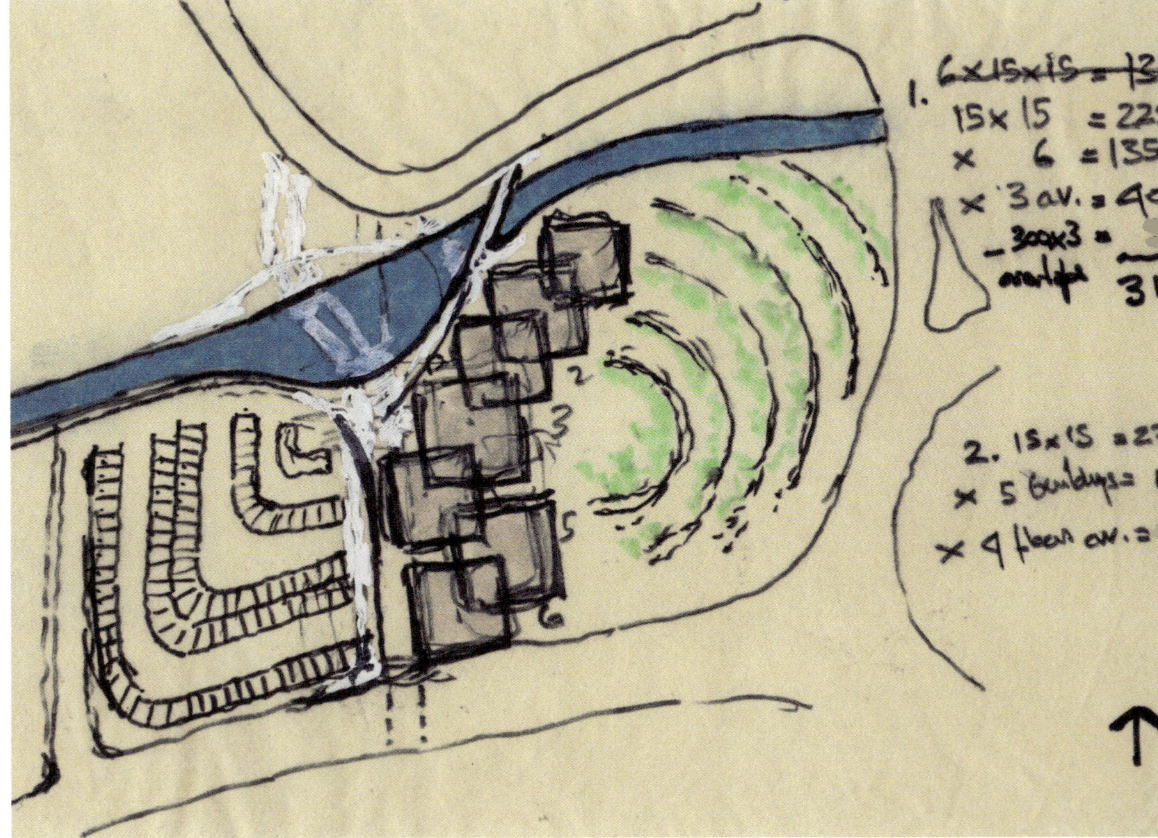

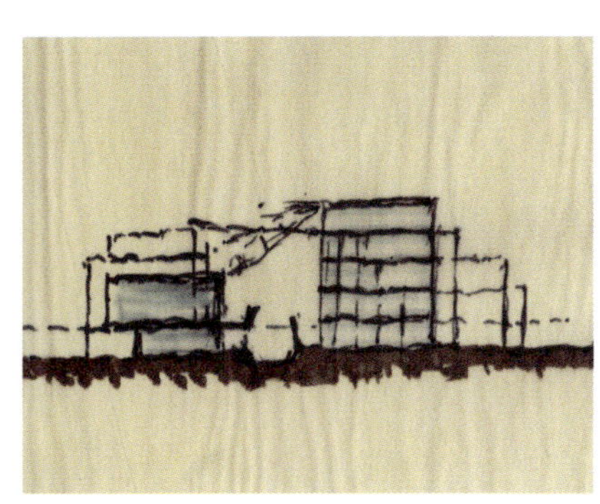

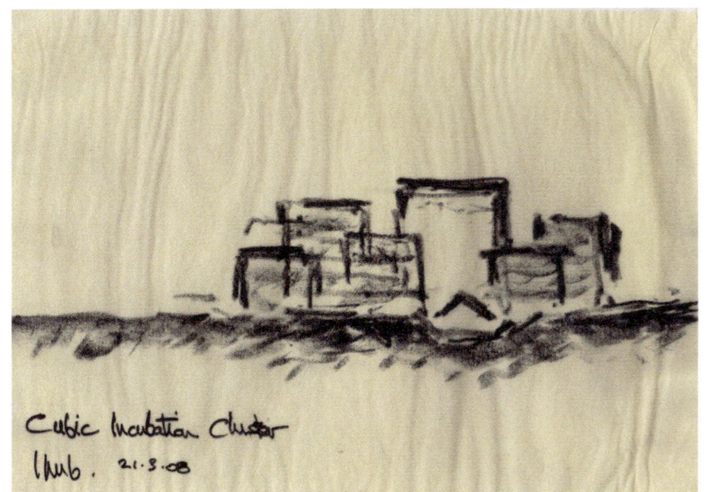

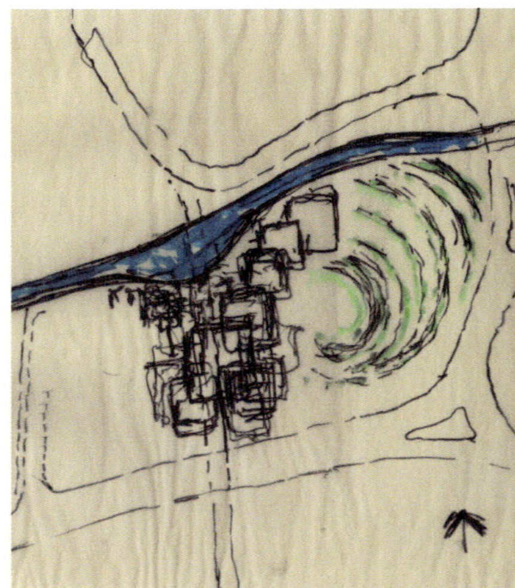

The Board of the Innovative Construction Network (ICoN), represented by the University of Northampton and the BRE, invited architects to enter an open competition to design an exemplar innovation hub and office building. Stage one of the competition received 71 entries.

This competition for a maritime museum in Falmouth also offered opportunities to make something lively of the harbourside area. These are often special places, and we felt good about the mix and layout of our initial ideas for an open space defined by the museum buildings and the mixed-use, low-rise housing.

Unlike the entrance-related interior ramp that we'd previously designed for our unbuilt Mary Rose Museum (a curved alignment beside the salvaged hull of the Tudor warship), here we proposed a diagonal external ramp rising to the entrance above and beside the somewhat boat-like curving wall of the museum. Internally, we formed a generous hall with a variety of boats facing downwards on a ramped 'slipway', as if ready to head out to sea through the adjacent harbour.

1996

An entry in the limited competition for the National Maritime Museum Cornwall.

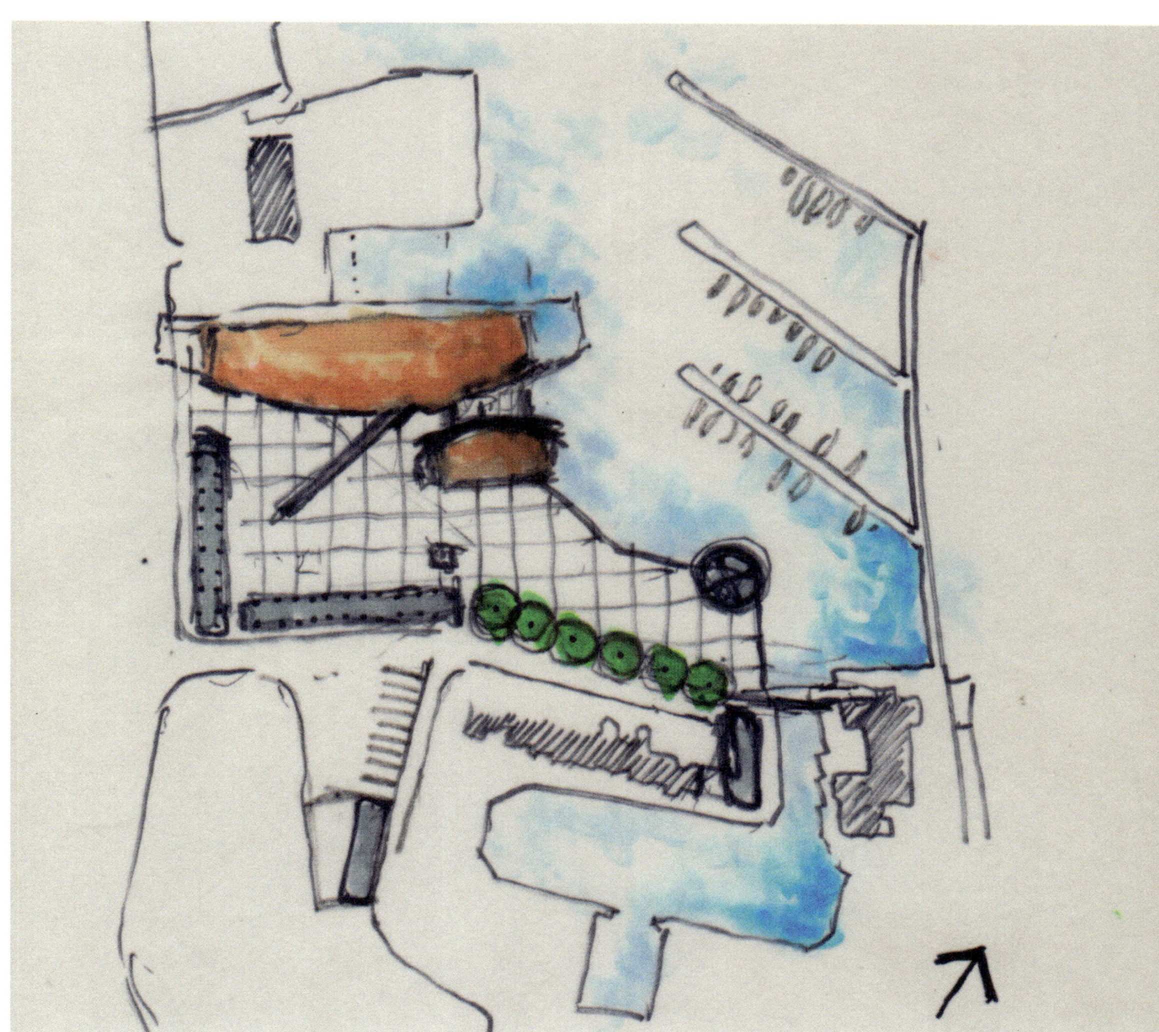

Cornwall County Council's competition to select an architect for a £28m regeneration project for Falmouth waterfront, and the new £19m National Maritime Museum Cornwall, attracted more than 70 applications. Long & Kentish won the competition and the museum opened in 2003.

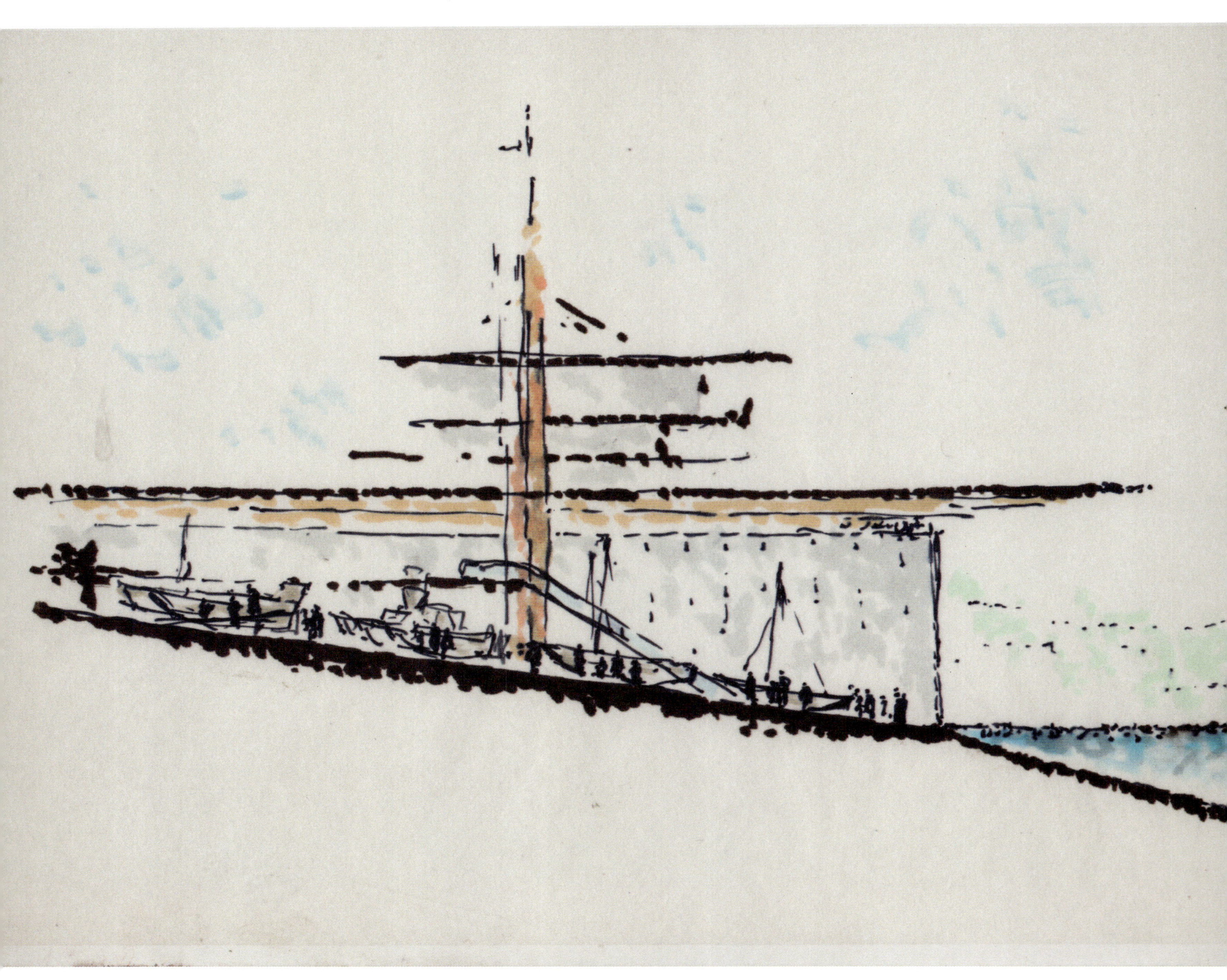

The waterside building would incorporate a sloping floor beneath a roof datum, with the boats exhibited as if on a slipway.

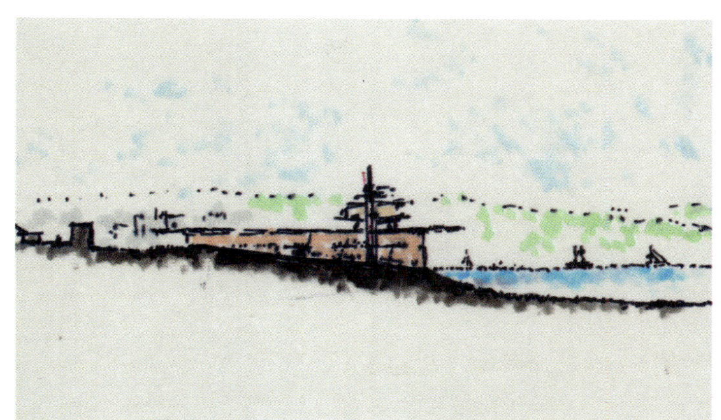

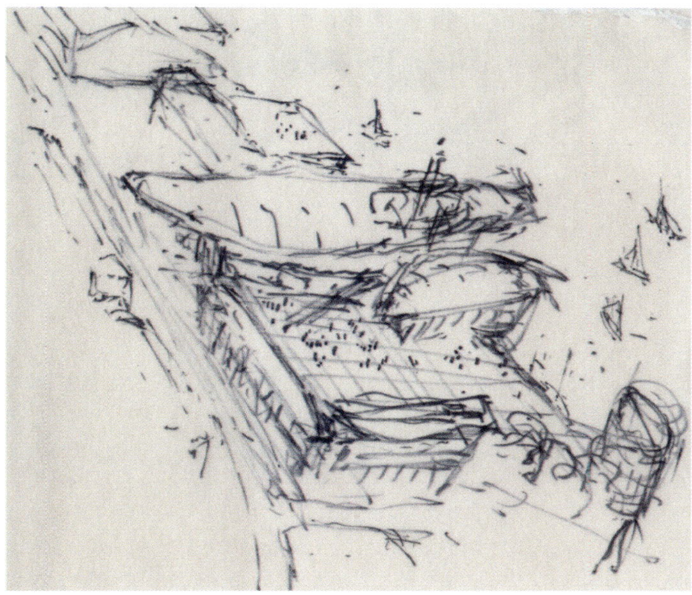

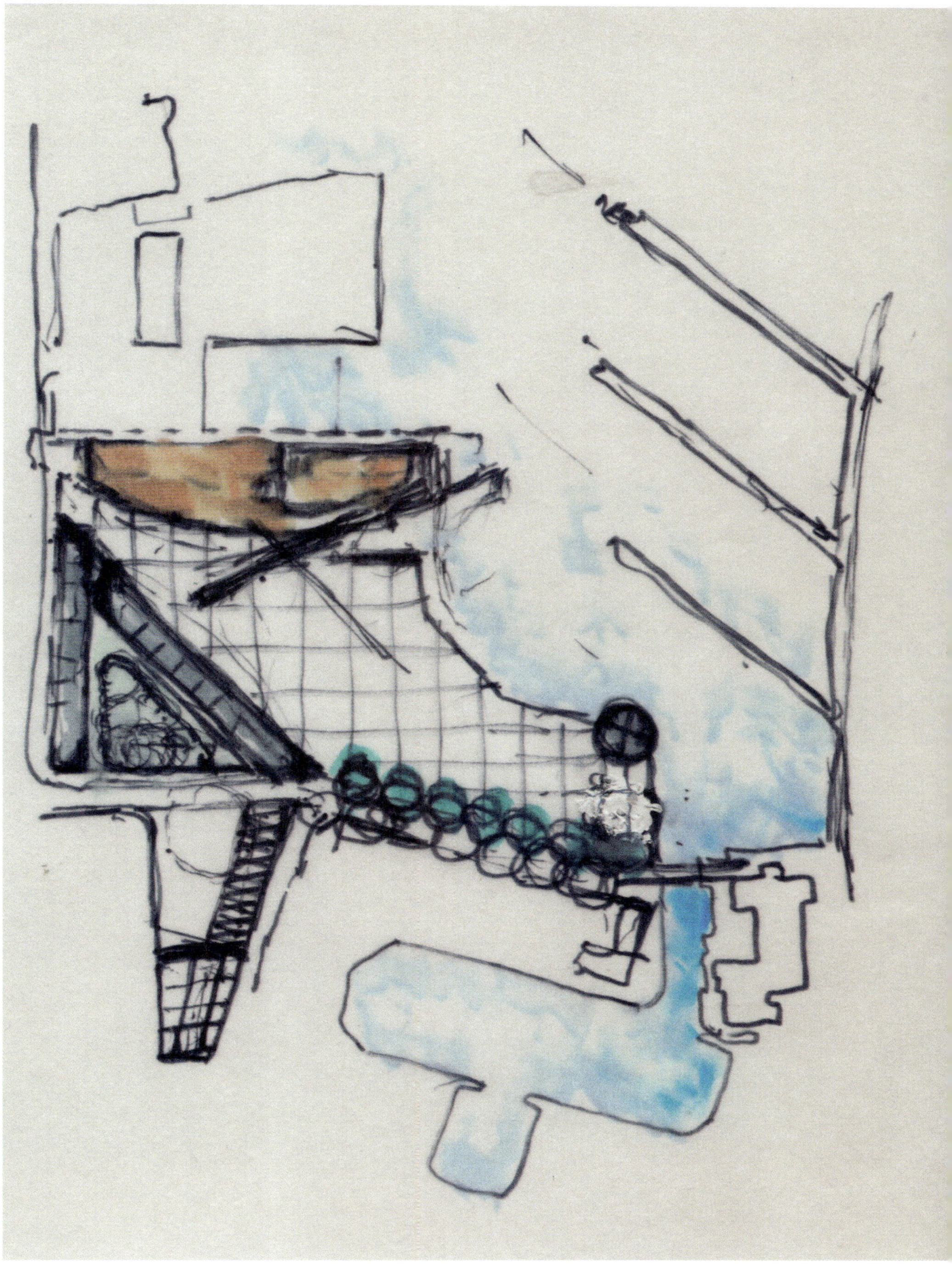

*The proposal was planned so as
to define a public plaza at the
harbour's edge.*

In the late 1960s we were commissioned to prepare a development plan for the newly established Oxford Centre for Management Studies, which in 1983 became Templeton College. On a greenfield site at Egrove Park, south of the city, we designed a series of buildings that were constructed in seven phases over a period of more than 20 years, on each occasion responding to the developing brief.

In the early years of the millennium Templeton College merged with Green College to become Green Templeton College. Initially the college gave consideration to a substantial expansion of Templeton's well-established campus, and in 2007 we were invited to consider possible planning options, some sketches for which are shown here. In the event, nothing further came of this as, instead, the college moved into the former Green College buildings in central Oxford.

2007

ABK was asked to revisit its 1960s Templeton College campus at Egrove Park to consider a further expansion.

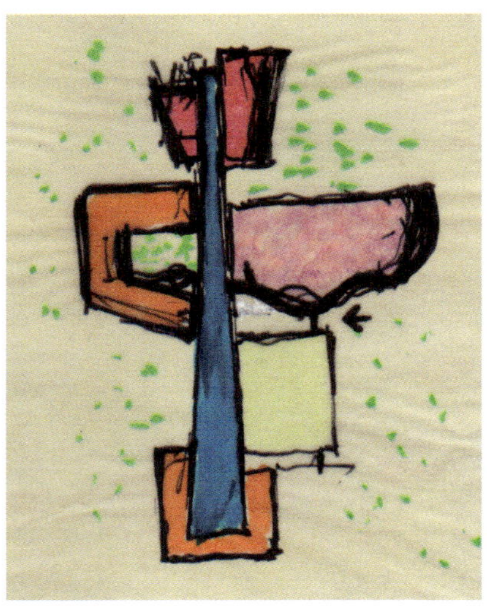

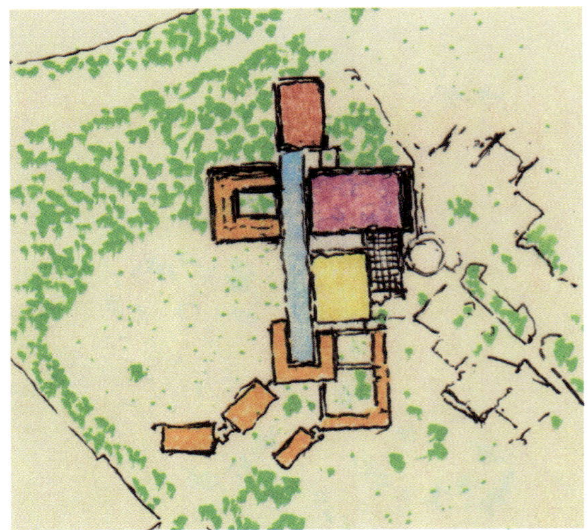

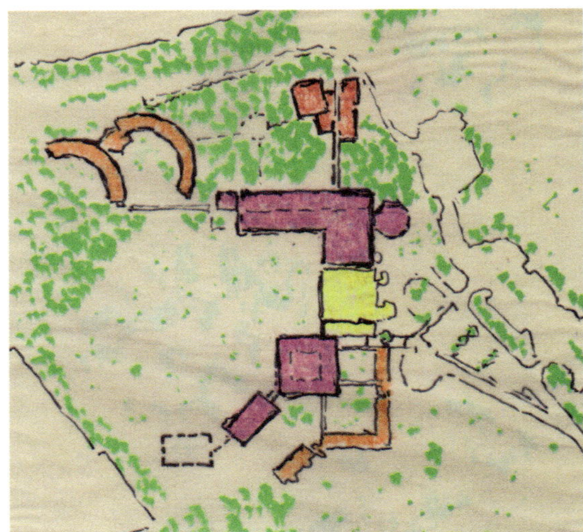

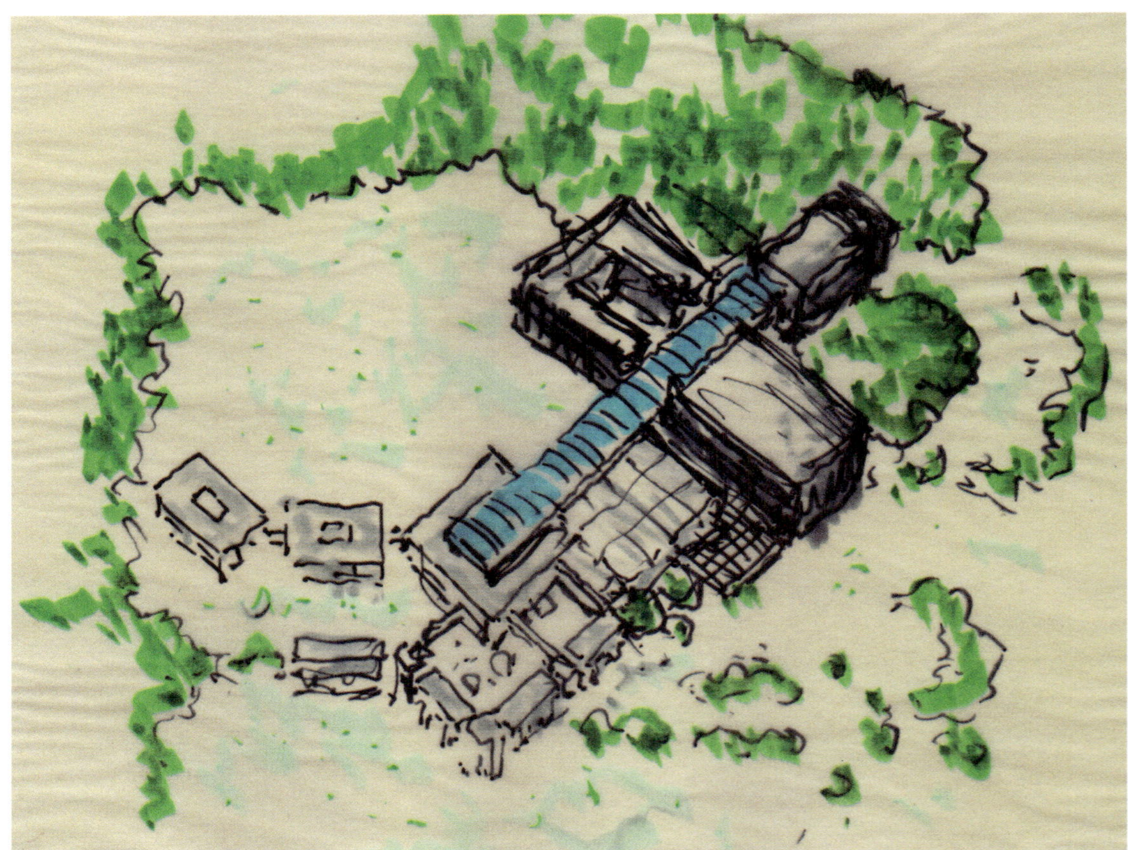

ABK's buildings for the Oxford Centre for Management Studies opened in 1969 and were listed in 1999. It became Templeton College in 1983, and in 2005 transferred its executive education business to the Saïd Business School, which still operates here.

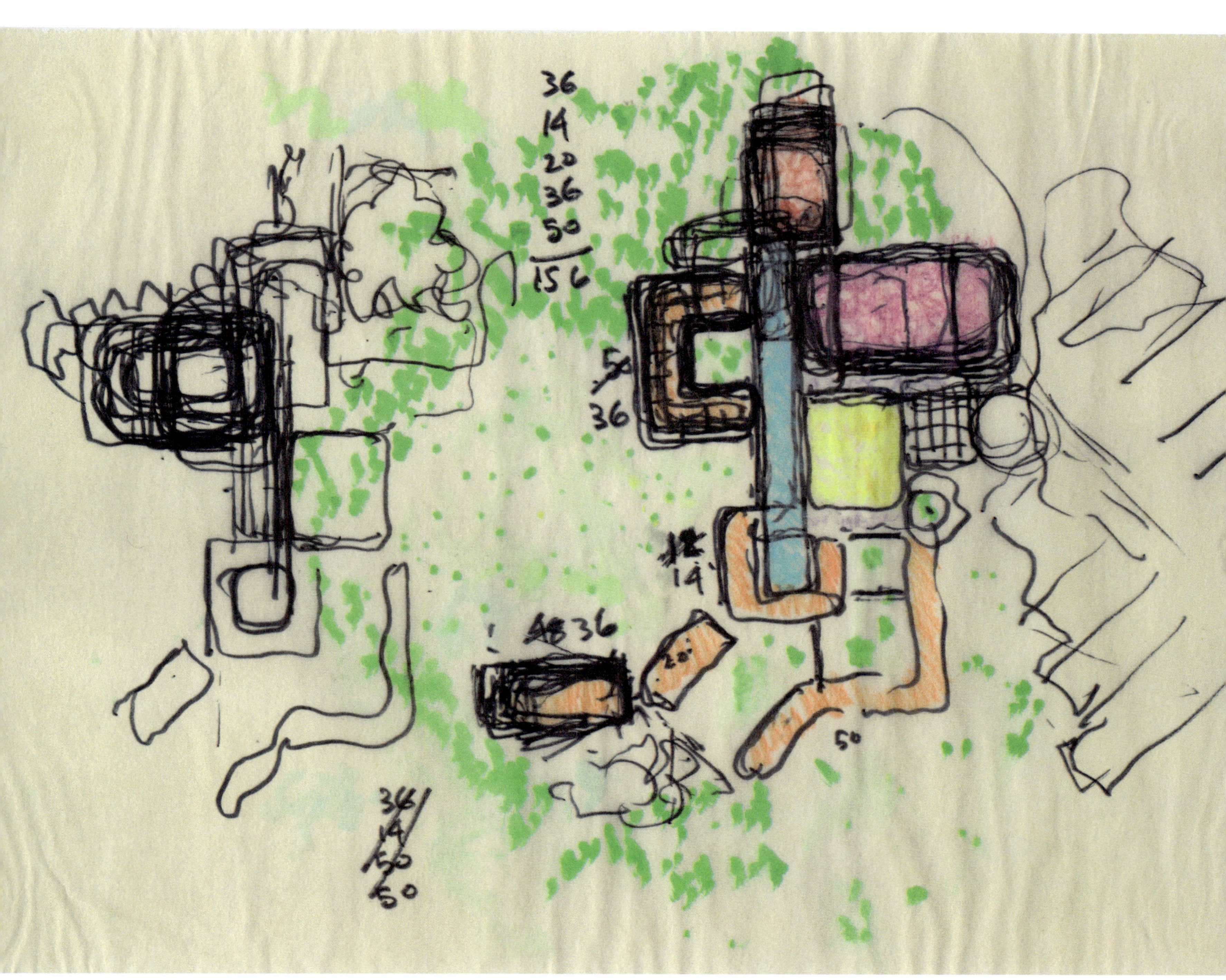

New interventions weave through
and lock into the existing
arrangement. The plan
incorporates conference facilities
(pink), a fitness centre (red),
residential accommodation
(orange), dining/bar (yellow) and
a linear concourse (blue).

These sketches illustrate some of our ideas for the 1989 competition for a new opera house at Compton Verney, on which we worked with the renowned acoustician Derek Sugden. We chose to set the building adjacent to the lake and across from the manor house in the beautiful rolling landscape.

I was taken by the idea of planning the building so as to engage with the slightly raised profile of the lake-edge hillside. Paul pursued a different set of ideas, proposing a largely glazed yet adaptable auditorium that was to be more or less 'open' in character to meet acoustic needs. Both ideas were strong, I thought.

1992

Competition entry for an opera house in the parkland, designed by Capability Brown, of the listed stately home in Warwickshire.

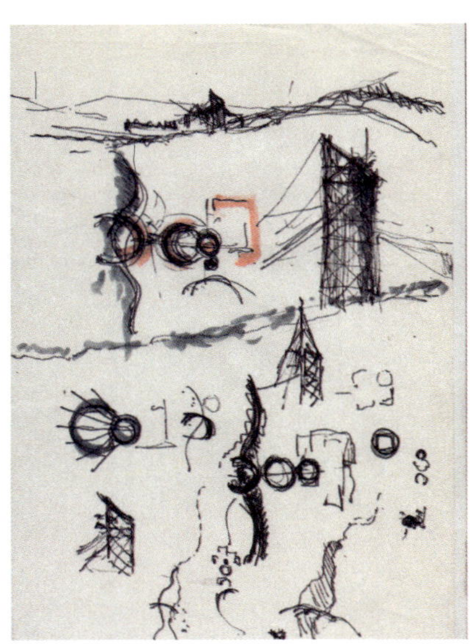

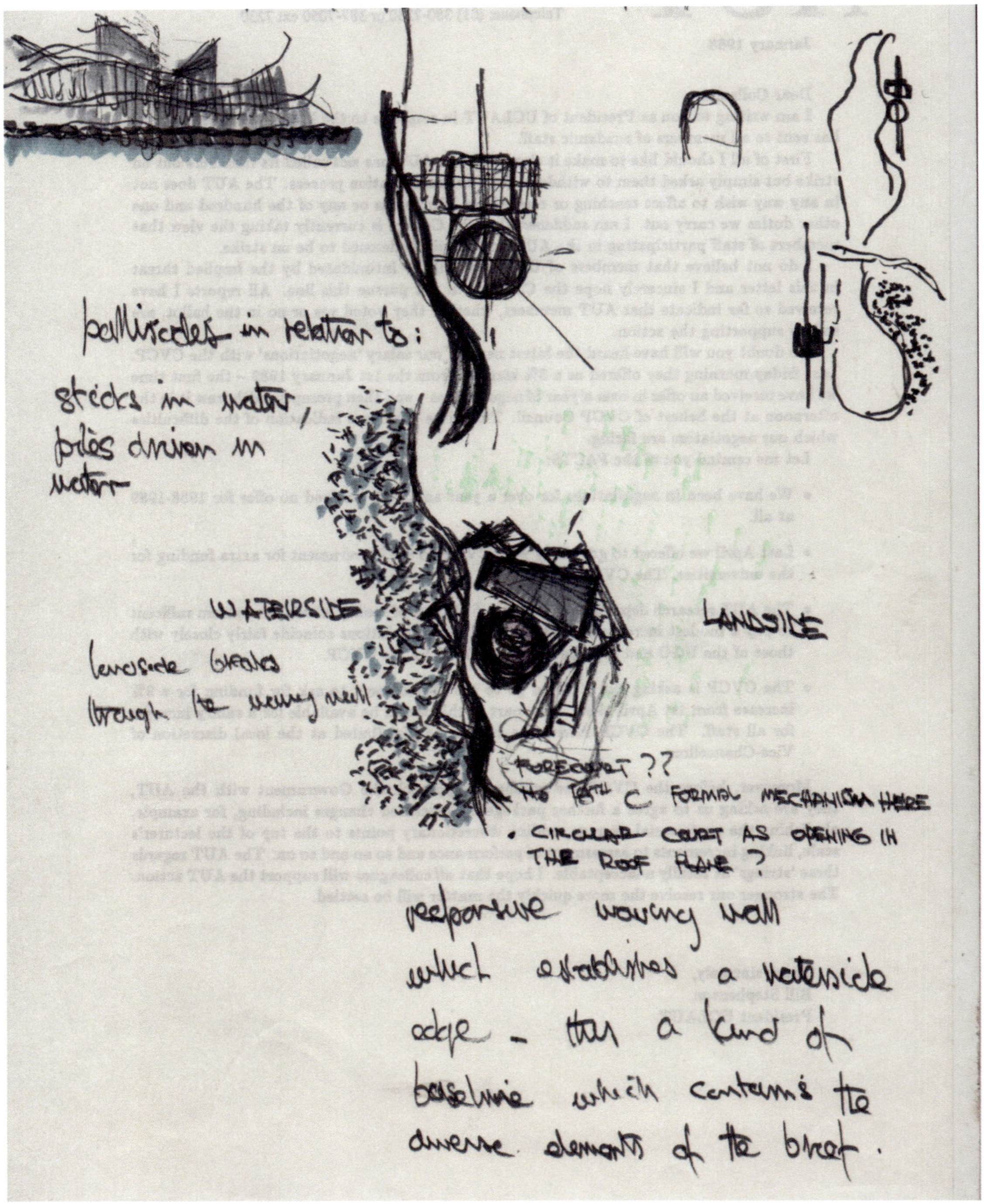

The architectural competition for a new opera house was won by Henning Larson, but remained unbuilt because of lack of funds. In the mid-1990s, the house was purchased by Peter Moores and extended by Stanton Williams to exhibit his art collection.

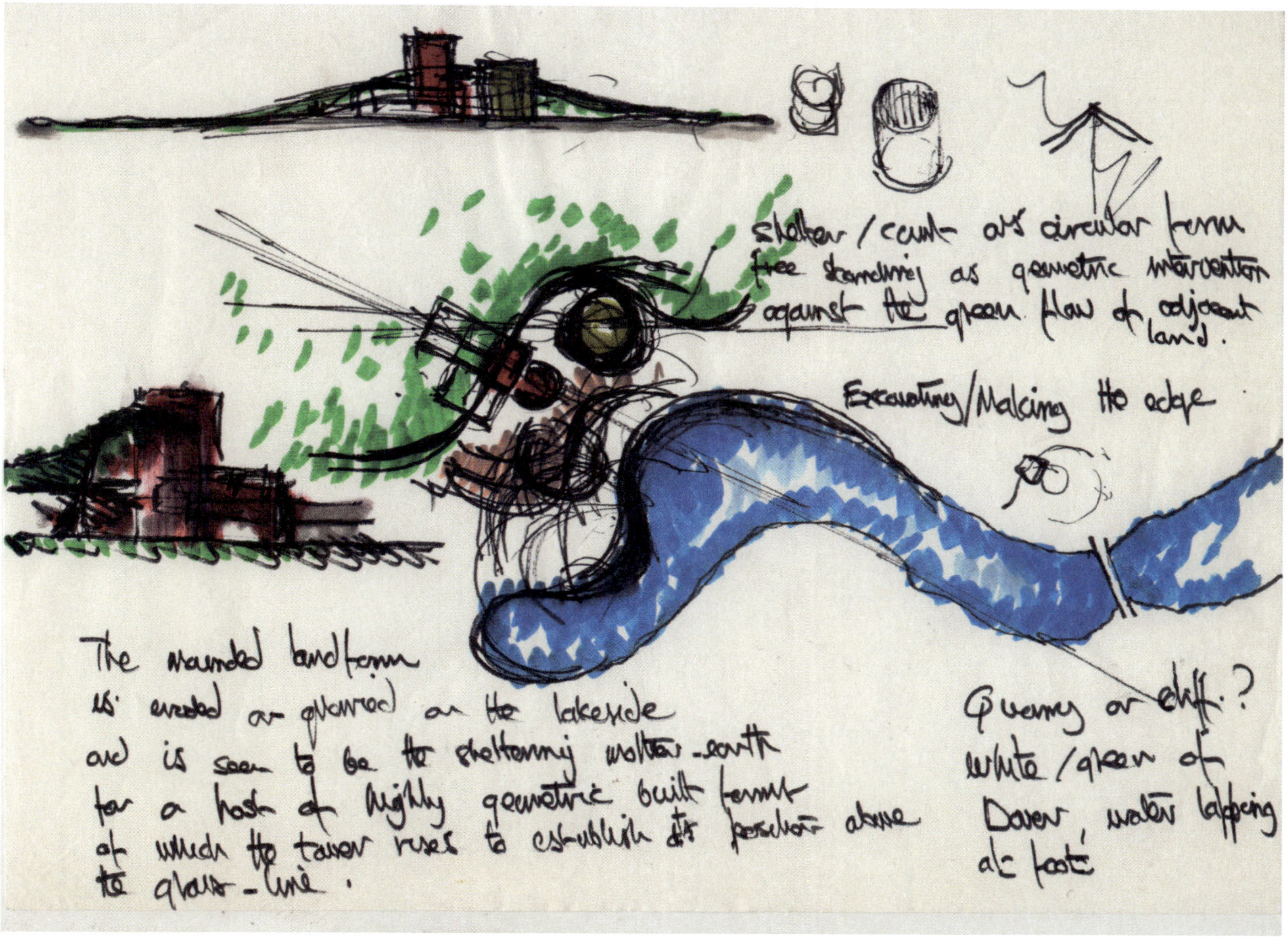

shelter / court as circular form
free standing as geometric intervention
against the green flow of adjacent
land.

Excavating / Making the edge

The mounded landform
is eroded or quarried on the lakeside
and is seen to be the sheltering wall to south
for a host of highly geometric built forms
of which the tower rises to establish its position above
the grass-line.

Quarry or cliff?
white/green of
Dover, water lapping
at foot

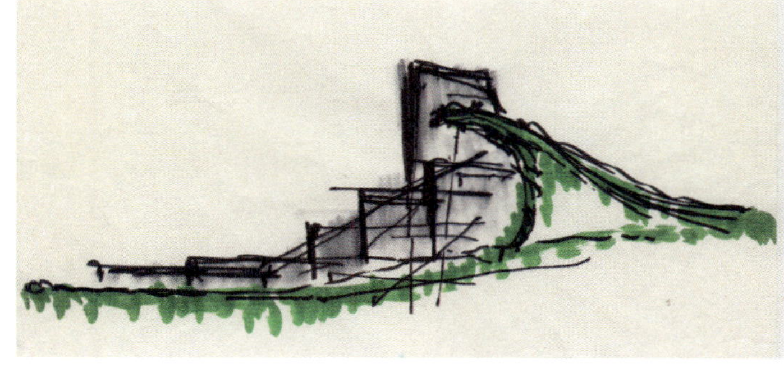

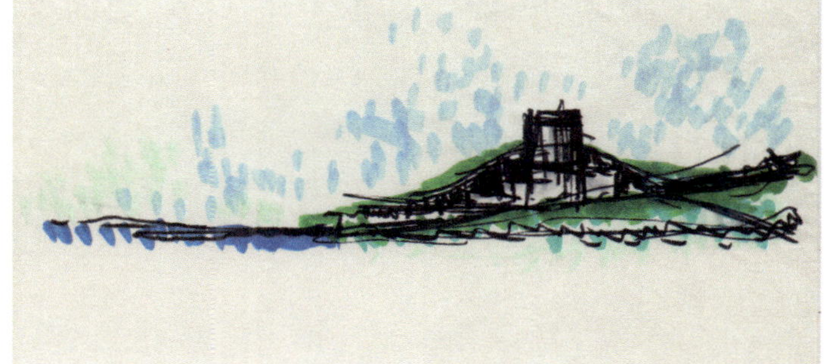

The substantial building was to be tucked into a fold in the landscape so as to minimise its impact in the sensitive parkland and draw the opera house into a relationship with the topography.

In the late 1990s we'd designed a self-build scheme, comprising four storeys of adapted shipping containers, for Urban Space Management on its site at Trinity Buoy Wharf, where the River Lea meets the Thames at Bow Creek. The developer's use of this modular construction method, both for its arts-related site and elsewhere, was tried, tested and interesting.

After the project was completed I found that these 'container construction techniques' lingered in the mind, presenting themselves as an opportunity for low-cost, fast-build social housing; an essential, well-established area of construction that had by then been long absent from the UK political agenda.

I met USM's Eric Reynolds in his newly-completed Riverside Building, suggesting that we should consider a design study for a substantial housing scheme in the largely underdeveloped area along the Tower Hamlets stretch of the Lower Lea Valley. As a first step this led to a brief and a set of ideas that were based upon low-rise container-construction methods. Time passed and the scope of the study grew, changing in discussion to meet a different client-based perspective. Within a loose association of other local land-owning bodies and in a mood of optimism, the brief developed, broadening in scale and type to become a first-thoughts, free-ranging planning study that was conceptual and ambitious. I hadn't expected this shift towards an 'area study', but welcomed the almost unreal nature of the prospect – no research, no consultation. The message was: just do it to expand horizons.

Here in a reflective mood of self-questioning of ABK's tendency to favour low-rise massing as a means of achieving integration in existing urban areas (say five or six stories, rather than 20),

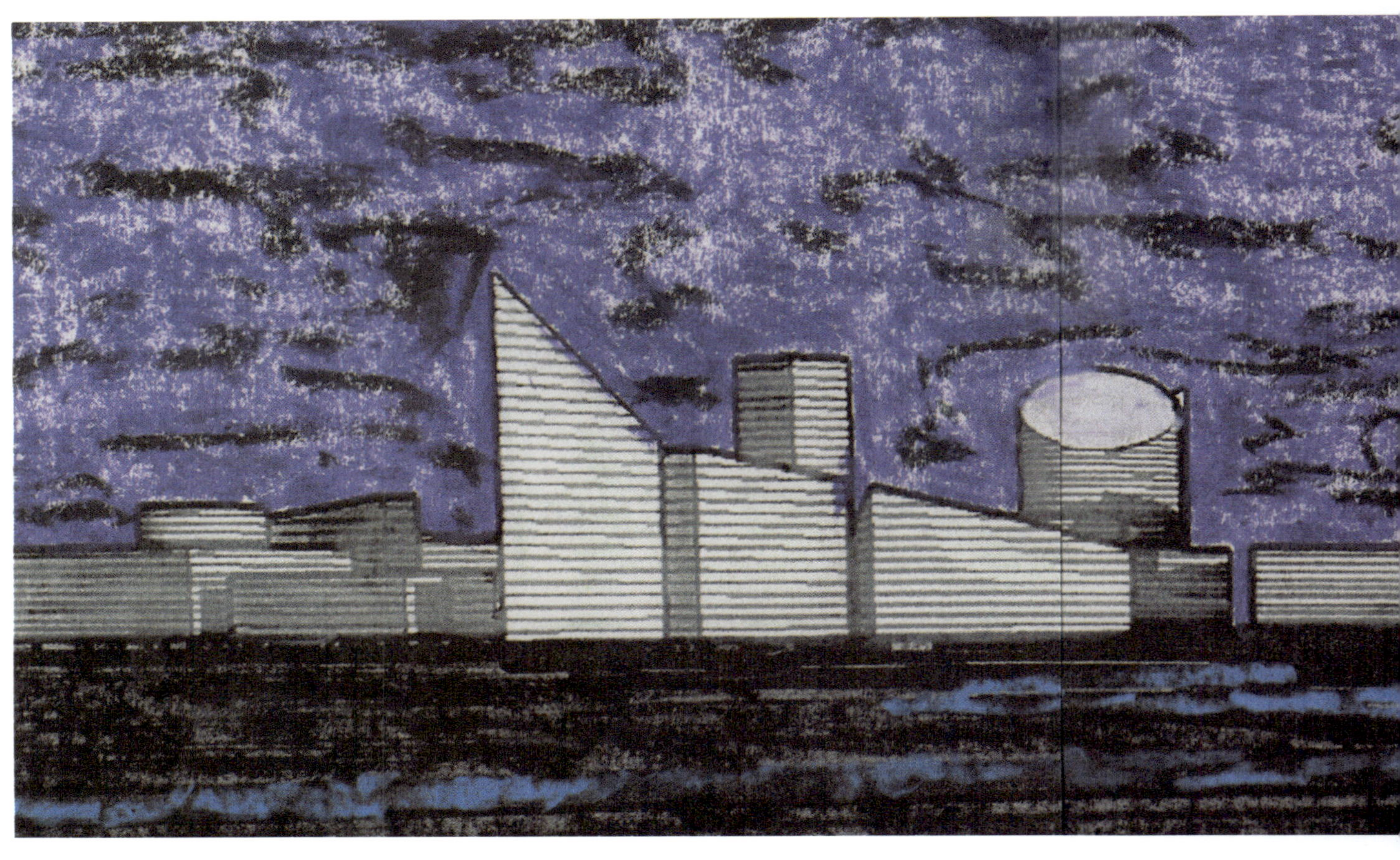

Elevational study showing the potential of a variety of building forms to produce a coherent yet varied development.

surprisingly I found myself instead drawn to a more typical Modern Movement alliance of mixed-use, high-rise buildings. Expressed by an angular set of linear alignments that were to be situated in a new parkland with new crossings extending over the Lea into Newham, this was to be, in every sense, an unfettered composition of high streets; not a new placement as an alternative Royal Mile but, I thought, a distinctive urban statement presenting and signalling an inbound/outbound connection with the financial hub at Poplar's Canary Wharf to the west, and eastwards towards the developing centre in Canning Town.

Historically, John Nash had demonstrated the value of edge-buildings with his West End alignment extending northwards from The Mall, along Regent Street, through the bifurcating crescent and onwards to form the stuccoed edges of Regent's Park – a bold city-move that made our east/west avenue of towers seem pale by comparison.

Some years later I tried to raise interest in making a documentary film about east London's urban history. 'London East' would examine the effect on the cityscape of the second world war, the impact of the new towns of Harlow and Basildon, the closure of the docks and the consequent break-up of the local communities and, in the last half-century, the accelerated development that has taken hold since Canary Wharf was first mooted. It's a powerful story that deserves a lively and politically analytical script, attracting a suitable production donor in order to make a strong documentary.

2005

Large-scale urban project in Tower Hamlets comprising a variety of building forms on a site owned by several major landowners.

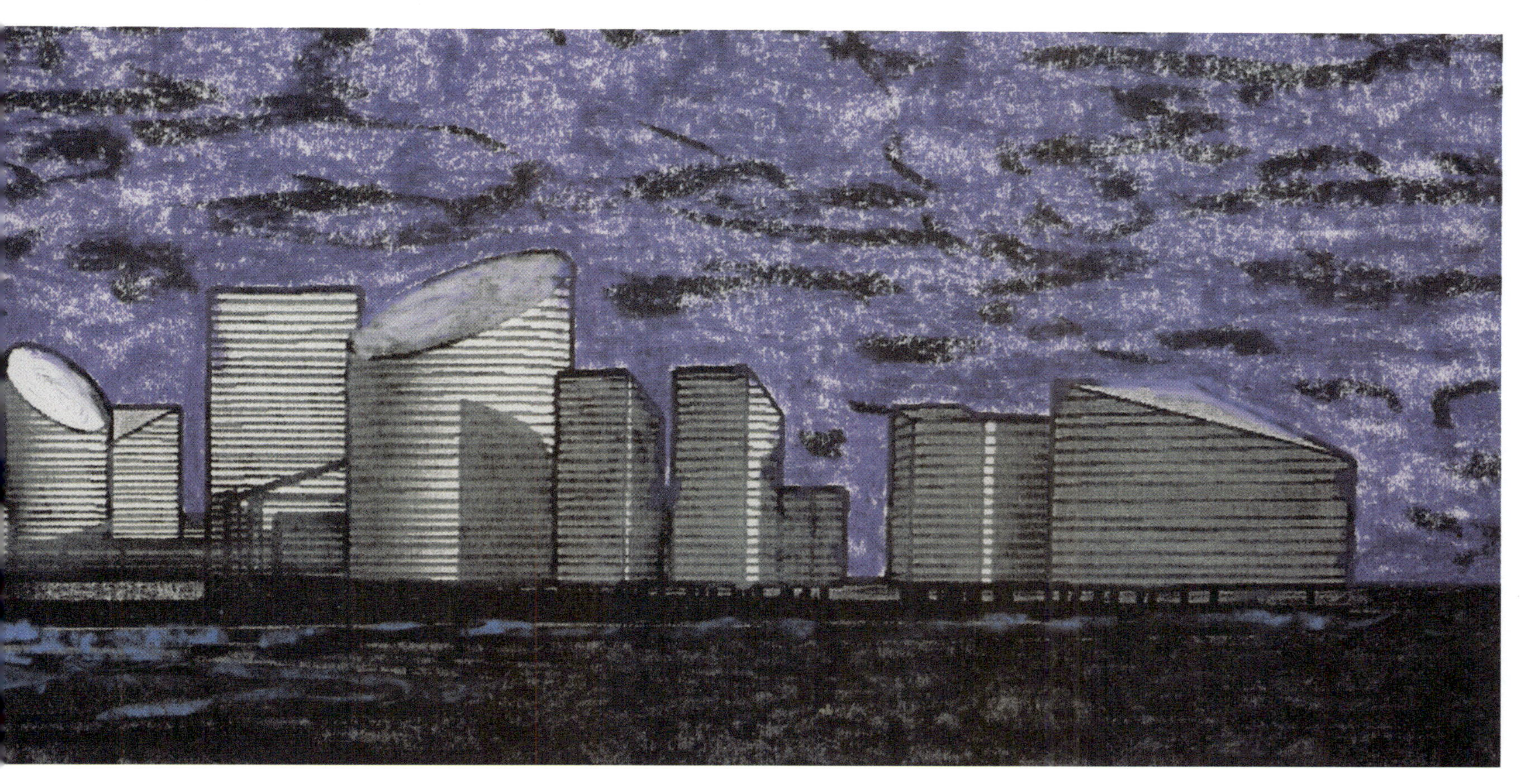

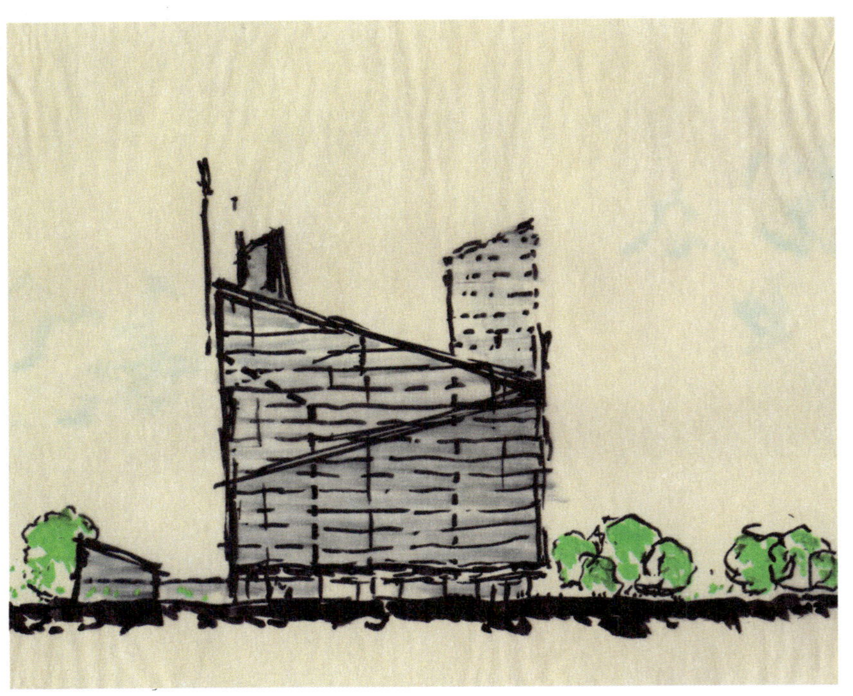

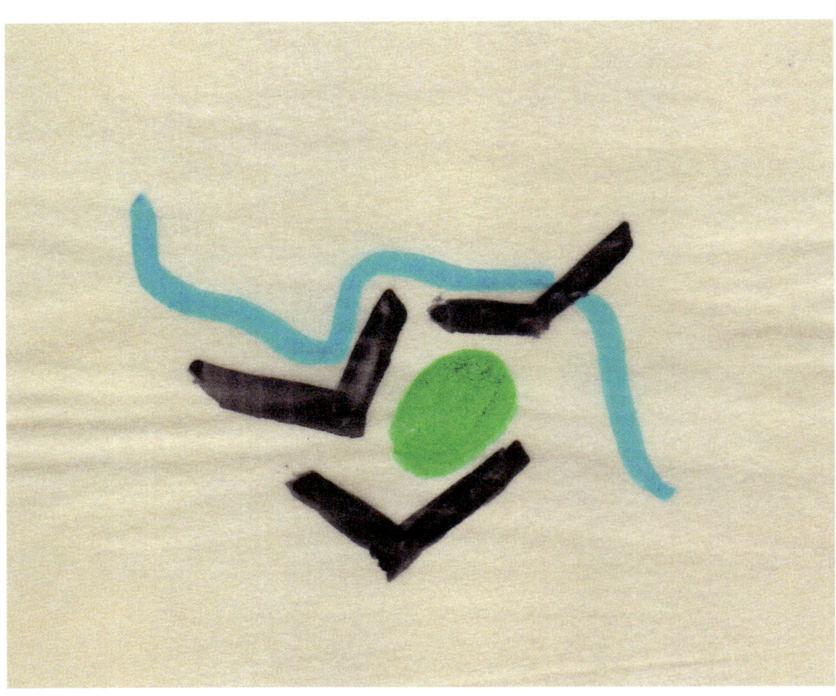

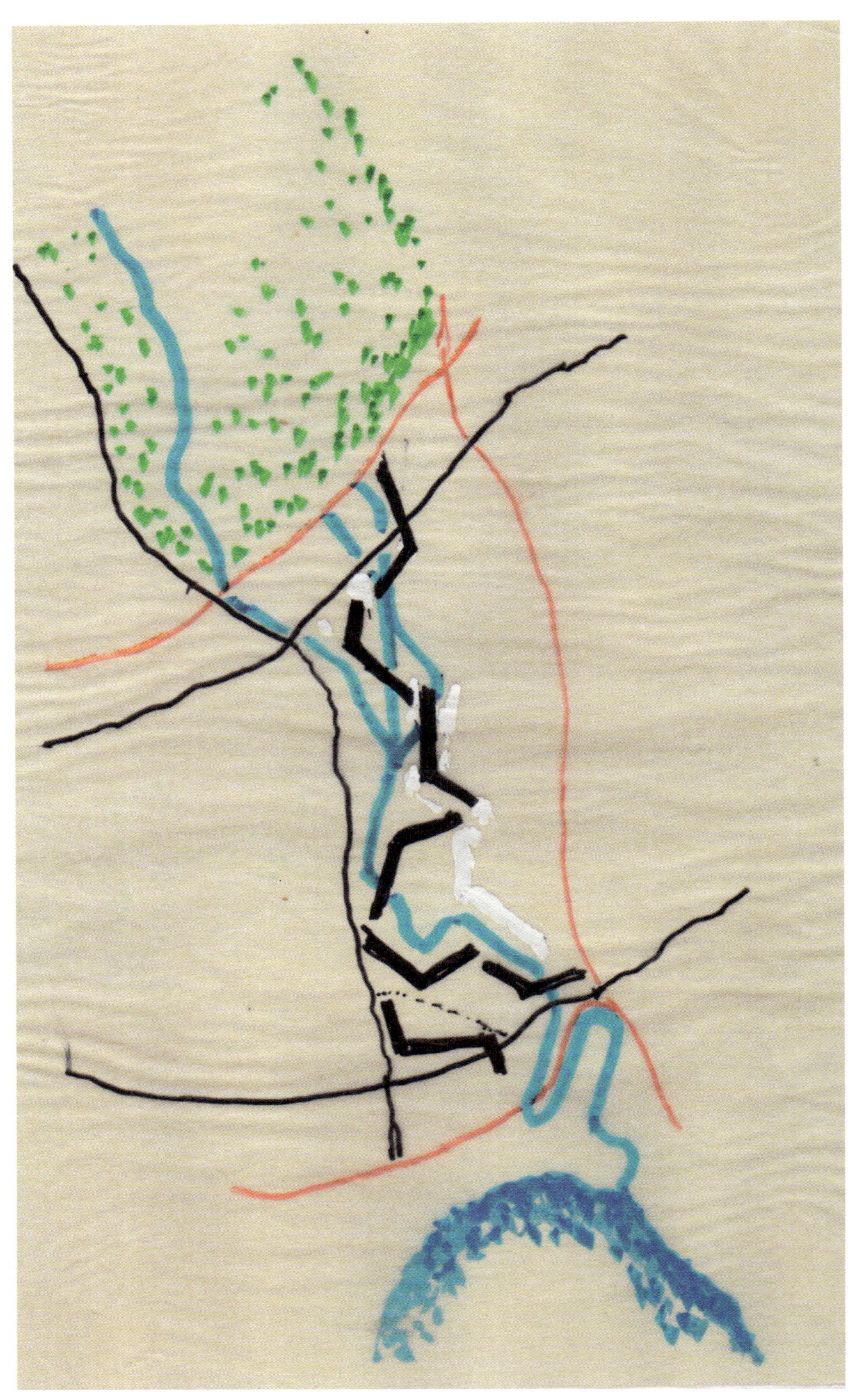

The area under consideration stretched from the Thames at Trinity Buoy Wharf northwards to the southern boundary of the site that would later be redeveloped as the 2012 Olympic park.

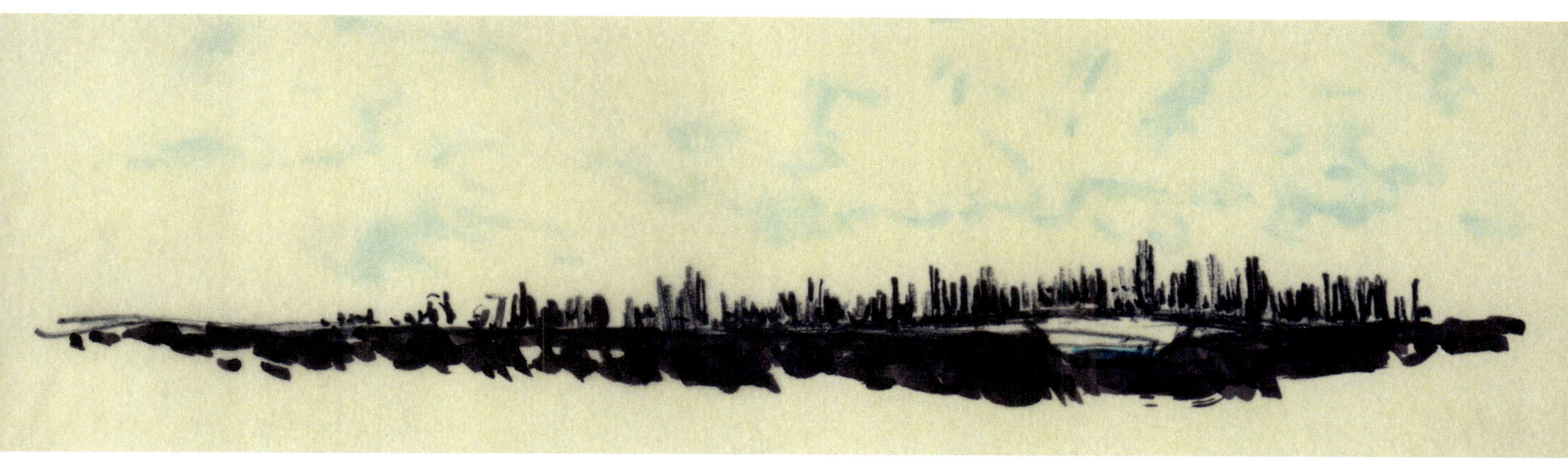

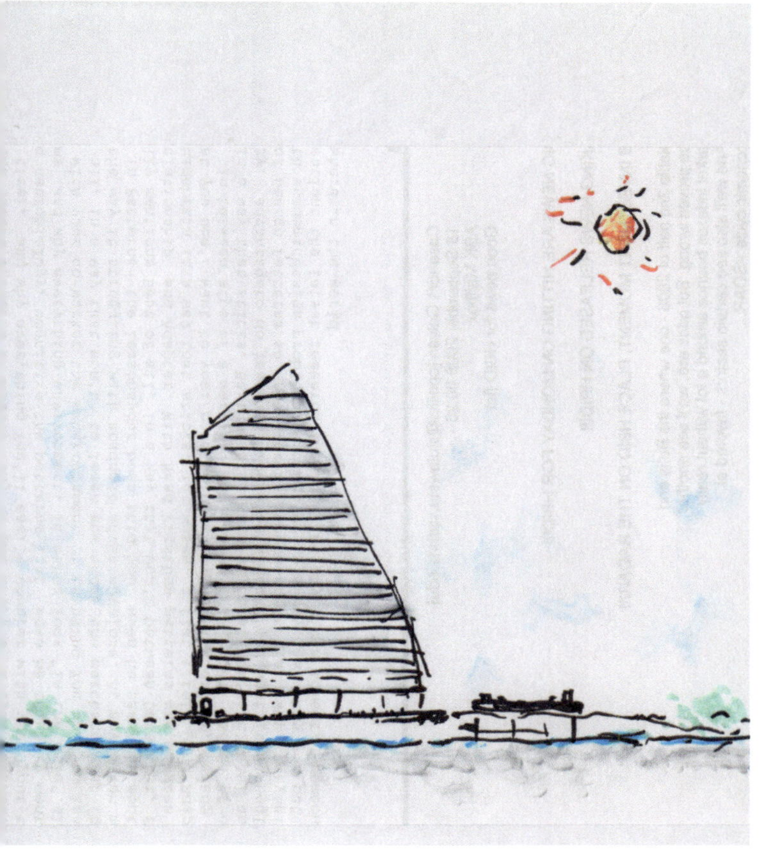

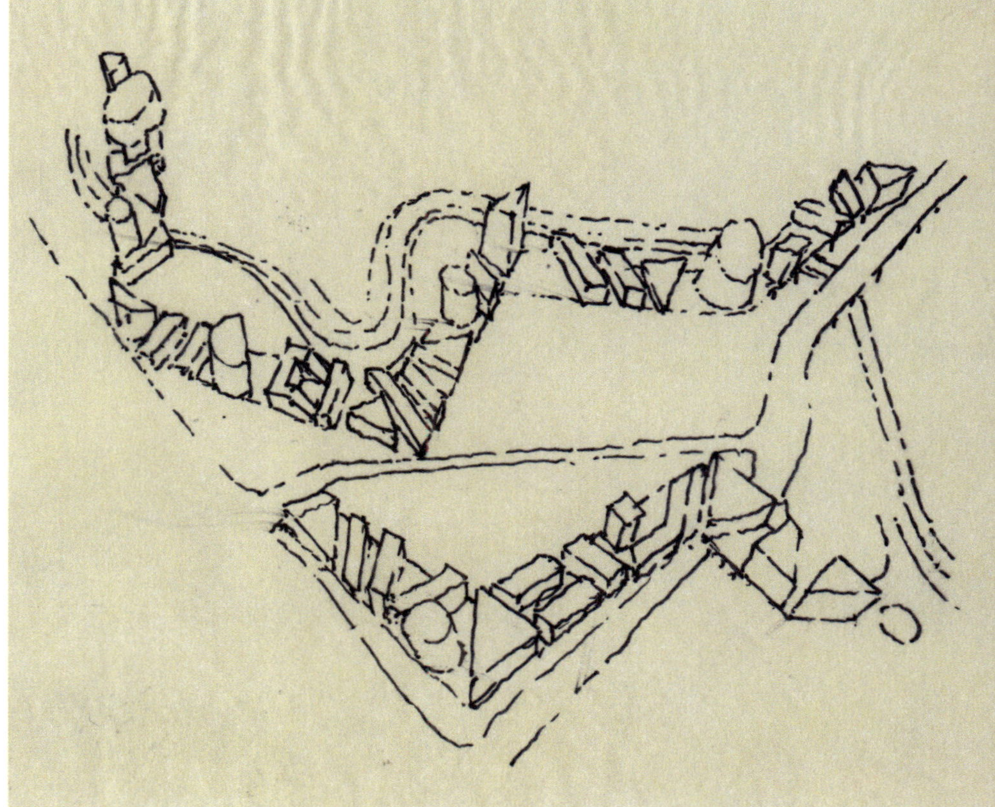

These sketches represent part of our work on the first-stage site layout for Leven Road, one of several options based upon a square-gridded pattern of three- and four-storey container-built housing elements extending across the inner part of the site; an informal checkerboard occupation of buildings and landscaped open space. In conjunction with, and in contrast to this matrix we proposed a discontinuous alignment of somewhat taller riverside buildings lying along the site's curvaceous edge to the River Lea.

The contrast with our earlier, very different set of design ideas for Leven Road reflects the extent to which our client's brief had developed. They now had a more confident view of a potential development, so they asked us to produce a conceptual area plan with ideas for the comprehensive development of this neglected part of Tower Hamlets.

2007

Following on from a more modest initial study, ABK began work on a more ambitious proposal for this extensive site beside the River Lea in east London.

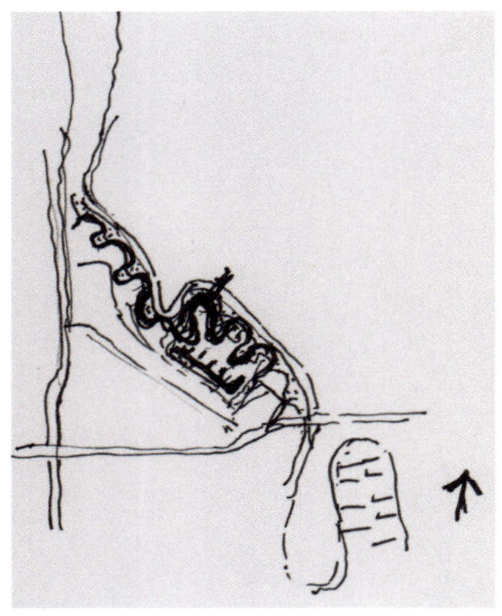

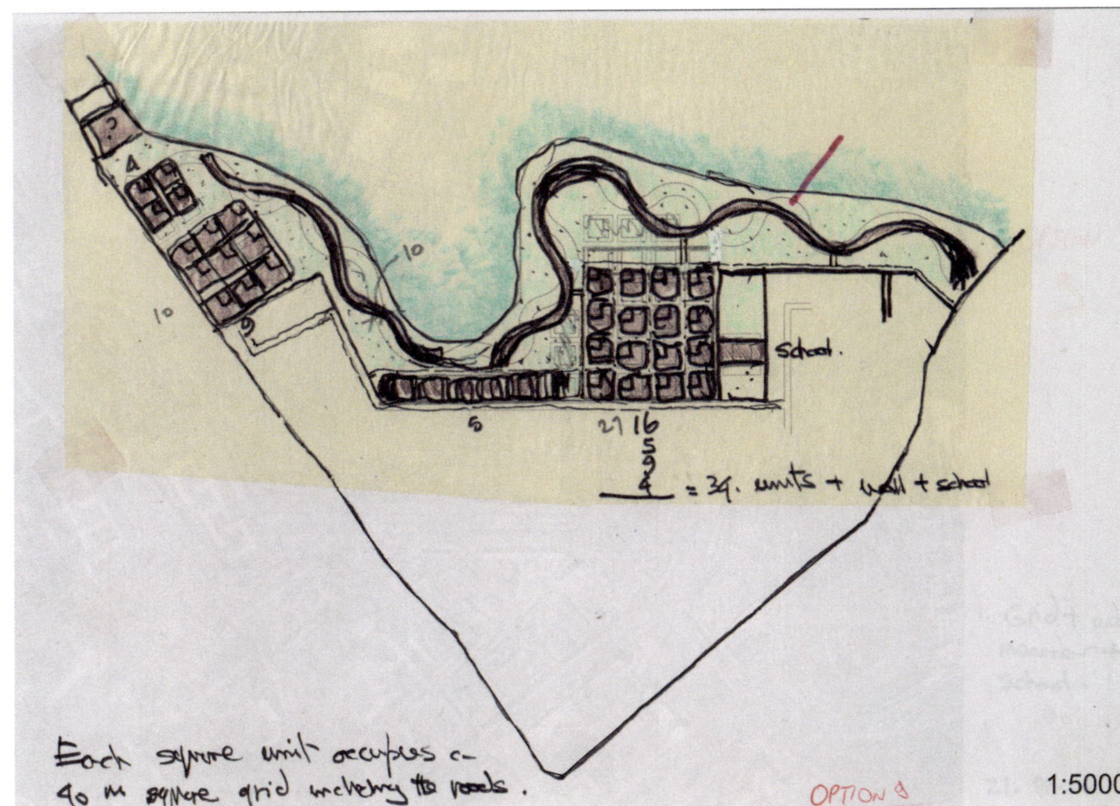

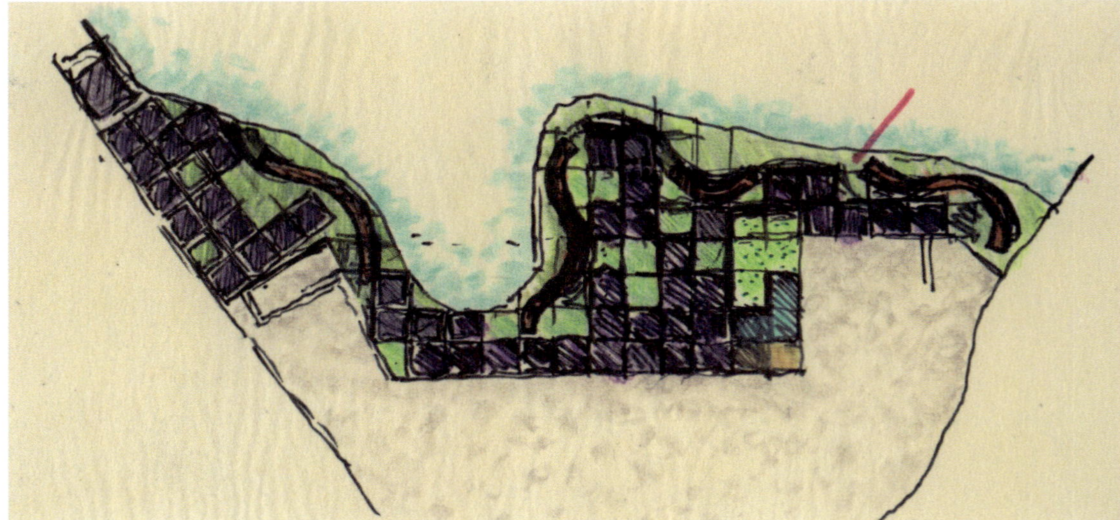

Initial planning ideas explore the combination of a meandering waterside building, echoing and exaggerating the curves of the river, and a gridded development that re-invests this ravaged part of east London an with an urban density and grain. The interstitial areas provide green spaces.

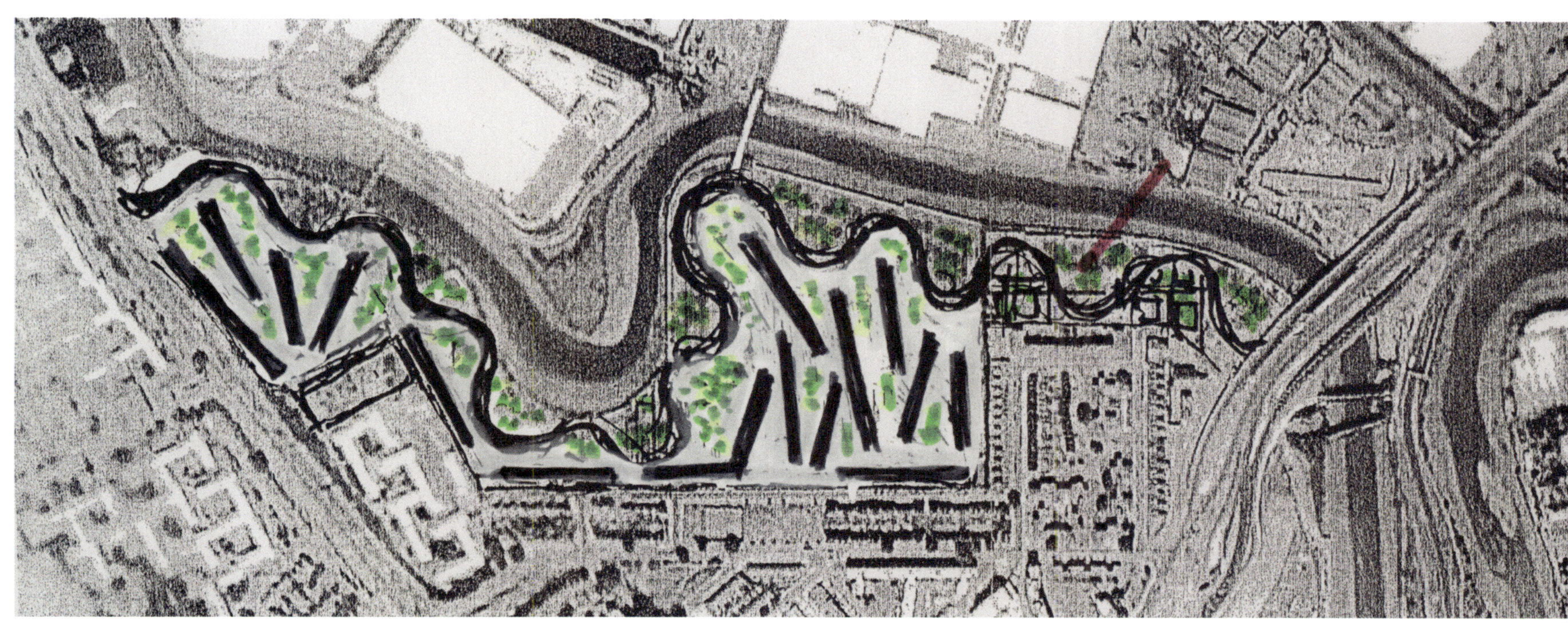

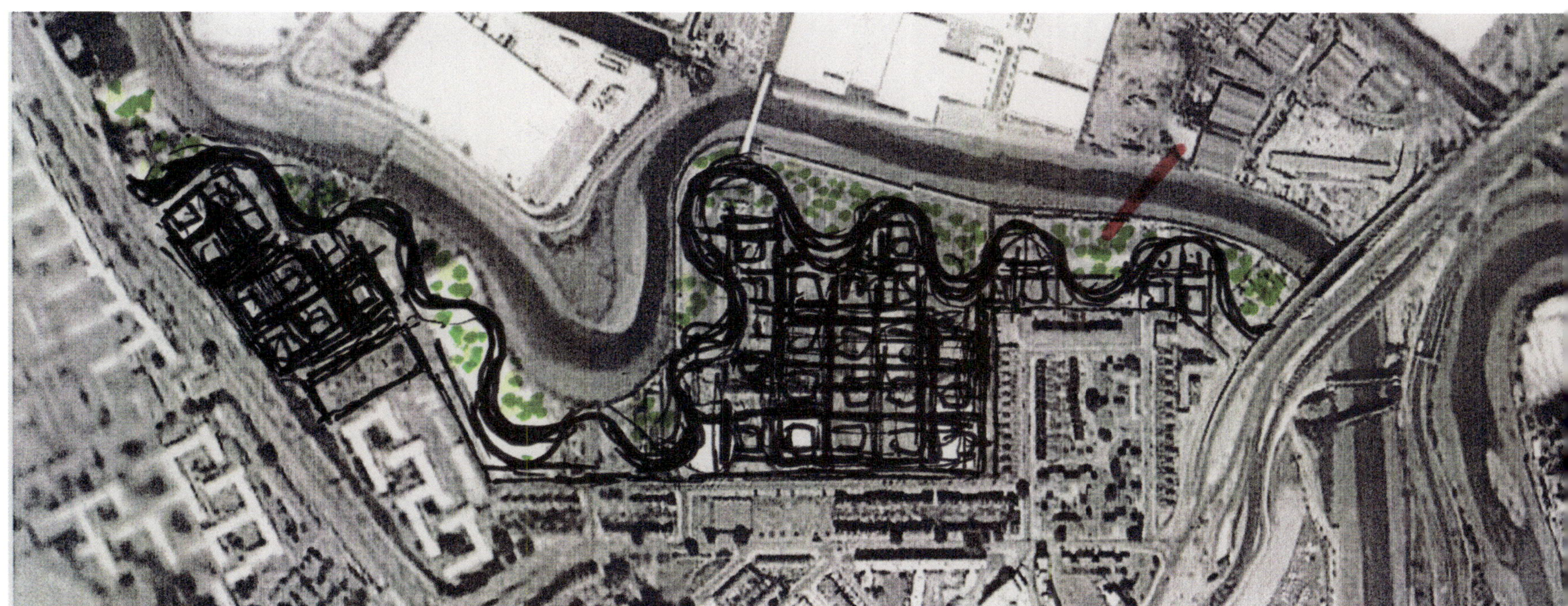

In reviewing these sketches for the North-East Inner City Civic Centre in Dublin, two particular points that relate to our design ideas come to mind:

First was the city architects' clear aspiration to initiate our development plan for this 'Convent Land' city block by commissioning a first-stage public building. The project was to accord with the massing guidelines that we'd laid down for the development, and thereby make a robust contribution to the future planning of this long undervalued part of central Dublin.

Second was the unusually complex brief that emerged from the three main occupying public bodies, whose separate and joint needs were clearly recognised. In the many briefing and design consultations, we found a willingness among all parties to accommodate our aspiration to control the massing of the whole in respect of the plan's retained existing buildings. Historic and modern buildings would form a well-fitting aesthetic coupling. Suddenly, however, we found that the funding for the whole development had been withdrawn.

2003

A new civic centre was to form a key project within the major regeneration programme for the run-down 'Convent Lands' in Dublin.

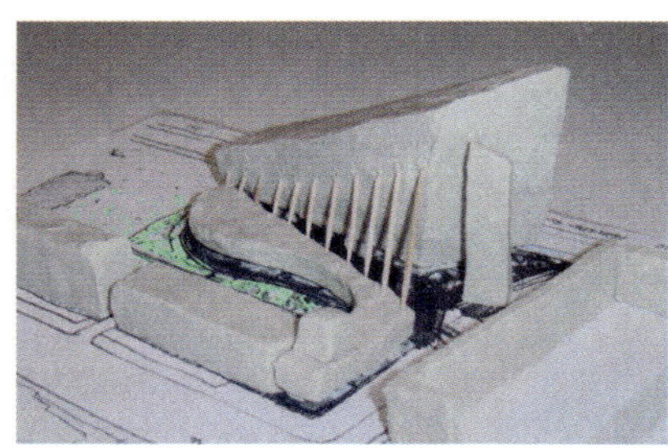

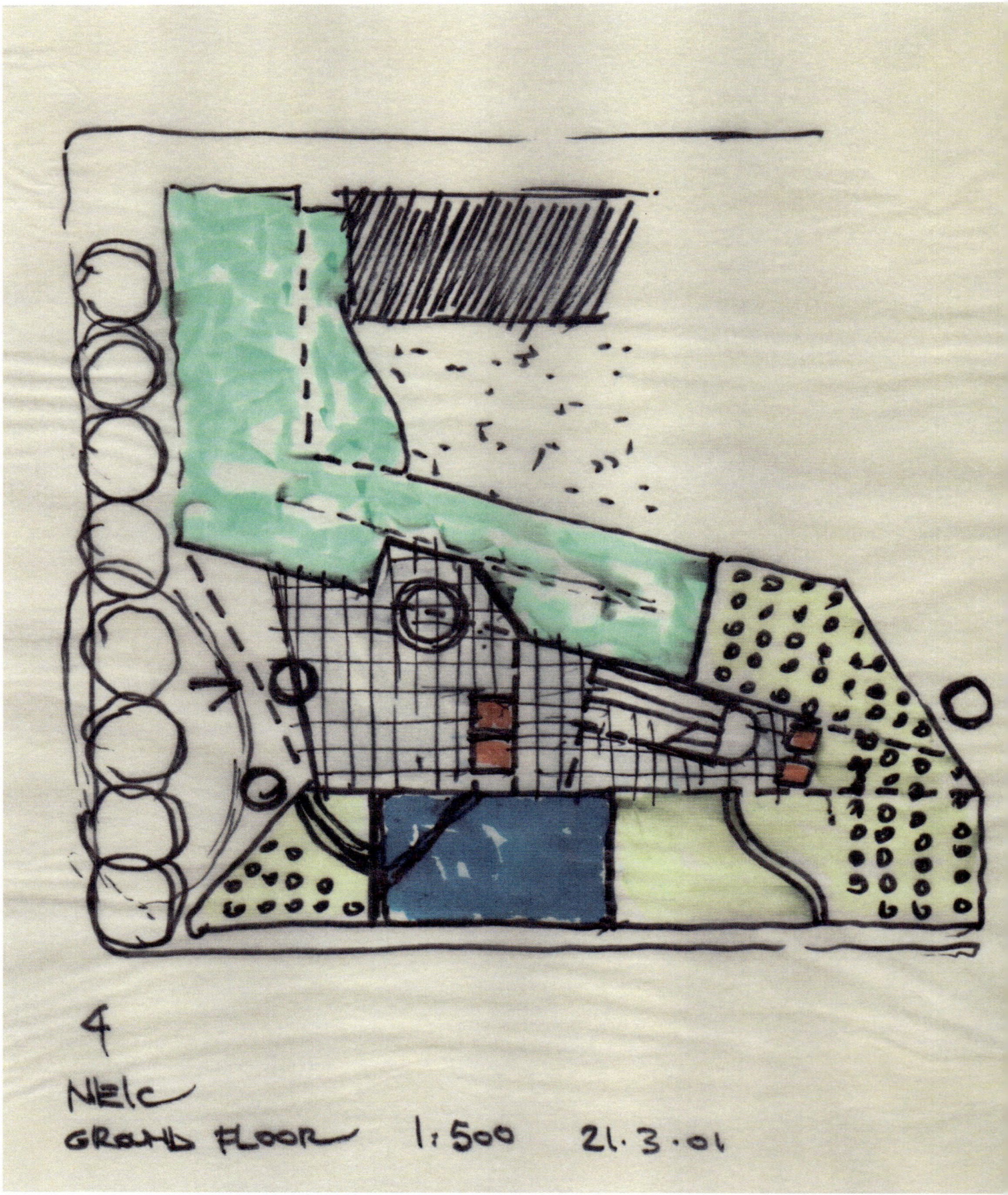

Commissioned by Dublin City Council within its North East Inner City (NEIC) development plan, this proposal is for the mixed development of a city block along Sean McDermott Street.

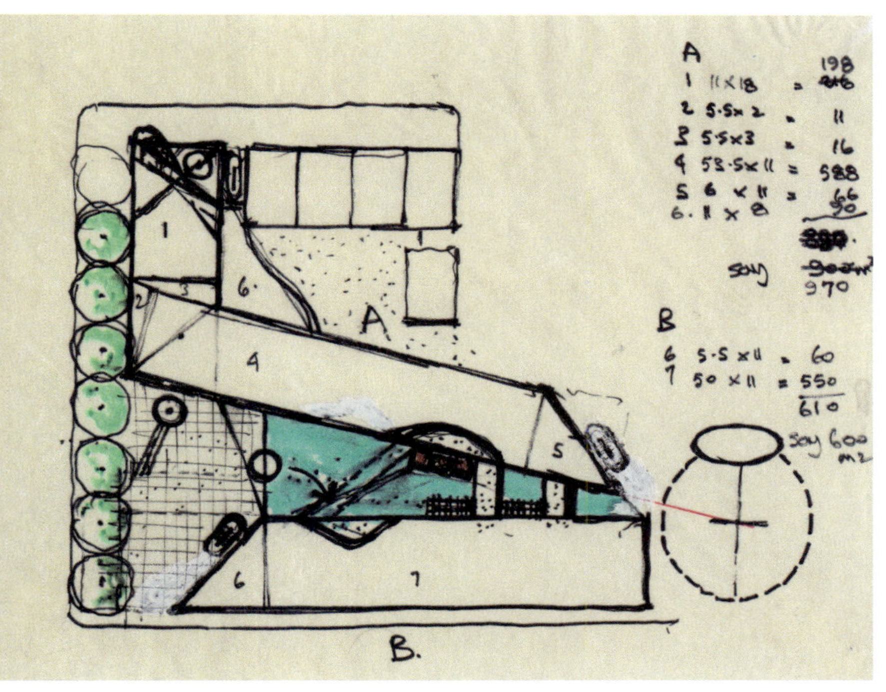

A
1 11 x 18 = 198
2 5.5 x 2 = 11
3 5.5 x 3 = 16
4 53.5 x 11 = 588
5 6 x 11 = 66
6. 11 x 8
say 970
B
6 5.5 x 11 = 60
7 50 x 11 = 550
610
say 600 m2
A
B.

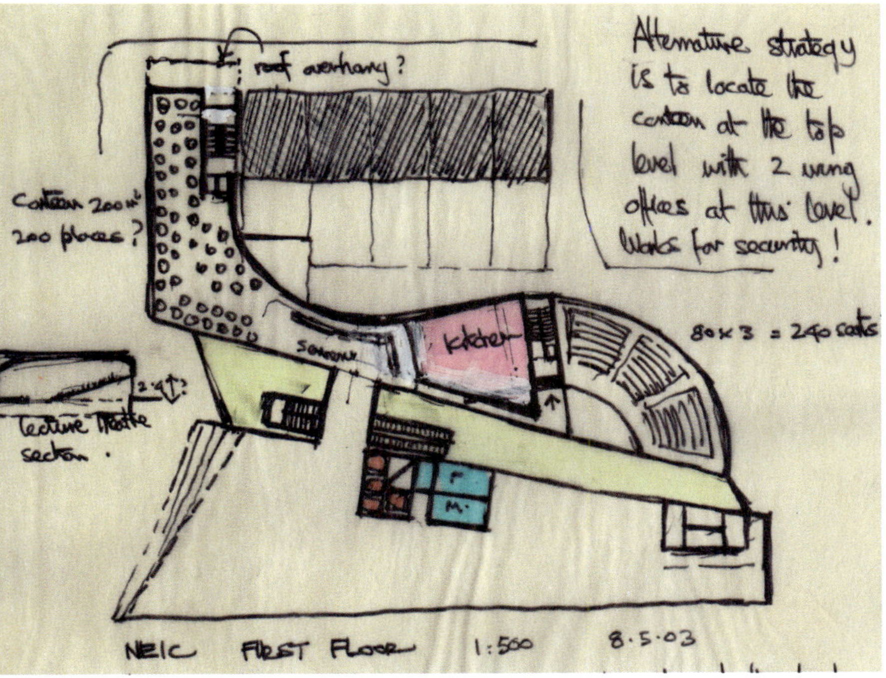

roof overhang ?
Canteen 200 m2
200 places ?
Lecture Theatre
section .
Servery
Kitchen
F
M.
Alternative strategy
is to locate the
canteen at the top
level with 2 wing
offices at this level.
Works for security !
80 x 3 = 240 seats
NEIC   FIRST FLOOR   1:500   8.5.03

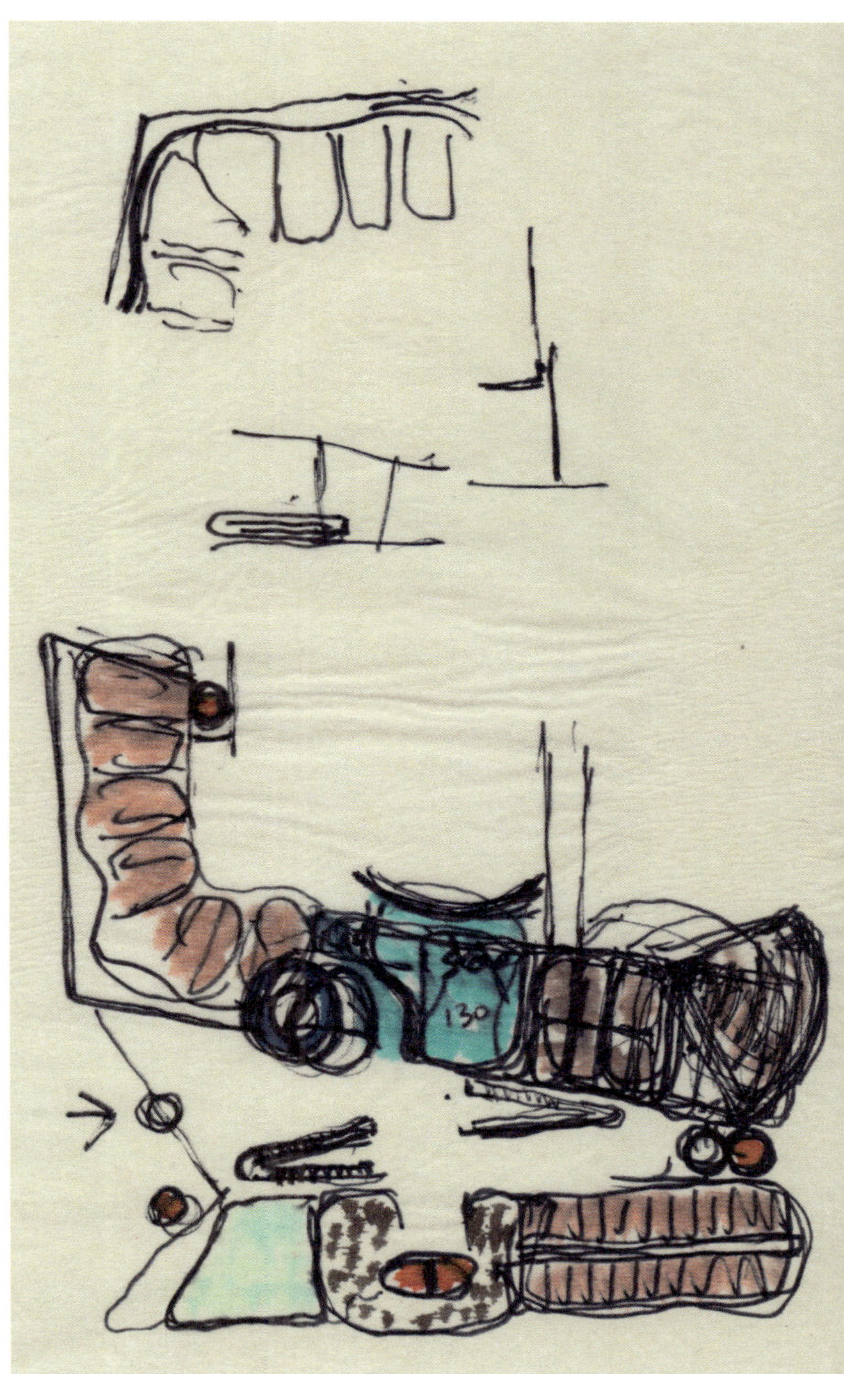

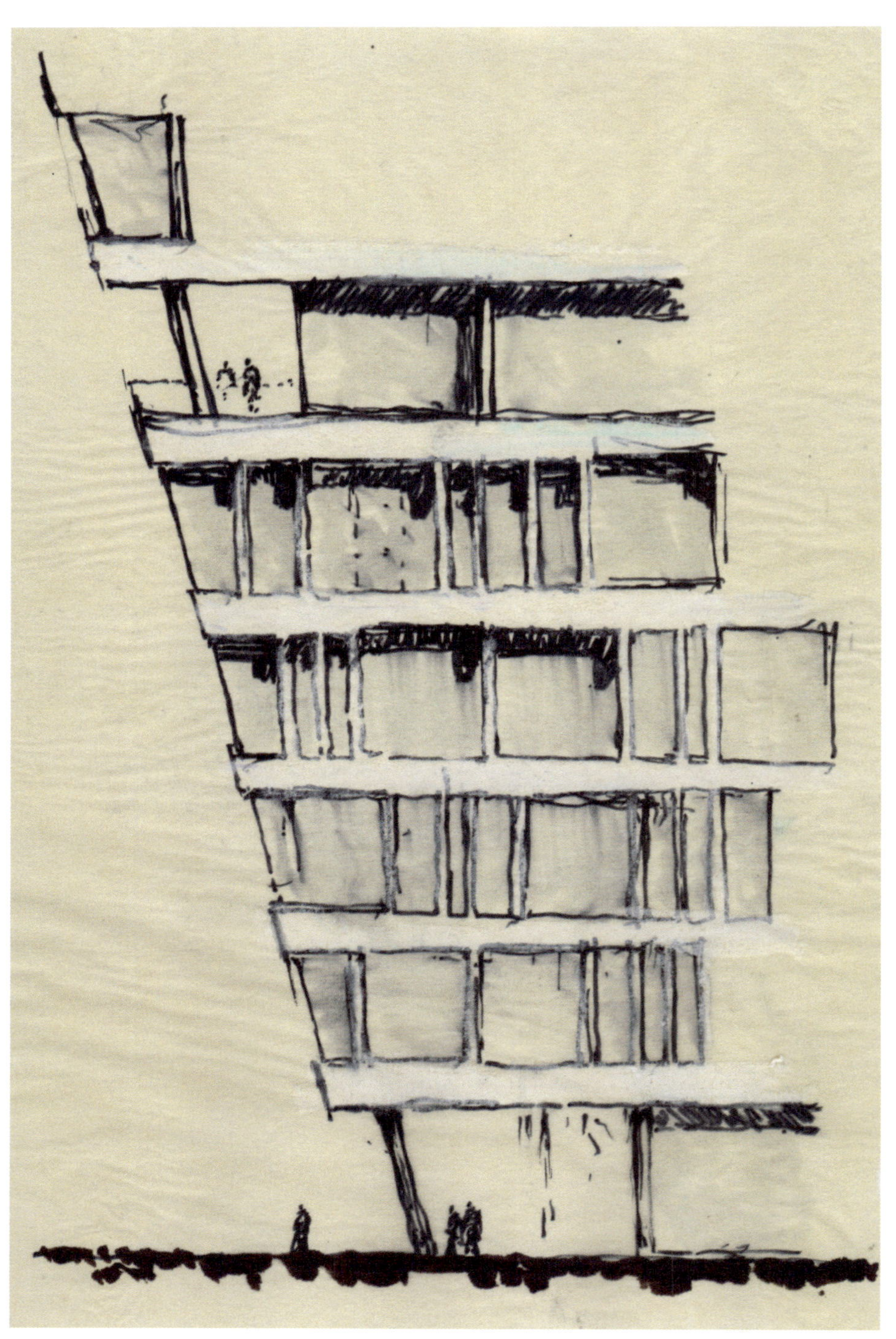
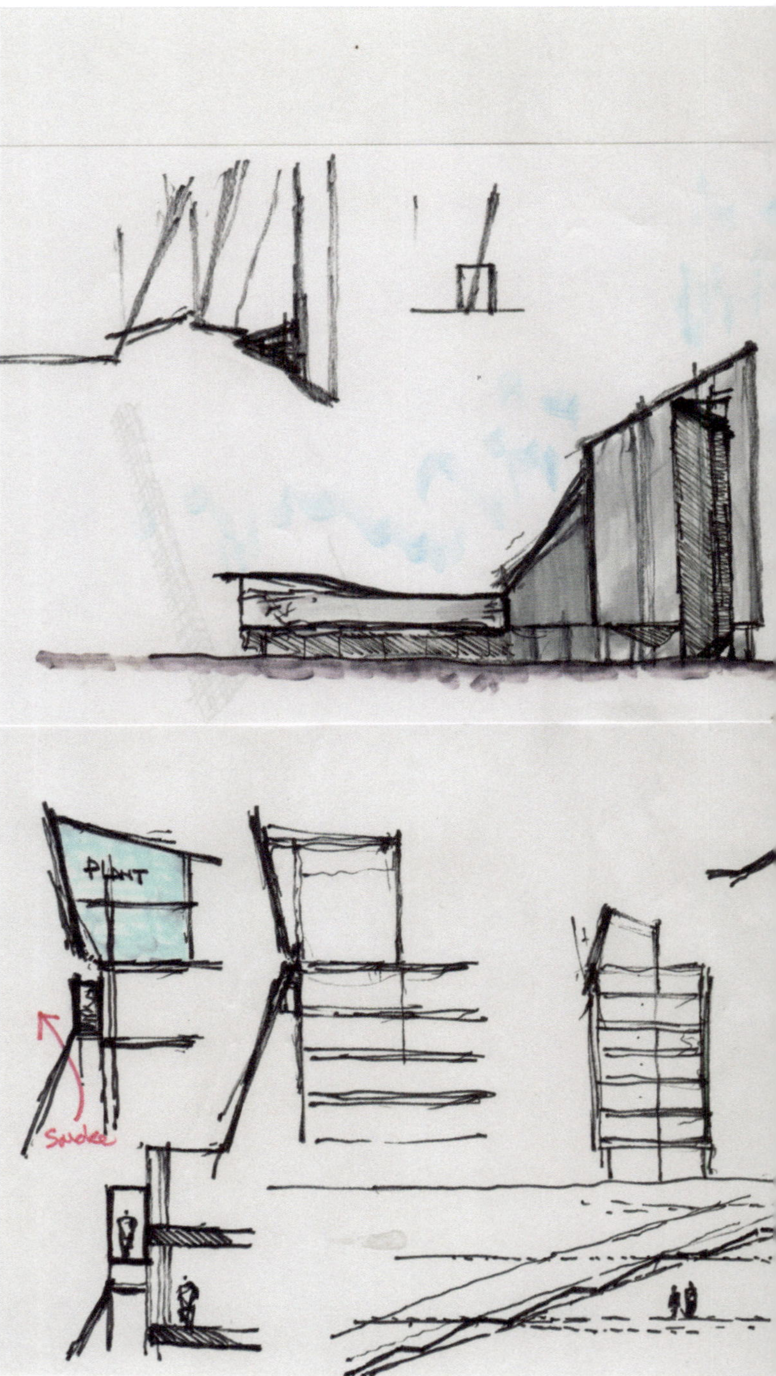

*Elevation and section studies for
the civic centre.*

Following on from our earlier scheme for
the Riverside Building, employing the
reused shipping-container system
pioneered by our client Eric Reynolds, we
were asked to suggest ideas for a higher-
rise design on the equally wonderful
Trinity Buoy Wharf site at the confluence
of the River Lea and the Thames.

Now, 10 years later, questions about the
structural and constructional constraints
that might arise in using containers to
form, say, a 10-storey building, remain
unanswered for me. Equally, might not
the modular nature of the containers
restrict the aesthetic dimension of a
design for this great site? At the time,
I thought not, so we started to design,
knowing that in this instance curved
forms would not be an option.

2006

**This project tested the capacity of shipping
containers to adopt a substantial urban form
that transcends their modular banality.**

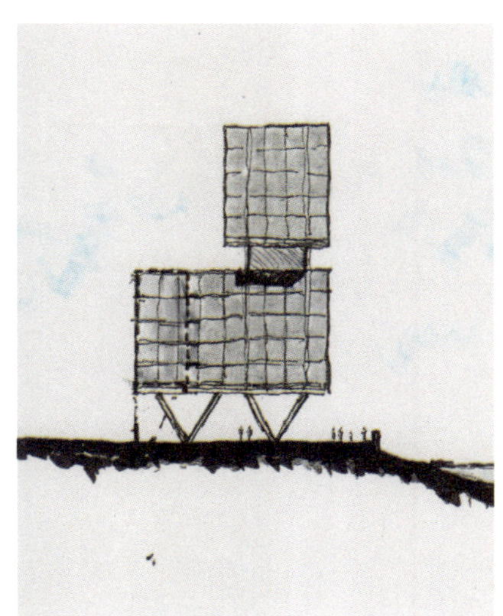

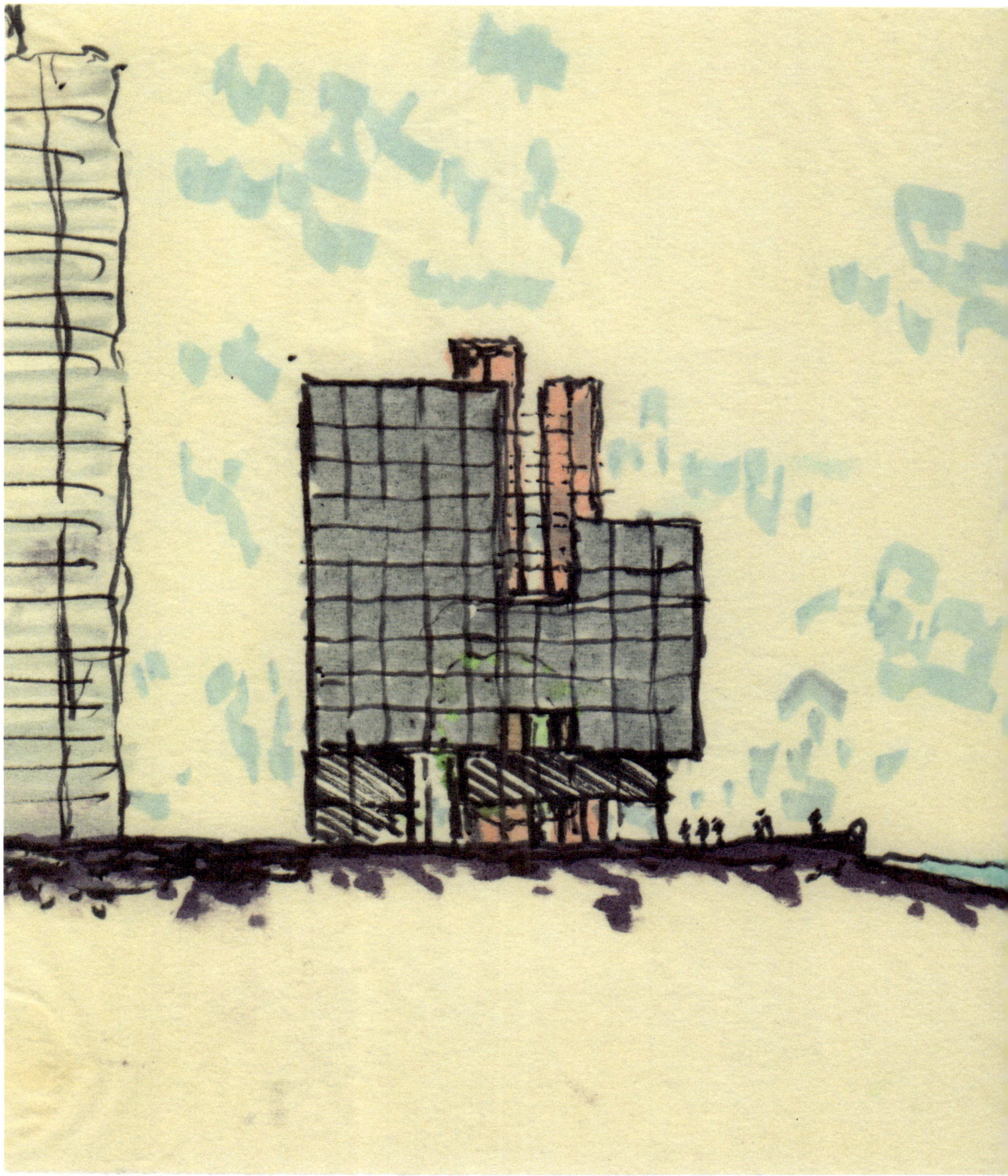

Leaside Building, Trinity Buoy Wharf

*The shipping containers are
stacked in clusters that are
articulated so as to create an
interesting and varied urban
arrangement.*

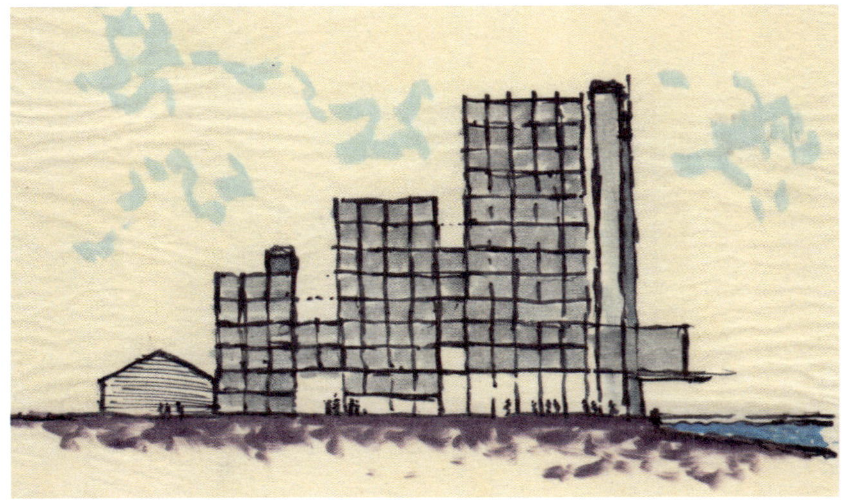

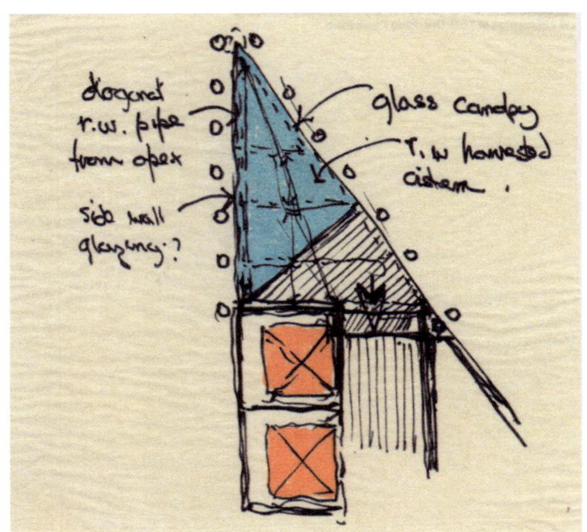

diagonal
r.w. pipe
from apex
side wall
glazing.?
glass canopy
T.w harvested
cistern.

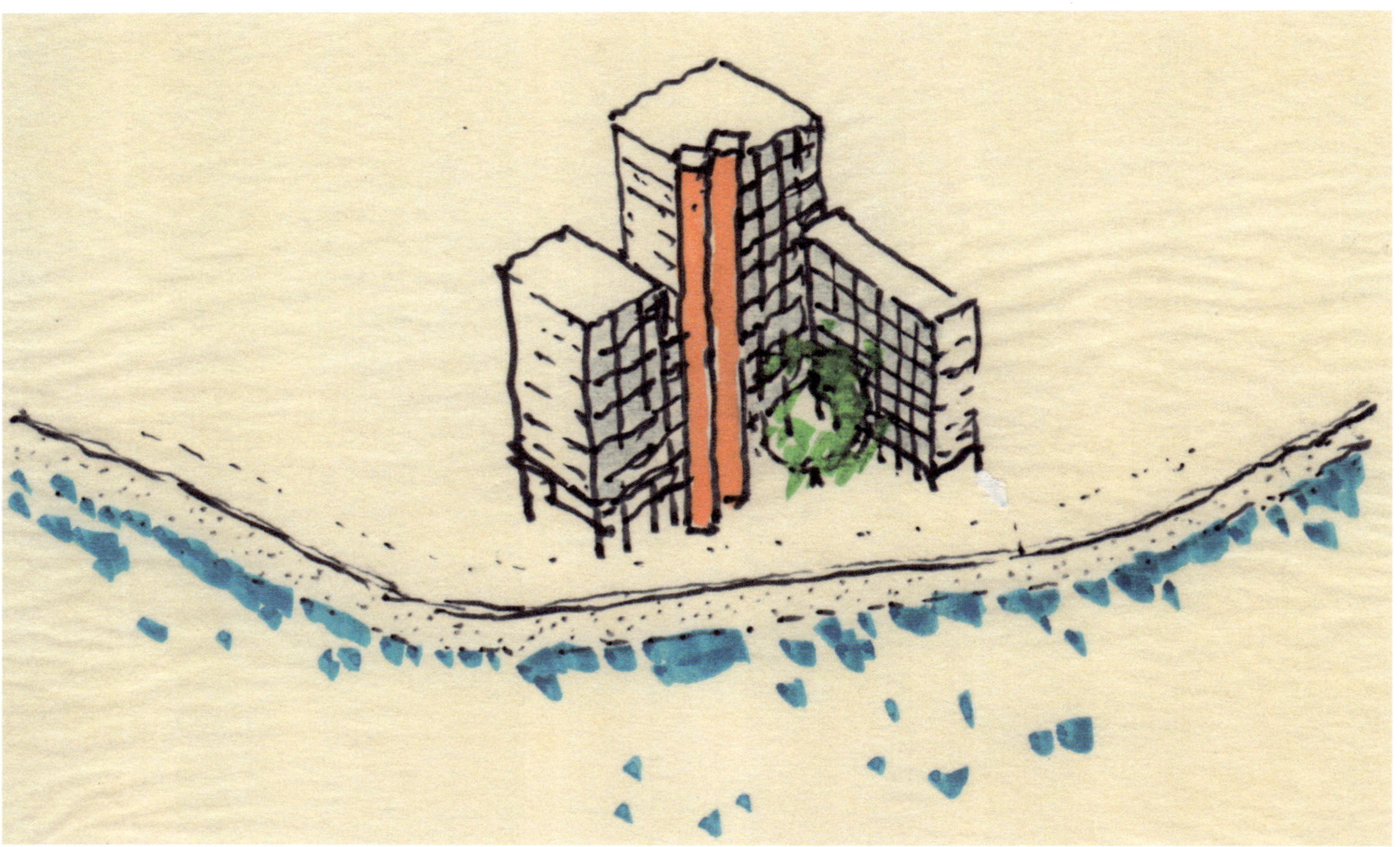

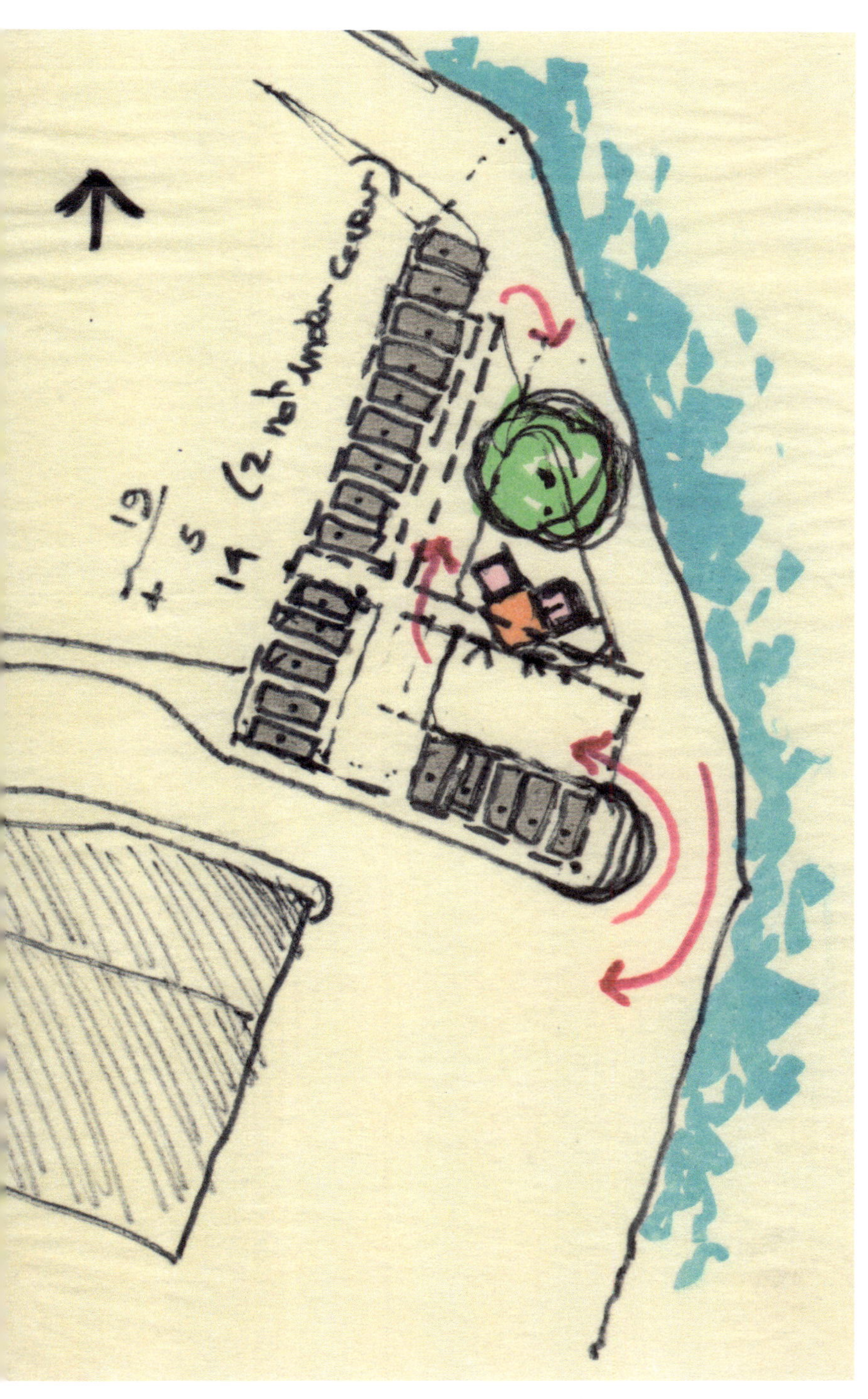

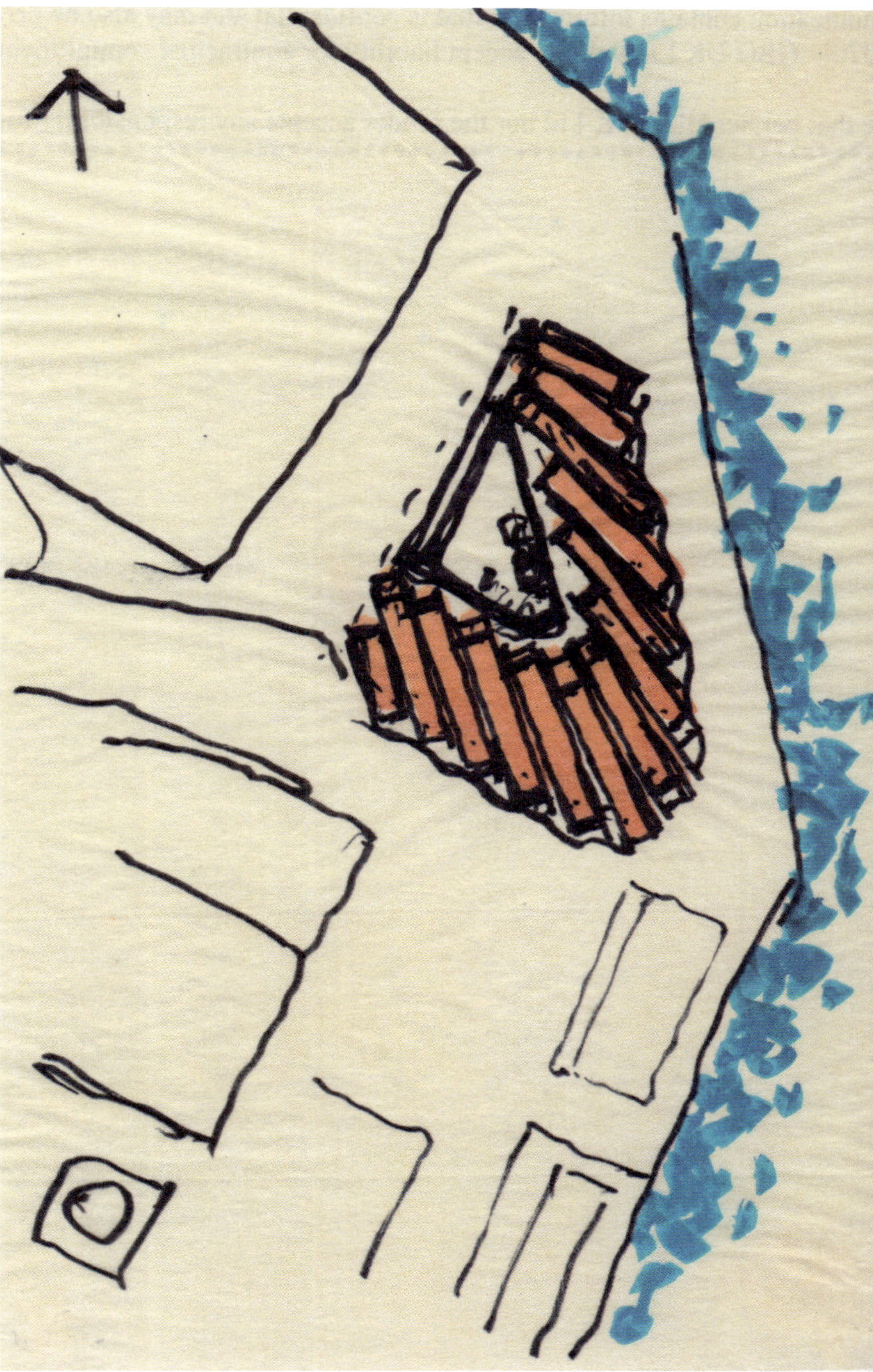

Plan options explored rectilinear arrangements, that follow logically from the container dimensions, as well as a 'splayed' configuration.

In the early 1970s we had completed a multi-occupancy family house on a great outward-looking site at the southern edge of the Jewish sector of the old city of Jerusalem. Years later I returned to Israel to speak at a conference on 'Bauhaus Tel Aviv', so it was pleasing to be one of two architects to be invited to compete for a multi-storey building in central Tel Aviv.

In recent years I signed a public pledge (Artists for Palestine UK), undertaking not to accept any work in Israel. Today, while typing 'Tel Aviv', I found that my entire draft for this book had disappeared. Happily, most of it was recovered, but not until I'd filed a complaint via my atheist guardian angel, suggesting that the draft couldn't reasonably be seen as breaking my pledge.

In carrying out some initial research into the urban history of Tel Aviv, I was taken by images of the city's early development in relation to the Mediterranean coastline. Visiting the beach, my interest was further stirred when I came across a piece of pale green glass that, smoothed by erosion, had become a beautiful object to hold. I later found that his curved form seemed to emerge in the plans – the freedom found by the erosion of the site's rectilinear outer corner helped form a small open space that, for us, became the Rothschild Plaza.

1994

Eroded glass shard inspiration in plans for a curving, glazed highrise tower.

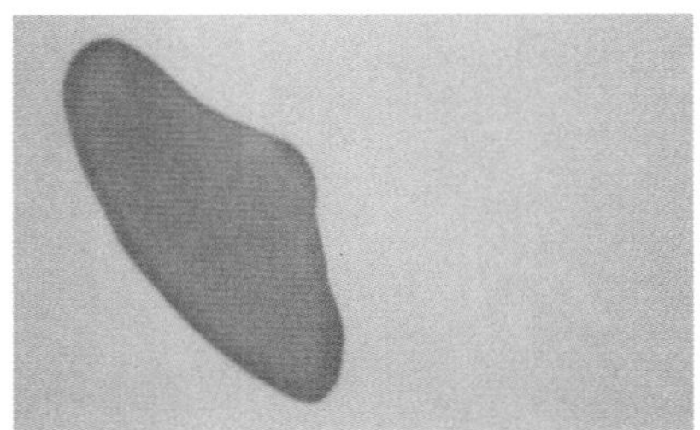

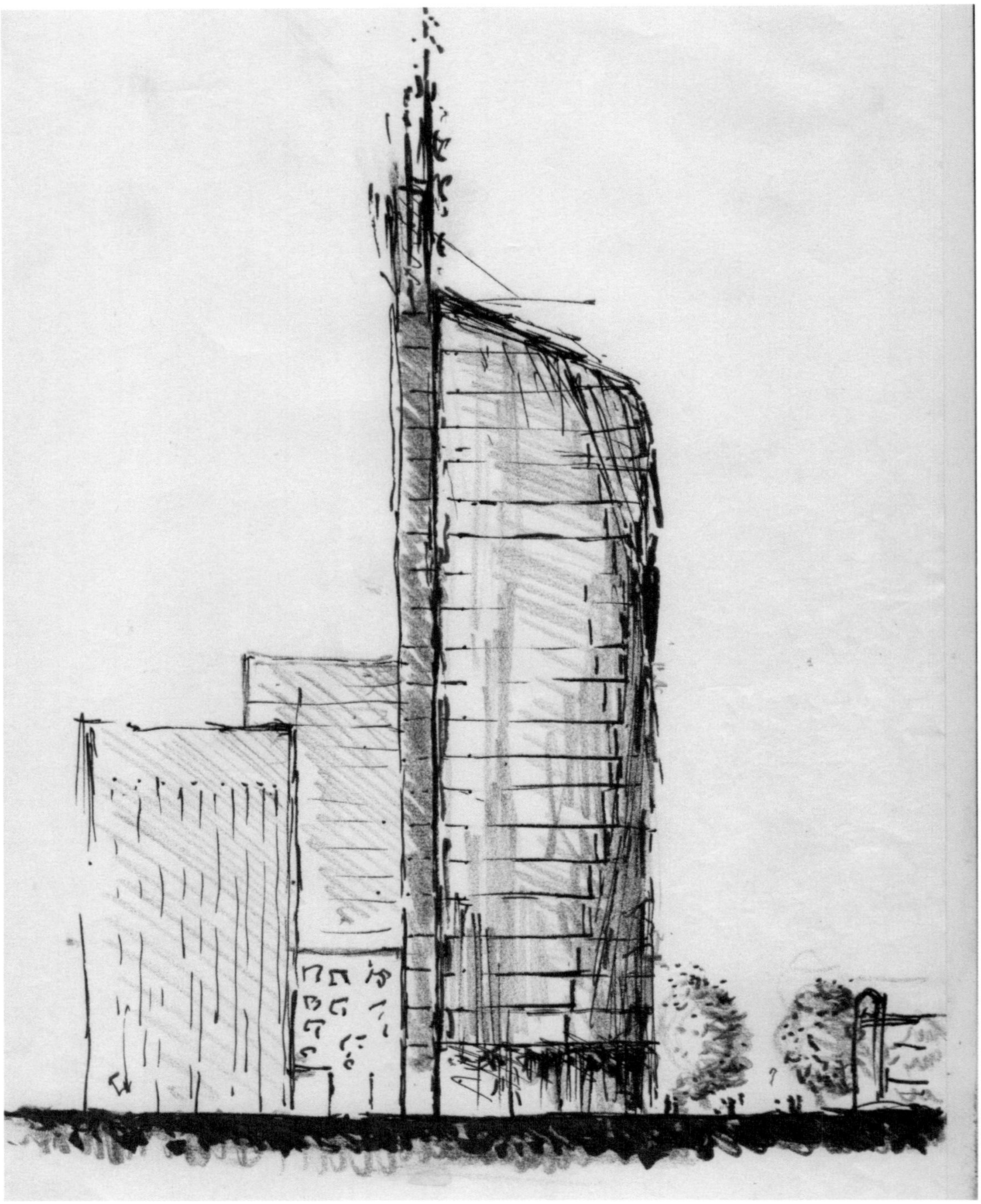

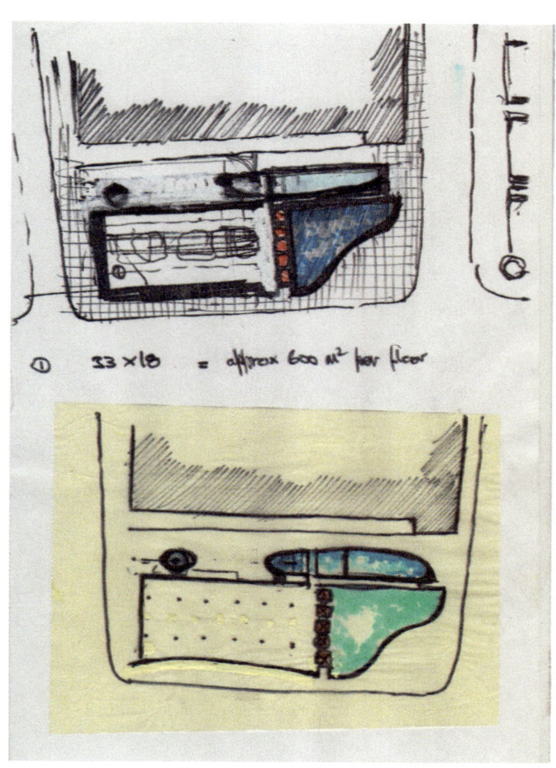

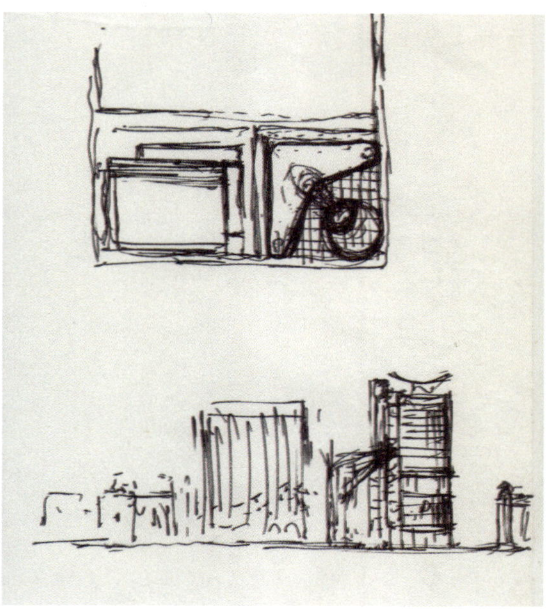

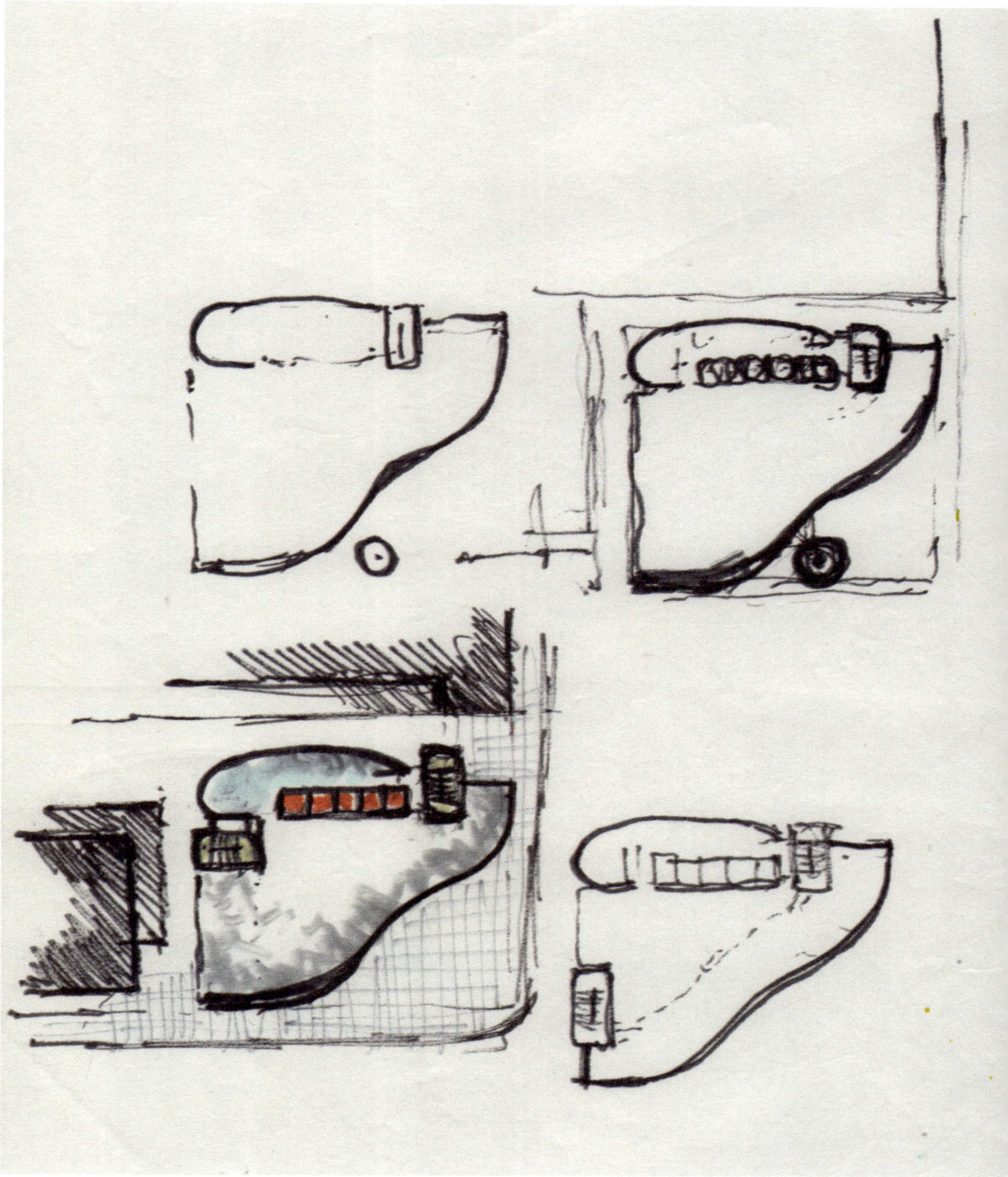

The tower occupies a corner site, and these sketches explore different ways to acknowledge this condition, most incorporating some form of concave inflection in counterpoint to the street junction.

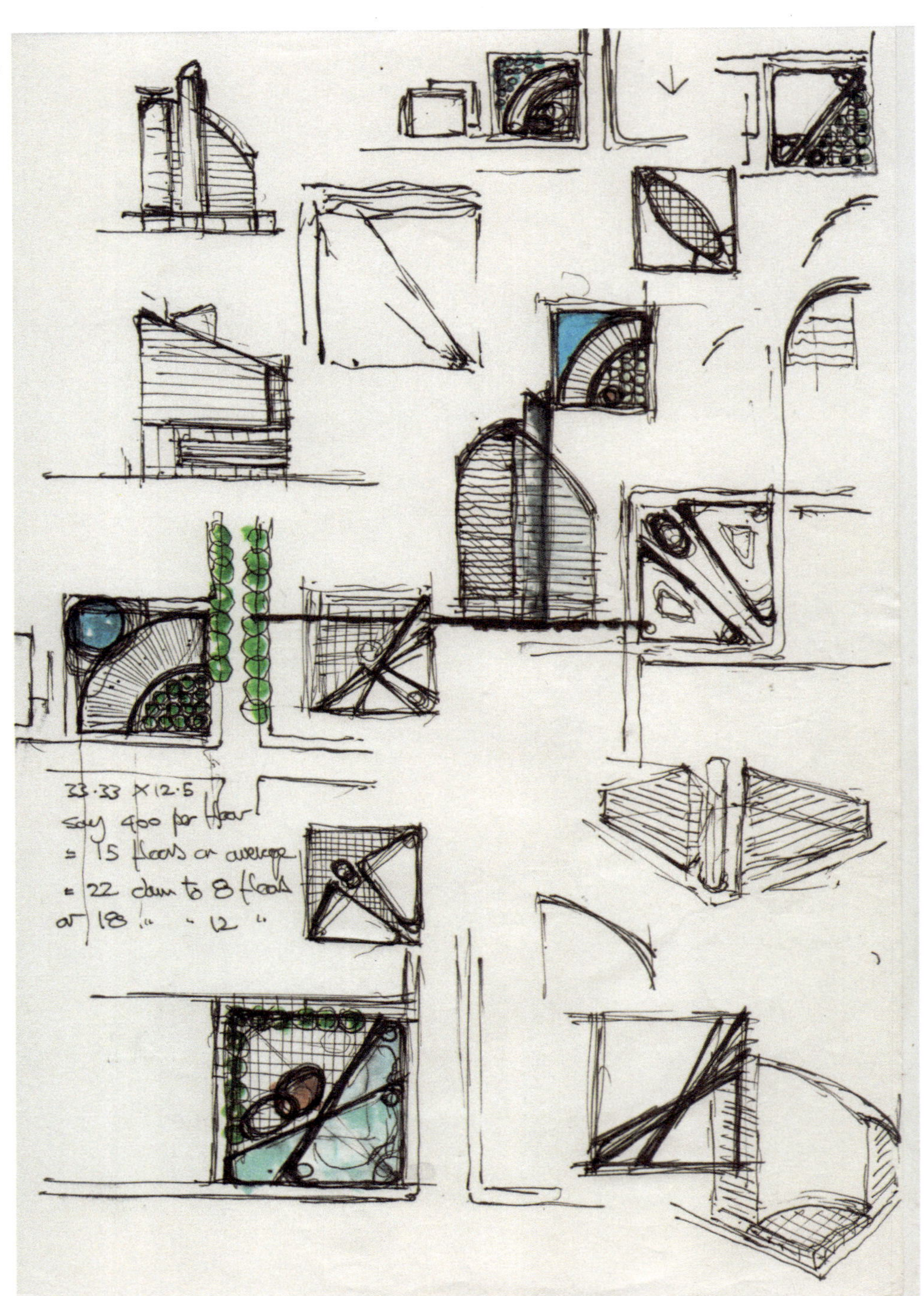

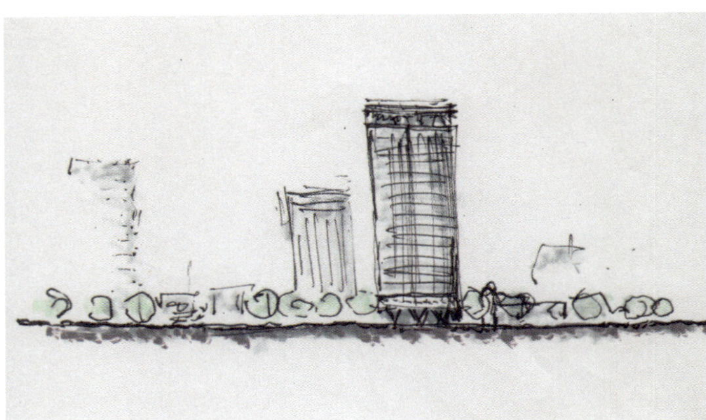

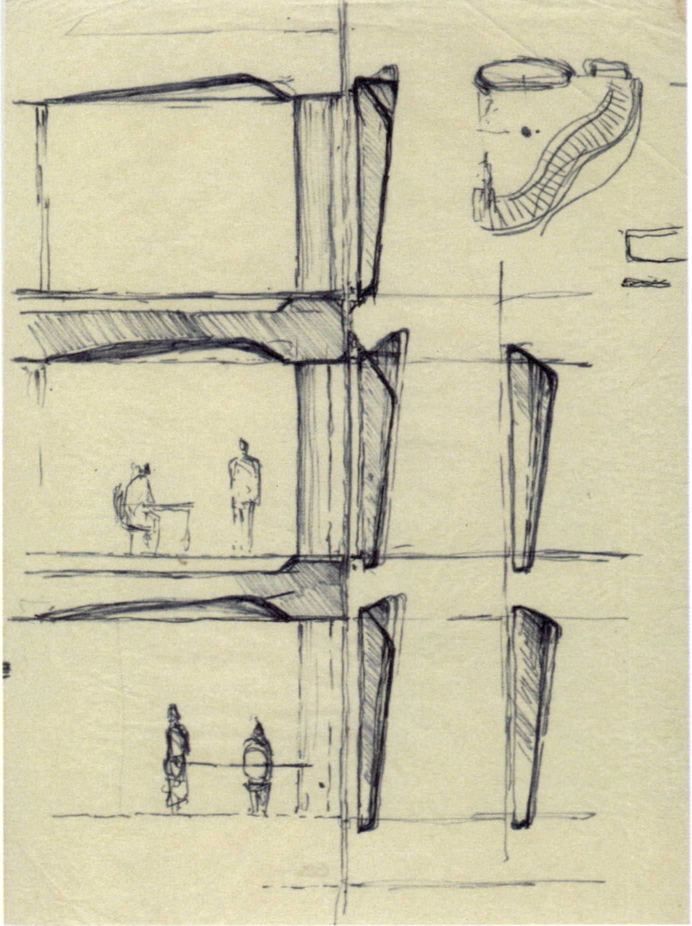

*While a high-rise tower inevitably
has a significant presence within
the urban context, particular
attention was focussed on its
impact at ground level so as to
create a space that contributes
to the life of the city.*

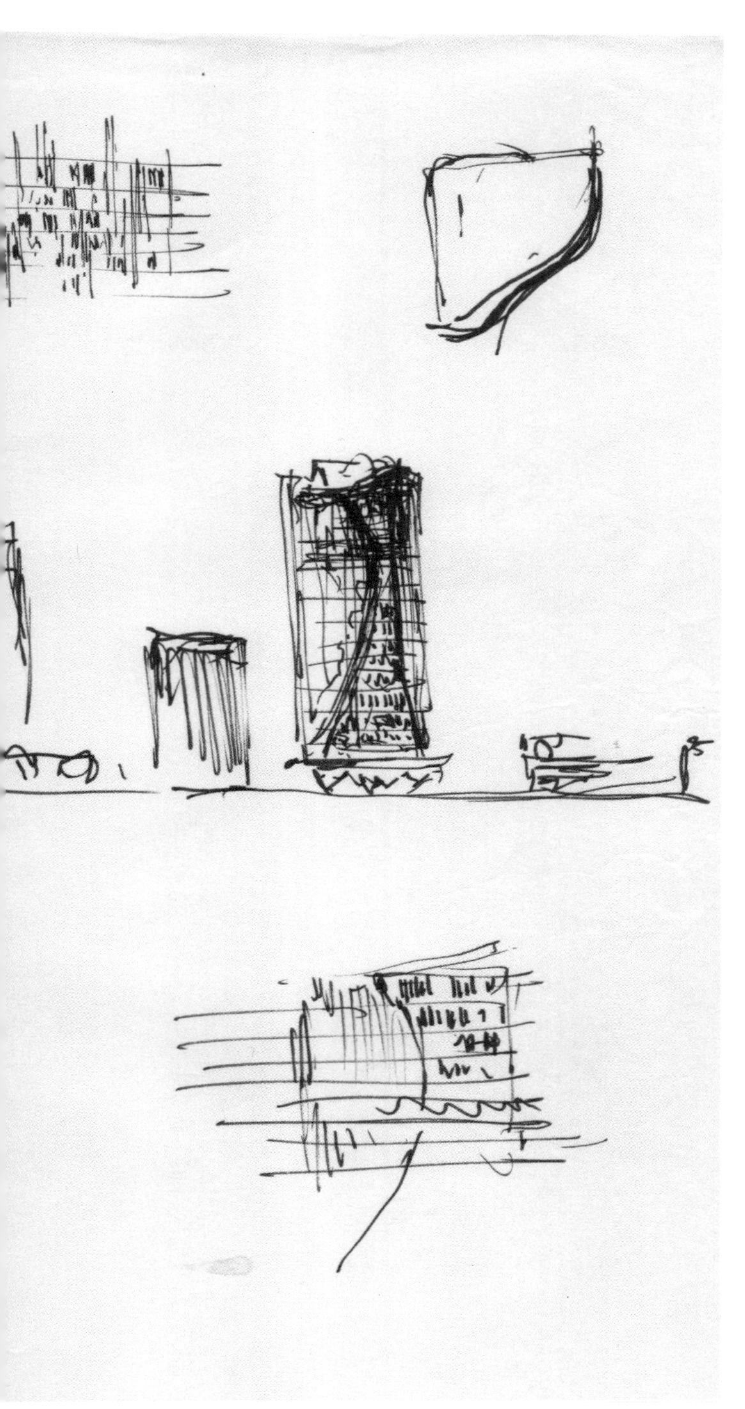

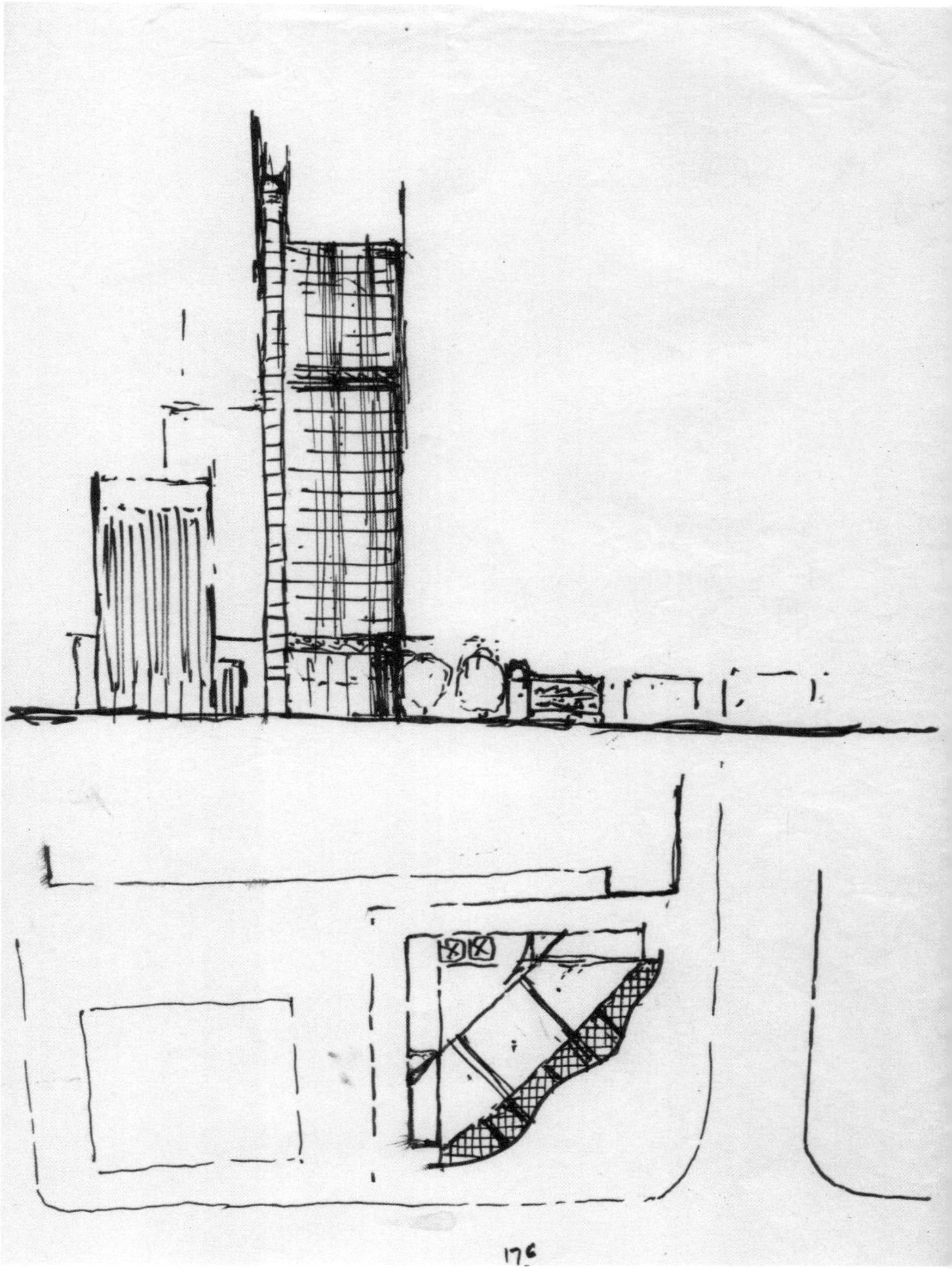

175

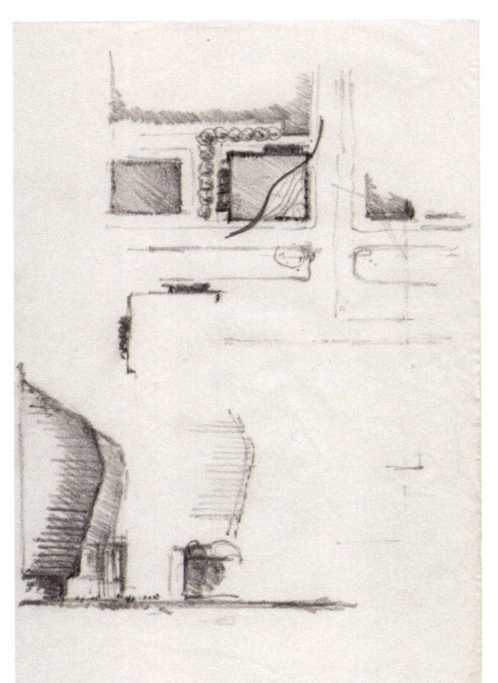

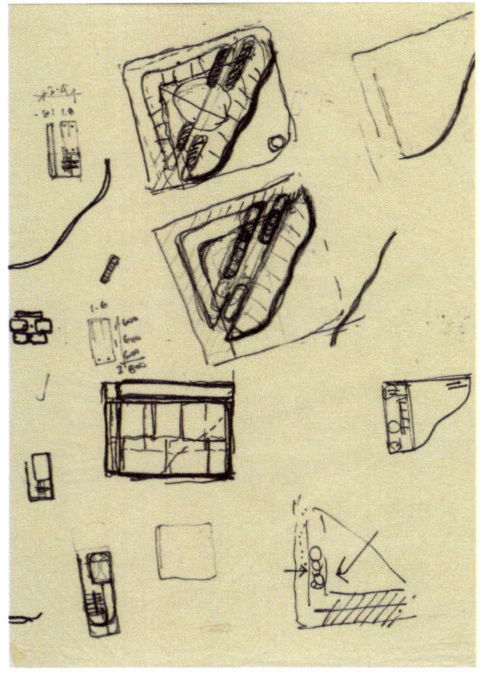

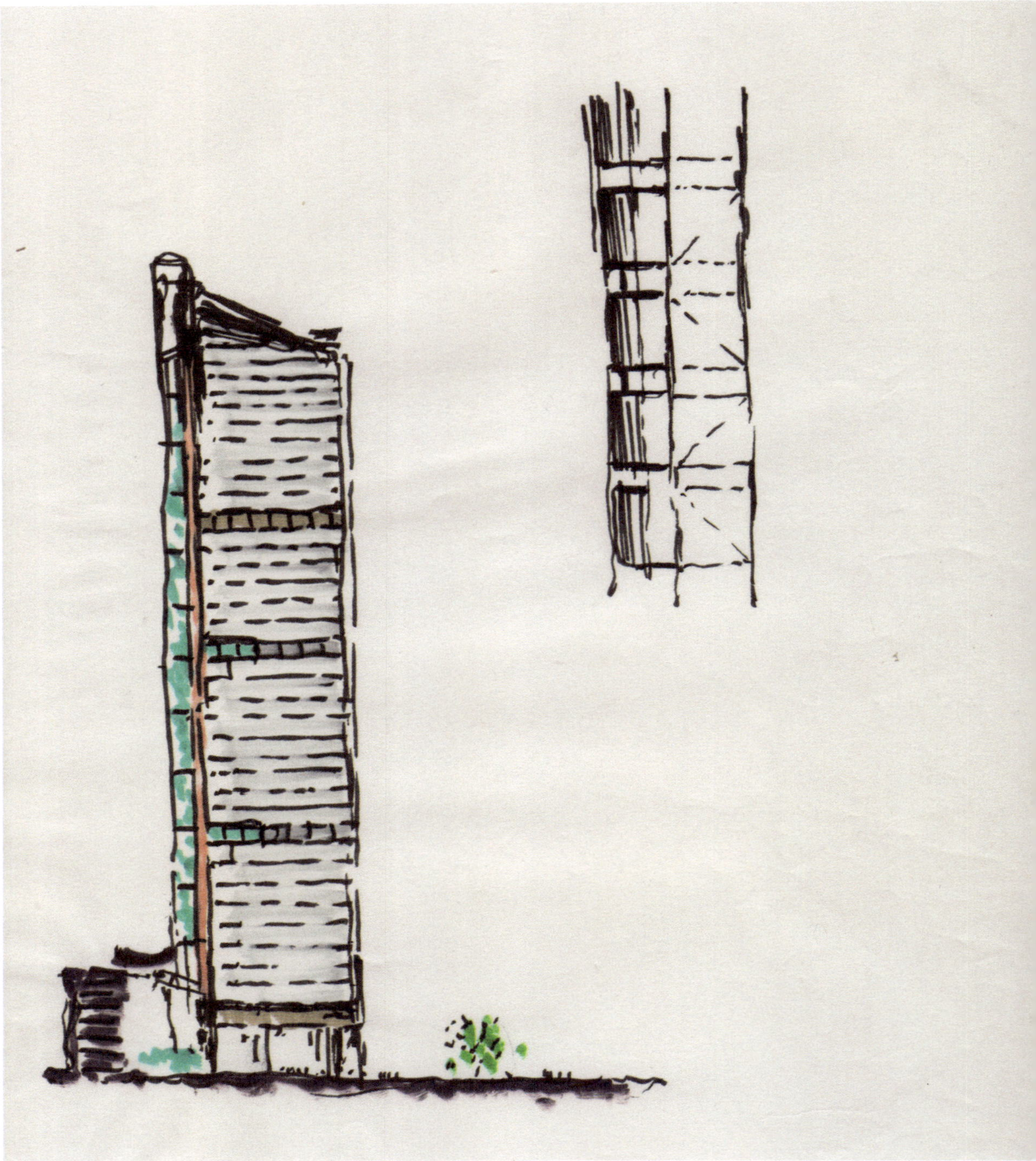

The Bartlett: A London Patchwork

This sketch shows the bones of an idea that I introduced at the Bartlett school of architecture, University College London, where I was professor from 1986-89. It shows an initial selection of three areas that were to form part of a 'London Patchwork' that I sought to introduce.

In view of the wide range of types, scales, complexities and contexts of the many design projects that would take place throughout the school's five-year programme, I thought that the teaching staff and students might effectively explore a common ground that was to be applied across the school. No better place than to situate the work within the broad and varied urban opportunities of our home ground, the inner city of London.

The idea was to additively create an 'urban patchwork' by selecting a different area of the city to serve as the design location for each of the academic years. This was not to be seen as an initiative to make a grand plan for the city but rather as an assembly and accumulation of ideas that would, in time, form an oeuvre of student-based contributions in an evolving urban scene.

1986-89

A strategy to focus the attention of multifarious student projects at the Bartlett school of architecture on the particular conditions of the London metropolis.

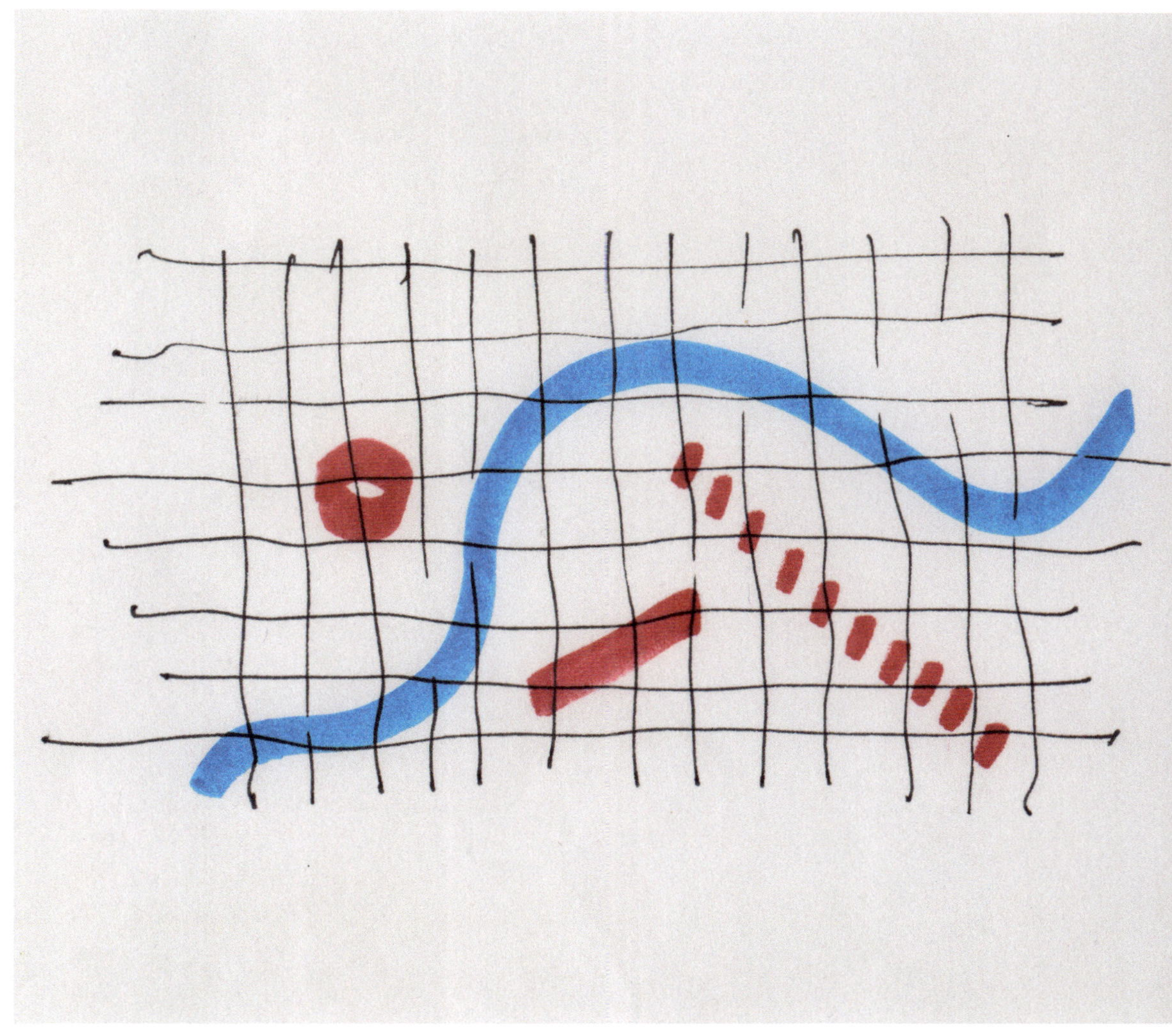

Coming upon these sketches again, without seeing the hard-line drawings that formed the basis of our submission for this competition, I find it difficult to recall either the substance of the brief or the format and details of our plans. What, I now wonder, does this loss of memory say about my feelings at that time, working on ideas for this central area of Berlin? Perhaps an ambiguity: on the one hand wanting to make some reconnection with my birthplace as an architectural gesture, yet on the other not wanting to connect with my childhood's still-buried and unrecognised feelings of expelled-pain and unvoiced outrage?

So, here are some sketches and notes that offer clues about a 'bridge-building' of strong forms and proportions. There's little doubt that the proposal was a bold, modern intervention, but I wonder why we never quite came to submit the scheme for assessment in Berlin?

1993

The Spreeinsel Urban Design Competition sought to reconfigure the historic heart of the reinstated German capital. The first round attracted more than 1000 entries.

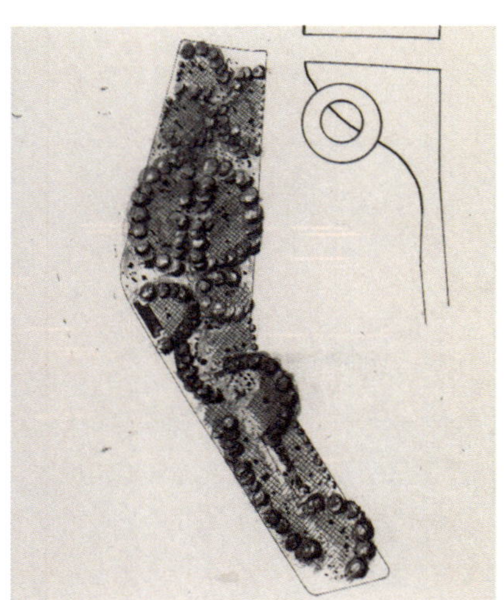

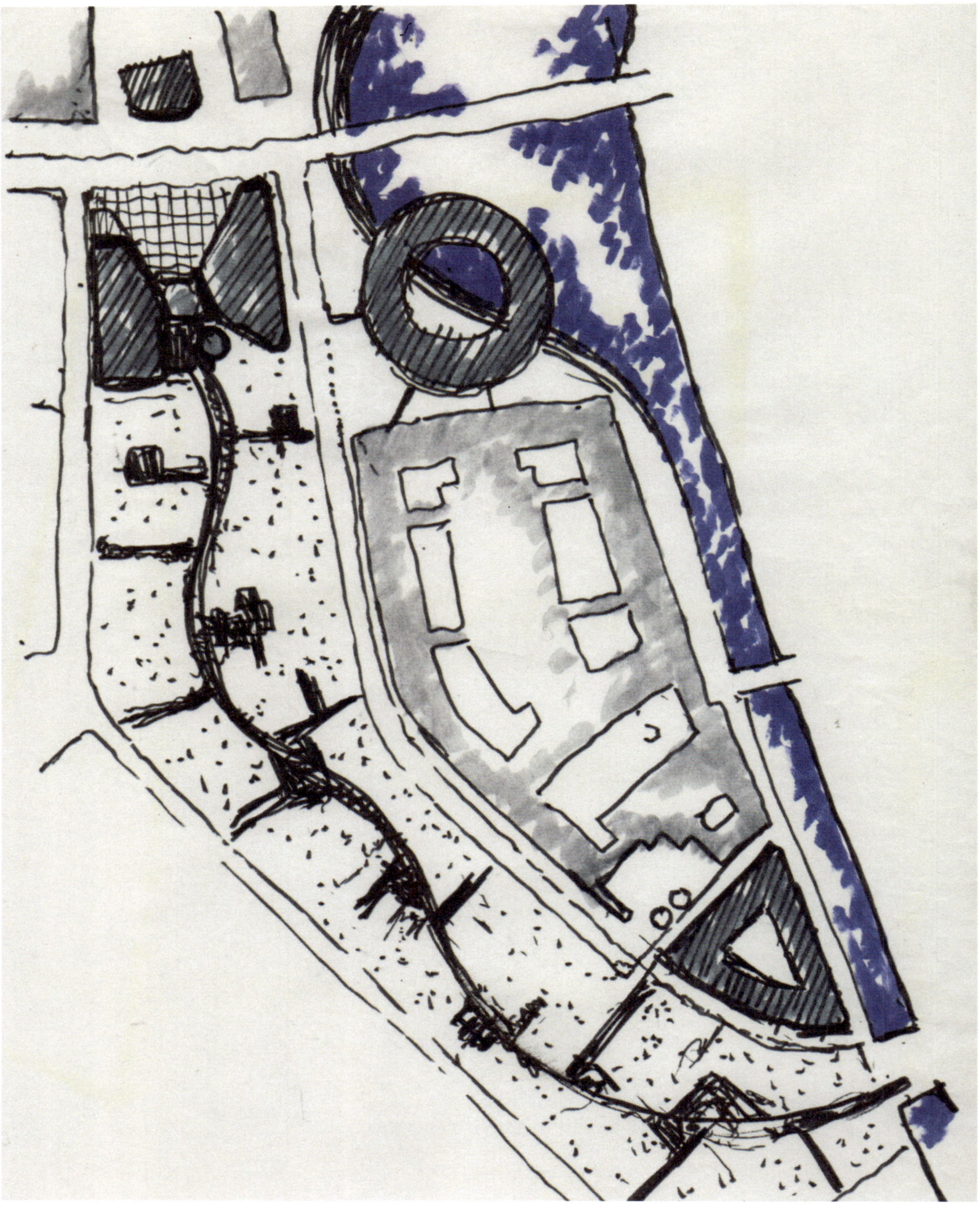

The island was destined to house the Ministries of Foreign Affairs and the Interior, forming a second new governmental district in the city as a counterpart to the Spreebogen development.

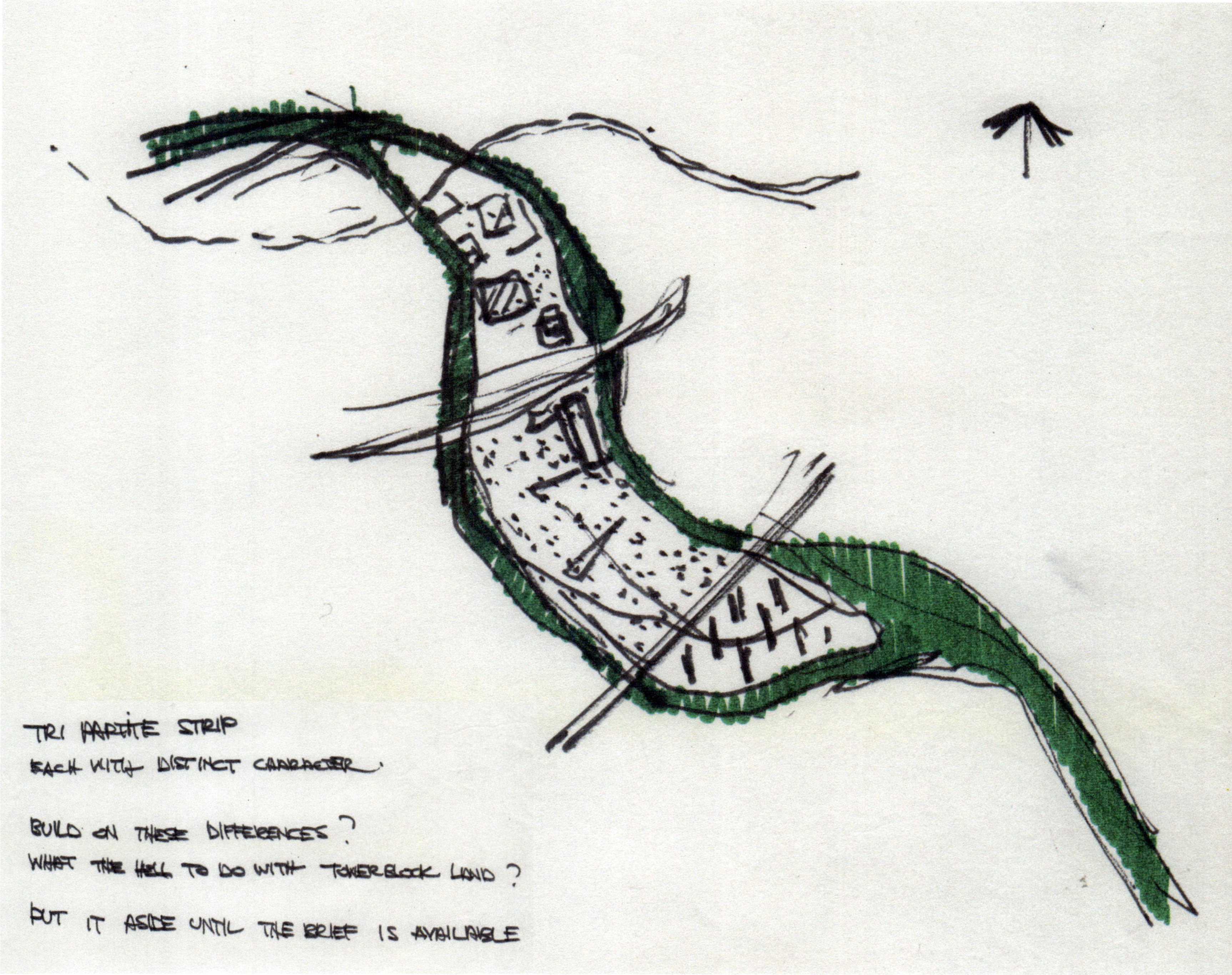

TRI PARTITE STRIP
EACH WITH DISTINCT CHARACTER.

BUILD ON THESE DIFFERENCES?
WHAT THE HELL TO DO WITH TOWER BLOCK LAND?

PUT IT ASIDE UNTIL THE BRIEF IS AVAILABLE

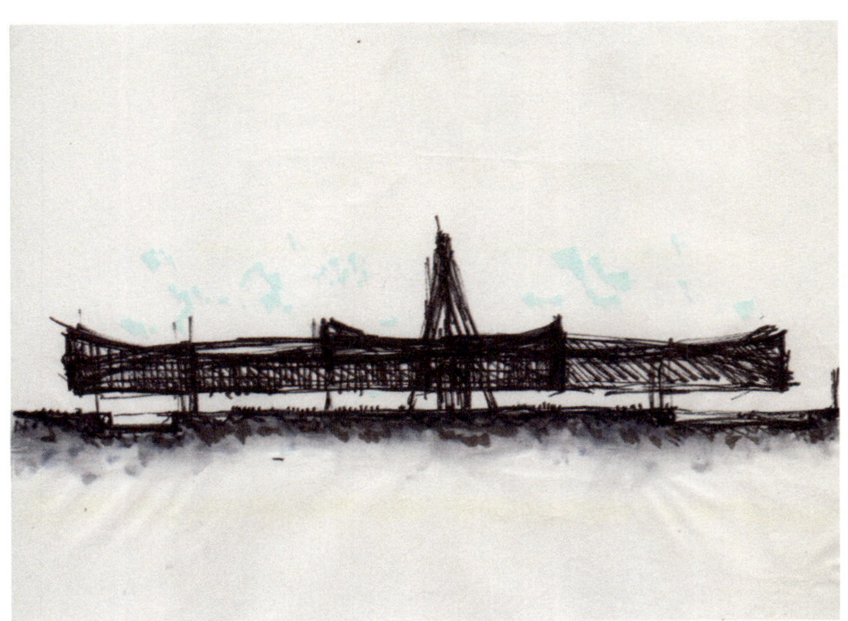

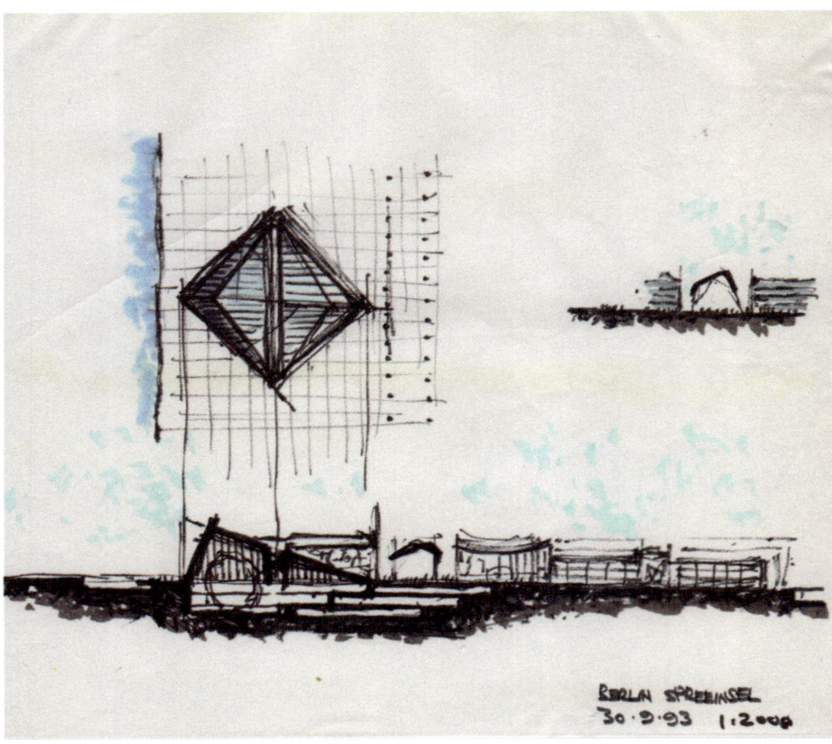

BERLIN SPREEINSEL
30.9.93   1:2000

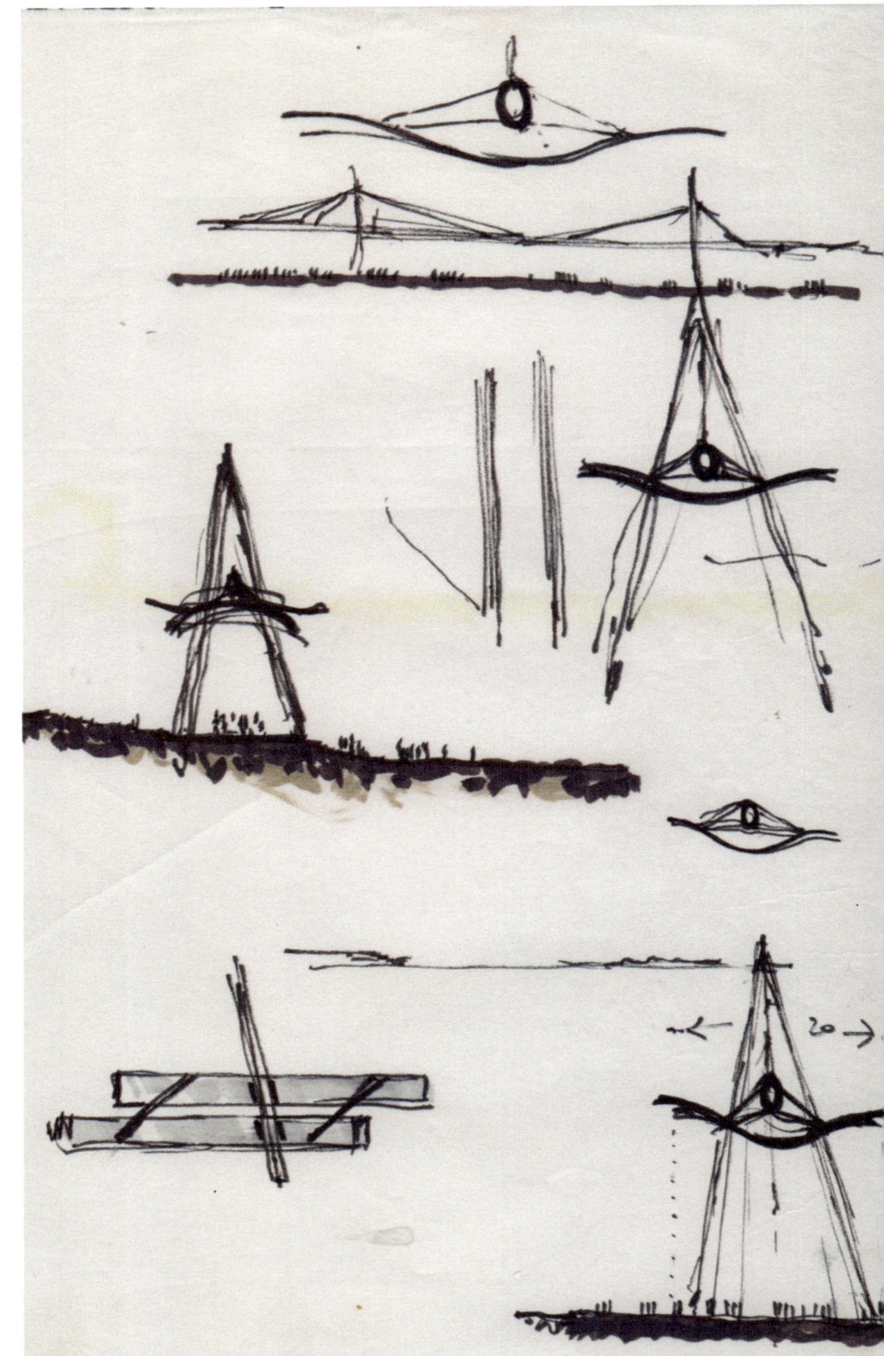

20

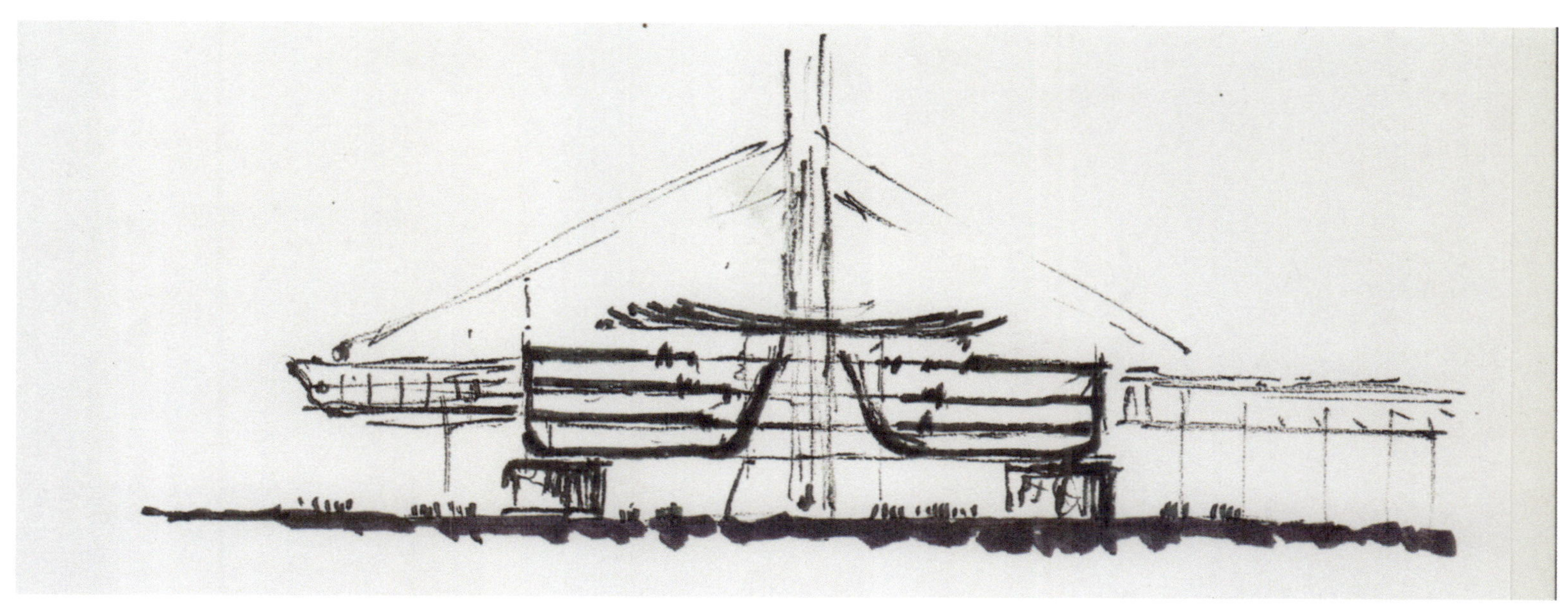

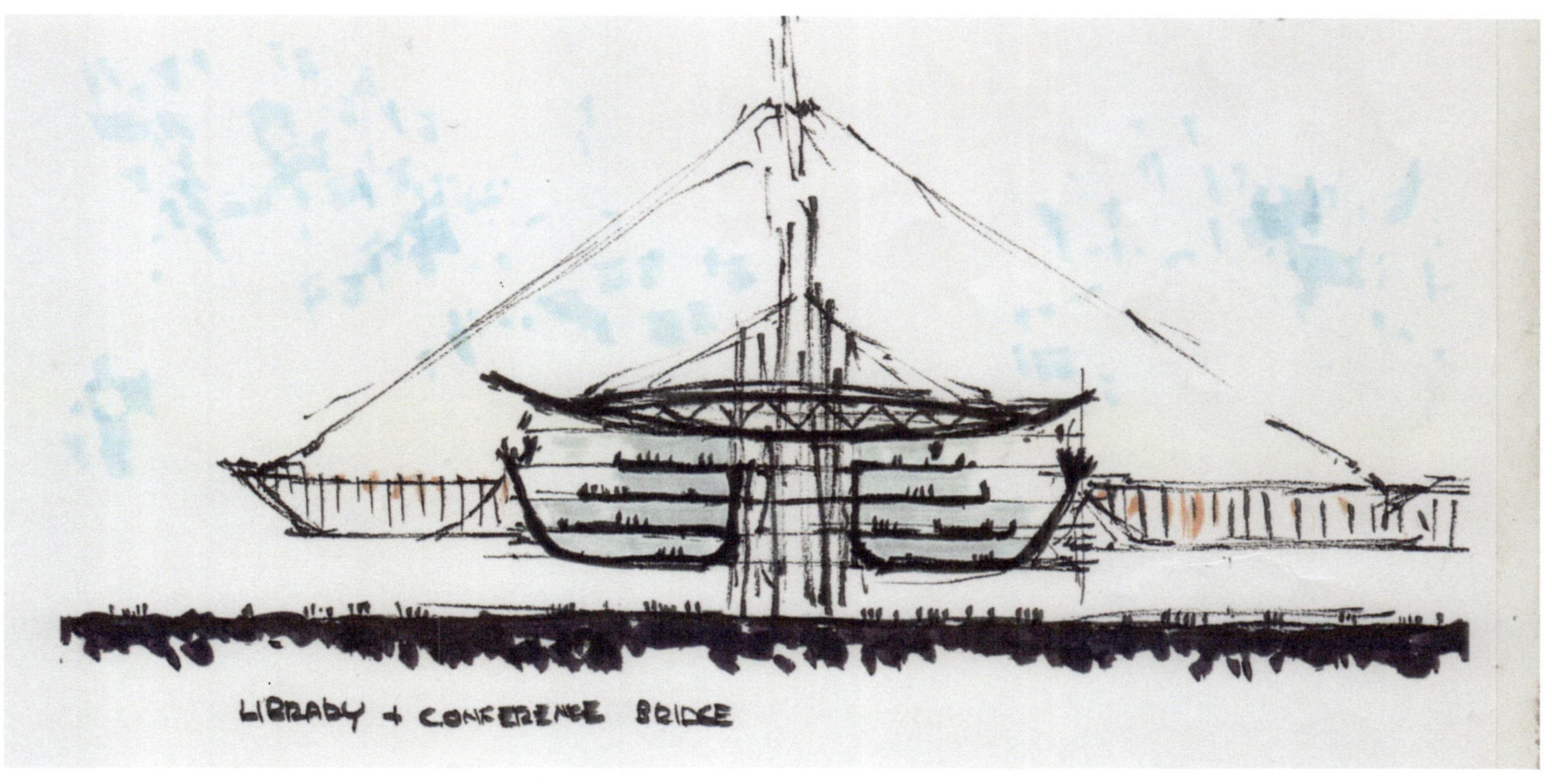

LIBRARY + CONFERENCE BRIDGE

In the mid-1980s, The Times newspaper invited a number of architects, including Peter Smithson, Will Alsop and ABK, to suggest design ideas for the River Thames. This was before the city-wide benefits of the South Bank river walk to London Bridge, and developments such as Tate Modern, the Millennium Bridge and London Eye had been realised. It seemed obvious to us that, with the proximity of Waterloo and London Bridge stations, the Thames shorelines of Southwark and Lambeth were assets that could contribute much to the capital's urban life. Without much research but with the expansive energy of optimism, we disregarded the brief to look only at the river, and included these shoreline areas in our plans.

We submitted our idea for 'Thameside', a vision that embraced the powerful presence of the river with a proposal for a series of new basins along its southerly bank. We also extended the study area southwards and formed a new type of linear park, a sweeping green link extending from London Bridge to Lambeth Bridge via a nodal crossing at St George's Circus.

1984

Earlier conceptual projects for piers, bridges and structures re-emerge in a speculative proposal to revitalise London's South Bank.

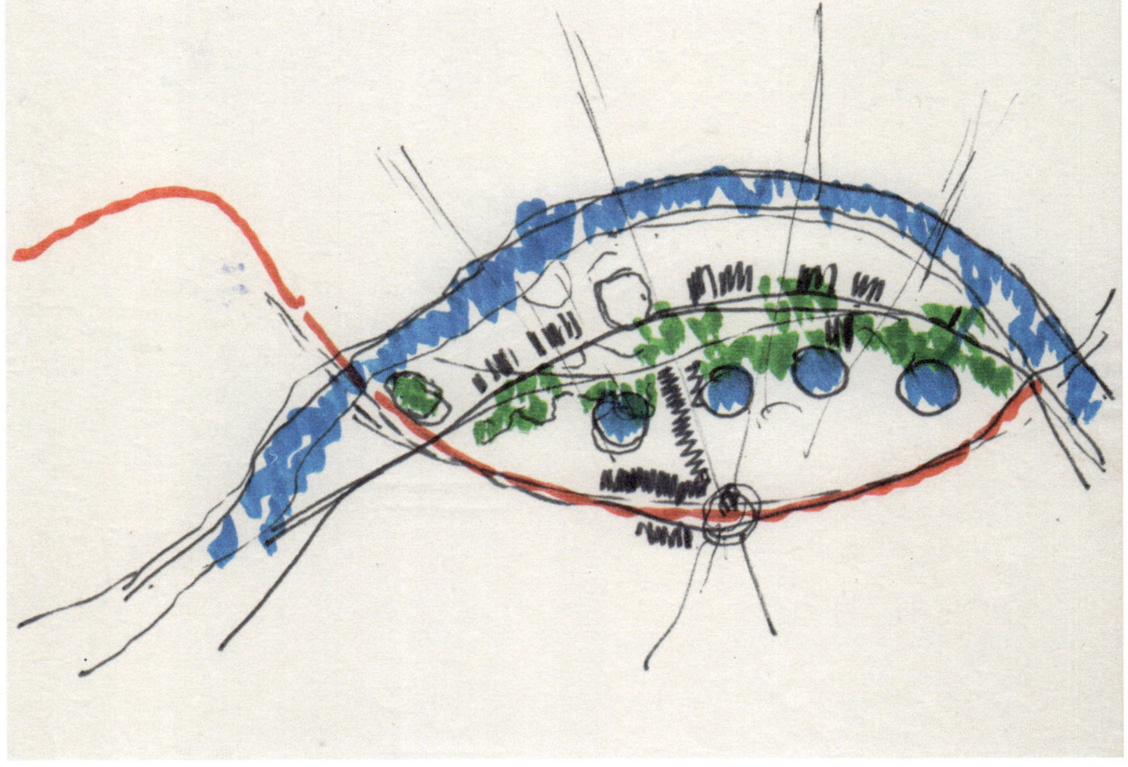

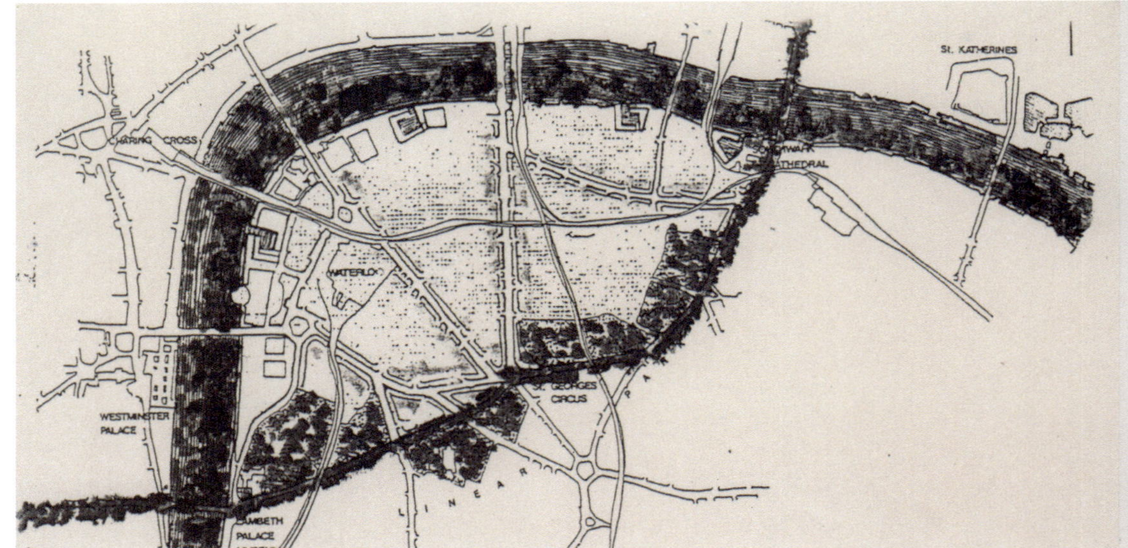

THAMESIDE

The South Bank and its hinterland lies dormant as a major resource in the heart of London. What is needed is a creative, strategic view rather than a tactical face-lift for the South Bank itself. Our plan identifies a whole new central area. We envisage London's centre of gravity expanding southwards in the 21st Century to meet new opportunities inherent in changing leisure and work patterns with better north-south links. We propose a travelator from Charing Cross to Waterloo and the South Bank.

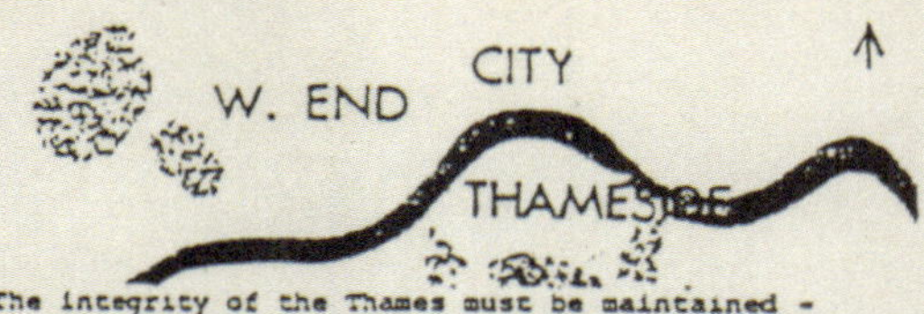

The integrity of the Thames must be maintained - avoid bridging with artificial land masses destroying the character of the river. Stop the development of a thin ribbon of office buildings "oriented" towards the City and West End. Such expediencies take no account of a broader potential for London.

Our proposal is in three parts: First, a new linear park. This would stretch in an arc from London Bridge, through St. Georges Circus to Lambeth Palace - an easy walk of 1½ miles. The gardens of Lambeth Palace and the Imperial War Museum would be integrated. The Palace would be opened to the public as a museum of religion. Morley College and the South Bank Polytechnic would form the nucleus of new education-for-leisure centres. Lambeth Pier would be developed as a major landing place.

Second, we plan a series of water basins along the river walk stretching from Jubilee Gardens to Southwark Cathedral. These will be similar in character to St. Katherine's Dock: a pattern of leisure, living and work.

Finally, we propose to reinforce and reconstitute the broken urban fabric along major roads; these will take on a boulevard scale terminating at the focal point of St. Georges Circus. The Channel Tunnel terminus at Waterloo will provide new opportunities for the whole area.

Thameside will become a place in which to live and work in the centre of London.

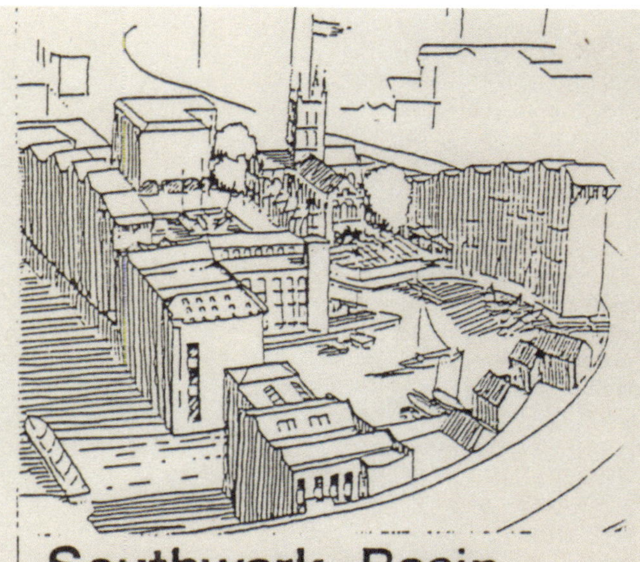

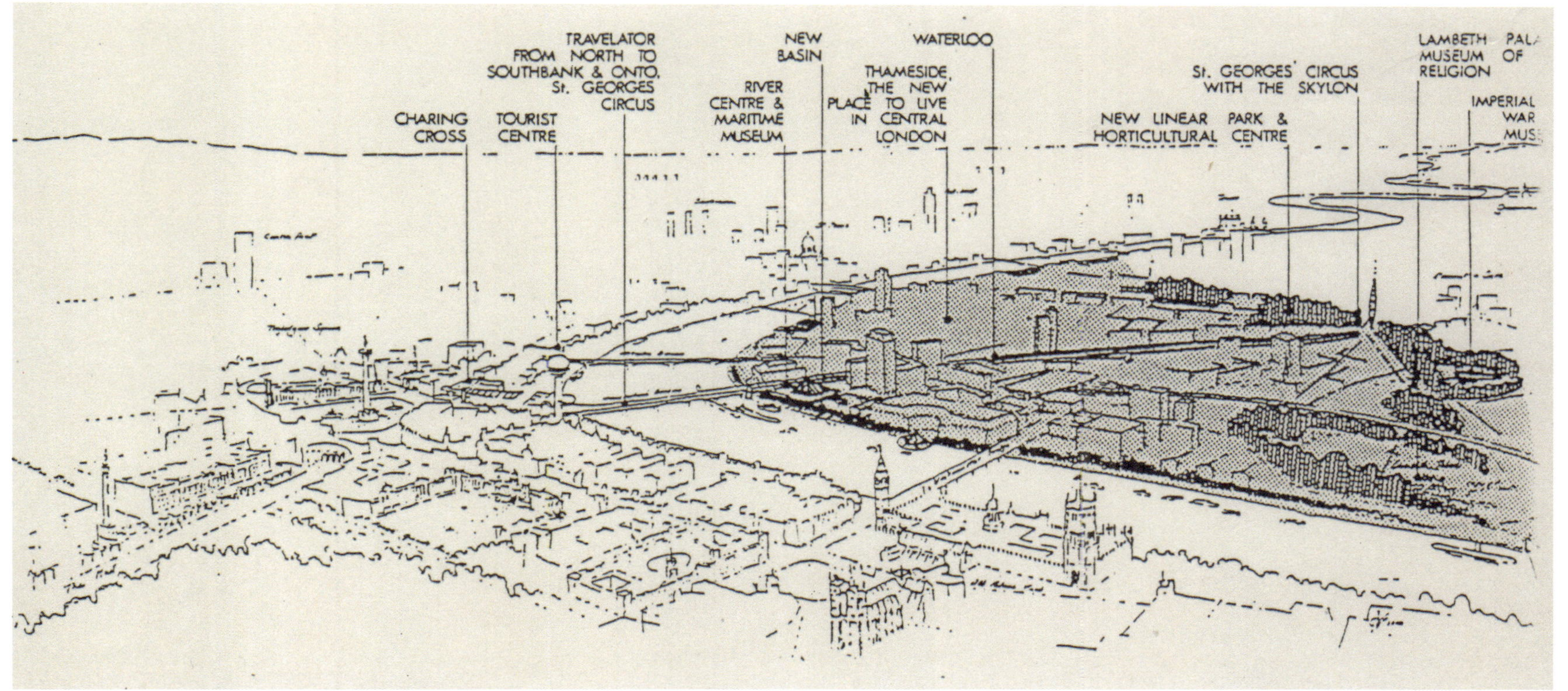

ABK's proposal comprised a linear park that followed an arc from London Bridge to Lambeth Palace, a series of water basins along the river walk between Southwark Cathedral and Jubilee Gardens, and built interventions aimed at reconstituting the fractured urban fabric.

Collaboration in Design. — Bergman & his views

This describes (indescribable?) the interaction in the dynamic chemistries that emerge in time and in relation to a developing sequence of design steps.

50 mins on these issues BUT

above all

the interactive process

with pictorial images

of the objects as built

COLLABORATION IN BURSTS
TIME IS FUNDAMENTAL
TO THIS PROCESS.

*Thank you Ian for your positive enthusiam,
your engaging encouragement and your fine
editorial skill which have been constant and
constructive as we put this book together;
it's been my pleasure to have worked with
you again.*

Peter Ahrends

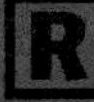